THE BIOGRAPHY OF THE
LATE MARSHAL FOCH

Au gal Graur
Cordial souvenir

F. Foch

THE BIOGRAPHY OF THE LATE MARSHAL FOCH

BY

MAJOR-GENERAL SIR GEORGE ASTON, K.C.B.

"Intellect, criticism—Pah! A donkey who has more character is more useful."—Foch, 1929

"More and more I see daily the tremendous truth that all our vaunted intellect is nothing—nothing but a noble mechanism, and that the source of feeling is the soul."

—Charles Kingsley, 1842

NEW YORK

THE MACMILLAN COMPANY

1932

DEDICATED

TO

GENERAL WEYGAND

in token of

Admiration of the Example of Loyalty and Devotion

to

A GREAT CHIEF

which he set to the Staff Officers

of

All Armies for All Time

PREFACE

"Prefaces? They bore me."—FOCH.

THE writing of the life of Marshal Foch has been to the author a formidable and at the same time an inspiring task.

He tenders his grateful thanks to many old friends and colleagues in the Service who knew the great Marshal personally for responding so helpfully to appeals for assistance; to General Sir John Du Cane, to Lieutenant-General Sir Archibald Montgomery-Massingberd, to Major-Generals Lord Sackville, G. S. Clive, and Charles Deedes, to Brigadier-General Sir J. E. Edmonds the official military historian, to Brigadier Charles Grant, and to Colonels Eric Dillon and J. A. F. Cuffe. Upon these, collectively, he has relied for much that he has written upon "Foch through English Eyes," but no one of them bears the responsibility for any individual statement unless his name is mentioned in connexion therewith. The author, knowing all his informants, has done his best to collate their evidence and to provide a fair summary. Amongst the many available printed sources of information, seen from the British standpoint, considerable use has been made of the late Field-Marshal Sir Henry Wilson's diaries, of Field-Marshal Sir William Robertson's *Soldiers and Statesmen,* and of the *Life of the late Lord Rawlinson.* Mr. Winston Churchill's *World Crisis* has also provided valuable material. Much reliance has been placed upon the excellent military operations, volumes I to IV, of the *British Official History of the Great War.* The thanks of the author are due to the Controller of H.M. Stationery Office for leave to reproduce some of the maps, and to the

Imperial War Museum authorities for excellent photographs. The Official British History "List of Principal Events, 1914-1918" and "Military Effort of the British Empire, 1914-1920," and Lord Edward Gliechen's *Chronology of the War* have been of great value. The pages of the Journals of the Royal United Service and the Royal Artillery Institutions, the *Army Quarterly,* and the *Cavalry Journal* and the *Household Brigade Magazine* have been consulted with profit, and the author is also very grateful for advice and assistance rendered by Mr. W. J. Baldry, War Office Librarian, Major Hughes, Librarian of the R. U. S. I., to Mr. Edward Salmon, the Editor of *United Empire* and to the Royal Empire Society, for leave to use certain pictures.

For French personal sources the author has relied much upon the personal authority of Marshal Foch contained in *Les Deux Batailles de la Marne* (Payot, 1928); also upon information supplied in correspondence by officers in the French Army whose names he is not authorized to quote. Amongst other printed sources, he has consulted the books of the following French authors: Réné Puaux (1918), Major A. Grasset (1919), Raymond Recouly (1920), "J. R.," *Ancien élève de l'École Supérieure de Guerre* (1921), J. Mortane, and Commandant Bugnet (1929).

The work done will achieve its purpose if the character and achievements of the great Marshal of France, and the sources from which he derived his power, provides as much inspiration for others as it has for the author.

GEORGE ASTON.

Woodford,
 Salisbury.
July, 1929.

INTRODUCTION

"IN MEMORIAM, IN SPEM"

WITHIN a few months of his lamented death, a life of the great French Marshal who led the Allied armies to decisive victory in the last year of the Great War conferred much honour upon its recipient. Acceptance of such an invitation involved a great responsibility. Had it not been for the knowledge that the life-long supporters of the great leader, and the Staff officers, both French and British, who had been connected most intimately with him in the days of his triumph would be willing to aid me in the task, the invitation would reluctantly have been refused.

Foch's strength lay in the "imponderables" beyond mortals' ken. In his own words: "What compels victory is, above all else, the conduct of the commander. 'Cæsar and not the Roman legions conquered Gaul,' said Napoleon, and Rome trembled before Hannibal, not because of the Carthaginian soldiery." And of these three Napoleon is the authority usually quoted for the estimate that in war the influence of moral causes is to that of physical as three to one. No great deeds, as the author of *Operations of War* put the matter long ago, have ever been performed by an army in which the qualities of courage and steadfast endurance were wanting. No commander has ever risen to fame who has not displayed great energy, perseverance and resolution. No nation has ever become great without fos-

[ix]

tering such qualities in its sons, nor has any remained great which ceased to foster them. Given realization of a just cause, there are times, in a community aroused by a moral purpose, when all that is virile vibrates with an impetus to put a stop to injustice, if necessary by ridding the world of its agents and such conditions provide an overwhelming incentive to overcome all obstacles to victory.

It was such an impetus that the character of their commander gave to the Allied armies which, after long endurance and steadfast resistance, were ultimately destined to be victorious. It has been written that a desperate corps-commander who was at the end of his resources reported to Foch that orderly retirement was no longer possible, and that he received this reply: "You say that you cannot hold on and that you cannot retreat, so the only thing left is to attack to-morrow morning," a tale which reminds us of the proverb of the old Zulu nation: "To go forward is to die, to go back is to die. Let us go forward." Wise saws and proverbs, however, are of little service to a multitude in a grave emergency without the help of what Foch himself called "the conduct of the commander," and conduct which remains steadfast to the very end depends upon character, not, as so many have imagined, upon some lucky improvisation of the moment.

"We must leave that to the verdict of history," is an expression constantly in use. Eminent historians maintain that history cannot be written for half a century or for a longer period after the event, until archives are opened, documents are accessible, and the passions of the moment no longer affect judicial investigation. In the past there is no doubt that reading the history of wars has exercised a great fascination upon mankind, and until quite recent years, the more remote the war the more thorough was the knowledge of it that was required of the young student. On the other hand, the fewer were the sources which would throw light upon that factor, all-important to success, the "character of the commander." Any contribution, however incomplete, to knowledge of that subject should therefore be of service to present and to future generations. The responsibility for writing this book has accordingly been undertaken in the belief that better indications of the character of the great French Marshal can be obtained from those who were intimate with him while these things are still fresh in their memories. We therefore aspire, in the light of such assistance, to trace the life of Ferdinand Foch from the day of his birth in the temporary family home at Tarbes on the northern slopes of the Pyrenees, to the evening when he passed quietly away at the advanced age of seventy-eight after enjoying at his window the air and sunshine of one of the beautiful days of last March which followed the most severe winter in our memory.

"Full of years and honours" was the expression that occurred most frequently in notices of his death. "Honour which is to glory what character is to reputation" is a phrase that was used by Mahan in his life of Nelson, the national hero of Britain. To the honour and character, rather than to the glory and reputation of Foch, the national hero of France, these pages will be devoted. The key to that character is to be found, undoubtedly, in a sincere faith in an Almighty Providence caring for the destinies of mankind, and this is best illustrated by the following story in which this faith is indicated though not publicly expressed: At the time, in April, 1918, when the powers of Foch to coordinate the Allied effort developed into the nominal command of the Allied armies, he said: "Materially, I do not see that victory is possible. Morally, I am certain that we shall gain it." Though he was well equipped with such knowledge as can be gained from history of the factors which make for success in warfare, faith was the impetus which inspired him to bear so great a part in the final triumph. It must be our object, then, to take due note of this feature in his character as it developed from his childhood through the years of education, of army experience, of achievement in the climax of the Great War and of subsequent service rendered in council affecting the destinies of France, the land which he loved and served.

CONTENTS

CONTENTS

CONTENTS

CONTENTS

[xvi]

CONTENTS

[xvii]

CONTENTS

CONTENTS

[xix]

CONTENTS

CONTENTS

CONTENTS

CONTENTS

CONTENTS

[xxiv]

CONTENTS

CONTENTS

ILLUSTRATIONS

SKETCH MAPS

PART I

BEFORE THE GREAT WAR

CHAPTER I

How can greatness be measured and how can genius be defined? Surely not solely by the "infinite capacity for taking pains," which Ferdinand Foch possessed in so remarkable a degree. As evidence of his greatness as a soldier and as a man we can point to his achievements; as proof of his genius to his power of endowing others with his own flaming spirit that no disastrous surroundings could dim. Certain qualities of greatness and of genius are inherent, and, it may be, inherited, so it will be well for us to endeavour to discover in Foch's ancestry some of the attributes which made him one of the riders of the storm in the world cataclysm of the years 1914-1918 and helped him to bear so great a part in the salvation of his beloved France. To that subject and to his environment in early years, this chapter will be devoted.

Hoping, it may be, to add additional lustre to one who needs no false halo to enhance his reputation, more than one biographer has tended to disregard the excellence of the stock from which the Marshal sprang, to ignore some of its military traditions, and to depict him as one of those comet-like figures that emerge from darkness to blaze across a page of history, a form of adulation which Foch himself would bitterly have resented.

Ferdinand Foch was, and had good reason to be, proud

[3]

more soldierly strain—an interesting point since it may show the original source of at least a part of his military qualities. His interest in military affairs was certainly fostered by the military traditions of his family. His maternal grandfather had followed a distinguished military career. After fighting as a private soldier in the French Army in campaigns on the Rhine and in Italy before the revolution of 1789, he later rose to the standing of Chevalier in 1809, the Emperor at the same time awarding him the Legion of Honour for his gallant war services. The Chevalier's coat of arms, engraved on some of his silver plate which is still in existence, shows a drawn sword and a Gallic cock, strangely symbolic of his grandson's career.

The Chevalier's portrait (which dates from about the year 1812) can still be inspected, and it shows that in addition to martial ardour Foch's maternal grandfather bequeathed some of his facial lineaments to his grandson, particularly the blue eyes and the strong, square chin. Foch's mother, the Chevalier's daughter Sophie, paid a visit to Tarbes to stay with her godmother, Mme. Barère, and it was there that she met and became betrothed to Bertrand-Jules-Napoléon Foch, the father of the great Marshal.

Tarbes was the actual birthplace of Foch but Valentine was his ancestral home, and the arms of the little town are curiously symbolical of his career. They are the plain arms of the old Kingdom of France, blue, with the fleur de lys in gold, surmounted by a crown, and supported by a lion and by two angels who are craving divine protection. Seekers after signs and symbols will also be able to find them in the family patronymic. Like most old family names it has suffered various corruptions, dating from the time when spelling was a matter of opinion. In the district the

Chapter I

ANCESTRY AND EARLY YEARS

How can greatness be measured and how can genius be defined? Surely not solely by the "infinite capacity for taking pains," which Ferdinand Foch possessed in so remarkable a degree. As evidence of his greatness as a soldier and as a man we can point to his achievements; as proof of his genius to his power of endowing others with his own flaming spirit that no disastrous surroundings could dim. Certain qualities of greatness and of genius are inherent, and, it may be, inherited, so it will be well for us to endeavour to discover in Foch's ancestry some of the attributes which made him one of the riders of the storm in the world cataclysm of the years 1914-1918 and helped him to bear so great a part in the salvation of his beloved France. To that subject and to his environment in early years, this chapter will be devoted.

Hoping, it may be, to add additional lustre to one who needs no false halo to enhance his reputation, more than one biographer has tended to disregard the excellence of the stock from which the Marshal sprang, to ignore some of its military traditions, and to depict him as one of those comet-like figures that emerge from darkness to blaze across a page of history, a form of adulation which Foch himself would bitterly have resented.

Ferdinand Foch was, and had good reason to be, proud

[3]

of his ancestry. He came of middle-class stock, one of those sound, sturdy, self-respecting families which, persisting through generation after generation, united in themselves the thrift, the industry, the endurance, and the patience of the worker, with the courage, the daring, the pride, and the honour of the aristocracy. These families are the backbone of every country having the good fortune to possess them.

Tradition tells us that four brothers Foch, ardent Catholics, arrived at St. Girons and St. Lizier during the period when the religious wars were at their height. With the industry which has continued to characterise the family they founded a paper mill, which prospered and passed from father to son with the result that a descendant is still engaged in the industry at Ledac. As time went on, one of the brothers left St. Lizier and established himself at Montsaunes, thirty kilometres from Valentine, and in turn his descendants settled in Valentine itself, where they were still flourishing in the eighteenth century. As is usually the case with large families, not all of the members flourished. Some went up and some went down in local surroundings, others migrated to America, but the branch to which the Marshal belonged throve and prospered, and by the days of Louis XIV they were important weavers and wool-merchants in the Valentine district. Gifted with the love of adventure and disregard of personal danger which they bequeathed in such strong measure to their illustrious descendant, they carried on a personal trade with Spain. Mounted on fine horses they braved the wild passes of the Pyrenees and the dangers for which the mountains in those days were famous. The strong religious faith which they also bequeathed to the Marshal was a dominant attribute of this branch of the family, and during their visits to Spain they lost no opportunity of offering homage at many of the great shrines in which the country abounded. The Christian names that were chosen in the family during that period showed both a Spanish and a religious influence; Joseph, Dominique, and Ferdinand were the names frequently bestowed upon the sturdy sons of the race.

At Valentine, the first direct ancestor of Ferdinand Foch of whom local history tells us was one Jean Foch. He died in 1693 leaving a son, Sieur Bruno Foch, who became one of the best-known citizens of the little town. This Bruno, as far as we can trace, was the father of the first Dominique Foch, and the great-grandfather of the Marshal. He married one Anne Subsol, daughter of a well-to-do family in the neighbourhood and died in 1768.

Of the second Dominique we know rather more. Like all the members of his family he possessed energy, foresight and enterprise besides "a lively nature, a warm heart, and a handsome face." The trading of this Dominique Foch with the Spaniards included traffic in mules, sheep and many other things besides the original wool of his forbears' business. The factory had been inherited by him from his parents and he rebuilt it, added improvements, bought land, and generally helped to increase the family fortunes. Being enthusiastic and patriotic by nature, this Dominique conceived a fervid admiration for Napoleon Buonaparte, and his admiration was destined in later years to have an influence upon the life of the Marshal. He called his son—Foch's father—by the names Bertrand-Jules-Napoléon. He did not follow the family tradition by attaining a ripe old age, and died rather suddenly when Ferdinand Foch's father was twelve years old.

Amongst Foch's ancestors on the distaff side we find a

[5]

more soldierly strain—an interesting point since it may show the original source of at least a part of his military qualities. His interest in military affairs was certainly fostered by the military traditions of his family. His maternal grandfather had followed a distinguished military career. After fighting as a private soldier in the French Army in campaigns on the Rhine and in Italy before the revolution of 1789, he later rose to the standing of Chevalier in 1809, the Emperor at the same time awarding him the Legion of Honour for his gallant war services. The Chevalier's coat of arms, engraved on some of his silver plate which is still in existence, shows a drawn sword and a Gallic cock, strangely symbolic of his grandson's career.

The Chevalier's portrait (which dates from about the year 1812) can still be inspected, and it shows that in addition to martial ardour Foch's maternal grandfather bequeathed some of his facial lineaments to his grandson, particularly the blue eyes and the strong, square chin. Foch's mother, the Chevalier's daughter Sophie, paid a visit to Tarbes to stay with her godmother, Mme. Barère, and it was there that she met and became betrothed to Bertrand-Jules-Napoléon Foch, the father of the great Marshal.

Tarbes was the actual birthplace of Foch but Valentine was his ancestral home, and the arms of the little town are curiously symbolical of his career. They are the plain arms of the old Kingdom of France, blue, with the fleur de lys in gold, surmounted by a crown, and supported by a lion and by two angels who are craving divine protection. Seekers after signs and symbols will also be able to find them in the family patronymic. Like most old family names it has suffered various corruptions, dating from the time when spelling was a matter of opinion. In the district the name has been spelt Foix, Foys, Fouch, or Fioch, and its derivation is uncertain. It may possibly have come from Fioch (fire), or from Fosse (a grave or ditch). Some have gone so far as to connect with it the fiery spirit of French valour, others the grave of German hopes in the Great War, but with such fantasies we are not concerned, and we can pass to the environment of the young Ferdinand in his early years.

Valentine is a small town in Haute Garonne, about two miles from Saint-Gaudens, a charming little place, nestling in delightful country at the foot of the Pyrenees. There Foch's paternal grandfather built a family residence which is still occupied by the Marshal's sister, and the town is hallowed for him, since both his father and his mother were laid to rest in its cemetery. Foch and his sister and brothers often spent their holidays at Valentine when they were children, and Foch explored the beautiful country, enjoying especially a walk to the Bout de Pay with its Chapel of the Virgin, from which he gained a glorious view over the entire valley of the Garonne.

Foch's father had inherited all the good qualities of his ancestors. Like them he was a deeply religious man, austere with himself but lenient and tolerant with others. His wide sympathies saved him from the bigotry and intolerance that sometimes spoil men of like austere character. He was loyal in all his relationships, extremely painstaking and conscientious in his business methods. As a parent he was excellent, and Foch owed much to his father's training. Brought up to strict obedience, the young Ferdinand gained the ability to command from having learned how to obey. Though strict, the father was neither harsh nor unjust. Under his wise rule the children preserved their independence of

[7]

spirit, while the love that they all bore their parents gives eloquent testimony of the spirit of the household.

The mother, the daughter of Chevalier Dupré, combined with her marked sweetness of disposition a strength of character and high ideals of life. Like her husband she was deeply devout, and like him she never allowed her religious leanings to tend towards over-severity with the high spirits of childhood, or to cause lack of sympathy with her children throughout the whole of her lifetime.

The Marshal undoubtedly derived from her his warmth of heart, while from both his parents he inherited his high sense of duty, his deep religious instincts, and the loyalty and the painstaking persistence in purpose which characterised him throughout the whole of his career. Both his mother and his father were of the Pyrenees, and he himself was a mountain man with the gaiety and vivacity of the southern race, tempered by the strength and steadiness of purpose of the uplands.

Foch's father did not find a place in the wool business according to the family tradition. Having completed his education under the care of his uncle, he entered the Civil Service and in course of time he became Counsellor of the Prefecture, in the department of Hautes-Alpes. In September, 1849, at the wish of Louis Napoléon who had been elected President of the Republic the previous year, he went to Tarbes, under the Pyrenees. The family took with them Mme. Foch's father, the Chevalier Dupré, but after he had lived with them there for three years he died of pneumonia in 1852. Of the old Chevalier, Foch used to say: "I cannot remember my grandfather because I was entering life just as he left it." He was a baby in arms at the time of his grandfather's death.

Foch was happy in the surroundings of his childhood, and Tarbes was even more attractive than Valentine to the young folk. It lies in a plain on the left bank of the Adour river which divides at that point, forking in several directions, so that the pleasant sound of running water pervades the town, while fine trees flourish in its squares, their roots deep in the moist soil. Tarbes is now the capital of the province of Hautes-Pyrenees, and its importance dates back to the Middle Ages when it was the capital of Bigorre. The Counts of Bigorre had a castle there, but all that remains of it now is the tower which forms part of the prison. The place was occupied by the English from 1360 to 1406, in the reigns of Edward III, Richard II, and Henry IV. Like many another French town, Tarbes suffered sorely in the religious wars of the sixteenth century when the Huguenots did great damage to the Cathedral of Notre Dame de la Sede. This building has now been restored, but it lacks the beauty of many French cathedrals, being heavy in design, and owing to the various restorations of very mixed architectural styles. Tarbes possessed the relics of a hero-priest, Saint Missolin, who defended his country against the Vandals and lost his life courageously. He was canonized in the time of Gregory of Tours, and many pilgrimages are made to his shrine. It is easy for us to understand how the tale attracted and stirred Foch's childish imagination, appealing both to his religion and to his patriotism, the two impulses which dominated his life and his career.

Besides the Cathedral there is the old Carmelite church at Tarbes, built in 1282, which stands in one of the tree-bordered squares with which the town abounds. There still exist, near the Jardins Massey—one of the chief attractions of the town—some fifteenth century cloisters, but though

[9]

these were made for the Carmelites of Trie four hundred years ago, they were not transferred to Tarbes until 1895.

Tarbes, like most other places, has altered greatly during the last generation. It is somewhat different in appearance from the little town which Foch knew. There is a new Hotel de Ville, and some of the promenades have names that would have meant nothing to the little Ferdinand, but at Forail, with its fine plane trees, the old picturesque fairs are still held, and life goes on in the old place much as it did when the great Marshal first saw the light of day.

Foch was not the eldest child. A daughter had come first, who is still living at Valentine where she is known to her neighbours as Genie Foch. After Eugenie came a son Gabriel, who followed in his father's footsteps and became a lawyer at Tarbes. Then on October 2nd, 1851, there came into the world the child Ferdinand who was destined to become Marshal of France and whose name was on every lip in the last stage of the Great War.

It is frequently stated that Ferdinand Foch was "born over a baker's shop." This is correct, but it gives a wrong idea of the actual circumstances. At the time of his birth his father was Secretary-General of the Prefecture, and a baker's shop chanced to be under the *appartement* or flat which the family was occupying at the time. The house still stands—an unassuming edifice at the corner of the Rue St. Louis—and recently there has been affixed to it a tablet bearing the rather inadequate inscription:

Here was born on 2nd October 1851
Foch (Ferdinand)
Chief of the Great General Staff of the Armies of the Republic

[10]

FOCH'S BIRTHPLACE AT TARBES

The *appartement* or flat as it would be called in England, is a large and roomy one. There are eight rooms on the same floor, and the room in which Foch was born is the same to-day as it was on his birthday in 1851. There are two large windows facing the street, and the usual alcove at the back, in which the bed is placed. It is an ordinary comfortable room, as simple and unpretentious as the Marshal himself.

Foch *père* went in due course to register the birth of his second son, and received this birth certificate of the child whose coming was to mean so much to the land of his birth:

Foch, Ferdinand, No. 327

Office of the Mayor in the Town Hall of the city of Tarbes, October 4th, 1851: there has appeared before us, Jean Bordes, Mayor of the said city and Officer of the Civil Service of the Commonwealth—Bertrand Jule Napoléon Foch, Secretary-General of the Hautes Pyrenees, aged 47 years, living at Tarbes, presenting to us a male child, born on the 2nd of this October, at ten o'clock in the evening, in the Maison Balomann, in this city of Tarbes, Rue de St. Louis, No. 43, the said child being the issue of the said Foch and his wife Marie-Sophie-Jacqueline Dupré aged 37 years, and declared that the said child is to be named Ferdinand.

Three years later a third and last son was born to the Fochs. He was named Germain and he displayed at an early age a vocation for the religious life. He entered the Jesuit novitiate in 1872, and he died in 1929. He lived, however, to attend the funeral of his famous elder brother between whom and himself there had always existed the closest affection. Ferdinand Foch was a man of strong family affections, and he had a very warm devotion for his younger

[11]

brother. Throughout his life they corresponded with unfailing regularity, and even in the War and during its most anxious phases, Foch rarely allowed a day to pass without sending at least a few words to Germain, whose name he gave to the only son who fell in battle in August, 1914.

From his mother's side of the family Foch derived his soldierly traditions and may perhaps have inherited some of his military genius. One of the influences that moulded his character in his youth was the family's enthusiastic veneration for Napoleon Buonaparte. Foch was reared in an atmosphere of Napoleon-worship, and constant reference to the Emperor and adulation of him cannot fail to have made a profound impression on the mind of a sensitive and intelligent lad, given to admiring fine deeds and heroic actions. It may be that his thoughts were thus set more firmly upon a military career.

Though naturally the maternal grandfather's direct connexion with the Napoleonic campaigns was most frequently mentioned in the family circle, they had another association with the Emperor. The children's great-aunt Jenny, in many ways a remarkable personality, married General Nogues, who after starting as a drummer boy in 1792, rose to his later rank by merit and war service in the field. At one time he was A.D.C. to Augereau, and he left behind him some curious and very interesting memoirs dealing with his campaigns.

Madame Nogues, who was godmother to Eugenie Foch, the eldest child, was known to the family as Aunt Ni, and Foch remembered her with strong affection throughout his life. She was a beautiful and vivacious old lady, full of spritely anecdotes of the past, and she was a most entertaining companion to her grandnephews and niece. Her main passion was Napoleon, and of him she was never tired of talking, recounting the occasions on which she had seen him, and recalling every word and every gesture of the man whom she revered as the greatest that his country had ever known. We must bear in mind that the Napoleonic tradition was very much in the air in France at about the time of the birth of young Ferdinand. The *Coup d'Etat* occurred in the following December. In February, 1852, the birthday of Napoleon I was appointed by Decree to be the only national holiday. In September the Senate prayed for "the re-establishment of the hereditary sovereign power in the Buonaparte family." In November the people cast an almost unanimous vote for an Empire, and on December 2nd, the anniversary of the *Coup d'Etat,* the Prince-President Louis Napoleon became the Emperor Napoleon III.

It is a curious circumstance that "Aunt Ni" was bent upon filling the mind of young Foch with stories of Napoleon, upon stirring his boyish and easily fired imagination with recitals of the Emperor's exploits, of his powers of captivating all with whom he came in contact, of his extraordinary military genius, and above all of his great services to France. Whether she was animated by some uncanny foresight of the destiny before him, or possibly by the fun of teasing the boy, she would pretend to try to recall to him events, always concerning her hero, which had occurred before he was born. After holding forth at length upon her favourite topic, she would turn to him and say: "You remember, Ferdinand, the ball which 'He' gave one night and where 'He' made me dance?"

"No," he would answer, "I do not remember, auntie, because I was not born then."

[13]

The old lady appeared to think this over for some moments, and then by a nod she would admit the justice of the objection. Soon she would begin again: "You remember, Ferdinand, the eve of the Battle of Austerlitz?" And she would ask many similar questions, to which Foch was compelled to return the same answer, but nothing daunted her. Her questions were so persistent that it must have seemed at times to the young Ferdinand that she really believed that he had met and conversed with the First Consul or Emperor.

Napoleon, the Chevalier Dupré, and General Nogues were idols of young Foch's boyhood, and on one occasion when a fête was in progress he dressed himself in the striking uniform of the General, which had been carefully preserved in the family. He made a gallant and martial young figure. His boyhood was happy. He led a simple life surrounded by the influences calculated to make him sound both in mind and in body. There was much family affection in the little household in the Rue St. Louis; both parents understood the joys as well as the duties of parentage, and while they exacted unquestioning obedience they demanded it in love and not in fear. A story is told in connexion with this quality which exemplifies not only Foch's boyish aptitude for obedience, but also his ability to find a satisfactory solution for a difficult problem.

Most children have a rooted objection to some article of diet; Ferdinand had an aversion for peas. He disliked them intensely, but he was often told to eat them. On one occasion they were placed upon the table, and Ferdinand was directed to eat his portion. His parents' attention was distracted for a moment from the reluctant little diner, and when they turned towards him again they saw that his plate was empty. Wondering at the phenomenon they questioned the child and he stammered out: "My heart heaves when I crunch them, so as I wished . . . as I wished to obey absolutely, I swallowed them all at one gulp."

The first few years of his life were passed much in the same way as those of any other child of his age and station, fortunate in having young companions in his own home. He and his brothers and sister played and quarrelled, romped and grew sturdy and strong, learning in due course from their mother their first simple lessons as a preliminary to attendance at the schools in the neighbourhood.

CHAPTER II

CHILDHOOD AND EARLY EDUCATION: 1861-1870

AGED 10-19 YEARS

THOUGH the boyhood of Ferdinand Foch was in the main uneventful, he displayed at an early age the attributes which were to be so strikingly manifested at a later date. While still a lad he encountered experiences and he was subjected to strong influences which all played their part in the moulding of the man.

He was sent by his parents with his brother Gabriel to attend the *Lycée* at Tarbes, in these days known as the *Lycée Theodore Gautier*. There, at the early age of ten, he began his serious education. The *Lycée* is housed in an old building with a curious old carved inscription over its gateway:—

Collegium Tarbiense stet domus haec fluctus donec formica Ebibat et totem testudo perambulat orbem—1699

"May this house stand until the ant has drunk the waters of the sea, and the tortoise has made the circuit of the world." There the little Fochs began the curriculum usual to their age and time, and although Ferdinand was of too active a temperament to be a book-worm in the usual sense of the word, he was of a studious turn of mind and from his earliest years a great reader. In addition to the books of ad-

[16]

venture which are favoured by all normal healthy lads of his age, he was particularly devoted to books on Napoleon. He devoured eagerly all the literature on that subject which came his way, and at the early age of twelve he was deep in Thiers' "History of the Consulate and the Empire." He knew most of Napoleon's campaigns by heart. His boyish imagination was naturally stirred by the powerful personality of the Emperor, whose relationship to his country was nevertheless the principal attraction. To Foch in his youth the great Napoleon Buonaparte was more than the hero of France. He *was* France. Reading about his exploits and career evoked as much patriotism as hero-worship in the boyish imagination.

The records of the printed page were enlivened and illustrated for him by memories of the stories told to him by his "Aunt Ni," and by the reminiscences of the Chevalier Dupré, which are carefully treasured in the Foch family to this day. The lively old lady's actual remembrances of the most outstanding personality in French history and the reminiscences of Foch's soldier-ancestor who had actually served with Napoleon and been decorated by him, supplemented the personal touches of the biographer and the chronicles of the historian.

Young Foch naturally studied other subjects besides French History, and at the school at Tarbes he gained the *"accessit"* for religious knowledge, Latin, History—in which he took a special interest—and Geography. At a very early age he was passionately devoted to the romances of Sir Walter Scott. Young Ferdinand had other interests besides his studies and other hobbies besides his devotion to the memory of *"Le petit Caporal."* There was a great stud farm at Tarbes for breeding the Pyrennean horses and in the sur-

rounding district great horse fairs were held so the young
Fochs were brought up in the knowledge and handling of
horses. The boys used to watch them being driven through
the streets of Tarbes to the fairs which they would attend
themselves, and so by degrees they learned something of
the points of a horse, its value, and the special use for which
each type was fitted. As boys will, they used to chatter with
the owners and drivers of the animals, and they secured
occasional rides, often bareback; it was at Tarbes that the
future Marshal, a natural lover of horses, laid the foundations
of his excellent horsemanship.

The holidays were nearly always spent by the young Fochs
at the family residence at Valentine, where the family has
always been held in high repute since and even before the
time of the Dominique Foch who played an important part
in the Revolution as a member of the Garde Nationale and
later as Mayor of the Commune under the Consulate in
1803. Ferdinand enjoyed these holidays to the full. His
studious turn of mind did not interfere with his love of outdoor pursuits; he was active and sturdy, and he spent most
of his leisure time in roaming about exploring the country-
side. Probably on account of the family enthusiasm for the
First Empire, the young Fochs were generally known to
the good folk of Valentine as "the little Napoleons," when
they appeared during the holidays wandering through the
meadows, up to the mountains, and through the quiet streets
of the old town.

Ferdinand's principal diversions during his weeks of
leisure were walking, fishing, and shooting, though we
know that he spent long hours poring over books in the
great library and we can imagine him in that old room with
the green shutters, trying to find more volumes concerning

[18]

the family hero, amusing and sometimes exasperating his playmates by his pursuit of literature when they wanted his company upon some boyish adventure. He was a great walker, fond of exploring new ways, and he particularly enjoyed climbing the mountains as far as he could penetrate, looking up at the lofty peaks, and trying to trace the paths over which his adventurous forefathers had driven their pack-laden horses into Spain. That love of the heights remained with Foch throughout the whole of his life, and in his career he displayed many of the attributes of the mountaineer in his iron courage, his serenity, and his endurance.

He continued to gain experience in riding at Valentine, and he also had opportunities of joining shooting and fishing expeditions in which he delighted. The father, anxious that his sons should be trained early in all manly recreations, used to take them with him on his shooting excursions, so Ferdinand learned early how to handle a gun and how to develop steadiness of hand and accuracy of aim. He enjoyed the fishing expeditions in the crystal streams in which the district abounded, even more than the shooting; besides trout there were crayfish to be found by those who knew how to discover them, and he proudly provided many a dish for the family dinner table as the results of a day's sport.

Even in his recreations he did not forget his Napoleon, and a good story is told in that connexion. His father, when searching for Ferdinand to join in an outing that he had planned for the family, found him sitting on the floor surrounded by various books dealing with the Emperor's life.

"What are you doing, my son?" he inquired. Young Foch looked up with a harassed frown. "I want to find out what

Napoleon did in his school holidays," he announced gravely, "but I cannot find out whether he went fishing. I should enjoy it so much more if he did!"

Like so many old French towns whose history goes back to the Middle Ages, Valentine was the home of countless legends. Most of them were of a religious nature, and some dealt with miracles that were likely to tax the faith of all but the most credulous. The young Fochs were assured that Pontius Pilate himself was born at Valentine, and the very house of his birth was pointed out to them, while the Virgin of Notre Dame du Puy, they were told, had worked for her favoured town legions of miracles; it was widely believed that she had stopped the Plague from spreading through the city at the end of the fifteenth century. When the Terror broke out in France, it was feared that some of the rabble, undeterred by the miracles that she had worked, might commit some desecration upon Her holy statue, and the good and pious Dominique Foch helped to hide the Virgin safely in a barn. There she remained until peace had been restored to the country, when it was said that of Her own accord She went back to Her shrine, and anyone who doubted this part of the legend was shown the imprints of Her knees left on the rocks to convince the most hardened sceptic. This and many similar legends were told to the youthful Ferdinand, and no doubt they all helped to foster the deep religious instincts which were inherent within him. On such matters few men talk to their fellows but definite evidence is available of the influence of Foch's early religious training and of his differentiation between essentials and legendary lore. Commandant Bugnet, A.D.C. to the Marshal during the closing years of his life, tells us a story of a correspondent who wrote to inquire his views on the immortality of the soul. "For myself, I cannot doubt it," replied the veteran soldier, tearing up the letter without replying to it, in no mood to air his beliefs. His faith knew no doubt, and admitted no intellectual argument. He was a fervent and devout Catholic to the end. "Happy are those who are born believers," was one of his sayings. "My religious faith has been part of my character, and hence of my conduct as a man and a soldier," was another. His habit was to meditate in churches, but he held that the Almighty was omnipresent and that doing one's duty was, for a man of action, the best method of paying him homage. Prayer with him was no movement of the lips but complete self-surrender. Religious observances he practised consistently and punctiliously, without parade of piety and without bigotry. For him example was better than precept, leaving his character to influence others as it might, but not seeking to proselytise, and, above all, like his parents, avoiding criticism of others with their own faith or views and their own problems to be faced.

His views on mysticism and on miracles were clearly expressed. When urged to dedicate his armies to the Sacred Heart he replied that he prayed to the Sacred Heart as he prayed to the Holy Virgin during the month of May or to Saint Joseph during the month of March, but added: "Is it he who will grant me the victory? That is outside my province." He used to add that the sort of people who urged him "mean well, certainly, but one cannot trust them. There is no knowing how far they will carry one." He had no sympathy with exaggeration or with the need of miracles. When reminded of the tale that Saint Thérèse of the Infant Jesus appeared to him at Verdun in the guise of a barefooted Carmelite Sister and gave him guidance in military matters

[21]

which helped him to victory, he replied that all that was a fairy-tale.

Faith, inherent or acquired in childhood, was his salvation from discouragement, doubt, unrest, hesitation, weariness, and all weakness of body and spirit. Such, in his own later opinion, were the effects of his early environment.

Daniel, the bellringer of Valentine, was a character well known in the neighbourhood, and one with whom the boys often talked. He told them of his church and the famous carillon that it possessed. Daniel loved his bells and played upon them three times daily, varying his tunes according to the weather and to the seasons. Ferdinand's great ambition was to be allowed to try his hand on those bells, and, though he never attained it, he gained many quaint, if not always infallible, items of ecclesiastical lore from the bellringer.

The country holidays did much to strengthen him both in mind and body. While he possessed a strong constitution he was rather inclined to be over-eager, nervous, and rather too energetic, so the open-air pursuits, the calming influence of the long days spent climbing the mountains or exploring the countryside exercised a thoroughly good influence.

When Ferdinand was about twelve years old his father became Paymaster of Public Funds at Rodez where the children went to school, by a somewhat fortunate chance, since it was at the *Lycée* at Rodez, not at Tarbes as has commonly been stated, that a master shaped Foch's future career. We can give the story in his own words:

I was in the 3rd at the *Lycée de Rodez* when my *horoscope de Polytechnique* was drawn by my mathematical master called Almeras, a man of amazingly simple, precise and forcible logical power. He said: 'You should send him to the Polytechnique. That is the best thing for him. He has a geometrical mind.' It was he who set my objective before me.[1]

When Foch *père's* post was discontinued he returned to Valentine, while awaiting a new appointment, and there he sent his sons, Gabriel and Ferdinand, to the local seminary, where they completed the second stage of their education.

About this time the Fochs moved frequently and Ferdinand attended the Jesuit School at Polignan for a time. We are fortunately able to give, on the authority of his A.D.C. Commander Bugnet, Foch's own opinion in later years of the marks left upon his character by the time that he spent at Polignan. It was the first occasion on which he had entered a religious community. What struck him most from the first was the devotion of the masters, who were all priests, to their vocation. They took real trouble with their pupils, and having received the previous reports of young Foch's mathematical tendencies they made him specialise, all by himself, in mathematics, in order to make a more rapid advance. He was fourteen or fifteen years old. The other pupils in the Seminary were two or three years older than he was, about seventeen years old. They were all preparing for the priesthood, and they worked enthusiastically, and were much more advanced than Foch. "They swotted all the time. They were stout fellows! They always had their nose in a book." In order to keep pace with them Foch had to "pull a stiff oar." "That's what I learnt over there —to pull a stiff oar!"

Later, when Foch was earning brilliant successes at the College of St. Michel, he and his elder brother competed with companions of their own age, and found themselves

[1] Bugnet's evidence.

more advanced than they were. People said: "How is it that these two little Fochs carry off all the prizes?" Foch's own reply to the question when he had thought things over in later years was, "We had been at a good school at Polignan."

In 1867, his father was made Collector of Taxes at St. Etienne, and moved there with his family, sending his sons to the Jesuit College of St. Michel.

It was the usual custom of that college to receive boarders, but Foch senior, though severe in some ways, was a devoted parent. He had the true welfare of his sons at heart and he wanted to keep his boys at home with him as long as it was possible. He held that influences of the home would be of more real advantage to them than those of the boarding-school, so before the lads entered the College he sought out the Principal, and made it plain that the boys would enrol only on the understanding that they would be day boys. An agreement was arrived at to take them on those terms.

Foch was prepared at St. Michel for his *"baccalauréat,"* and later he received a degree in Arts. The Jesuits at St. Michel and at the other colleges under their direction had a great reputation for preparing boys for the military colleges and it was while Ferdinand was at St. Michel that his military career was definitely decided.

Both the young Fochs did well there, and the prize-giving day was a proud event for their parents. They watched their sons carrying off prize after prize and heard the parents of less studious sons murmuring to each other: "Who are these little Fochs that they succeed so well?"

As we can readily imagine, the boys' prize-books were carefully treasured by their parents. Those of Ferdinand alone made quite a respectable show in the salon at St. Etienne and at Valentine, but though father and mother were proud of their family, the children were not allowed to be vainglorious over their successes. One of the younger ones, delighted with a school prize, showed it to one of Mme. Foch's friends exclaiming:—

"See how clever I am!"

"My child," came the maternal rebuke, "cleverness that must be mentioned does not exist."

Ferdinand's ambitions for a military career had been steadily growing, and he looked forward to his time at the Jesuit school at St. Clément at Metz with eager anticipation. His father had hesitated about St. Clément, because it was impossible for his son to enter that college as a day pupil, though some students resident at Metz lived at home. The Foch parents liked their sons to live under their own roof-tree, and this would be the first occasion on which Ferdinand would leave his home. If, however, his son was really to be trained for the military career upon which he had set his whole heart, there was no help for it.

M. Foch believed in "the morality of the fireside" and he was doubtful about the habits that were acquired in those days by boarders in the *Lycées* in their spare time, but though he was convinced that his boys were better at home in their leisure hours, he overcame his scruples in the interests of Ferdinand's career, and early in the momentous year 1870 young Foch joined the *Internat,* or resident side of the College of St. Clément.

Though he looked forward to his new life and to the career to which it was the preliminary, this first break with his home was a great wrench for a youth with strong family affections. His home life had been of the happiest and he

[25]

said good-bye to his family with mixed feelings. His father had talked much with him about his new experiences and about some of the moral and other difficulties that he might be expected to encounter at so critical a stage in life, and his son had listened attentively. The depth of the impression which his father's advice made upon him will be gathered from a later account of his time at St. Clément, and the prizes that rewarded his endeavours.

Mme. Foch probably felt the temporary loss of her son even more than her husband did, but she felt few misgivings about the wisdom of letting him go. "We have trained him well," she said to her husband. "We have done our best—of what use was our care if our son cannot be trusted? He is a man. He must go into the world. Under God we have done our best to arm him and I have faith in Ferdinand." And he never betrayed her faith.

St. Clément was to afford young Foch a preparation for the *Ecole Polytechnique*. Marked ability in geometry had originally caused that school to be considered his fitting destination and to the Ecole he eventually went, though as matters turned out he was destined to have his first experience of army life before he actually sat for his entrance examination. From all accounts the Foch of this critical period of adolescence seems to have presented some contradictory features both in his outward appearance and in his temperament. He was fair, with clean-cut features and very clear blue eyes, kindly in expression. His whole face showed a sympathetic and amiable nature, redeemed from weakness by his firm lips and square determined chin. When he was not conversing his eyes were usually fixed upon the ground, but when he was talking to anyone, he looked them full in the face, as he did to the end of his life.

By temperament he was still inclined to be as impulsive as he had been as a child, but his manner was quiet, almost gentle, and though his disposition was really friendly he was not sociable in the usual sense of the word. He promised to become a man of a few friends, rather than one of a host of acquaintances, and though genial with his fellow students, he was inclined to be reserved about his own thoughts and feelings, a reserve that grew with his years. Like all great men Foch was never loquacious. The young student of St. Clément has already developed the habit of saving words by the use of gestures, a feature that struck many observers during the course of the Great War.

His youth, as one well acquainted with him tells us, gave a kind of first sketch of his future maturity. The main features remained the same, only more deeply marked and constantly gaining in depth and in power.

CHAPTER III

EDUCATION: 1869-1871

AGED 18-20 YEARS

As might be expected young Foch found the College of St. Clément very different from the schools which he had previously attended. Situated in the Rue de Pontiffroy at Metz, it had been disestablished at the time of the Revolution, but Napoleon III had restored it to the Jesuits who now conducted the establishment.

The College made a great point of "congregationalist" teaching, for the purpose of preparing boys for the great military colleges of St. Cyr and the *Ecole Polytechnique,* and students came to St. Clément from all parts of the world, particularly from Poland, while the big neighbouring towns such as Nancy and Strasbourg sent many day pupils.

The students thus formed a cosmopolitan gathering, and in mixing with them young Foch gained much useful experience and an insight into various types of character that served him well in later days. He was popular with his colleagues, and well liked by the masters. While he formed many of the usual school friendships, his strongest attachment was for a young man called Rivet de Chaussepierre. Soon after Foch entered the College, he was hurrying one day to a lecture and was running down a corridor when he crashed full-tilt into another student also in a great hurry. There were mutual apologies and explanations, and from that moment he and Rivet de Chaussepierre were firm friends. He showed considerable ability in his studies, enjoyed his life at the College, and when, in the summer of 1870, he went home to St. Etienne for the holidays, he took with him a prize that pleased his parents more than any award for scholastic proficiency would have done, the *"Grand Prix de Sagesse."*

This award was not presented by the masters, but by the students. It says much for the high esteem in which young Foch was held by the other lads and the excellent impression that he had made, that the youth of several nations and of very varying temperaments had united in judging that his behaviour had merited the most signal mark of approval that it was in their power to bestow.

In the ordinary course of events Foch would have returned to St. Clément to resume his studies in the autumn term, but on July 19th the Franco-Prussian War broke out, and the whole French nation was thrown into a state of turmoil. The classes at Metz, soon to be besieged, did not reassemble. St. Clément was turned into a military hospital, and Ferdinand remained at his home awaiting the course of events.

He was not of a nature to remain inactive. From the day when war was declared he longed to be able to take his part in the conflict and to fight for the country which from infancy he had aspired to serve. He followed the progress of the war with keen interest, and he heard of the tragedy of the Sedan with a grief and horror shared by all his countrymen.

Levies were already being called for, and many already were in Paris preparing to assist in withstanding a siege which the German armies were threatening as, in the far north, they marched steadily westward. The danger threatening the capital strengthened Foch's resolve to take part in his country's defence, so at the next call for levies he presented himself as a recruit at the local depot of the 4th regiment of infantry.

His one ambition was to serve first as Private Foch, and in the course of time to emulate some of the brave deeds of his ancestors. How he more than fulfilled his ambition in the course of time all the world knows, but for the present his military career was destined to be brief.

He spent some weeks at the depot in the 24th company of the 4th battalion, and then he was drafted to Châlons-sur-Saône, not far from the scene of the last fighting of Bourbaki and the tragic and disastrous march to the relief of Belfort. Once there, he had high hopes of seeing the active service for which he hankered.

The Germans had invested Metz, the town he knew so well, and Foch followed the fortunes of the French troops with a heavy heart. Marshal Bazaine and his army had sought shelter behind the fortifications, and the Germans thereupon besieged and surrounded the town. Metz was invested for ten weeks and then Bazaine was forced to capitulate, surrendering to the Germans nearly 180,000 troops, several hundred cannon, and a vast quantity of military stores.

The effect all this had on the patriotic mind of young Foch can well be judged, but to his bitter disappointment his battalion was still kept on garrison duty. In January, 1871, an armistice was signed, and his chance of seeing active service passed away.

This brief experience of army life was nevertheless of

great value to him. He had been given his training as an infantryman, he had gained knowledge of life in barracks and of the routine of the parade ground, and what, in the light of after events, was much more important, he had acquired some understanding of soldiers and some insight into the minds of men whose like he was to command in later life. From the days of his youth Foch's judgment of his fellow men was excellent. He was not given to expressing his opinion unless it was necessary, but he could sum a man up almost at a glance and decide upon the work for which he was best fitted. He detected at once any weakness that might make his work of little value.

When the armistice was proclaimed Foch's battalion was immediately disbanded, and he returned home, there to await the resumption of the studies which the outbreak of war had interrupted. Peace was finally proclaimed, and Foch returned to St. Clément with his fellow-students to resume his education.

No period in the years of his youth made as deep and bitter an impression upon young Foch as did those days of his return to Metz after the war. The town was now a German fortress, with the Prefecture as General Headquarters. The Germans had occupied the place for some months and those of this generation who know something of what that can mean, can well guess at the feelings of the inhabitants. To Foch's ardent patriotism and to the military strain in his blood something more was added at this time that had its influence on the events of later years—a hatred of the German character as exemplified in warfare, and a determination to avenge his country for the indignities which had been heaped upon her. His mood has been described as one of patriotic exaltation. Life was opening to him, and he

[31]

had chosen the profession of arms. Must he not avenge his country? *La Revanche* was to be his life motive.

It was bitter for the sensitive and sympathetic youth still under his majority to walk through the streets of the old town and to see traces of the invader on every hand, to hear the clank of Prussian sabres on the esplanade, or to see the conquerors swaggering in and out of the ten city gates. It was tragic to know that in the graveyard of Chambière there lay the bodies of over eight thousand French soldiers who had perished in the defence of their country, but young Foch had a more personal reason for his bitterness. His best friend, Rivet de Chaussepierre, who had become a Second Lieutenant, had been killed in action. This was a heavy blow to Foch who, loyal in friendship and deep though reserved in his affections, had been devoted to his college friend. It is significant that when he first heard of Rivet's death he is said to have muttered: "A great death, and one to be envied. You shall be avenged." He kept his vow.

With some strange foresight of what was to come, Foch seems to have made a special study of German psychology. During those weeks at Metz he often mentioned to his companions that he had noticed certain attributes of the Germans which in his opinion should never be overlooked in any dealings with them, and throughout his life he retained the impressions which he then formed of the German temperament. He seems to have realised in some strange way that the conflict in which his destiny was to be so deeply involved would be renewed at some future period. He said himself not long before he passed away that he had pursued his military ambition with a single purpose: "I strove to apply the conclusions of an essay which had been given to us to work upon at St. Clément at the very moment when the country was being invaded by those Germans whom I meant one day to pursue."

The weeks passed and still the Germans occupied Metz, but the French inhabitants hoping against hope, strove to believe that the invaders would soon be forced to go, and that Metz would once more belong wholly to France. Their hopes were doomed to disappointment. One of the students, Josselin Lenotre, gave a poignant account of how the pupils of St. Clément heard the bitter tidings:

All at once the cannon of the Fort thundered out a salvo, so that the vibration shook the windows.

At one bound the pupils were on their feet! The superintendent rose suddenly from his chair. "My children," said he, and then, not able to speak, he bowed his head, joined his hands and crossed his fingers as though in prayer.

We knew then. The abominable treaty had been signed. Metz became German. All heads were bowed. Heavy silence brooded in the vast space, but many tears coursed down upon the open books.

You were with us at that moment, Foch, and you also, Maud'huy.[1] Who could have forewarned us that you were marked out to re-enter victorious, and to bring back joy and pride into that city which, in the despair and consternation of that night, saw fall upon her the first night of her long captivity?

The signing of the Treaty which gave Alsace-Lorraine to Germany was a bitter blow to France, and a tragedy for Metz. On the same night the students of St. Clément prayed for France that one day her full glory might be restored to her, little dreaming that in their midst knelt the man who was to play so great a part in that restoration.

[1] Commanded the Tenth French Army early in the Great War.

Foch did not allow his grief at the death of his friend, and the humiliation of his country, to interfere with his studies. His reading became much more varied at St. Clément, but he had by no means lost his boyish enthusiasm for Napoleon, and during the events which happened while he was at Metz, he was often heard to wonder what the Emperor would have done in like circumstances. As can be imagined, he was intensely interested in M. Rouher's attempts to form a Bonapartist Party, but neither at that time nor at any future period did he take any part in political issues.

Many things happened at Metz to strengthen his determination to see his country avenged. On one occasion, much against his will, for he was never at any time of his life given to violence, he was drawn into a street brawl, in which some Bavarians behaved with great brutality, and this seems to have made an indelible impression. Another incident at about the same time was described by Foch himself: "Some Pomeranians who kept guard over the students took away their ball on the pretence that they had thrown it into a forbidden area. Then I got together all my friends. We dashed to the assault and got our ball back from them!" His talent for quick decision and leadership seems to have developed early. He said to a friend at St. Clément: "It is necessary to take back Alsace-Lorraine; it is necessary that France should no more be defeated; it is necessary that I should be one of her liberators;" a curious speech for a lad of twenty, apparently with no prospect of anything but an ordinary army career, but even allowing for legend and *esprit d'escalier* there is much evidence to show that after those months at Metz there was present in Foch some strange sense of his destiny. It was not boasting. No man could have been less of a braggart. It was hardly ambition, for it was strangely impersonal. It was as if he felt within himself the seeds of a greatness that in due course must surely come to maturity.

In some inexplicable way his consciousness of future greatness communicated itself to others, even to those who did not know the young man with any degree of intimacy. One of the professors at St. Clément who knew Foch merely as one amongst his large class of young men looked intently at him one day, noted his eyes and his forehead, and remarked to a colleague: "That young man will accomplish later something immense."

On another occasion a friend of the Foch family, a well-known doctor, was showing his children the famous Arc de Triomphe, and when describing it to them he uttered a curious prophecy: "Look," he said, "one day we shall conquer Germany which has just beaten us. I cannot say how, but I am certain that it is Ferdinand who will lead our troops under this glorious arch."

Though Foch at this age was good looking, with fine eyes and regular features, there was nothing outstanding about his physique to cause this strange faith in his future; it must have been intimate knowledge of his character, his quiet steadfastness, great tenacity of purpose, determination, and the power shown by his expression: "the lamp of the soul shining through its fleshly covering."

Foch remembered Metz and his experience there all his life. In after years he told students at St. Clément that it was there that he had learned to work, and added: "Work you, too. The greatest heights will be accessible to you, but you must work to reach them, work hard. Go, too, to your Chapel to look to the light without which nothing avails."

And then he gave them the lead, kneeling in the same old oaken pew. One evening, after the signing of the Armistice in 1918, he walked all round the town, accompanied by a single staff officer, recalling his college days there, and conjuring up memories of his youth when, angry and revengeful, he had paced the streets dreaming of the time when Metz would once more belong to France, and the invaders would in their turn be conquered. He has placed on record his own account of this experience which will be given in due course.

For his final examinations Foch had to go to Nancy, and there again he experienced the bitterness of finding the town occupied by German troops, under General Manteuffel. Nancy, with its chequered history stirred his young imagination. He roamed about the streets, hating the traces of the invader which he encountered everywhere and admiring the wonderful old gates, so like triumphal arches, through which the enemy had marched. He paced the Royal Square which was built by Stanislas and contained fine buildings which the Germans found so useful; and he turned into the cathedral to pray for the liberation of his country.

France was still in a state of chaos and the Versailles Assembly was causing trouble. Thiers had resigned, and all who loved France had grievous doubts as to her future. Foch was an exception. He had no such doubts. He saw his country reborn more glorious than she had ever been before, her enemies defeated, her security established; and he determined to work for those ends.

With his family he was the Ferdinand that they had always known, with the same strong filial and fraternal affection. He was always glad when his studies allowed him to go home, where he occupied his holidays very much as he had always done, showing affection for his mother and deference towards his father. His steady progress through the various colleges at which he had completed his education gave great satisfaction to his parents and justified them in their belief that they had done well to allow him to follow his inclination. There was always a strong bond of affection between Foch and his brother Germain in whose novitiate as a Jesuit novice in 1872 he took great interest. The brothers talked over constantly the different paths in life that they were to follow, and though Ferdinand had, and retained, strong religious instincts, the army rather than the priesthood had attracted him from his boyhood. The idea of his brother being a priest was nevertheless attractive to him, and all details of Germain's new life were studied with avidity.

"We shall both serve France," he said, "you to pray for her; I to fight for her; and who knows which is the better service?"

His elder brother Gabriel was training to be a lawyer, a profession that had no attractions for Ferdinand. He had no mind for legal hair-splitting. His intelligence was direct and penetrating, but for subtlety either in speech or in action, he had little taste. His view of what Napoleon called "idle phrase-making" may perhaps have been tinged with contempt, but even if it was, the Foch family affection was so strong that each member was interested in the welfare of the others. He was always fond of his only sister Eugenie, and she in her turn was devoted to her younger brother who was never boyishly rude or patronising. His attitude towards her partook rather of the nature of protective affection.

He was still as well liked by his fellow students as he was when they awarded him the *"Grand Prix de Sagesse."*

He was genial and responsive with them, always willing to help his comrades in any way that was possible. He was attentive to his studies, a good companion in all the usual recreations of the students, alert and good-humoured; but he retained a strict reserve about personal matters.

It was a great day for Ferdinand and his family when they heard that he had passed his final examinations at Nancy, and that he had qualified for the *Ecole Polytechnique* at Paris. The capital with all its historical associations fascinated the young student, and before he left home he studied its history anew, reading of the past glories that emphasized the bitterness of its present humiliation. By that time Foch senior had grown accustomed to his sons quitting the parental roof, and Ferdinand's behaviour had convinced him that he was really to be trusted in any circumstances, even in the rather trying environment of students in a military school in Paris.

Foch himself had no doubts as to his career. His one ambition was to wear the uniform of the French Army, and he set his face steadily towards this goal. It sometimes happens that the first taste of army discipline cures a martially-minded youth of his military fervour, but the brief experience that Foch had acquired of life in the French Army in 1870 had, if anything, intensified his longing for a military career. Consequently, with this end in view, he read all the books on military matters that chanced to come his way, often surprising his masters by his knowledge of subjects not in the curriculum. "He will go far," one of them remarked. "To get the students to do what is necessary is often an achievement; here is one who exceeds all the tasks set for him."

At last the great day came, and on November 1st, 1871,

soon after his twentieth birthday, young Foch left his home for Paris to become a student at the great *Polytechnique*. His number in the entrance order was seventy-six, and with the powers of application learned at St. Clément he was soon to rise higher in his class. To Father La Couture, a distinguished mathematician, and to Father Saussier, once in the French Navy, he owed the development of some of his best qualities, a debt that he acknowledged freely in after life when looking back at his career.

On arrival in Paris he found the place sorely stricken, the horrors of the Commune were a recent memory and thousands were still languishing in prison awaiting trial. Only a few months earlier the *Polytechnique* had been the scene of bloodshed. Communists had occupied and had tried to hold the school but a battalion of chausseurs had driven them out at the end of May, executing a certain number of the insurgents in the courtyard of the buildings.

CHAPTER IV

MILITARY TRAINING AND EARLY EXPERIENCE: 1871-1878

AGED 20-27 YEARS

At the *Ecole Polytechnique* young men who have passed
a very difficult preliminary examination and wish to prepare
themselves for high positions in the public services receive a
highly specialized scientific education. Founded by Gaspard
Monge in 1794, the College has attracted students from all
parts of France, but though many of France's finest soldiers
were educated there, the College is not only for those preparing for a military career; civilians are educated there
such as engineers and those who wish to prepare for the
ordnance office.

At the time when Foch entered the College on November
1st, 1871, the *Polytechnique* occupied the old buildings of
the College of Navarre, and one of the pupils of Navarre,
wishing to express in stone his wishes for the school, had
chiselled above the door the same quaint motto which was
above that school at Tarbes where young Foch first began
his education:

May this house stand until the ant has drunk the waters of
the sea, and the tortoise has made the circuit of the world.

The house had stood, but the engraver of the motto might
well have wished to see it fall before it endured the humilia-

[40]

tions which it had undergone shortly before young Foch first made its acquaintance.

Foch did not go to Paris in very high spirits. He had seen and endured things during the previous year that were to remain as an indelible impression throughout the whole of his life. The months at Metz had been bad enough. Certain portions of the College itself had been occupied by German troops, so when he was on his way to and from the lectures of Father Saussier—the old naval officer, who had taken orders and was then attached to the College, who took a great interest in young Foch—or to the mathematical classes of Father La Couture, the young Ferdinand continually encountered German soldiers, and these incidents caused bitter humiliation in a youth so sensitive and patriotic.

From Metz he had carried away two historic memories of 1870. He had seen Napoléon III in front of the Préfecture, in the square filled with carriages; the Emperor was leaving in a barouche, looking ill, tired, and depressed. He had also seen Bazaine's Headquarters established in the Grand Hotel with the General Staff in complete chaos and Bazaine himself playing billiards. Foch had not left Metz until investment was imminent, and he was among the last to leave, having first completed the oral examination for the *Polytechnique* on August 4th-6th. He left on the 11th accompanied by an old peasant woman, a refugee from Strasbourg, carrying her sole treasure—a geranium in a pot!

At Nancy his experiences if anything had been still more trying. This city formed the headquarters of the German Army of Occupation, and General Manteuffel who was in command decided to have a daily musical "Retreat," his soldiers playing triumphant German airs as they marched through the streets of the city. The effect upon the feelings of the loyal inhabitants of the French city can well be imagined. Foch witnessed these cruel parades, and for forty-two years the hostile airs of triumph seem to have echoed in his brain, producing a longing that France might be avenged and a craving for a triumph to erase from his memory the sight of swaggering German soldiers marching through Stanislas Square. In course of time his ambition was fulfilled (in November, 1918), and when, on August 23rd, 1913, he had assumed the command of the XXth Corps, "guardians of the frontier," he arranged that on the day when he entered Nancy there should be a grand musical "Retreat," in which the bands and trumpeters of the six town regiments should take part. By his wish *Marche-Lorraine* and the *Sambre-et-Meuse* resounded through the streets that once in his memory had echoed to strains of German martial music. The experience went far towards blotting out painful reminiscences.

If his memories of Metz and Nancy were bitter, his sensitive nature must have been still more deeply wounded by his environment in Paris when he went there so soon after the worst days of the Commune. That France should be still in the iron grip of the enemy was galling to him; that her capital had been unable to withstand a siege was mortifying enough, but he was destined to witness the results of the work of the Communists, his own compatriots, and to mark the ghastly ruin wrought by the *pétroleurs* and *pétroleuses*. Armed with cans of petrol they had set on fire many of the noblest buildings of the city. Accounts reached him first-hand of the street fighting in which horrible excesses had so recently been committed. He heard from eye-witnesses of the mass executions in the prisons, in which

Frenchmen had shot their fellow countrymen in batches, inflamed with a blood-lust against which the holiness of an Archbishop or the power of a President had been of no avail. Twenty-five thousand Communists were still awaiting trial in the prisons late in September, and the evacuation of the Paris forts by German garrisons had only begun at the end of the month.

The *Ecole Polytechnique* had not escaped from the mania for violence that possessed the city for a time. When the scum of Paris, under the leadership of a deformed cobbler inflamed with a maniacal lust for destruction, had installed themselves in the school buildings in May, their triumph had been short-lived. It was the 17th Battalion of Chasseurs belonging to the Versailles Army that stormed the school. The Communists fled by way of the chemical laboratory.

The buildings had not escaped damage. They had been hit by some shells from the *Père la Chaise* batteries, during a bombardment of the Panthéon. One shell burst in the hospital, seriously wounding one of the male attendants.

Depressed by the suffering of Paris, Foch went to the *Polytechnique*. He entered somewhat at a disadvantage. As a *"Postard"* (one prepared for the entrance examination at a Jesuit college, rue des Postes), he had to submit to the lecture that was delivered to all such by a senior cadet, recommending them *"à se défaire de la tournure d'esprit qu'ils avaient dû contracter dans les établissements d'où ils sortaient."* We can imagine the effect at that age upon so sensitive a nature, but such incidents strengthened rather than reduced his faith, and though in after years his strong religious convictions did not improve his prospects in the Army, he rose to power in spite of them and by them he was strengthened in fulfilling his purpose.

Joffre—the "Papa Joffre" of whom Foch had so high an opinion when he served under him in the Great War—belonged to an entry senior to that of Foch at the *Polytechnique*. While the war was in progress Joffre and the other students had been called to arms. They had served with the garrison of Paris and they did well in minor commands, holding various positions, so Joffre had his "baptism of fire" early in his career.

We have mentioned the tragic memories attached to the recreation ground or courtyards of the School, where after the failure of the Commune the leaders of its activities in the neighbourhood were ranged for execution. Amongst others, Maurice Treillard, the Chairman of the Public Relief Committee of the Commune, had there met his death, and the billiard-room had been used as a temporary mortuary. We can imagine the inmost thoughts of young Foch on coming into such an atmosphere. To him it seemed that France had suffered grievous enough humiliation at the hands of a ruthless and insolent enemy. She had then experienced the horrors of internecine strife. He saw traces of ruin all around him, and we are told that at that time the *Ecole* itself was more like a monastery than a college for young men on the threshold of their careers. Some of the students had just lost their lives in battle. Others, Gazet among them, had died in the School hospital, and the whole place bore an aspect of mourning which even the presence of normally high-spirited youth could not dispel. There were no gaieties and no youthful amusements of any sort. Even the games common to such establishments were forbidden by the authorities. The disasters of the war and the horrors of the Commune weighed so heavily upon everyone that throughout the whole of the time that Foch spent there no entertainment of any kind took place. Even the traditional "Point Gamma" was omitted. But how was the future Marshal of France affected in his youth, outwardly at least, by such depressing surroundings? On the occasion when he put on his uniform for the first time he went with his friend Graef for a walk in the streets of Paris, and this is how he himself described the experience: "We walked about tapping the ground with our heels and we held ourselves very straight as if something had changed in the aspect of the universe!" If there is truth in the proverb that those whom the gods love are young when they die, Ferdinand Foch was certainly a favourite in such quarters. He retained that youthful buoyancy of spirit to the end of his days.

There is no doubt that young Foch dreamed constantly of the future glory of France. He had seen her not only conquered by external enemies but riven by internal strife. He longed to see her triumphant after she had been trampled in the dust. He saw in himself her champion, her defender, and one of those who would help to restore her former greatness at a time when all around him was chaos and despair. It must have required determination, trust in the future, and great faith in himself to cling to that ambition, to follow the path that he had marked out for himself, to force himself to put aside gloomy thoughts, and to concentrate on the studies that would help him to advance towards his ultimate goal.

Though Foch, born and bred amid rural surroundings, had no great love for cities and was faithful to the scenes of his early youth, he explored Paris very thoroughly while he was at the *Ecole Polytechnique* and he must have had a melancholy experience. When the first swagger of wearing a new uniform wore off, he is said to have paced the streets, gazing at the havoc wrought by the riff-raff whose defeat had been too recent for any attempt at restoration to be made even at the *Arc de Triomphe,* through which the Germans eleven months before had marched in triumph into the capital and remained for two days. The Hôtel de Ville, the Palais de Justice, the Palace of the Legion of Honour, the Ministry of Finance, and above all the Tuileries had been damaged by fire in the senseless destruction by French hands that followed. He explored Notre Dame, which only by great good fortune had escaped being blown up by the insurgents, and he lingered by the Panthéon where barrels of gunpowder had been placed in readiness. Returning to the School, he used to read in the great "Bibelo" library, now dispersed, the Napoleonic literature of which he already knew so much, and to wonder whether the words that the hero of his boyhood had given to the School as a motto in 1804 would ever be fulfilled: "Everything for liberty, knowledge and glory." What was French liberty, and what was it worth at that time? Knowledge he could certainly acquire, and there still remained to him the stubborn conviction that he would yet win glory for France. Such, we are told, were the imaginings of his nature at the time, and, in his own words: "Nothing makes us so great as a great grief."

Foch entered the School as Number 76; he was Number 47 when he left prematurely for a reason to be explained in due course. Several of his fellow students at the *Polytechnique* became famous in course of time. Joffre, the most eminent of them, after taking his part in the defence of Paris, had returned to complete his training. Foch also made great friends with a young Ruffey, a Bourguignan, with whom he had much in common. They were destined to meet in later life under very different circumstances, for Ruffey commanded an army corps in the Great War.

The surroundings of the School may have outraged Foch's ardent patriotism and caused him to find little pleasure in his time at the *Ecole Polytechnique* but he made good use of his opportunities. In later years he described the instruction of the College as excellent. They did not teach everything, which would be an impossibility, but "when one left there, one was able to understand anything"; in other words he learned how to learn. He would have stayed his full time at the School, but as he was beginning his second year, there came an appeal of the sort to which he was always ready to respond. It was at the *Polytechnique* that *La Revanche* as an object in life seems to have been fixed most firmly in his imagination, and the first step thereto was obviously to perfect himself in his profession.

As a result of military disasters, officers were urgently needed to restore the French Army to its proper strength, and with this end in view an appeal was issued to the *Polytechnique* students to enter the *Ecole d'Application* at Fontainebleau. Artillery and engineer officers were specially required, as soon as possible.

Foch was one of the first to respond. It may be that the thought of Fontainebleau and all its associations stirred his imagination, but, however that may be, he was accepted and he entered Fontainebleau on February 10th, 1873, remaining there until October, 1874, when he left as a Second Lieutenant in the Artillery.

At Fontainebleau he was enabled to forget, at least temporarily, some of his previous surroundings. The town, set in the midst of the forest, showed little trace of the turmoil of the war, and its broad streets brought back to him no unhappy memories of the swaggering conquerors of Metz, the triumphant martial music of Nancy, or the wreckage left by the Commune in Paris.

As a *"Petit Chapeau"* Foch worked at the Artillery School, but his duties there did not absorb all his time. In his leisure hours he took long rides into the forest, and visited scenes intimately connected with Napoleon. For a youth learned as he was in Napoleonic history and tradition, it was easy to conjure up visions of bygone days and to people the Palace with ghosts of the past. He spent many hours in the great salons, imagining the little Emperor pacing through the Palace—on which he had spent six million francs—thinking out new campaigns, or recalling the experiences that had raised a young artillery subaltern to be Emperor of France.

Foch took special interest in the Court of Adieux. It was there that Napoleon, at the foot of the Horse-Shoe Staircase, bade farewell to the Old Guard in 1814. It was easy to picture the scene, and to contrast the France of those days with the France of his own, though the years of Napoleon's glory doubtless made more impression than did the year of his fall upon a temperament just emerging from adolescence. Our young cadet spent much of his time alone when he was at Fontainebleau—alone, but never lonely, as his mind was well stored with the history of his surroundings. There were reminiscences of others besides the Emperor. Of Josephine, against whom the decree of divorce was pronounced within the walls of the Palace; of Pius VII, who had twice visited the place, once in 1804 when he came there to consecrate the Emperor, and again between 1812 and 1814, when he was there under less happy circumstances, as the Emperor's prisoner; and of many other courtiers, princes, and potentates who had fawned upon the Man of Destiny in his triumph or schemed for his downfall.

Foch used to say that after the time at the *Polytechnique* he had to plunge into the world to assimilate the theory that he had learned and to put practice in its place. He was happier at Fontainebleau than he had been at any time since his early days at Tarbes and Valentine. France seemed to be recovering; matters were slowly righting themselves; the first bitterness of defeat was passing; and schemes were already afoot for restoring the damage in Paris. The National Assembly were facing a difficult task and they showed some hesitation in undertaking the political reformation of the country as they did in reorganizing the military forces, but the Army ardently worked for its own regeneration, the only mistake made being the reinstatement of too many of the officers of the Second Empire when they returned from captivity. Foch's view was that the Second Empire had been brilliant. The Army contained fine fellows, fine talkers, elegant and effervescent and therefore worthless. "The leaders knew how to make war as well as elephants know how to climb a ladder." There were no commanders. Colonels were fit to command companies. ("And even more, for walking in front and crying 'Forward!' with cigar in mouth.") They were followed, for they were brave, but bravery was quite beside the point. Though they were fine soldiers, they were not *leaders*. What was wanted of leaders was aptitude for command. They were really not stupid; they were even intelligent, with good manners, plenty of go, and plenty of good humour. "But it is not enough to strut about and march past in brilliant style"—a lesson for armies for all time.

The spirit of reform that permeated the French Army at

this period undoubtedly gave Foch encouragement in his career. The spirit was spreading to the Artillery School. Foch enjoyed his life there. It suited his simple tastes, and the disciplined routine was no hardship to him as he had been reared amid healthy, hardy surroundings. He realized the necessities of his training and he fulfilled all his duties cheerfully, giving satisfaction to those in authority over him. As at St. Clément he was popular with his comrades. In 1874, when he had completed his time at Fontainebleau, he passed out third. The young officers were given their choice of a post, and Foch chose the garrison of his birthplace, Tarbes, where the 24th Artillery Regiment was stationed.

His choice gives a good indication of his character at this period. Most of the young subalterns when they were offered a similar choice voted at once for the gayest garrison town of which they knew, but life of that kind was never to Foch's taste. Sport and an outdoor life, with facilities for riding and for reading appealed to him most strongly. At Tarbes he renewed his acquaintance with the old town in which he had passed his childhood. His fondness for horses had increased, so it was good to be among the horse-fairs again. He spent two years at Tarbes, during which time he went through the routine common to all young artillery officers, and in 1876 he was transferred to the Cavalry School at Saumur.

Riding-school put the finishing touches to his horsemanship. He naturally had a good seat and hands from an early age and as he was a good judge of horseflesh he usually secured good mounts. He was so keen and he spent so much time in the saddle that he always walked like a cavalryman, and there are grounds for believing that the illness from which he was suffering at the outbreak of the War—an affection of the kidneys which caused him considerable suffering—was attributable to his devotion to spending long hours in the saddle.

Foch liked Saumur, and he enjoyed long rides in the beautiful surrounding country. With his usual craving for knowledge he explored the Roman and Celtic remains in the district, in spite of his well-known saying: "The past—let it alone!"

Foch was now gradually expanding his experience. The youth of ideas was developing into the man of action, and a favourable opportunity is afforded to study what he told others of the philosophy of life which had begun to grow in him when his comprehensive education had taught him how to learn and he had begun to put theory into practice. Foch was by temperament a man of action. "Ideas? However good they may be, they are of no use unless they are translated into facts. . . . Act, and you will be taken into account." He emphasised the need for keeping an object in view and for choosing a course to pursue. Thought before action. Then one must persevere in one's studies, not a difficult matter if one reduces everything to simplicity, ignoring the non-essentials. He had no belief in natural gifts. Intelligence was wanted, but above all will-power. Everything depended upon will, and given an average intelligence, understanding comes with will. If a man directs his whole will to a fixed goal and perseveres, seeing to it that his mental powers are kept up to the mark, he is quite certain to reach that goal. Grasp some idea, establish it as a guiding star, keep your eyes steadfastly fixed upon it, and then combine a strong will with well-directed work.

"Know what you will, and do it," was his precept.

Throughout his own life he knew what he "willed" ("resolved," "decided," or "determined," would perhaps be good substitutes). He also had no doubts about his ability to achieve his purpose, and he had little patience with others who were content to drift with the tide.

"Do as I have done," he once said. "When a man of ordinary capacity—I repeat, of ordinary capacity—concentrates all his faculties and his means upon the attainment of a single purpose, working hard, and not being diverted from his goal, he is bound to attain it."

He took no account of arguments, prevalent at the time, on the influence of heredity and environment upon character and career, nor of the "eternal inequality of human fate" in the matter of opportunity. With him, it was simply a question of wise selection of purpose, and of concentration upon that purpose. To that quality his own strength and achievement can undoubtedly be attributed. Whether his own original capacity was "ordinary" is not susceptible of proof.

Foch's concentration of purpose seems to have impressed almost everyone with whom he was brought into contact, but he did not parade it. He was not a prig, quite "human," with his fair measure of little weaknesses and foibles, but they were never allowed to interfere with any task that he had set himself nor with any intention upon which his will had been fixed. This story is typical:

While he was at the Cavalry School one of his brother officers said of him: "Foch is very agreeable; he will fall in with any of your plans, always providing that he has not already made one of his own!"

Though he was not easily offended he was capable of strong dislikes. He was impatient of weakness in any form, and like all men with such a nature he had little sympathy with pretentiousness. Even as a young man he was not easily taken in by appearances. Direct, truthful, and inclined to be blunt himself, he appreciated like qualities in others. He passed out fourth from Saumur, leaving behind him an impression that his career would differ from that of most of his brother officers. For Foch himself the future seemed to be brighter; he was advancing in his career; France was recovering; and he looked forward to his next appointment with satisfaction.

In 1878 he became a Captain in the 10th Regiment of Artillery at Rennes in Brittany, a place that twenty-one years later was to become notorious as the scene of the Dreyfus Court Martial.

Chapter V

FOCH'S ARMY TRAINING: 1871-1878

AGED 20-27 YEARS

In the preceding chapter details of the training that applied to Foch as to other officers of the French Army of his day have been omitted in the belief that they would appeal less to the general reader than to the professional.

The qualifications for appointment as sub-lieutenant with commissioned rank depended upon the arm of the Service which the candidate wished to join. Those destined for the cavalry, infantry, and colonial troops went to St. Cyr, which corresponds with the English Sandhurst, and those for the artillery and engineers to the *Ecole Polytechnique* where the course lasts normally for two years. This establishment also trains candidates for the *Ponts et Chaussées,* telegraphs, State factories, and other public departments in which technical knowledge is required. The initial cost of outfit, subscriptions, etc. amounts to about £30, and the annual cost of the education is £40. There are other roads of entry into the commissioned ranks of the Army, but with these we are not concerned.

Artillery and engineer cadets who qualify in the two-year course are sent under normal conditions to regimental duty for a year, when they go to the *Ecole d'Application* at Fontainebleau, already described, for two years' further instruction. The artillery also possessed schools for senior officers of

[54]

artillery, and courses of instruction are given at the Head-quarters of each brigade. The Cavalry School at Saumur is the *Ecole d'Application* for the cavalry, and at the time it was intended both for training young cavalry officers who had just obtained their commissions and also for further instruction of lieutenants both in the cavalry and in the artillery. It was under these conditions that Foch joined the School after performing a period of regimental duty and training at Tarbes, the scene of his early education. To for-eigners the designation of the School at Saumur is a little confusing. *Ecole de Formation* is the name applied to St. Cyr and the *Polytechnique,* the name implying that the instruc-tion is specially designed for special arms of the Service, but Saumur, though called the *Ecole d'Application* also performs the functions of an *Ecole de Formation* for the cavalry. In order to picture to ourselves Foch's participation in what we should perhaps call a "course" in the British Army, a de-scription of the celebrated establishment at Saumur will not be out of place, especially in these days when the machine is doing so much to supplement and to replace the horse in all armies. In Foch's day mobility depended upon the horse, though the machines, especially motor-lorries, were being introduced in 1914 and rapid developments followed.

The little town of Saumur with its fine old feudal chateau is situated on the left bank of the Loire between the river and the surrounding white cliffs. The climate is proverbially mild, and the great wine country extends in every direction. A riding academy was founded by Henri IV, and first opened in 1771 when every cavalry regiment sent four offi-cers and four non-commissioned officers there every year. It was swept away by the Revolution and not revived until 1815. In 1824 it was established on its present site. During the forty years which preceded the Franco-Prussian War French cavalry officers had only the regulations of 1829 to guide them, so there was much leeway still to be made up at the time when Foch joined the school in 1876, but the best riders and the best horses in the French Army had already begun to find their way there. From that date onwards Saumur has witnessed a period of unbroken progress. A British artillery officer [1] visiting the place reported in 1908 on the "picked horses, judicious expenditure and well-directed energy which had been combined to build up a unique establishment which is the pride of the French Army and justly celebrated throughout Europe;" and four years earlier a British cavalry officer [2] furnished an exhaustive report on the school and on the system of instruction there given:

The Staff included a Colonel as Commandant, a Lieutenant-Colonel as second in command, six Majors, about forty-five Captains or Lieutenants as instructors, about one hundred and fifty cavalry reservists to look after the horses, and four officers and about three hundred and fifty men to provide guards, officers' servants, and to do the necessary work of the establishments. Everything was on an elaborate scale, and the courses of training were comprehensive, including equitation, *Exercices Militaires,* and theoretical instruction, with special schools for veterinary work, telegraphy, and signallery, horse-shoeing, fencing, and the manufacture and fitting of saddlery. Four classes of horses were to be seen, thoroughbreds, heavy and light half-breeds (hunter class), and Anglo-Arabs, bred in the south of France

[1] Major G. T. M. Bridges (now General Sir Tom Bridges), *Cavalry Journal,* 1908.
[2] Major G. K. Ansell, 6th Dragoons (killed in the Great War).

in the district that Foch knew so well. A specialty was made of training horses to be sufficiently supple, well-mouthed, and responsive to the legs of the rider to acquit themselves creditably in the tricks of the *Haute Ecole*. This training was carried out by a large special staff of *écuyers*.

The *Exercises Militaires* included staff rides or regimental tours working out schemes which lasted for half a day; field exercises in various duties that would be performed by small bodies of cavalry in war; cavalry work in combat and drill; foot drill; fencing, physical drill and gymnastics; musketry and revolver practice; and *viva voce* instruction by question and answer. The schools of veterinary work, telegraphy, farriery, and saddlery performed the functions that these names denote. The object of the officers' courses was to train them not only as leaders but also as instructors, an important point when, owing to their short service, so many men were passing through the ranks and required intensive training to become efficient in so short a time. The object of *Haute Ecole* or trick-riding was to add a little more *éclat* to the horsemanship of the *écuyers* and show the students what a perfect horseman can make his horse do by judicious use of hands and legs. No time was wasted in teaching all that to the students. It is an interesting point that up to the date of that account (1904) more fencing than musketry was done at the school, the object being to keep the men slim and active as they grew older.[3] Foreign officers as well as French were attracted to Saumur, and there were American, Spanish, and Swedish officers there at the time of reporting.

These brief notes on the Cavalry School at Saumur will

[3] Full information about the scope of the examinations for Saumur and other *Ecoles d'Application* is to be found in the *Programme des examinations,* published by Charles-Lavauzelle, Boulevard Saint Germain, Paris.

suffice to enable us to understand the thoroughness of the training undergone by Foch as a lieutenant of artillery. The classes attending at that establishment included *sous-lieutenants* from St. Cyr, *Elèves-Officiers,* cavalry non-commissioned officers qualifying for commissions, and *Lieutenants d'Instruction,* of whom about one-third were artillery or engineer officers, the remainder belonging to the cavalry. There remains the question of recreation, which in Foch's day seems to have been very much as it was when visited in 1908, and it was reported by Major Bridges that:

The Saumurians believe with the late Mr. Gladstone that change of work is the best recreation, and most of them may be seen schooling a horse in the short hours of leisure. There is, truth to tell, not much else to be done. In winter, however, there are several packs of hounds within reach, and the nominal leave for one day's hunting a month is liberally extended. Pupils hunt their own horses or their *chevaux d'armes* chargers. There is no polo, but Paris, the sovereign remedy for *l'ennui,* lies but four hours distant, and there is a fast afternoon train. . . . All ranks appear to throw their hearts into their work with a devotion calculated to ensure success in any undertaking.

Such was the nature, while the French Army was rapidly reviving in the years after the Franco-Prussian War, of the experience that was undergone by Foch between the years 1876 and 1878. As he was soon to be selected for further training in Staff work, a few notes on that subject in the French Army will not be out of place in this chapter.

In 1821, soon after the death of Napoleon, a Staff School (*Ecole d'Etat-Major*) was set up to train embryo Staff officers as distinguished from the regimental officers in the Army. The cavalry and infantry cadets at St. Cyr and the artillery and engineer cadets at the *Polytechnique* were given an opportunity if they passed sufficiently high in the final examinations to go direct to the *Ecole d'Etat-Major,* and if they succeeded in graduating there they became Staff officers for the whole of their period of Army service. They did no regimental duty at all and in fact never belonged to any unit or corps, and this system proved most undesirable. The Staff were out of touch with the troops and had little knowledge of their requirements, their opinions, or even of their nature. These points came into prominence in the disastrous war of 1870-71 when it was imagined that the troops were ready "to the last gaiter-button" for immediate service. Soon after that experience we know that many of the senior officers of the Army of the Empire, of whom Foch spoke so caustically in later years, vigorously contested reform, being still imbued with the old ideas.

In 1878, the year in which Foch left the cavalry school at Saumur, the name of the Staff School was changed to *Ecole Militaire Supérieure.* Candidates for the Staff were then drawn from the regiments in order to be trained as Staff officers, but the reform was only half-hearted since once they had been so trained they remained on the Staff permanently, as they had in the days before 1870. About two years later (1880) there was a strong agitation for reform, the calamity of 1870-71 being directly attributed to a faulty Staff system in a series of articles in the press by Major Maillard. This officer was destined subsequently to teach infantry tactics at the Staff College from 1882 to 1890. Foch was to be one of his pupils, as we shall see in due course. In spite of the "die-hards" the spirit of reform was abroad, and in 1880 the name was changed to *Ecole Supérieure de Guerre,* as it is at present. In due course it will be desirable to describe that establishment in greater detail. Meanwhile we can take note of the point that with a change of name there was a change of policy. Permanent service on the Staff ceased and the special corps apportioned to that service was abolished. Regimental officers who had qualified at the Staff College spent the remainder of their service alternating between Staff and regimental duty until they reached the higher commands. We shall find, therefore, in due course, that after going through the Staff College, Foch was given practical experience with troops, and entered the Great War not only as a leader of academic thought and war philosophy, but also as an experienced leader of troops in so far as peace conditions can provide experience.

In other matters of Army reform which gave Foch great encouragement to look hopefully at the future, a very important law was passed in 1873 which contained the basic principle of raising and maintaining military forces in France which obtain to this day. In 1875, the year of a renewed German menace when the French stood at arms, ready to receive an attack, another law was passed that had a good influence upon organisation, strength, and efficiency, and from 1883 onwards progress was marked by further legislation.

In 1889, on account of the growth of the German Army, further steps were taken. In order to increase the available numbers for the French Army, liability to Army service was extended and three years were spent with the colours and ten in the Reserve for the Regular Army, six in the Territorial Army, and nine in the Territorial Reserve.

These notes will suffice for the time being to enable us to follow the principles underlying the selection of Foch for further military experience.

Chapter VI

REGIMENTAL DUTY AND THE STAFF COLLEGE: 1878-1887
AGED 27-34 YEARS

RENNES was Foch's next post after Saumur. He went there in 1878 with the rank of Captain to join the 10th Artillery Regiment. Rennes at once made a special appeal to him, and Brittany became in course of time the land of his adoption. This Celtic country with its traditions, its legends, and its ancient history, appealed to the imagination of so devout a Catholic, and owing perhaps to the fact that he met his wife there, Brittany ever afterwards held a strong attraction for him. Soldiers coming from that neighbourhood were always, with him, "My Bretons."

In 1880 he lost his father, to whose early training and example he had owed so much. Bertrand-Jules-Napoléon Foch died on the 30th of March in that year at the age of seventy. Members of the Foch family were said to "die young" at such an age, owing to the healthy life that they led, and we know that when an A.D.C. asked the Marshal some time after the War whether his parents lived long, the reply was "No. My father ate nothing when he woke in the morning, and at 11 o'clock he only had a couple of eggs. He did not get enough nourishment." The A.D.C. (Bugnet) claims to have got a smile out of the Marshal when he expressed surprise at the idea that passing the three-score years and ten could be described as dying young.

[61]

At Rennes Captain Foch met for the first time the lady who was to become his wife, and here, as in other matters, his wisdom and prudence did not forsake him. He was fortunate in his choice. He recognised in her the one woman with whom he could be happy, whom he could make happy; and he found an ideal helpmeet.

Mlle. Julie Bienvenue was an orphan and an only child. She came of very much the same class as Foch himself, with a line of ancestors intelligent, intensely self-respecting, and noted for the same strong religious faith that had characterised her husband's family. Many of her direct ancestors had been lawyers, and the family were well known in Brittany; both her father and grandfather were barristers, of the Court of Rennes. Her grandfather, a ripe scholar possessing the sensitive, retiring nature which so often distinguishes the learned, had also been a Councillor, and Mlle. Julie had inherited many of his qualities. A cultured yet an excellent housewife, and afterwards a devoted mother, pleasant to all but showing no signs of weakness, she was a worthy mate for the future Marshal with whom she lived in complete accord until the day of his death.

The wedding took place on the 5th of November, 1883, at St. Brieuc, and the bridegroom was destined within a few weeks to face one of the great sorrows of his life, the death of his mother which took place in the same year. His father having passed away three years before, the death of his mother meant that the old home must be broken up. To a man of such strong family affections, the loss of both parents came as a severe blow, but one happily softened by the affection and companionship of his wife and by the new interests in life which had come with marriage.

Foch, like his father, believed firmly in home life. He

wanted a settled existence, and in the intervals of his military service he showed the love of the hearth which, contrary to popular belief, is a strong feature of the French temperament. Soon after their marriage the young couple settled down in an old château with estate of Traoufeunteniou at Ploujean near Morlaix in the extreme west of Brittany, between the Montagne d'Arree and the Atlantic coast.

In its simplicity and surroundings the château was a fit residence for a man of Foch's temperament. Like him the house had no outward pretensions. It was massive and designed to withstand the encroachments of time, a rather long house, built of solid grey stone, with a high-pitched roof, innumerable windows opening to the sun, and the wide spaces which Foch loved. The gnarled stems of ancient vines and tendrils of fragrant honeysuckle clung to the grey walls, which were surrounded by great trees, the last survivors of the vast forests of Broceliande.

Like so many men whose chief characteristic has been simplicity, Foch was fond of trees. Forestry was one of his favourite recreations and he would work happily for long hours, making new plantations, cutting down the old giants which had succumbed to the onslaughts of time, and planning new vistas and new rides through his estate.

The period succeeding his marriage was happy and peaceful. He enjoyed his military duties; there seemed to be every prospect that he would advance in his chosen career, and he was able to spend all his leave with his wife at his château, enjoying the peace of a home, walking with his wife, planning with her improvements on the estate, reading and studying, or working among his trees. The château was not far from the village church at Ploujean, and, good Catholics as they were, the Fochs built a domestic chapel in the grounds at the side of the house, which they often visited for their private devotions.

Sometimes Foch would go out shooting with his dog, and he took long walks in the neighbourhood exploring the country, reconstructing its past history, and chatting with the inhabitants with whom he soon became popular. He understood and sympathized with the folk of the country-side, and he used to listen patiently and with real interest to the stories that they told him. He generally knew all about the men and women who stopped to tell him of some small, but to them highly important happening: that the family cow had presented them with a calf which he must certainly come and see; how the bees had been of a laziness incredible—Rennes was famous for its honey—how *le petit* Jacques had cut a double tooth, and so forth. To all such happenings Foch lent a sympathetic ear, finding in the chatter of these folk memories of his boyhood in the old home at Tarbes.

In due course four children were born to the Fochs, two daughters, who much to their father's satisfaction married soldiers, one Captain Bécourt and the other Captain Fournier, and two sons, one who died in his early youth, and the other, who had been christened Germain after Foch's favourite brother, whose fate it was to lose his life in the first few months of the War—a terrible blow to his father and a further incitement to the fulfilment of his life-purpose.

Of the seven years spent in regimental soldiering at Rennes there is little to write. We have evidence that Foch was reading widely to increase his knowledge and thinking deeply to assimilate it. That he "stood out of the ruck" is undoubted as he was selected to join the *"Section technique"* at the Ministry of War and in 1885 was chosen for a course at the *Ecole Supérieure de Guerre,* the equivalent of the British Staff College at Camberley, whither Ruffey, his friend and comrade at Metz, had proceeded earlier. It was at the *Ecole Supérieure* that he was to become more widely known in the Army. At the time when he entered the College it was just recovering from the depression and loss of prestige from which the Army had suffered since the experiences of 1870-71, and it is doubtful whether he found the place all that he hoped. In his *Principes de la Guerre* he wrote later:

It was not until a little before this period, in 1882, that a reasonable and practical teaching of War was given at the *Ecole de Guerre,* though the School itself dated from 1875. It is not sufficient to carve an inscription on the walls of a building to create a Staff College. Something is needed within.

He was himself to take a great part in providing "that which was needed within" from the time when, on joining the College, he reached the first step in the ladder of advancement toward the pinnacle of fame. A favourable opportunity is now offered for us to deal more comprehensively with the subject of the *Ecole Supérieure de Guerre,* with Foch's influence, with the influence of education and study upon his development, and with the position which the French Staff College now holds in the eyes of the world largely as the result of his pre-war writings and of the world-wide reputation earned by the armies of the Republic in the Great War.

It has been written of Foch by one who was intimately associated with him for nearly eight years that by the time he left St. Clément at Metz in 1871 for the *Polytechnique* his character had been finally formed. It rested on the deep

[65]

and solid foundations upon which he built the whole edifice of his career. His youth gave the general design of his future maturity, the main features were the same, only more deeply marked and constantly gaining in depth and in strength. While at the *Polytechnique* he was well taught and made to realize that the true mission of education is not to cram the brain with knowledge but to increase its faculty of acquiring knowledge, to teach how to learn. "When I left there," said Foch himself, "I was able to understand anything."

This faculty of understanding was in due course to prove of infinite value to the future Marshal of France when he secured his entry as a student at the *Ecole Supérieure de Guerre* in Paris, where he was destined to spend so many years, first as a student, then as a lecturer and professor, and finally as Commandant. There he learned in the end, as so many have learned before him, that though one has perhaps studied for many years most assiduously it is not until one has been charged with the responsibility for teaching a subject that one gains knowledge which is really deep and thorough. The mere fact that the teacher, if he has a vocation for such work, must see so many new aspects of his subject suggested by the inquiring brains of a succession of students, incites him to broader and to deeper thought, culminating in a knowledge which no other experience can provide as a preparation for the practical application of the increased understanding that has been acquired.

The *Ecole Supérieure de Guerre* is now the pride of the French Army, in that it attracts students of all ranks from General to subaltern officer, of twenty foreign nations, to learn what French leaders of military thought are so well qualified to teach them about the conduct of land warfare, more especially that branch of it which has been, and again may be conducted in theatres of war in Europe. The large building in which this Staff College for officers of the French Army is situated is an imposing edifice with a fine façade dating from 1750, and situated in a "live" quarter of Paris. The fact that it is sited in the metropolis confers a great advantage, though there are also some disadvantages, as, for instance, the distance from suitable ground to use for tactical and strategical exercises. These disadvantages have been much reduced since the Marshal was there as a student and as a professor by the improvement in facilities for transport, by the excellent motor-roads that radiate from Paris, and by the existence of high-power motor cars and motor coaches. The advantage which has always remained is the surrounding atmosphere of progress and learning and the presence in close proximity of leading civilian authorities in historical, literary, financial, economic, and scientific worlds. These men can be induced to convey through lectures and other channels their views to the future leaders of thought in the Army, thus broadening their outlook far beyond the purely military horizon and enabling them to become the men of wide views and culture for which the best French soldiers have carried such a well-merited reputation. "One must take a wide view. You all know I hate blinkers. One must not have an exclusive military outlook," was Foch's conclusion in the matter.

The great building in which the *Ecole Supérieure de Guerre* is situated also provides accommodation for the *"Centre des Hautes Etudes,"* a school of higher strategy for the more senior officers in the French Army which has its equivalent in the "War Course" at Greenwich for the British Navy, and, on a somewhat wider basis, in the "Imperial

College of Defence" recently established in London for senior officers of all the three natures of fighting forces in the British Empire. Excepting for the Commandant, there are no residential facilities, the space available being fully occupied by lecture-halls, studies, and offices of the *Centre des Hautes Etudes* and the *Ecole Supérieure de Guerre,* and at present by the residence of the Chief of Staff of the Army and by the necessary accommodation for married servants of these establishments. The members of the instructional staff and the students find their own accommodation in apartments or houses in Paris, but there is also a mess in one part of the building for "officers of the garrison of Paris," and here some of the unmarried students take their meals on occasion. The remainder of the accommodation in the great building is occupied by a riding establishment, fencing hall, and gymnasium.

Each new annual entry of officers is called a *"Promotion,"* which is divided into eight *"groupes"* for performance of the work. The course lasts for two years, and each Promotion includes about eighty officers of the French Army and about thirty foreign officers. These latter are nominated by their respective Governments, and they differ widely in rank, capacity, and attainments, but only the very best of the applicants in the French Army can expect to secure an entry. Several commissions composed of senior officers interview each French candidate before he can qualify for entry as a student, and the entrance examinations are both personal by oral tests, and on paper. The instructors, of whom there are no less than fifty, in addition to a central and organizing staff of ten, are men of high standing in their profession who retain their appointments for five years at a time, sometimes returning for a second period, and they nearly always earn

[68]

early promotion to higher rank. As "lookers on see most of the game," it may be apposite to quote here the opinion of one of the few officers of the British Army who has had an opportunity of gaining an intimate knowledge of the *Ecole Supérieure de Guerre:* "The Staff and instructors are as charming as they are competent and the students as good and as pleasant a lot as one would wish to meet." [1]

The annual course begins early in November, and the period from that month until about the middle of May is occupied mostly by indoor work, with two short vacations each of ten days, one at Christmas, the other at Easter. The second or outdoor period closely follows the first. It is spent in the practical application of theoretical knowledge, and it lasts until the end of August. The months of September and October can be spent by the students as they like, excepting by those who have not gained enough knowledge, before entering the college, of arms of the service other than their own. Roughly speaking, it may be said that the first-year course covers the handling of bodies of troops up to the size of a division. In the second year larger formations, up to the size of army corps, are studied. The work is always strenuous and the practical part of it involves long days in the saddle followed by much brain-work in writing orders and in organizing imaginary troops. Every detail is mastered, and the working day sometimes lasts from 7 A.M. to 2 A.M. For the more extended exercises large convoys of Citroën cars are used nowadays, and the training culminates in the performance of the Staff work for a large army of several corps, with the senior officers of the *Centre des Hautes Ecoles* taking the place of the higher commanders. The eastern frontiers of France are visited, and lessons are now carried on

[1] *Journal of the Royal Artillery Institution,* April, 1929.

[69]

at the actual scenes of the battles of the last Great War. During the whole two-year period the work of each student is constantly scrutinized and assessed, the results being finally collated, and it is from this setting of zeal, constant application, and crucial tests that Marshal Foch emerged with the air of distinction as a leader of thought that he was destined to confirm in later years as a leader of great armies.

As the *Centre des Hautes Ecoles* has here been mentioned in addition to the Staff College proper, it will be as well to take note of the point that Weygand, who was Foch's chief Staff officer in the days of his fame, did not pass the Staff College. He attended one of the senior officers' courses there, which were introduced by Foch in the days when he was Commandant, and were nicknamed in the French Army the course for budding Marshals (*Cour des Elèves Marèchaux*). Foch's periods at the Staff College, first as a student, then as a professor, and finally as Commandant seem to have caused him to dread the vogue of excessive theory unless it was combined with abundant practice and experience: "the power to get things done" was his ideal in an officer:

Some men have superior intelligence, which shows them all possible solutions of a problem; but they do not know how to choose one of these, still less to apply it. Others, if offered decisions, will choose the best, but will be incapable of showing initiative. *The power to get things done* calls for certain qualities: intelligence, judgment, imagination, decision.

Foch was to find these qualities in Weygand, who not only had not passed the Staff College, but had had no previous experience of Staff work when he came to Foch, so he brought a fresh mind to bear on the subject and was not bound by regulations which his Chief abhorred. He "got things done."

Reverting now to our narrative, we find that Foch spent nearly two years as a student at the School where he was later to be one of the most brilliant masters it had ever known. In 1887 he left Paris to spend a probationary period on the Staff at Montpellier, afterwards becoming an officer on the Divisional Staff in the same town.

By virtue of his personality, knowledge, and hard work he was placed fourth in order of merit amongst the large number of officers who formed the "Promotion" of his year, and the placing does credit to those who were in authority at the *Ecole Supérieure de Guerre*. It is not always easy to pick out leaders in embryo by virtue of the evidence of academic exercises.

Chapter VII

THE RISE TO REPUTATION: 1888-1895

AGED 37-44 YEARS

HAVING been so well reported on at the Staff College, Foch had not to wait long for Staff employment, and there was little delay over his further advancement. The divisional Staff work at Montpellier covered more or less a probationary period, and in 1891 he was promoted to the rank of Major (Commandant). His good work as a student at the Staff College had subsequently attracted the attention of those in power, and Major Delanne, one of his former Commanders, invited him to come to Paris to join the Third Section of the General Staff of the Army. This widened his experience considerably. He took up his work in February, 1891, and these later times in Paris must have contrasted very strongly with the first visit that he had paid there when he was a cadet in the *Ecole Polytechnique*. His memories of the city of those days were never entirely effaced, but the new Paris was very different from the city which, desolate and ravaged, had confronted the young cadet directly after the Franco-Prussian War. All traces of the Communist riots had disappeared. The public buildings were restored to their proper proportions, many of them better than they had been before the attack of the incendiaries. The Grand Opera House had been completed and there were several fine new buildings the sight of which was likely to cheer the heart of an intense patriot. The recovery of France after the War had exceeded all expectation. The indemnity of £200,000,000 in gold had all been paid off in September, 1873, every peasant contributing, and the last German troops—occupying Verdun—had left French soil within a fortnight. So rapid was the recuperation that in 1875 the militarist party in Berlin, fearing a war of revenge, were anxious to smite again, and in the same year four great volumes of addresses from towns in France conveying thanks to England for relief in the war and containing 12,000,000 signatures were presented to Queen Victoria. During these years Bazaine had been tried and condemned to twenty years' imprisonment. The fortifications of Paris had been renewed in 1876. The Army had been affected by political unsettlement which led in 1877 to the dismissal of a general (Ducrot) from his command for suspected association with a proposed *coup d'état*. In 1880 the heads of departments in the War Office were dismissed, and in the same year the Order of Jesuits, to whose system of education Foch had owed so much, was dissolved by Decree. In 1887 there had been military scandals at the War Office. In 1889 all the world had flocked to Paris for the great Exhibition.

The two years (1889-1890) preceding Foch's arrival in Paris had witnessed the public activities and popularity of the celebrated General Boulanger, at one time a thorn in the side of the French Government, now only remembered by a music-hall refrain and by the nickname of *"l'hero du Café Concert."* Foch's rigid rule to have nothing to do at any time in his life with anything connected with politics may have stood him here in good stead. His views on the subject were clearly expressed in later years. He was told that unless he took part in politics he would "never get anywhere." He re-

[73]

plied that no politician would prevent him from being promoted and from getting the *rosette* of the Legion of Honour when he retired. Then he was told that he would never become a Commander of the Order. He reminded his hearer [1] in later years that this statement had not affected him much. He had gained the *cravate,* the *plaque,* and eventually the *Grand Cordon.* And the others who held that intrigue was essential in order to succeed? . . . There was no need to answer. His principle, as he put it, was to "work and to follow the paths of honesty," which with him was not a copy-book maxim, but a genuine principle followed throughout and governing his career. He kept out of political matters altogether, even in conversation, and it was well that he did so as there were plenty of *"affaires"* during the time that he spent in Paris. He seems to have had little sympathy, perhaps almost an aversion, towards men of words. He had Napoleon's maxims by heart, especially "Deeds take priority over ideas, actions over words, practice over precept." He seems to have found the Army Staff rather old-fashioned at that time, and confessed afterwards to having been considered somewhat revolutionary in his ideas, as he had a strong objection to red tape and to "pigeon-holes." When he was criticised he asked whether he had put every point bearing on a question. When told that he had, he said: "What more do you want?" He did not think much of the Autumn Manœuvres as they were in the early nineties. On one occasion he was entrusted with the work of organizing the Review with which they always concluded. He astonished them by massing troops in so small a rectangle and by the speed and smoothness of his arrangements. At 8 A.M. the ground was empty. Within ten minutes it contained 100,000,

[1] Commandant Bugnet.

men, who had arrived from all directions in columns, and the parade ground was empty again a quarter of an hour after the march past. Every unit had made for its entraining station by a separate route and they had disappeared "like a flock of sparrows."

In spite of the various political *"affaires,"* the French Army had reformed itself from within, and it had made gradual and steady progress during the twenty years which had intervened since the war of 1870-71. The officers were good, the discipline was good, and so were the arms and equipment. Perhaps one of the most important reforms, affecting vitally, as it did, the strength of the French Army, was the passage of a Bill in July, 1889, to reduce the term of compulsory service in the Army from five years with exemptions to three years, nominally without exemptions. The writer was in Paris at the time, and remembers well the cries of *"La nouvelle loi militaire, cinquante centimes!"* on the Boulevards and the avidity with which copies were purchased. Public opinion supported the Army reformers.

After Paris Foch went to Vincennes for regimental duty, to command the 3rd Battery of Horse Artillery. He found the experience interesting, though it is doubtful whether he thought the connexion between Vincennes and Napoleon was quite as palatable to him, as a hero worshipper, as the associations of Fontainebleau had been. The fosse of the castle was the scene of the shooting of Louis, Duc d'Enghien, by order of the great Corsican after a hasty trial early in the morning of March 22nd, 1804. On the 18th of May in the same year Napoleon was proclaimed Emperor. The State prison at Vincennes held more tragic memories than when it was the Royal Castle of the French Kings.

In 1894 he was recalled to the General Staff at Headquar-

[75]

ters in Paris. On the 31st of October, 1895, he became lecturer (Associate Professor) of military history, strategy, and applied tactics at the *Ecole Supérieure de Guerre*.

Throughout the years when Foch was passing from post to post, doing both regimental and staff duty, he constantly studied the theoretical side of his profession, and worked at the problems connected therewith. It is surely one of those strange contradictions to which humanity is subject that Foch, who, as he tells us himself again and again, was first and last a man of action, should have first earned fame through his devotion to the theoretical side of his profession. Even at that time accounts of his brilliance in that direction had been spread in the Army, and this led to his selection for the Staff College lectureship. Within a year he was promoted to Lieutenant-Colonel and became Chief Instructor, giving lectures that attracted the widest attention and caused something of a sensation in military circles both by reason of their matter and of their form.

Up to this time Foch had trained himself, mentally and physically, as far as peace conditions permitted, to be himself a leader in the field. Now he was to have an opportunity of influencing others and he said, in after years, "what forced me to work at my profession was having to teach it." An audience of Staff College officers, of men of high mental capacity collected from afar, is highly critical of instruction. Once converted to any special views, the members of a class leave as missionaries to all formations in the Army. A Staff College lecturer who can convert his hearers to any doctrine of war spreads his views throughout the Army, and the lesson that Foch taught was that there is *no* doctrine of war and *no* dogma. To deal with a situation wisely and promptly, a leader must be so soaked in the knowledge that he has acquired that he applies it automatically, without searching his brain for precedents. There are no precedents. He must think deeply of the factors in the actual situation with which he is called upon to deal. *"De quoi s'agit-il?"* What is the problem? This he must decide, and then *act*. Above all, act. It was always by their actions, by their deeds, that Foch judged others. Never by arguments or by dialectics. His test of a good soldier was the Biblical test of a good Christian, and he was both: "I will recompense by their deeds."

From the outset his lectures attracted attention, and, as it is rarely possible to obtain the candid opinions of students on the subject of the capacity of their teachers, we are fortunate in being able to quote, from an article by a well-informed writer in the *Correspondent,* an extract reproduced by M. René Puaux and Major Recouly. He tells us that the successive classes of officers who passed through the Staff College between the years 1896 and 1901 never forgot the impressions which they received from Foch's personality and lectures. His special course in strategy and applied tactics was one which always aroused lively interest and attention. It was regarded as the foundation of all that was taught at the College. The forty-eight officers selected to form a class arrived with a keen desire to form and to develop their military knowledge and judgment, but in addition to that they looked forward to the chance of coming into contact personally with the expert who had been specially chosen to impart to them the doctrine of scientific warfare. Foch more than fulfilled their hopes and expectations.

The writer then gives a valuable personal touch in a description of Foch's appearance at this time and the impression made upon those whom he taught. The description shows him as slender and distinguished in appearance. He wore with an air the jacket and dolman then worn by artillery officers "which a deplorable mania for uniformity has since abolished." The first impression which Foch made upon his hearers was one of quiet strength and of intellectual honesty. His forehead was that of a thinker, his nose straight and clean-cut, while his greyish-blue eyes looked straight into those of his hearers. He spoke as one having authority, in a grave and rather a hoarse and monotonous voice, weighing his words carefully and often using long sentences to make every point of his close argument clear.

Then comes a point which throws much light upon what occurred in later years when Foch was entrusted with colossal power over a great army. "His discourse was not always easy to follow on account of its wealth of ideas and suggestions." We shall find in due course that the same was said of him by many of those with whom he dealt in the great crises of the War, and even Weygand, the brilliant Staff officer who became the future Marshal's second self, confessed, according to Bugnot, that he sometimes found difficulty in plumbing the depth of his Chief's mind. At the Staff College Foch was always ready to encourage discussion, provided that it was accompanied by logical reasoning. He had a great regard for logic, and also for mathematics, in which he had been pre-eminent in his youth, and through which he received as a boy the first impetus, given to him by a master at the *Lycée* of Rodez, to adopt a military career. He often employed mathematical terms in his lectures. Even when hard to follow, they repaid the very closest attention, not only on account of the keen insight which they showed into all branches of the subject dealt with, but also because of the evident sincerity and conviction of the lecturer.

The *Ecole Supérieure de Guerre* at that time had men of

distinguished mental "gifts" (Foch never believed in gifts) and brilliant lecturers, but amongst them all Foch stood out, in the opinion of the officers under instruction, as the most original thinker and the most profound student. They listened with avidity to his lectures and they all felt that by his influence their minds had been stimulated.

Foch, however, did more than stimulate men's minds. He also stimulated character and enthusiasm, and before he gained the power to do so he went through an experience of which few, excepting one so intimate with him as Weygand, ever heard the details. He felt very deeply the grave responsibilities which must be borne by all who aspire to teach their fellow men. Like all men truly great whose influence has been widespread, he realized that only bare truth can endure and prevail to the end (Zola's *La verité est en marche —et rien ne l'arrêtera*), and in the wilderness of war-doctrines and formulæ which he had encountered during many years of voracious reading he had become tortured by doubts. He felt himself to be sinking in a quagmire from which he was determined at all costs to struggle before he lectured to others. We can find in the decision at which he then arrived the solution to the widespread influence which resulted.

"Example," as Edmund Burke held, "is the school of mankind, and *they will learn at no other*," and, in the words of a living statesman,[2] "The strongest personalities are the outcome not so much of striving for personal success or fame as of patriotism and faith in an ideal." Foch's ideal at that crisis of his life was to spread truth. He knew that no lecturer, orator, or divine, however eloquent, can influence others permanently unless they themselves believe

[2] Lord Grey of Fallodon.

what they wish others to accept. Torn from one theory or idea to another, almost abandoning hope of discovering bare truths, his thoughts in a whirl, he suffered from a brainstorm or soul-storm, call it what we will. Easter-time, which meant much to him, was approaching, and he took the opportunity to leave Paris and to take refuge in complete solitude in the woods of Brittany.[3] The result, after many days of mental struggle and misery, was that at last truths were first dimly and then clearly discerned through the fog of formulæ which had kept his keen brain struggling so miserably.

We cannot trespass upon his privacy while he communed with himself in the wilderness. Others have been through periods of mental torture and self-distrust; few have spoken of their experience, but some, like King David of old and Charles Kingsley of modern times have given some indication of their sensations. Kingsley went so far as to say that the deeper a man fell into that horrible pit the better it was for him at the last; he rose from it all the stronger, with more sympathy for others giving him increased power and influence. Nevertheless it was a "horrible pit, mire and clay, where one can find no footing," and one sinks all the deeper for struggling; a place of utter loneliness where all men seem to be liars; a place in the outer darkness where a horrible dread overwhelms; a pit with no shape, no order, nothing but contradiction and confusion, the ground a bottomless quagmire of doubt, change, and shapeless dread. But the deeper a man sinks into it the more certain he is to find his feet upon a rock and the nearer he is to deliverance.

Foch found his deliverance by the same method as King

[3] The incident is described by Weygand in the *Revue des Deux Mondes* for May, 1929.

David and others—*De profundis ad te clamavi*—and he returned to Paris ready to deliver the lectures which were destined to produce the influence which has been described. The main lesson taught by those lectures to tortured brains, seeking solutions to complicated problems, is to be found in Foch's constant phrase *"De quoi s'agit-il?"* What is it all about? What is the definite problem? Sweep everything else out of your mind.

While he was holding his post at the Staff College, one of his contemporaries said of him that he had no personal ambitions for advancement; all that he worked for was to secure the triumph in the French Army of his ideas to which he clung with the faith of an apostle. The substance of his lectures was published subsequently in two volumes: *Des Principes de la Guerre* (1893) and *De la Conduite de la Guerre* (1894) which have had a wide circulation both in the French and in the English editions. They were recommended to all desiring to be candidates for entry at the Staff College, and extracts from them have been widely quoted. That they influenced thought and opinion in the French Army before the Great War is undoubted. It has been written that lack of his guiding hand and the reservations that he applied to the universal offensive (*"Attaquez! Attaquez!"* as the solution for all war problems), these reservations being the need for reconnaissance and *"fixation"* of the enemy,[4] was the cause of much that happened to the French Army in the early days of 1914.

[4] This quotation from Foch's doctrine is apposite here: "When one comes at night, without a light, into one's house what does one do? Does one not extend an arm in front of one, so as to avoid knocking one's hands against the wall? The extended arm is nothing but an advanced guard which keeps its suppleness while it advances, and only stiffens, more or less, when it meets an obstacle."

[81]

Lest future aspirants to the command of armies should rely upon Foch's writings rather than upon themselves—a course which would have been anathema to Foch himself—it is important to note that, in founding his deductions upon close study of the Napoleonic campaigns and on the Franco-Prussian War of 1870-71, he did not seek for the principles of successful strategy so much as for the underlying psychological basis of victory. In several accounts of the life of the Marshal many extracts, taken almost at random, have been made from his books to fill up the pages, but they must be read carefully as a whole and pondered over. They are not easy reading, and if delivered verbatim as lectures they would not be likely to grip an audience. Like all successful orators and lecturers, Foch probably felt the soul of each audience and used different words to each, but he taught the same lessons. "Reading out" whether from the pulpit or the rostrum, tends in course of time to fail to inspire and even to produce a soporific effect upon most brains.

As we are dealing with the life of the great leader of armies "through English eyes" it will not be out of place to quote, on the subject of Foch's teaching and practice, the opinion of the British official historian, Brigadier-General Sir H. Edmonds, who has had access to masses of material, on this question.[5] "Delving amongst the phrases and aphorisms," he writes, "with which the text abounds, one finds, however, that his main operative thesis is 'There is no salvation outside the offensive.' There continually occur such dicta as:

" 'Henceforward strategy can no longer prevail against that which assures and aims at practical results, Victory in battle . . .

[5] "Foch," *R. U. S. I. Journal,* May, 1929.

It is the initiative which must be secured everywhere. It is the offensive that must be launched at every point . . . There is only one method of dealing with an opponent: that is to fight him, and, for that matter, to overthrow him. Hence the idea of shock, composed of two elements, mass and impetus. . . . Modern war knows only one argument, the tactical act, battle . . . Attack equals victory . . . and forgetting Austerlitz and Waterloo never can the defensive lead to the enemy's destruction.' "

The historian reminds us, in this connection, that in Flanders in the autumn of 1914 Foch acted up to his precepts by showing the greatest objection to a defensive attitude, and he allowed rear lines to be made only as a concession to the odd ways of the British. Foch had laid down at the very beginning of his teaching *"un seul criterium, la raison"*; but now that the War has been fought it is quite clear that there was some false reasoning in his early views. It appears that he came to that conclusion himself. It has been said by M. Engerand, in his *Secret de la Frontière,* that, after the stabilisation of the front, Foch had the intellectual courage to say to his Staff:

Gentlemen, it remains for you to forget what you have learnt, and for me to do the contrary to what I have taught you.

More vital, as it turned out, than his cult of the offensive was his insistence upon the force inherent in the power of will of a commander, and in practice it was his own "will to victory" which went more than half-way to ensure his success. His favourite quotation was "A lost battle is a battle one believes lost." One can realize the effect of Foch's words on General Maud'huy at Arras in October, 1914:

There are three courses. You can retire, stand fast, or attack.
I forbid the first. You can take your choice of the other two.

It was in the power of driving others "to the battle" that
Foch was supreme. With a minute Staff, little more than
a personal one, he wielded great masses, appealing not to
the troops, but only to the higher commanders whom he
trusted to pass on his spirit.

Leaving the guidance of the trained and experienced
historian, we can add for ourselves, remembering that Foch
himself was to earn the name of Generalissimo, his remarks
concerning that position:

The Generalissimo alone indulges in art, in Strategy in the
fullest sense of the word, while the others confine themselves to
tactics, to Prose. He alone makes music and leads the orchestra;
the others only play their parts in this orchestra.

Throughout the whole of his life the characteristic that
stands out above all others is his consistency. What he
preached he practised, what he believed he endeavoured to
carry out in his actions, and all that he taught, all that he
himself learnt (for he confessed to have learnt as well as
taught during those years at the Staff College) he carried
out in many of his operations when he occupied commands
in the French Army. But his warning to others held good
with himself:

Let no one look for a complete, still less for an academic
treatise on the Art of War; this is simply a setting forth of the
principal points concerning the handling of troops, and its chief
object is to show that if a commander has the proper orientation,
he will always plan his manoeuvres in a rational manner.

Conceding the skilful manœuvre of the strategist and "proper orientation" in the views of the tactical leader, it is well worth while to give in Foch's own words his ideas on victory, for which both are working. These words, if we look back at his achievements, seem to embody the very essence of his thoughts and conduct:

The moral factor is the most important element in war; the will to conquer sweeps all before it. There is a psychological phenomenon in great battles which explains and determines their result. One hundred thousand men leave ten thousand of their number dead upon the ground and acknowledge themselves beaten; they retreat before the victors, who have lost as many men if not more. Neither one side nor the other knows, when they withdraw, what their losses have been nor how heavy those of the opposing force, therefore, it is not on account of material damage, still less from any computation of figures, that the losers give up the struggle. As General Cardot says in a very keen analysis: "Ninety thousand vanquished retire before ninety thousand victors, solely because they do not wish to fight any longer, and this reluctance is because they do not believe that they can win, and are therefore demoralized and unable to hold out any longer."

Thus the lecturer, destined in course of time to inspire the leaders of armies not of hundreds of thousands, but of millions, to apply that lesson and so to emerge victorious from the greatest battle in the world's history.

CHAPTER VIII

TEMPORARY ECLIPSE: 1900-1907

AGED 49-56 YEARS

FOR the proper understanding of the temporary setback in Foch's career which followed the increase in his influence described in the preceding chapter, it is necessary for us to go back for a few years and to recall the circumstances of the Dreyfus case, which created such bitter feelings in the French Army and nation, and so great a regret to all France's friends abroad.

Captain Alfred Dreyfus was arrested in October, 1894, and tried by Court Martial *in camera,* convicted on the evidence of War Office documents, sentenced to life imprisonment, degraded publicly, protesting his innocence in January, 1895, and by February he was undergoing his sentence in the penal settlement of the Isle du Diable, an island not inappropriately named in French New Caledonia. The incident followed closely upon the Boulanger *affaire* to which reference has already been made, and both these occurrences had the effect of intermingling Army and political issues. Further inquiries into the Dreyfus case were constantly demanded and he was ultimately brought to France and retried at Rennes, where Foch had spent several years in regimental duty, in August, 1899. Feeling ran very high and led to attempted assassinations and to duels. Dreyfus was "pardoned" by the President and released in

[86]

September, 1899, but it was not until July, 1906, that the Court of Cassation quashed the judgment of the Rennes Court. Finally, in July of the same year, Dreyfus was presented with the insignia of the Legion of Honour in the courtyard of the Staff College where he was degraded in 1895, the year in which Foch joined the College as a lecturer. Feeling in the intervening period ran high and political issues were involved.

In addition to the Dreyfus affair, a heated politico-religious controversy seriously affected the Army. There was much unsettlement in Paris over these and other incidents, accompanied by anarchism, suspicions of plots against the republic, and general unrest. In October, 1890, the Embassy of the Vatican was suppressed. In January, 1900, the Superior and Monks of the Assumption Fathers were accused of plotting against the Government. In the same month the stipends of several bishops were suspended by the Government. In June strong action was taken against highly placed officers, and the Chief of the General Staff and others resigned. So matters went on. There was a feeling of insecurity abroad, and a strong anti-clerical movement. Politics were unhappily allowed to mix themselves up with Army affairs, with unfortunate results that can easily be imagined, one of them being an intensely bitter feeling against all Catholics.

This feeling grew so strong and assumed such extraordinary proportions that it is said that the Ministry of War in Paris prepared secret *dossiers* in which a black mark was put against the name of every officer who was in the habit of attending Mass on Sundays.

Foch, an earnest and deeply religious man, made no parade of his faith but certainly never attempted to conceal

[87]

it. Religion was not with him a matter of mere words. He carried his beliefs into his life, and they formed the inspiration of his work. He said once that in the old days at Metz he always used to say to himself that he would not like to die until he could hang his sword up as a votive offering on the walls of the Cathedral, and that "once my motto was knowledge and conscience but I now say conscience and knowledge. Conscience first, for that is what matters more." He held that religious idealism, the devotion to the Divine, gave a man strength and courage for whatever might be his duty to do, and to him the fear that his religion might interfere with his worldly success carried no weight whatever.

To many at that time at the Staff College it was obvious that Foch might have remained if his religious opinions had been less well known. Foch himself would have sacrificed all prospect of any further advancement rather than give up any of the religious observances to which he had been accustomed and which he had followed all his life. "Do what you ought, and let circumstances take care of themselves," was his rule, and though he could no longer close his eyes to the fact that his career was in danger, he saw no reason to abandon his principles.

In 1900 General Bonnal, a military writer of world-wide reputation, succeeded General Langlois as Commandant of the Staff College, and in the same year Foch found that, by direction of higher authority, he was obliged to leave and to take up regimental duties once more. Putting matters more bluntly Bugnet, the A.D.C. who discussed the matter with the Marshal in later years, says that he was dismissed as a reactionary, unjustly sent in disgrace to Laon, kept under suspicion and deprived of advancement for three years although he was on the list for promotion to Colonel. Others similarly treated wanted to resign their commissions, but Foch called that desertion, adding: "You have no guts! When war comes you will have to put up with worse things than that. If you can't stand it now, what will you do then?"

The Army officers who were not prejudiced by the doctrinal controversy of the times sincerely regretted his departure, knowing that in Foch they had found not only a military professor with remarkable ideas but one who had the gift of being able to impart his knowledge and even his enthusiasm to the students. As an example of his inspiration to zeal by his own procedure: on one occasion he was conducting a Staff ride and on arrival on the ground he was "perhaps feeling a little tired," but owing to the large attendance of students who could not be sent back he determined to see the thing through. While on the way home, he was "peeling," so he consulted a doctor who diagnosed scarlet fever in a late stage. "Oh, it was nothing serious," said Foch when telling the tale. There were many who did not hesitate to say that his absence was only temporary and that it was inevitable he would return to the College where his influence had been so far-reaching.

The authorities had their way, and Foch joined the 29th Artillery Regiment at Laon there to be "buried" for the next three years according to those who understood his genius and wished to see it fully acknowledged. He is said to have left in good heart, and to have thrown himself into his routine work. This left him leisure which favoured the ripening in his mind of the knowledge that was to be of such great value to France.

It seems by some curious chance to have been his fate to be sent to places which were in some way connected with

Napoleon. He had last been stationed at Vincennes, with its memories of the Man of Destiny's dealings with those who stood in his path; he had been previously at Fontainebleau, and now he came to Laon, the scene of defeat of the French by the Prussians in Napoleon's brilliant but disastrous campaign of 1814.

Although Foch probably regretted leaving the Staff College and its associations, he wasted no time in regrets, and he soon gained as thorough a knowledge of Laon and its history and surroundings as he had of the other places to which he had been posted. Knowledge of Laon was to stand him in good stead in the appointed time. When he was there with his regiment it was not a place of much importance, apparently unlikely to grow. But it marks the junction of several railways on the line between Amiens and Rheims, of which much use was made during the German invasion in the Great War.

From the time when the incidents of Metz and Nancy had made so profound an impression on him in the days of his youth, Foch had made a diligent study of German psychology, losing no opportunity of exploring the mentality of Germans whom he happened to meet, particularly their outlook in military matters. He constantly studied German military text books ("I read Clausewitz. . . . There was a man for you!" was one of his sayings), and by the time that war broke out he had made himself so familiar with the workings of the German mind, and he was so thoroughly versed in their views on warfare that his knowledge sometimes helped him to foretell with extraordinary accuracy what the enemy would do under given conditions, though he professed in the early days of the War to lay little stress upon caring for the enemy's intentions. He concentrated on

his own. We shall come across examples when we arrive at
the period of the Great War, especially one when, early in
July, 1918, Foch staked not only his own reputation but the
safety of the Allied Armies in France upon his forecast of
the German intentions. This he confided only to his own
Staff for fear that the secret of the counter-stroke which he
was preparing should reach the enemy. By his reticence he
risked not only his control over the Allied Armies but the
support of the Allied Governments to whom he owed his
position.

On the other hand we have it on his own authority that
he was taken by surprise on the Marne in 1914 when the
enemy withdrew before the attack that he was staging, and
in April, 1918, when a British officer who knew him asked
what he thought that the enemy's object had been in making
a certain attack, Foch brushed the question aside with a
characteristic gesture and said "How should I know?" As
a matter of fact whatever he may have thought about the
enemy's intentions, he did not like discussing them. He used
to say that it was guess-work, and not worth while. The
study of German psychology from the days of his youth at
St. Clément onwards seems to have been the logical outcome
of the life-purpose formed at that time—*La Revanche*.

While he was at Laon Foch was urged by his friends and
some of his superior officers who knew the value of his
Staff College teaching, to prepare for publication in book
form the lectures that he issued under the title of *Principes
de la Guerre*. We have already touched upon the essence of
the teaching in that volume and further quotations from
it will probably be desirable to point out the moral when
his principles were tried by practice. One extract is, however,
apposite at this juncture:

When young officers join their regiments, and propose to study the conduct of troops in the field, they hear talk of certain principles which govern war.

They attempt in vain to discover these guiding principles; they cannot find them . . .

It has been attempted in the present book to define these principles, to explain from what necessities they arise, to what results they lead, and how, being unchangeable, they can be applied in practice with the arms of to-day to modern war.

To his views upon relying upon other people's opinions and "ideas" where it is a question of one's own, we shall refer in due course.

Though he had left the College, Foch continued to take a great interest in the careers of the students who had seemed to him to show promise while under his instruction, and nothing pleased him better than to hear that one of them had gained some special advancement. Though he was quiet and apt to be reserved, he was always generous to youth, mindful of its possibilities, and tolerant of its impulses, and the fact that while admiring him as a teacher they also respected him as a man helped in his influence upon the young officers. His test of capacity was action—as he put it himself: "One judges people by their achievements."

During the year 1903 in which he published his book Foch was promoted to the rank of Colonel and joined the 35th Artillery at Vannes, and two years later he published his second book, "The Conduct of War; Manœuvres in the Field," applying the principles to the war of 1870-71 and concluding the preface with the words: *"In memoriam, in spem"*—after sad remembrance, the hope of better days.

It is interesting to note, as an indication of his character and motives, Foch's scornful account therein of the method

employed by Bismarck to make the war of 1870 inevitable—
the forgery applied to the celebrated Ems telegram when
Moltke, Roon, and Bismarck were lunching together on
July 13th, as boasted of by Bismarck himself:

Then I took my pencil and deliberately struck out the passage
which stated that Benedetti had asked for another audience,
leaving only the beginning and end of the message, which gave
it quite another meaning. When I read the version I had just
made to Moltke and Roon they both cried "Splendid! That is
sure to produce one effect—" and we went on eating with better
appetites. Everyone knows what followed.

And Foch finds no words to express an opinion which
he would have conveyed to an audience by silence and a
gesture. He writes: "This story needs no comment."

He returned to Brittany, the land of his adoption, with
much satisfaction, and Vannes, with its narrow streets, its
old castle and its ancient history reminded him of his boyhood spent in provincial towns. Refusing to be overwhelmed
with administrative routine, he concentrated upon the one
essential—to teach his men to fire their guns.

Though his advancement had been arrested, it had not
been stopped. Wiser counsels prevailed in high places and
in 1905 he was appointed Chief-of-Staff to the Vth Army
Corps at Orléans—an invaluable experience for one who
aspired to high command.

To a man of Foch's imagination, deeply read in the history
of his country and an ardent patriot, the repulse from
Orléans of Attila the Hun in the fifth century may have
held an appeal, and doubtless the figure of Jeanne d'Arc
reminded him of one with the same ambition as his own—
the salvation of French territory from foreign occupation.

[93]

Knowing his habit of solitary walks, we can imagine him pacing the narrow streets or the quays by the riverside with such thoughts in his mind. These thoughts, however, certainly did not absorb his attention when engaged on Staff duties in which he was pre-eminent though sometimes revolutionary when confronted by hidebound routine.

Orléans was soaked in the history of France, and was the scene of heavy fighting in the "People's War" in 1870, when the place was taken by the Germans in October, retaken by the French in November, and lost again in December. Through it flowed the Loire, river of many memories, to which was to be added that of providing a base for the British Army on the Marne until the tide of invasion had been rolled back and Havre was again available.

In 1907 he was appointed *Général de Brigade*—two years after Ruffey, his old friend, whom up to this period he seems constantly to have followed, had been given this advancement—on the General Staff in Paris which again brought him into close contact with the authorities. Those who had the real good of the Army at heart and realized the folly of allowing politics or religious prejudice to interfere with its welfare, had never ceased to regret Foch's departure from the Staff College, and hints were conveyed in the right quarter that it was the duty of his superiors to reinstate him there. Reports of his genius for teaching reached high places, and Bonnal, his predecessor as a Professor, was just completing his time as Commandant.

Though at the time the years spent in the provinces seemed to him sterile, Foch did not regard them so in later years, according to his own showing. He gained experience of the details of Army life; he acquired a wider personal knowledge of the men who were the Army, which academic

FOCH, GENERALE DE BRIGADE

appointments could not teach, and this all helped him in later days when as much depended on his judgment in choosing his instruments as upon his knowledge of the conduct of warfare.

In those seven years Foch had changed but little. In his appearance there was a more pronounced suggestion of the cavalryman. His blue eyes still held the same serious expression; the curiously level voice, and the air of suppressed activity were those of the Foch who had left Paris seven years before, destined to return to the capital to earn greater fame than his most fervent admirers had expected.

With plenty of time for reading he had never ceased to study progress in the art of war, which had a profound attraction for him. He read every military manual issued in Europe, and he made a special study of the progress made in military affairs in other countries. As a looker-on he paid due attention to political questions, and even at this time it seemed that he had some presentiment of a coming conflict, in which he would be able to put at the disposal of France the results of his studies and his own genius, a genius in which he did not believe; with him it was simply a question of hard work and will-power. The great General Staff in Berlin had already worked for three years on the Schlieffen plan of invasion.

It seems to have been at about this time that he contracted the habit of substituting gesture for speech. Unlike many Gascons he used gestures to take the place of words rather than to accompany them, and with a movement of his expressive hands he could convey the meaning of a whole sentence. As he advanced in life this habit grew upon him. It is mentioned by many of those who came into contact with him during the years of his war command. A man of action himself, he had little patience with a meaningless flow of words, and to a long speech addressed to him by a colleague whom he thought too verbose, he sometimes answered with a single gesture, rather disconcerting, but quite unmistakable in its meaning.

In coming back to Paris, Foch must have had some inkling of an approaching change in his fortunes. He never seems to have expressed any bitterness over his eviction from the College. To one of his religious beliefs these things seemed ordained and therefore to be accepted without complaint, but he could not help knowing his own strong points or where he could put them to the best use in the interests of the country. So far his most influential work had been at the *Ecole Supérieure de Guerre,* where he had taught six classes of students who were now serving in influential appointments and had carried his fame all over the Army.

In October, 1906, shortly before Foch was summoned to join the General Staff in Paris, M. Clemenceau, the "Tiger" of the Great War, became Prime Minister, and the change of government at that particular time was destined to have a dominating influence upon French history.

CHAPTER IX

THE year 1907 in which Foch returned to Paris marked
the turning point in his career. It was in that year that he
first met Clemenceau and those two, of all Frenchmen, did
the most to save France in the most critical days of her
adversity.

The authorities were looking out for someone to succeed
General Bonnal at the Staff College. The political prejudices
in the Army which had caused the departure of Foch had
produced a bad effect upon the *Ecole de Guerre*. Its admin-
istration had deteriorated, its policy had grown weak, and
it sorely needed a new Director whose efficiency was indisputable—a man capable of reorganising the whole system and of putting more vigour into the intellectual centre
of the Army. As far as the public knew, the war-cloud was
still below the horizon, but only six years were to pass before
the storm broke.

To all who knew anything of Foch's previous work at
the College, it seemed that he was the man for the post and
that his religious faith should certainly not be allowed to
stand in the way of giving him the chance to do work for
which he was so eminently fitted.

As President of the Council, which roughly corresponds
to the position of the British Prime Minister, Clemenceau

wielded great power which he was destined to hold for only two years. Reports were brought to him of the genius of Foch, and of the desirability of getting him back to the *Ecole de Guerre*. Having no personal knowledge of Foch, he listened to all that was said to him. He was impressed by the unanimity of praise, and by the quarters from whence it came, so finally he sent for Foch and there took place the conversation of which so many different reports have appeared. After very few preliminaries Clemenceau, as was his wont, is said to have come straight to the point:

Clemenceau: I have some news for you, General. You are appointed Director of the *Ecole de Guerre*.

Foch: But I am not even a candidate!

Clemenceau: Possibly not, but you are appointed all the same. And I am sure you will do good work there.

Foch: Thank you, but you are doubtless unaware that one of my brothers is a Jesuit.

Clemenceau: I know that, but I don't care a damn! You will make me good officers; that is the only thing which matters.

That is the generally accepted version of the story, but it will be better to have Foch's own version as told to his A.D.C.[1] about fifteen years later. Foch, according to Major Bugnet, said that it was a fact that he had told Clemenceau that his brother was a Jesuit, but that the above version of Clemenceau's reply was not quite accurate, though it might be taken as a good paraphrase. The business took a great deal longer than has been generally stated. Foch took a firm attitude and said that his brother was a Jesuit who at the time was in Holland, and Foch himself was over forty

[1] Bugnet: *Foch Speaks*, 1929.

years old and beginning to act upon his own responsibility, without asking the advice of others. When Foch said that, Clemenceau "flew at him." A "long and pleasant" talk followed and the result was that Clemenceau, who had summoned a Cabinet meeting for 9 o'clock, kept them waiting, and Foch did not leave him until 9:25. In saying good-bye Clemenceau said that he intended to give Foch a command. All that happened on July 15th, 1908.

Foch then went to the manœuvres and he had so much to do that he had no time to think of anything else. In September the War Minister (Picard) who was watching his operations said to Foch: "So you are going to the Staff College?" Foch simply replied "Oh?" in a tone of surprise. Picard then remarked "The President says so."

Nothing happened during the next eight days, and then Clemenceau, who was acting as War Minister at the time, sent for Foch. This second interview is specially interesting in the light that it throws upon methods and feelings that were still running rife in the French Army up to that date.

Clemenceau opened the conversation by telling Foch that the Prefect of the Aisne had reported on him as "A good officer, but a doubtful Republican" and asked Foch what he had to say. The reply was "Nothing." Clemenceau then said: "Is that so?" Foch added: "Is that all?" to which Clemenceau replied: "Yes." Then this important conversation followed:

Foch: Then you are not in possession of reports which the Prefects of the Loriet and Morbihan made on me?

Clemenceau: That is so.

Foch: Then your dossier is incomplete and meaningless.

It is General A. who has trumped up a case against me.

Clemenceau: Yes, you are right. But what are you going to *teach* at the Staff College?

Foch: Nothing, as I shall be in charge.

Clemenceau: Yes, but in what way are you going to take charge?

Foch: I shall do just as I did when I was a Professor there.

Clemenceau: But they did not like you, because you favoured students who came from Jesuit schools?

Foch: That is surprising. I did not know who they were . . . mention some of them.

Clemenceau: De Grandmaison, de Lafontaine.

Foch: They are A.D.C.'s to General Tremeau [a distinguished General of the day] or on the General Staff . . . Not such a bad choice! What about the others?

Clemenceau: X——, Y——, Z——.

Foch: Where are they?

Clemenceau: I don't know.

Foch: You see . . . And even now you have only mentioned five or six, and I have had over 500 students through my hands!

"After that he appointed me," was Foch's final comment. The name of General "A" is given in the original, but there is no need to perpetuate ill-feelings. "A rose by any other name smells as sweet." It was fortunate for France that "The Tiger" knew a man when he saw him.

Thus the appointment was ratified. The interview, brief but very much to the point, marked the beginning of an understanding between two men, who, while they differed widely in many ways—Clemenceau was as much a sceptic as Foch was a believer—agreed in one great essential, a fervid patriotism. Their future intercourse was always to be on the same frank footing, and during the War, when they were brought much into contact, Clemenceau was, as a rule, a supporter of Foch's plans. Rumour, which must always be taken for what it is worth, says that Clemenceau seemed to take exception to some of Foch's alleged statements which appeared in a French book dealing with his life. He is said to be writing a book in answer to them, but it is certain that at no time did he doubt Foch's military genius, though it was remarked by some that Clemenceau "took charge" for a time in those fateful days in the spring of 1918, until he saw that Foch was firmly in the saddle.

Foch joined the Staff College at once as Commandant and resumed the class of work for which he had become famous. He has confessed that in the training of others he helped to train himself for the great part he was to play in the European conflict.

The effect of his presence was immediately felt. On his return he at once set to work to make the changes that were badly needed and to inaugurate some sweeping reforms, one of the most important of them being the remodelling of the two-year programme.

Conversant as he was with the real needs of the students, Foch soon came to the conclusion that too much had been crowded into the two-year course. The time was insufficient, and one of the first things that he did was to obtain permission from the authorities to make some changes. Amongst these there was a course of training in higher strategy, which the fifteen best students would continue to follow in a third year. It was started in 1909 and only one such course was held. Foch, with the possibility of war in view, was anxious to find leaders. It was in leadership, he thought, that the French Army had failed in 1870, so he also established at the Staff College a "Centre of advanced military study," with courses lasting for nine months for Lieutenant-Colonels in all arms of the Service; this was the course that was dubbed in Army chaff the School for budding Marshals (*Elèves-Maréchaux*) referred to elsewhere. Weygand, Foch's future *alter ego,* attended this course.

Foch was not above using the experience of others, and he admired certain Teutonic qualities and systems, whatever he may have thought of German mentality. He made no bones about taking what was best out of the system of training at the *Kriegsacademie* in Berlin, especially his three-year course for fifteen selected students. His experiment was a marked success, so much so that the inevitable happened. The jealousy always attendant on successful reform was aroused. There were murmurs of favouritism and suggestions that certain men were chosen arbitrarily for the extra privileges. The criticisms were unfounded. Foch, who had an unerring instinct for real ability in the students, did not choose them arbitrarily, but because it was his belief that they were the men who would profit by the extra tuition, and that their gain would in due course be to the country's advantage. It seemed to him to be of little moment whether the officers stayed for one or two extra years, if, as a result, they were fitted to fill high commands with credit to themselves and to their regiments. However, many of those about him lacked his breadth of vision, and, much to his regret, the feeling against the special class became so strong that after a year it had to be abandoned.

The "School for Marshals" made its mark, and exercised over its students an influence that was shown by their later careers. Many rose to high rank, and had brilliant records. Weygand afforded an outstanding example. The School may be said to have turned out a new generation of picked officers.

We now come to a momentous meeting which was destined in course of time to have a material influence upon Franco-British policy and the issue of the Great War. In 1906, the general tendency of the Schlieffen plan of 1904—the movement across Belgium to attack the French Army—was beginning to be apparent to all experts who visited the district in the neighbourhood of Aix-la-Chapelle and Malmédy. Amongst these was Brigadier-General Henry Wilson, who became Commandant of the British Staff College at Camberley in that year. Henry Wilson, who was a *persona grata* at the War Office, also knew of the conversations between the French and British Staffs on the steps to be taken in the event of the British Government deciding to come to the aid of France if attacked by Germany.[2] Foch's books were well known at the British Staff College though they had no great vogue in England until some years later, and when Foch was appointed Commandant of the *Ecole Supérieure de Guerre* in 1908, Wilson lost no time in arranging to visit the College. Further details on the subject of the friendship which ultimately developed between Foch and his friend "Henri," its influence upon Franco-British relations, and its various vicissitudes, must be reserved for a later chapter [3] which will be devoted specially to Foch as

[2] These notes are based on the personal memories of the writer, who was Professor of "Imperial Strategy" under Sir Henry Wilson at the Staff College to the end of 1907.

[3] The writer, who became the head of the General Staff of the British Army in South Africa, saw a good deal of the late Sir Henry Wilson during visits to England between 1909 and 1912, and again in 1913—August, 1914.

seen through English eyes at the time when Joffre, during the "race for the sea" in the autumn of 1914, used Foch as his deputy to coördinate the efforts of the French, British, and Belgian troops to prevent a further advance by the enemy in Flanders, and, if possible, to drive him back.

About Foch's early impressions of Wilson there is no first-hand evidence. Of Wilson's early impressions of Foch there is plenty. He frequently spoke about them himself. At their first meeting a surface impression was formed by him of Foch as a rather contemptuous, almost hostile man in elastic-sided boots. The entertainment of Foch by Wilson in England caused a gradual thawing and finally a genuine affection between them. They both had the same object in view: that a British Army should be sent across the Channel to the assistance of the French Army in the event of an attack by Germany. Neither man looked beyond that object. They both concentrated their energies upon that single issue. Both of them looked upon warfare as a matter solely of military operations and of success in land battles, but of neither of them could it have been said, in the words of Sir Edward Grey about militarists, that they did not understand, and were incapable of understanding, the soul which exists in nations.

When the first meeting was suggested by Colonel Fairholme, the military attaché, Foch at first showed no special enthusiasm at the suggestion. He was, as we know, hard at work reforming the Staff College. He always concentrated the whole of his energies upon the object which he wished to further, and this was his task at the moment. Foch had no great desire to parade his methods, or even to talk of them, unless it was necessary. The work of the *Ecole* seemed to him to be of paramount importance so the best thing to do was to get on with it. The last rôle that he cared to play was that of a proud pedagogue conducting distinguished visitors round his school and describing the improvements that he had introduced, but when Wilson arrived on December 2nd, Foch received him with courtesy, and, as Wilson records in his Diary: "was exceedingly nice as the day wore on. We went to four lectures and a conference, and then had tea and a couple of hours talk." Further extracts from the Diary give a good idea in Wilson's own words of the impression made upon him by the French Staff College:

Dec. 2nd. The teaching I saw to-day could scarcely be bettered. Very fine. There are 40 on the Staff for 180 students, two years course, each of 90, and this year they are keeping on 15 for a third year.

Dec. 3rd. Another most satisfactory day.

When the visitors left at the end of the first day, Foch bade them a courteous farewell, being under the impression that the visit was concluded and that as far as he was concerned the College had done with them. Wilson, who had ways of his own, coolly announced that he intended to come again on the morrow to see more of the man who was his "opposite number."

Foch's sense of humour, of which he possessed a due share, overcame his surprise. He was attracted by Wilson's pertinacity as well as by his personality, so he agreed to the return visit. On the second day the discussions between the two men were conducted much more frankly, and their friendship was established on a firmer basis. Their relations became so cordial that it was arranged that Wilson should pay another visit early in the next year. He went to Paris again during the following January, and wrote in his Diary:

Jan. 14th. Spent three hours with General Foch at the *Ecole Supérieure de Guerre.* He was most open. Explained the whole working of the College to me again. How the staff is allotted Infantry, Cavalry, Artillery, Strategy and Tactics, Staff duties, running through both years.

Also told me much of the Russian unpreparedness and we talked at great length of our combined action in Belgium. Most interesting.

He asked me to come over for a Staff Tour in the summer which I certainly will do. He is coming over to stay at the end of May.

It is interesting to note that at this period there was some idea in Foch's mind of the concerted action which was destined to have so great an influence in the War, as we shall see in due course.

It is possible that Wilson may have over-estimated his influence over Foch who was not a man to be easily influenced by anybody, especially in war matters, but the cordial relations that did actually exist made, on the whole, for a better understanding between the military authorities of the two countries, if not of the Governments. The French Government gained an impression from the military conversations that the British Government was irretrievably committed to send an army to help France in the event of attack by Germany, while the British considered that it was open to them to decide when this emergency arose, using their own judgment upon the actual circumstances. In the actual event the matter was simplified by the German violation of Belgian neutrality, whereby the British were involved by a Treaty obligation.

Foch at one time confided in Wilson more freely than he did in any other Englishman, as Wilson bears witness in his private Diary. Foch seems to have had a great respect as well as an affection for Wilson, and in the days of his nominal "supreme command" [4] he sometimes listened to him when other counsel would have gone unheeded. One of the main difficulties with which Foch was confronted when coördinating the efforts of the Allied forces was the fact that few foreigners, and not all Frenchmen, could understand him. Wilson was one of the few who did.

Wilson himself had his own methods of explaining what he meant according to his audience. When discussing the gravest matters, of which he realized the great importance, he spoke with apparent levity and adopted a vocabulary all his own, which might have irritated those who did not realize that he was wide awake to the situation with which he was dealing, and usually competent to deal with it. Mr. Winston Churchill has drawn such a clever verbal picture of Wilson's methods and mannerisms that we cannot do better than quote it *in extenso* if we want to imagine Foch and Wilson together. They had some of these methods in common. Here is the passage, from "The World Crisis": [5]

Sir Henry Wilson constantly corrected the clarity of his mind by whimsical mannerisms and modes of expression. He spoke in parables, used curious images and cryptic phrases. He had a vocabulary of his own. The politicians were "frocks"; Clemenceau always the "Tiger." He even addressed him as Tiger. His faithful Aide-de-Camp, Duncannon, was "the Lord." He wantonly pronounced grotesquely the names of French towns and Generals, in discussing the gravest matters he used the modes of levity. "Prime Minister," he began one day to the War Cabinet, at a meeting which I attended, "to-day I am a Boche." Then

[4] Which, in the actual event, was neither "supreme" nor was it a "command" over Allied troops.
[5] Part II, pp. 392-393.

followed a penetrating description of the situation from the standpoint of German Headquarters. On another day he would be France or Bulgaria, and always out of this affectation there emerged, to my mind, the root of the matter in hand. But some ministers were irritated. He did not go as far as Marshal Foch, who sometimes gave a military description in pantomime; but their methods of displaying a war proposition had much in common.

I can see him clearly as I write, standing before the map in the Cabinet Room giving one of his terse telegraphese appreciations. "This morning, Sir, a new battle." The reader will recognise it when it comes. "This time it is we who have attacked. We have attacked with two armies, the British and the French. Sir Haig is in his train, Prime Minister, very uncomfortable, near the good city of Amiens. And Rawly [6] is in his left hand and Debeny is in his right. Rawly is using five hundred tanks. It is a big battle,[7] and we thought you would not like us to tell you about it beforehand.

Incidentally, the extract carries a special interest. The success of the attack on the occasion referred to depended entirely on secrecy, and this shows that Haig in August, 1918, had ensured secrecy by the same method that Foch had employed in July, by keeping his counsel to himself, taking special care not to tell "politicians" on the plea that they cannot keep secrets.

Wilson and Foch evidently had some characteristics in common. They were both men of intense patriotism; they had both studied the problem of a war between France and Germany, and they both believed in the great importance of brain-work.

It must at times have seemed a little strange to some

[6] The late Lord Rawlinson of Trent.
[7] The 8th of August, 1918, the turning-point in the War.

people that a man of Foch's directness should have been attracted by the Englishman's less direct methods, but Foch could see beneath the surface, and appreciate Wilson's qualities and quickness of brain. After their first meeting Wilson fully appreciated Foch's military genius. He continually spoke of him, and constantly quoted his sayings. He was greatly impressed by the method in which technical schemes were carried out at the *Ecole de Guerre,* and Foch gave him every opportunity of watching. According to Foch's system this work was conducted at top speed and those who were in charge of the class stimulated the students' efforts by crying *"Vite! Vite!"* and *"Allez! Allez!"* When he went back to the Staff College at Camberley, Wilson introduced exercises on this plan, and in due course they became part of the curriculum and were known as *"Allez! Allez!"* operations. Wilson gained valuable experience of French military mentality in Foch's time at the *Ecole Supérieure de Guerre.*

It is interesting in the light of after events to recall the value that Foch set upon England as an ally. He was a firm supporter of the *Entente Cordiale* from the first moment of its inception, and when relations between the two countries were inclined to be strained at a certain period after the War, he never failed to emphasize the need for an Anglo-French understanding. His views on the British soldier will be given in due course.

In some of his characteristics Foch presented a curious contrast. Of set purpose he had devoted his life to the study of war. He almost believed at one time that it could be reduced to the level of an exact science; and he was more than a soldier—he was immersed in the study of soldiering in the abstract. To him armies were moved to defeat or victory solely by the skill and driving power of the mind and character behind them, and in logically following out his ideas he could be quite ruthless, if he believed that, from his country's point of view, the end justified the means, but having once achieved his purpose he did not believe in war. At the British Legion's Annual Conference which he attended in 1928, the delegates heard from the Chairman of the Paris branch an account of the activities of the *Fédération Interalliée des Anciens Combatants,* and when the speaker said that in Allied countries the views of old soldiers were becoming more influential, that their power in the community was growing, and that that power was devoted to peace in our time and in all time, Foch vigorously nodded his agreement.

At the same time, if war must be, he held that it must be conducted with a strong will and by a character capable of facing its realities—and these include casualties. Such was his teaching in pre-war days at the Staff College, and he had the strength to apply that teaching when he himself was put to the test. Many legends already surround the name of Foch, but so many of them give examples of this quality that it is not out of place to give a sample of one of the most recent. It possesses a personal touch, since Foch smoked incessantly, which lends verisimilitude to the story.

A commander came to Foch at his headquarters to report that his troops were so situated that they would have to retire if they were attacked. Foch listened so intently that he let his cigar go out, at the same time making one of his accustomed gestures by pushing his cap back off his forehead. Some of his intimates said that they could read his thoughts on such occasions by the way in which he smoked. This time he chewed the end of his cigar, listening silently until the commander who was reporting to him had finished. Then he set his cap at the right angle, deliberately relighted the remains of his cigar, and gave his decision.

"You must not retire. Your troops must hold on at all costs."

"That means that we must all die?"

Foch stared hard at the stump of his cigar, stood up, and threw it away.

"Exactly. You have hit it," he said and walked away, leaving his subordinate staring after him.

"Victory"—said Scharnhorst—"is won by teaching soldiers how to die, not how to avoid dying," and there is a tale of Stonewall Jackson who, when a subordinate claimed credit for having fallen back without loss, remarked: "Do you call that fighting, Sir?" and put him under arrest; and we read in Hamley's "Operations of War" [8] that a commander has to bear many responsibilities and to take many chances. If he has, in addition, to be thinking constantly of every man he loses . . . he will certainly never perform great deeds. Generals are not made of iron. They can quite safely be trusted to consider losses, without any urging.

This was what Foch taught in time of peace, and practised in war, with the proviso that casualties, to be justifiable, must be directed towards some object to which profound thought has been devoted. With Foch there were no parrot principles. His art of leadership did not lie solely in the monotonous repetition of the words *Attaquez! Attaquez!* A parrot could thus have led great armies, or better still a gramophone record as being more portable and more susceptible to reproduction and wide distribution. The essence of leadership lay in personality, and in the inspiration which that quality could convey.

[8] Seventh edition, p. 432.

[111]

Foch held his appointment as Commandant at the *Ecole Supérieure de Guerre* for three years, and his teaching there can be summarized quite briefly.

While other exponents of the art of war constantly harped upon the need to look into "the enemy's brain," he taught the need to look into an opponent's soul. This principle, at first but dimly perceived, gradually dominated all others in the knowledge gained first by his studies and his teaching, and in course of time by actual experiences. Those who try to derive from the text of his writings formulæ composed of dead words and parrot phrases as guides for action in the conduct of warfare do him but scant justice.

In our account of Sir Henry Wilson's visit to Foch at the *Ecole Supérieure de Guerre* in December, 1909, one important record was omitted. Wilson, in his diary for December 3rd, mentioned an item in the conversation which he had with Foch on that day. The entry runs:

His [Foch's] appreciation of the German move through Belgium is exactly the same as mine, the important line being between Verdun and Namur.

This brings out clearly the point that Foch could hardly have approved of the French "Plan 17" which was in force when war broke out in 1914, and on the other hand neither Foch nor Wilson conceived the probability that, if Germany decided to violate the neutrality of Belgium at all, she would be likely to make the most effective use of defying what Bismarck called the "imponderables"—the moral factor—and make a wider sweep, north of the Meuse, a procedure which was actually adopted.

Foch responded in June, 1910, to Wilson's suggestion that he should cross the Channel to pay a return visit to the British Staff College, of which Wilson was the Commandant. On arrival at Camberley Foch spent some hours in his inspection and he and Wilson passed the next day together.

[113]

It was noticed that Foch was particularly observant. He surprised everyone there by calling attention to details that no one else had noticed, and it was certain that nothing of the workings of the College, which Sir Henry did his best to explain to his distinguished visitor, escaped his attention.

Sir Henry mentions the visit in his diary, and another meeting which was momentous for both the men concerned:

June 7—I took Furse [1] in car and we met Foch and Huguet [Military Attaché in London] at Farnborough, and we went out to Long Hill. Saw a small field-day there, then round Lincolnshire barracks, lunched with Jimmy Grierson, after that Supply Depot, then Field Stores, and back here [to Camberley]. Then on to Englemere, tea there with the Chief, and the Chief and Foch made great friends, neither understanding a word the other said.

"The Chief" was Lord Roberts, and the two men, each recognizing the other's greatness, did become real friends, in spite of the language difficulty which Wilson slightly exaggerated.

One can imagine the scene of the meeting at Ascot between the two soldiers, so similar both in their simplicity and in their greatness, in the large hall of Englemere decked with Indian and South African war-trophies, and in the garden in which the great "Little Man" with the keen blue eyes used always to walk with visitors—a wistful look on his face as he passed the gun in saving which his only son had gained a Victoria Cross, and had lost his life. Foch, less than four years later, was destined to face the same sorrow.

Lord Roberts, who was constantly in touch with Camber-

[1] The author's successor on the Staff at Camberley. Now General Sir William Furse.

ley in the days of Wilson and his predecessor, the late Lord Rawlinson, had been one of the earliest to realize the German menace. He had at once started a crusade for better military preparedness and for national service. In this crusade he enlisted the help of Colonel Repington, the military correspondent of *The Times,* of whom more anon. While Rawlinson (who left in 1906) was still Commandant, Repington came to the Staff College for a long discussion with Rawlinson and the writer on the subject of Lord Roberts's campaign. Repington came down in a London taxi-cab, which waited for him until the talk was over at about 1.30 A.M. At that time the crusade for military preparedness was based upon home defence, upon the fear of invasion. Repington's view was that by such means alone, by frightening people about the safety of their homes, was it possible to induce them to press for a larger army. We parted without coming to an agreement, Rawlinson's view being that it would pay better in the long run to tell the truth. He agreed with the "Blue Water School" of the day that it would be better to have a Navy to prevent invasion than a large Army to repel invaders who had landed, and that the Army was really required for service abroad.

Lord Roberts's scheme for national service and military preparedness had a small measure of support for a time and when it fell flat for want of official support [2] he continued to preach his crusade all over the Empire, even when he was derided and ridiculed in the Press. His was a "voice crying in the wilderness," and the echoes of that voice sounded in many memories when he passed away in Fland-

[2] The writer retains a vivid memory of a talk at a Foreign Office reception on July 30th, 1909, between Lord Roberts and the Prime Minister, in which Mr. Asquith seemed to show respect for the obvious sincerity of Lord Roberts but to treat him as one would humour a foolish child.

ers within the sound of the guns on November 14th, 1914. Whether he and Foch understood each other without the medium of speech we do not know. That they became real friends at first sight we do know on Wilson's authority.

In October, 1910, some months after this meeting, Lord Roberts spoke at Quebec at a celebration on the Heights of Abraham, and he then uttered a striking prophecy which indicated the profound impression made upon him by his meeting with Foch:

They refuse to believe me, and we sleep under a false security, but I do not hesitate to affirm that we shall have a frightful war in Europe, and that England and France will have the hardest experience of their existence.

They will in fact see defeat very near, but the war will finally be won by the genius of a French general named Ferdinand Foch, professor in the Military School at Paris.

The memory of the fulfilment of these prophecies is a recent one, and it seems a hard fate that Lord Roberts should have lived to see the first accomplished in full measure but not the last. When he met Lord Roberts, Foch can hardly have forgotten the years when his own message to France and to the Army had been obscured, and this may have helped to excite his sympathy and respect for the older veteran who was devoting the last years of his life to trying to warn a nation which would not take him seriously. Both, in their own ways, were trying according to their lights to save their fellow countrymen from impending disaster.

Legends always crop up about men of achievement in the years that follow their fame, but those surrounding the name of Foch are unusually abundant, and based upon good evidence. We know, for instance, that in the days when the family used to spend their holidays at Valentine, Ferdinand and his brothers were commonly talked of as "the little Napoleons," [3] and from that date school-teachers, professors, many military superiors, and numerous students recognised in him a great leader in embryo. There is clear evidence that Sir Henry Wilson spread this view in the British Army and elsewhere as early as 1909.

On the 8th of June, the day following the visit to Lord Roberts, Wilson met Foch and Huguet again, this time at Andover, and took them to Bulford Camp and then up the Avon valley to see the Cavalry School at Netheravon, now the Machine-Gun School. On the 9th, they witnessed artillery practice at the Larkhill ranges on Salisbury Plain and they saw some Yeomanry Camps, having spent the intervening night at Salisbury. Our yeomanry came as a novelty to Foch who kept his guides busy answering his very pertinent questions. On June 10th Wilson took Foch to the War Office and introduced him to Mr. Haldane, to the Adjutant-General, the Quartermaster-General, and the Director of Military Operations, after which they went on to the Royal United Service Institution, which Foch was anxious to see.

Sir Arthur Leatham, Secretary of the Institution, has given an account of Foch's appearance there. He was, he says, sitting quietly in his office when the door was thrown open and Sir Henry Wilson walked in.

"I've got a French General outside," he announced, "General Foch, boss of their Staff College, whom I want to introduce you to. And, mark my words, Leatham, this fellow's going to command the Allied Armies when the big war comes on."

Then he brought Foch in, and while he was there chaffed

[3] Raymond Récouly: *Foch,* p. 22.

him about his future rôle of Generalissimo, after which they inspected the Museum and the rest of the building, in which Foch showed great interest. He was so impressed that he insisted upon paying another visit, examining the exhibits which particularly attracted him, and spending some time over the well-known Waterloo model, by Captain Siborne. He had an argument about that with Sir Arthur Leatham. The subject was one that Foch knew by heart, having devoted much time in his younger days to studying the details connected with his early hero's downfall, and he maintained that the model was incorrect in certain particulars. After some further criticism he finally admitted that "for a model" there was not much wrong with it.

From this widespread recognition of Foch's genius, before he had had an opportunity of demonstrating it in actual warfare, it seems that Mr. Lloyd George's claim to have "discovered" Foch would be difficult to establish. Foch himself said that Lloyd George "invented" him, rather implying that he would have found it difficult to secure a patent on his invention, but we must make allowances for Foch's well-known dislike of politics and politicians. Of one he said: "He is a coward in a rage"; of another: "He is a peacock; he has all its pride and all its futility"; and of another: "He is an eel. . . . He slips away like macaroni."

Lord Roberts and Sir Henry Wilson seem to have been the first to "discover" Foch from the British point of view; in France there was no doubt for many years about his outstanding ability.

During his first visit to London one of the "sights" which Foch saw by accident was the march of the relieving guard, which passed by him on its way from Chelsea Barracks to Buckingham Palace. Foch watched the procession in silence.

His comment was unexpected. It was not the bearing of the Guards, or their fine physique, or the martial music of their band which most impressed him. Turning to his companion he asked: *"Mais pourquoi les agents de Police?"* (Why the policemen?) He could not imagine a reason for two constables heading a procession of soldiers, but he did not know his British public or the powers of constables over the London traffic.

Foch's visit to England cemented his friendship with Wilson who was destined to find it of great value during the four years preceding the Great War. Wilson became Director of Military Operations, responsible for details of war preparation, immediately after he left the Staff College.

In the summer of 1910 Sir Henry Wilson carried out his intention of accepting Foch's invitation to go to France in order to attend a "Staff Tour." [4] This particular tour promised to be very satisfactory. It doubtless helped to promote the understanding between the two men and to teach Wilson much about the French outlook, but just as it was getting well started Foch was ordered back to Paris. He had been selected to attend the Russian manœuvres, which he found very illuminating, and he returned with very definite ideas about Russia's military future, and the part that she was likely to play in what was once somewhat inaptly called the "concert of Europe" on the principle *Lucus a non lucendo.*

On October 12th of that year, one of Foch's daughters was married, and the growth of friendliness between him and Wilson can be estimated from the fact that Wilson was invited to the wedding. Foch was always very reserved about his private life. He held, and every right-minded Englishman agrees, that a man's domestic life is something entirely

[4] An exercise by commanders and Staff officers, without troops.

apart from his professional career, and it has no share therein as far as the public is concerned. He resented every attempt to invade what he regarded as the privacy of his household, and he had no hesitation in administering a snub to those who attempted any intrusion.

He was an excellent husband. His married life was uniformly happy, and he was a devoted and affectionate father, but he kept his family affairs from all suspicion of publicity. He had no desire to parade his domestic relations. The life of Foch the soldier had necessarily to be public property; it was dedicated to the service of the nation. The life of Foch the husband and father was his own affair; it had to do with nobody but himself and his family.

Wilson was evidently on business as well as on friendship bent. After the wedding of Mlle. Foch he had an interview with Foch at the *Ecole de Guerre* which lasted for over two hours. He gives an account of it in his diary (October 13th):

General Foch has just been to Russia as the Tsar's guest. He tells me that the Russian Army is getting on, but very slowly ... that the Russian Secret Service report that the Germans consider the French Army very fine; he says that he doesn't think Russia would actively interfere if Germany and France were to fight over Belgium, but Russia would do all her possible if war broke out through the Balkans. He tells me that the Emperor Bill has actually offered his army to Russia to quell internal disturbances, and always does all he can to get into Russia's good graces. This is in order to pacify her, if, and when, he moves West.

Foch tells me he believes Germany will absorb Belgium peacefully and throw the onus of war upon France, and, in short, Foch is of opinion that in the coming war in Belgium, France must trust to England, and not to Russia, and that all our plans must be worked out in minutest detail so that we may be quite clear of the action and the line to take.

He finished off by warning me that, for many reasons, which he could not give, I was to remember that the year 1912 would be a dangerous year to live through.[5]

From this extract, quoting Foch's exact words, it is clear that his forecast of the coming struggle was in the main correct, and that his study of the German mind had enabled him to foretell, almost to a certainty, the course that they would adopt when the day of war actually arrived. In his opinion that Germany would absorb Belgium peacefully, he did not foresee the sense of honour of King Albert or the patriotism of his people.

For his own country his vision was clear, and Wilson was not alone in thinking him "one of the foremost authorities on the art of war in Europe." Up to this time the "military conversations" had been more or less of an academic nature. Wilson in 1910 gave them a practical form.

In December Foch paid a second visit to England, seeing Wilson again, and also having an interview with Sir Arthur Nicholson, Permanent Under-Secretary of State at the Foreign Office. Shortly afterwards Wilson recorded in his diary (January 14th, 1911) Sir Arthur's opinion that "Our power of intervening on the Continent being almost nil, and Germany's position being enormously strong, she almost ignores us."

In 1912 Foch came to England again for the Army manœuvres. He saw a good deal on that occasion of Sir James Grierson—the "Jimmy Grierson" of Wilson's diary. The manœuvres were highly successful, and Foch was genuinely interested in them. He admired Grierson's work, and after the manœuvres were over lunched with him.

[5] The "Agadir Crisis" came in 1911.

Foch expressed his admiration for the work, and congratulated Grierson on a display which had strongly appealed to him. Grierson, according to Wilson, had at one time been destined to be Chief-of-Staff to Sir John French who commanded the British Expeditionary Force. He went to France in August, 1914, to command the IInd British Army Corps, but he died in the train on the 17th of August, before the battle of Mons.

In 1911 Foch was made a Divisional General by Millerand and he left the Staff College to take command of the 13th Division at Chaumont. This time he left the College in very different circumstances from those in which he had quitted it in 1900. He left it on this occasion without any deep regrets, as he had completed his work of thoroughly reorganising the system of teaching, and matters were on a satisfactory basis. His previous lectures there had become famous. Under his command the College had turned out batch after batch of officers who had profited by one of the finest courses of strategy and tactics that had ever been given. It has been established that he knew that there were stormy days ahead for his country and, apart from his own prospects, that the students who had been under him at the College might soon have an opportunity of putting into practice some of the doctrine that he had established.

In December, 1912, Foch was promoted to the command of the VIIIth Army Corps at Bourges. He met Sir Henry Wilson, who was on his way home from winter sports in Switzerland, on the 16th of February. Wilson had had an interview with Generals Joffre and Castelnau about some articles in *The Times* by Colonel Repington, claiming that the British Navy was worth 500,000 bayonets to the French at the decisive point. Wilson had written to F. S.

Oliver—the historian who brought out "Ordeal by Battle," a brilliant book, in 1914—his opinion that the British Navy was not worth 500 bayonets to the French, and, except for the moral standpoint, Joffre and Castelnau did not value it at one bayonet. Then Wilson, with Huguet, the French Military Attaché in London, dined with Foch, talked until midnight, and recorded "Foch is exactly of the same opinion . . . as are Castelnau and Joffre."

Comment on the narrowness of outlook which that entry in Wilson's diary discloses is hardly necessary in these days.[6] The quotation has been given because it throws so much light upon the subsequent difference of outlook between the Allies which added so seriously to the difficulties that confronted Foch in coördinating the efforts of the Allied armies. The question whether Repington was wise in his methods is a different one. Wilson records that the French generally considered the statement to be a most serious one, coming at that moment, and an agreement was arrived at, Wilson concurring, that "it should be thoroughly exposed in the French Press," the presumption probably being that any-thing which conveyed to the German General Staff an idea that the French would have no military support, however much in the right, in the event of attack by Germany would encourage such an attack. In that view there was some rea-son, as was proved by future events.

Foch himself was always very cautious about expressing his views publicly. Save for his books, in which he had dealt only with technical matters, he had avoided as far as possible airing any views in the Press at all, and though always

---

[6] As matters turned out, British Sea Power, by its direct and indirect influence, could have been described without exaggeration as the main factor in the ultimate victory of 1918.

courteous in his dealings he did not exactly welcome the pressmen and interviewers who would fain have dogged his footsteps. Holding such views, he had very little tolerance for the military "expert," familiar to the readers of the journals of all countries.

Foch was now one of the outstanding figures in the French Army, and all who had any knowledge of his abilities foresaw that he would soon rise above the command of the VIIIth Corps. As usual, he did nothing to curry favour or to accelerate his own advancement.

CHAPTER XI

THE CALM BEFORE THE STORM: 1912-1914

AGED 61-62 YEARS

FOCH held the command of the VIIIth Army Corps with his headquarters at Bourges from December, 1912, until August 23rd, 1913, when he was transferred to Nancy to take over the command of the XXth Army Corps, guarding the German frontier. It was of this command that Foch had said that all the leading generals who had held it became obsessed by the local situation. He looked wider afield, while at the same time following his usual practice of concentrating upon the work of the moment.

While he was still at Bourges the situation in Europe had seemed somewhat alarming. The Agadir crisis of 1911 had been followed by local wars in the Near East, but before he moved to Nancy the mutterings of the storm had passed away over the Balkan Mountains, largely through the influence of "diplomacy by conference," an assembly of the Ambassadors of the countries concerned, with the British Foreign Minister, Sir Edward Grey, presiding. During the most critical period in the negotiations Foch seems to have thought that his prediction that there would be a great crisis in 1912 was likely to be fulfilled, as it might have been, had it not been for the handling of the situation by Grey whose prestige in the chancelleries of Europe then stood at its highest. It is on record that Foch as commander of

[125]

the VIIIth Corps spoke of the need of preparedness at this period, and also of the amount of extra preparation needed for modern warfare, as compared with the past. "It is against Germany that we shall have some day to fight: it is against her that we must be prepared." [1] He thought, too, that the war of the future would be a far more terrible drama. Bismarck, he knew, had said forty years before that the war of 1870 was child's play to what the war of to-morrow would be, and that the struggle would require the whole of the national resources (not for any participant an affair of "business as usual" as an unwise statesman was to pronounce in 1914). Foch added that, if France wanted to have men able to conduct such a war, it was essential to arouse the enthusiasm of the "intelligent few" in order to have men capable of leading the nation and the army when the hour arrived. They would be called upon to face tremendous responsibilities and they would need great courage. Where would they find it except in character? ("Intellect? Criticism? A donkey who has character is more useful.")

Then came his transfer to the celebrated XXth Corps at Nancy, when he was approaching his sixty-second birthday. The Balkan storm having passed without breaking, he seemed like most others to have thought that the danger had passed away for the time being. "I was beginning to think that I was to end my days without seeing it," after forty years of expectation and self-training. That, however, did not do away with the need for preparation. His was the Army Corps upon which the first blow was likely to fall, and he saw to it that the defences of Nancy, from which it would debouch when the hour struck, were kept in an efficient state and improved. His troops were kept up

[1] Bugnet, p. 201.

to full strength, trained up to the highest pitch, and organised to move at short notice to take up a covering position, if required, in order to protect the mobilisation of units more distant from the frontier.

The murder of the Archduke Ferdinand at Sarajevo on June 28th, 1914, which ultimately proved a pretext for Austria-Hungary to make war upon Serbia, did not at the time seem likely to disturb the equilibrium between the great European Powers, still less did it appear that the hour which Foch had expected for forty years had arrived. Early in July he took part in the regular peace programme for divisional manœuvres.

A young cavalry officer, Captain André Dubarle, has left on record a valuable pen-picture of the future Marshal as he appeared to others on the eve of the War. The writer was a picked man.[2] He had recently passed seventh out of the Staff College, and the description occurs in a letter written by him from Humbeauville to his father and mother on July 5th, 1914:[3]

Here we are nearly at the end of our camping period . . . On Saturday we shall be in Nancy. We have just been having a good time manœuvring with the 11th Division—the "iron division of Nancy" as it is called. General de Castelnau, inspecting, and General Foch commanding the XXth Army Corps took part in the manœuvres. The presence of these two great men and their criticism made things very interesting.

General Foch . . . is still quite a young man [few generals over sixty years of age would have earned such a tribute from a young officer], thin and supple, and looks slightly fragile;[4] in-

[2] Quoted by Puaux, p. 49.
[3] Captain Dubarle was killed in the War.
[4] It is interesting to compare that with the "physically he was thickset and stocky" of "Trois Maréchaux." (Author.)

deed his head almost looks like a flower that is too big for its delicate stalk. What strikes one first is his bright, penetrating glance, full of intelligence, but in spite of that great energy, still luminous. This "luminosity"—there is no other word for it—quite spiritualises a face that otherwise would be almost brutal, with its great moustache and protruding jaw. When he speaks, drawing lessons from the manœuvres, he gets extraordinarily animated, almost passionate, and yet never fails to express himself with simplicity and purity.

His language is sober and direct; he points out the principles of warfare, condemns faults, makes an appeal to one's best energies, all in the same brief and contained style.

He is a priest who judges, condemns, and teaches in the name of a dogma [the one thing which Foch abhorred!][5] that inspires him, and to which he has devoted all the strength of his brain and heart. General Foch is a prophet inspired by his God.

You can well understand that criticism from such a man was full of interest.

The outstanding words in that letter, coming, as they do, from such a source, are those which describe the appeal made by Foch to "one's best energies." In that characteristic, exercised under conditions against which few even of the bravest characters were proof, lay the secret of Foch's great achievements in the days that were to come. He got the very last ounce out of all with whom he was in personal contact, and in that way he achieved his purpose.

When the divisional manœuvres were over and the troops had returned to their barracks, there was, apparently, not a cloud upon the political horizon, and on the 18th of July Foch obtained a fortnight's leave, to be spent as usual with his family on his estate in Brittany. His two sons-in-law,

---

[5] The author has, unfortunately, not had access to the original French. If "cause" were substituted for "dogma" the sentence would pass.

Captains Fournier and Bécourt, came there at the same time, the one with seventeen days leave, the other with twenty-five.

A short summary of important political events during those fateful days of July, 1914, may be of service to us here.

On July 5th the Kaiser received at Potsdam a special envoy from the Emperor of Austria and promised "the full support of Germany" in the event of Austrian action against Serbia, and he consulted his naval and military advisers before he left for a cruise in northern waters in his yacht, the "Hohenzollern," on the 14th. The Council of Austro-Hungarian Ministers finally determined upon taking action against Serbia, and on the 19th they approved of a draft ultimatum to that country.

On July 23rd the Austro-Hungarian Government sent the ultimatum to Serbia. On the 24th the German Government submitted to the Entente Powers a note approving the ultimatum; on the same day Sir Edward Grey initiated a proposal for an international conference to avert war, and the Belgian Government declared that, in the event of war, Belgium would uphold her neutrality "whatever the consequences." On July 25th the Serbian Government ordered mobilisation, and, on the same day Austria-Hungary severed diplomatic relations with the Serbians, who had accepted all the vital demands in the ultimatum, and withdrew her Ambassador, who left Belgrade. The Serbian seat of government was at once moved from Belgrade to Nish.

During this period Foch had been spending the last peaceful days that he was destined to experience for four years and a half. The whole family were gathered at the old château near Morlaix, with no foreboding of the cataclysm so soon to follow. M. le Goffic [6] has given us some local colour for realising the life of Foch with his family during his last leave:

On the 19th of July, 1914, at the hour when the smoke of the morning cigar drifts out into the streets, Morlaix, that old romantic city of the pointed roofs, that half-Spanish town with patios and staircases sculptured with trees of Jesse, saw coming from the railway station an alert traveller of military aspect who crossed the Grand Place, passed under two arches of the immense viaduct and by the Quai de Triguier with its severe Louis XIV bastions of black stone and grey granite, and so arrived upon the road to Ploujean to gain the woods of Trofeunteuniou.

There goes General Foch, who returns home again.

That's all right! The war can't be coming yet!

In the early days of July Foch had been present near Nancy at the manœuvres of the 11th Division, the "Iron Division." This man was the "Eye of France" upon the Vosges. So who would believe that if a storm really menaced the frontier an official so vigilant would have quitted his post and have come to so distant a spot for his rest, in this far country of Ploujean where Captain Fournier and Captain Bécourt, his two sons-in-law, are awaiting him.

Thus reason the folk of Morlaix to whom this General officer, born at Tarbes but dwelling amongst them for more than a quarter of a century, had become almost a compatriot.

Having arrived at his home, Foch settled down to his fortnight's holiday with his wife and children and the grandchildren, taking his usual walks and supervising various work on the estate. Even when in plain clothes—he was addicted to a morning coat, striped trousers, and rather a flowing tie—he looked what he was—a born commander

[6] *Entretiens avec Foch.*

—but in his own neighbourhood he preferred to sink his military rank and be treated as Monsieur Foch the landowner, rather than as the Commander of the XXth Army Corps, the pick of the French Army. He now seems almost to have made up his mind that the great Armageddon, for which he had trained himself for so long, would not come in his life-time—or at all events while he was on the Active List; but suddenly it was upon him, coming as a bolt from the blue. On the 26th of July, seven days after he had reached Morlaix, he was recalled to his post.

On that day the Austro-Hungarian Government ordered partial mobilisation as against Serbia, and Montenegro followed suit. The Kaiser returned hurriedly to Berlin, and the British Admiralty countermanded the dispersal of the British Fleet which had been collected for exercises. On the 27th of July the French and Italian Governments accepted Sir Edward Grey's proposals for an international conference, and the German High Seas Fleet was recalled from Norway to its war bases. *On the 28th the German Government rejected the British proposals* for an international conference and thereby, as matters turned out, made the Great War inevitable. The British Fleet was ordered to its war bases. Austria declared war against Serbia. On July 29th the Russian Government ordered partial mobilisation against Austria and in the evening the Russian War Minister ordered general mobilisation without the knowledge of the Tsar. Austrian artillery bombarded Belgrade. The German Government made the notorious overtures to Great Britain to secure her neutrality, and on July 30th the French Ambassador asked that Britain would range herself on the side of France. On the same day the German proposal was rejected and France was told that Great Britain could not as

[131]

yet promise active intervention. In the evening the Tsar signed an order for mobilisation of the Russian Army. On July 31st the Russian Government issued the mobilisation order, as did the Austro-Hungarian and the Belgian and the Turkish Governments. Germany ordered a state of war-danger (*Kriegsgefahr*) and sent an ultimatum to Russia which was presented at midnight. On the first of August the German and French Governments ordered general mobilisation and the British, naval mobilisation.[7] Germany declared war upon Russia, and hostilities began on the Polish frontier. French troops had been withdrawn six miles from the German frontier, but on August 2nd hostilities began on that frontier, and German troops crowded into Luxembourg. The British Government guaranteed naval protection of the coasts of France against German aggression via the North Sea or the Channel. In the evening Germany presented an ultimatum demanding a passage for her troops across Belgian territory. (The ultimatum had been written seven days earlier, and it had been lying at Brussels in readiness.)

On the 3rd of August Germany declared war against France. The British Government guaranteed armed support to Belgium if Germany should violate Belgian territory, and the Belgians refused to comply with Germany's demands. Germany declared war against France, and the British Government ordered army mobilisation.

Early in the morning of the 4th of August German troops crossed the frontier of Belgium, and Germany declared war against that country, which severed diplomatic relations at once with Germany.

[7] The order reached the author, who was serving at Portsmouth, at 3 A.M. on Sunday, August 2nd.

At 11 P.M. (Midnight Central European time), Great Britain, having received no reply to an ultimatum dispatched earlier in the day, declared war upon Germany.

According to Foch's estimate of others by their actions rather than by their words, the War was brought about by deeds, and those deeds were the bombardment by Austria, supported by Germany, of Belgrade on July 29th, the crossing of the frontiers of France and of Luxembourg by German troops on August the 2nd, and the frontier of Belgium early on the 4th of August.

Bugnet writes, claiming first-hand knowledge of his views, that to Foch war had suddenly loomed on the horizon and become a reality which had to be faced. He had done nothing to bring it to pass. He did not rejoice; matters were too serious; and he had hardly a moment for consideration. He was neither surprised nor disconcerted. He himself was *sans peur et sans reproche*. War was inevitable. "The Germans were bent upon it: they would have had it by hook or by crook." It was no longer a time for making leaders, but for being one. Henceforward what was important was "deeds and not ideas, action and not words, practice and not precept." Those with force of character must display it. Every resource must be brought into play, every force concentrated, every particle of will-power used so that—come what may—the final object, victory, might be attained.

These were the views of Foch as a clear thinker in the great crisis. To those who hold, with him, that the War was brought about by deeds and by the men of action, rather than by words and by the men of words, the years that have since been spent by historians, propagandists, and archivists delving in the pigeon-holes and waste-paper baskets of statesmen, diplomatists, and officers have been simply wasted labour. They have not even searched, for instance, the archives of the men of action, the great General Staffs of Berlin and Vienna upon whom the responsibility rests for the actual deeds. Among the wilderness of words in the English language which have emanated from the British Empire and the United States on this subject of war-guilt (Foch's supreme test—the justice of his cause) the writer has found only one author—Mr. Winston Churchill—who has gone to the root of the matter in after years as Foch did at the time of crisis. The passage is worth quoting *in extenso* on account of its bearing upon the future:

The only test by which human beings can judge war respon-sibility is Aggression; and the supreme proof of aggression is Invasion. Capacity to invade a neighbour implies superior capac-ity to defend the native soil. The past has many instances of invasions for the purpose of forestalling a counter-invasion. Dis-putes as to the responsibility for bringing about conditions which led to various wars are endless. But mankind will be wise in the future to take as the *paramount criterion of war-guilt the sending of the main armies of any State across its frontier line,*[8] and to declare that whoever does this puts himself in the wrong. The violation of Luxembourg and Belgium by the German armies marching upon France will stare through the centuries from the pages of History.[9]

Mr. Churchill adds, very wisely, that "Mobilisation justi-fies only counter-mobilisation and further parley."

With thoughts of actions rather than of words in his mind, Foch had returned from his home in Brittany to Nancy, where he had ordained that the streets should re-sound with French patriotic airs to eradicate his memories of humiliation.

[8] The writer's italics.   [9] *The World Crisis.*

PART II

The Great War

1914-1918

CHAPTER XII

THE GREAT WAR, AUGUST, 1914 (INTRODUCTORY)

AGED 62 YEARS

FOCH embarked upon the Great War with certain definite ideas in his mind. "To hell with history and principles! After all, what is the real question?" Verdy du Vernois is credited with having made that remark when he arrived on the battlefield of Nachod in the Austro-Prussian War of 1866, and Foch, in commenting thereon, once said to a member of his Staff: "Confronted by the difficulties which were present, Verdy du Vernois racked his brains in the hope of remembering some example or precept which might tell him what to do." When he once realized that it was a matter of deciding upon a real and not upon a theoretical question, and of "taking action," then, as Foch put it, "he immediately made up his mind what to *do*. That is the objective manner of handling a problem."

The story brings out the difference between what Napoleon called the many "good generals who saw too many things at a time" and a leader like Foch who confined his attention to the essentials of a problem. These, as Foch maintained, vary to an infinite degree, and for no situation in practical warfare is there an exact precedent which can be followed with advantage. He once summed up the subject of strategy as he understood it in a very few words: "merely a matter of character and commonsense," but he

[137]

added that although easily understood after it was performed it was not at all a simple thing to put into practice. These were the conclusions at which he had arrived when the Great War broke out in 1914.

What was wanted in a commander was the ability to appreciate the situation as it existed in special circumstances, shrouded in the mystery of the unknown—to form a sound judgment upon what was actually seen and known, to divine what was unseen and unknown, and then to make a quick decision and to act vigorously upon it without any further hesitation. Above all, to bear constantly in mind two factors, one of which should be known to oneself, one's own *will;* the other the will of the enemy, a subject for conjecture. It is impossible to accentuate too much the outlook of the great Marshal upon the importance of the will-power of a commander of armies and upon its influence on the issues at stake. "It is enough to know what one wills, and that is half the battle," was one of his sayings. "Know what you *will,* and do it!" is another. It will be necessary to revert to this subject in tracing his rise to the pinnacle of fame in the Great War, and meanwhile we will take note of some of the other factors that cause the practical to differ so materially in Foch's opinion from the theoretical strategy which is so dear to the "arm-chair" critic.

Foch rightly maintained that to the factors under human control must be added those that are incalculable, such as weather, temperature, sickness, railway accidents, misunderstandings, mistakes by subordinates, in fact everything of which man is neither the originator nor the master, and that it mattered little whether we chose to call them "chance," "fatality," or any other term. Theoretical knowledge was of no value in such matters; what was wanted was a pre-

vious development of mind and of character, founded upon
military knowledge already acquired, and guided both by
military history and by constant practical experience gained
in the incidents of every-day life. Strategy was far more
than a science—it was the application of knowledge to
actual life, and for success therein it was necessary to develop, during events that were constantly changing, some
primary governing influence of thought—"the art of acting
under the pressure of the most difficult circumstances."
What he had always aimed at during his many years of
academic experience was to evolve certain principles of
war as "beacons kindled on a stormy shore to guide
the bewildered mariner," or as "guiding principles for
the mind to enable it always to conceive a rational application," and we are faced with the problem of recon-
ciling with all this his warm approval of Verdy du Vernois'
remark: "To hell with principles!" with which this chapter
begins.

In Foch's view, as expressed by himself, a knowledge of
principles without the power of applying them is useless.
Teaching would be a waste of time if it did not lead to the
application of principles. After precept we should aim at
practice, and constantly to apply principles already acquired
is the only possible way to develop judgment and character. "Principles of war" were described at the British Staff
College at Camberley in the days of the late Lord Rawlinson as *"Warnings, never Rules,"* and Foch maintained,
when it was stated to him that a doctrine of war can be
evolved from the study of history, that all that is meant
thereby is the establishment of a certain number of
principles, indisputable when once they have been laid
down, while their application depends entirely upon cir-

cumstances and upon personal conditions. It does not mean the establishment of dogma or the collection of intangible truths to depart from which would be mere heresy.

"Now let us have a look at your mule-harness," a British Field-Marshal once said to a Brigade Commander in South Africa who had been holding forth on a small field day to the officers of two battalions on the way in which Napoleon, Scharnhorst, and others would have handled their commands. The harness did not fit, and the mules had sore backs.

Between the date of Foch's dismissal from the *Ecole Supérieure de Guerre* in 1901 and his return there as Commandant in 1908, and again between the years 1911 and 1914, he had gained much practical experience of the details which affect the efficiency and movement of troops, but— as he himself put it—those who are equipped only with such knowledge remain only of mediocre quality. They are incapable of providing in emergencies what he called the true test of leadership: "the spark or impulse given from above." The story of his services between the years 1914 and 1918 provides abundant evidence of the inspiration and impetus "from above" with which Foch quickened the armies which he led to ultimate victory.

The outbreak of the Great War found him in command of the celebrated XXth Army Corps which, according to the preconceived plan of campaign, formed part of Castelnau's Second Army. His headquarters were at Nancy, and according to him the idea of a great Battle of Nancy to decide the issue in the event of a war with Germany had become an obsession amongst the leaders of French military thought. In later years he said to his aide-de-camp:

General Millet was always telling me: "What is wrong with the Higher Council is that all the generals have held the Nancy Command. They know every inch of the ground there. They have studied every position—the Grand Couronné, the Haricot de X..., Z... Ridge. The Battle of Nancy! That is the only one for which they have prepared."

This remark is typical of all his teaching and practice. In his lecturing days at the *Ecole Supérieure* he used to say that the first point always was to grasp the fundamentals, next to bring an open mind to bear upon them, quite freed from prejudice and from undeveloped ideas, guarded against opinions blindly accepted because one has always heard them advanced, or even seen them executed, without question. "No sentiments, no preconceived ideas. First of all let us look at the facts," was the motto in his mind when he left Nancy at the head of his XXth Corps for Lorraine in accordance with the "Plan 17" which was to cost the French Army and nation so dearly. On the 7th of February, 1914, each of the French Army Commanders had received a copy of the section of that document which referred to his own command. Foch had no hand in its compilation. The task allotted to Castelnau's Second Army of five army corps, two cavalry divisions, heavy artillery and other troops and three reserve divisions was to be ready to attack in the general direction of Château Salnis—Sarrebruck. It was responsible for the protection of the Nancy bridgehead, and it was to occupy a front from Lunéville to the Grand Couronné de Nancy, from which line it should be ready to advance on the twelfth day of mobilisation (August 13th). The assumption had been made, in the general plan, that "from a careful study of the information obtained" it was probable that a great part of the German forces would be concentrated on the Franco-German frontier, and that they might cross that frontier in places before the French general operations could be developed. Little account was taken of other possibilities, and whatever the actual circumstances might be it was "the Commander-in-Chief's intention to advance with all forces united to the attack of the German armies." [1]

The main point was that the enemy's plan of turning the French northern flank in overwhelming force, violating Belgian neutrality, was not provided against. Lanrezac's Fifth Army on the French left was told, it is true, that the northern boundary of the zone of operations would vary according to circumstances and that it could not be specified beforehand. Lanrezac was to "operate against the right wing of the enemy's forces." The theatre of operations might extend into neutral territory—Luxembourg and in particular Belgium. If the enemy did violate that territory, the Fifth Army was to "move north-eastwards for an advance into Belgian Luxembourg by way of the Neufchateau and Florenville districts, echeloned on its left for flank protection," but it was not to move in that direction without orders from the Commander-in-Chief. The Fifth Army was at first to be in readiness to move either east or northeast, the five army corps of which it was composed were to establish their headquarters at Ville sur Tourbe—Vouziers—Amague—Auberton—Stenay. The outstanding feature, in the light of events, was that when they determined to strike a decisive blow in overwhelming force at one point—round the French left flank—the Germans considered and prepared for the

[1] An English translation of "Plan 17" is given *in extenso* in Appendix No. 9 to the first volume of the British Official History of the War: Military Operations.

possibility of being thrown on the defensive elsewhere. The point was put succinctly to the author by one of the most brilliant members of the younger generation of the French General Staff, soon after the Armistice, in these words: "Our biggest mistake was that on the outbreak of war we had prepared no defensive positions on our left flank to enable us to hold out against superior forces there if necessary. On the other flank the Germans had constructed formidable field defences in the precautionary stage, before actual mobilization, and with those our great attack was confronted." [2] The introduction on a vast scale of those two factors favouring the defensive, barbed wire and machine guns, was thenceforward destined to teach many lessons to leaders of the old school who were obsessed, as Foch put it, by "ready-made principles and preconceived ideas" when they were faced by what Clausewitz called the "bloody solution of the crisis."

It has been necessary to touch upon these broad aspects of the struggle on the "Western Front" as an introduction to a short recital of Foch's part therein. There is no need to dwell at any length upon the logical development of "Plan 17" in its early stage,[3] or upon the butchery at Morhange which resulted in the retreat that was enforced upon the French Second Army. The XXth Corps which Foch commanded in that army suffered heavy losses but it was kept well in hand by him, so that in the subsequent stand made by the French on the Grand Couronné to cover Nancy, Foch was able to launch a counter-attack which saved the

[2] This point is further developed in the 7th edition of Hamley's *Operations of War.*

[3] General Lanrezac has published a valuable monograph, called *Le Plan de Campagne Française et le Premier Mois de la Guerre,* which merits careful study.

situation by gaining the time that was sorely needed for reorganisation and reinforcement after the two disastrous battles of Sarrebourg and Morhange. *"Attaquez!"* even in the most desperate straits, was Foch's watchword, especially when morale was at its lowest, in order to impose on the troops their commander's determination not to acknowledge defeat.

Here are some extracts from Foch's own description of those early days of the War:

When one of his divisions was held up in front of Morhange he wanted to put another one in, but he then received the order to retire. "If ever I were tempted to disobey, it is to-day!"—but since the Corps on his left was held up and the one on his right had retreated, leaving his own flank in the air, he soon saw reason and began to fall back:

The roads were blocked by supply columns and by magnificent motor cars from Nice. On the 21st we had to continue the withdrawal, and cross the Seille in order to hold the heights of the Meurthe . . . I went to Nancy. They wanted to evacuate it. I said: "The enemy is five days from Nancy, and the 29th Corps is there. They won't walk over the 20th without protest!" . . . Between the 23rd and 25th I attacked strongly . . . We had to stop their advance and I gave them a good hammering . . . For three days we were at it hammer and tongs. They did not break through. They did not get to Nancy.

Foch was soon to leave his XXth Corps for wider work. Joffre, the Commander-in-Chief, needed the influence of his personality and inspiration elsewhere. By the 29th of August, the Third, Fourth and Fifth Armies and the small British Expeditionary Force beyond the French left flank had been very sorely pressed. That flank was swinging back like a door on its hinges before the advancing German Armies of which the right columns had passed through Brussels and had swung round on the arc of a circle towards Paris. On that date Joffre thought it desirable to divide the Fourth Army by detaching two of its Corps (the IXth and Xth) and other troops and so forming a *Détachement de l'Armée* under the command of Foch, who received his orders on August 27th. This detachment, with the addition of a division from the Third Army on its right, became on the evening of the 4th of September the Ninth Army with which the name of Foch was connected so intimately during the momentous days of the First Battle of the Marne.

Here, if we wish to place ourselves by his side during the subsequent events which brought his name into prominence, we must take account of an ordeal and test of his devotion to the cause to which he subjected his life. The news was soon brought to him of the deaths in action of his son-in-law Captain Bécourt of the 26th Battalion *Chasseurs à pied,* and of his only son who had been killed at Gorcy (Meuse) on the 22nd of August. Young Germain Foch, aged twenty-five, a subaltern in the 131st Infantry, fell in action and was buried in a grave with others. Only the common grave, making a low ridge in the ground, and a small wooden cross marked the spot for the next eight years. A monument was raised in 1922. The depth of the wound to the father's spirit can best be estimated by our knowledge of the fact that until the end of his life Foch made an annual pilgrimage to Gorcy. There he uncovered and knelt on the ground in prayer by his son's resting-place. During the first minutes of poignant sorrow when the news was brought to him, he asked to be left alone for a while in his office. At the end of half an hour he called to his Staff officers: "Now let us get on with our work!" and from that time forward anyone who approached him expressing sympathy was met with the remark: "Yes, yes, never mind that!"

Of the losses in general, he once said: "It is hard to see so many fall. The sacrifices were bloody, cruel. And the more cruel they were, the more deeply they laid on us a higher duty: they must not have been in vain."

With him, casualties were no measure of victory or defeat. These are his words on that subject:

Defeat was thought to be a condition constituted solely by material losses, whereas it is, on the contrary, a purely moral result caused by the discouragement and fear infused into the loser by the combined and simultaneous employment of moral and material forces on the part of the victor.

Without going unduly into detail, we have now traced the part taken by Foch in such of the events up to the 29th of August as give us indications of his character and his methods. His part in the first Battle of the Marne must form the subject of another chapter. We can conclude this chapter by quoting, from the preface to Colonel F. N. Maude's English edition of "Clausewitz on War," the advice given by Krishna to Arjuna when the latter trembled before the awful responsibility of launching his army against the hosts of the Pandav. It bears upon subsequent events.

This Life within all living things, my Prince,
Hides beyond harm. Scorn thou to suffer, then,
For that which cannot suffer. Do thy part!
Be mindful of thy name, and tremble not.
Nought better can betide a martial soul
Than lawful war. Happy the warrior
To whom comes joy of battle . . .
. . . But if thou shunn'st

[146]

This honourable field, a Vishittriya—
If, knowing thy duty and thy task, thou bidd'st
Duty and task go by—that shall be sin
And those to come shall speak thee infamy,
From age to age. But infamy is worse
For men of noble blood to bear than death!

. . . .

Therefore arise, thou son of Kunti! Brace
Thine arm for conflict; nerve the heart to meet
As things alike to thee, pleasure or pain,
Profit or ruin, victory or defeat.
So minded, gird thee, to the fight, for so
Thou shalt not sin!

To that we can add a favourite quotation by Foch from Napoleon's memoirs:

People have but a slight idea of the strength of mind needed, after one has thoroughly considered the consequences, to launch one of these great battles on which the history of an army and a country or the possession of a throne depend. And so it is rare to find generals who will willingly engage the enemy in battle.

Foch himself added some illuminating notes on this which were intended to be helpful to commanders fearful of their own errors, which make the loss of life caused by their orders still more difficult to bear. His view was that when we think that we can do without an ideal, reject what we call abstractions, and live on realism, on rationalism and positivism, reducing everything to questions of knowledge or the use of more or less ingenious expedients manufactured for the occasion, we have not yet found any way for commanders to avoid error, mistake, and disaster, excepting the exclusive cult of two "abstractions" belonging to the moral domain—duty and discipline, and in order to produce the happiest results the culture of these requires knowledge and thought.[4] Foch had no *nostrum* for those who had not done their best to acquire these qualities before bearing the responsibilites of command.

On the subject of his own personal loss General Foch wrote on September 20th to his old friend of twenty-seven years standing, General Millet (who died on October 8th— his son-in-law was killed and his daughter died of grief) as follows:

The affairs of my family are lamentable. Bécourt and my son were killed on the 22nd of August near Yprecourt, on the Belgian frontier. I heard of it on the 13th, and I have told my wife who is still at Ploujean, Finisterre. One knows nothing more, and I tremble on feeling the despair which will reign there, and the desolation of my poor wife, and also your desolation.

For myself I try to find support in remembering my duty, but not without difficulty. The cruel sacrifices which we are enduring ought not to remain sterile. I shall work with all the energy of which I am capable, absolutely confident of the issue of the fight, with the mercy of God helping us.

Farewell my General, and in your sorrow believe in my profound and attached regret.

[4] *Marshal Foch,* by René Puaux, 1918.

GERMAIN FOCH DIED UNDER FIRE
AUGUST 22ND, 1914.

This photo of Marshal Foch's son was taken on manœuvres
in 1913.

CHAPTER XIII

THE RISE TO FAME: AUGUST 29TH TO SEPTEMBER 12TH, 1914

AGED 62 YEARS

"It was on August 27th, at 9 o'clock in the evening, that I received the order from Joffre calling me to General Head-quarters. I was then to the north of Vitrimont Wood, at the inn called 'Les Oeufs durs.' They were giving me Colonels Devaux and Weygand as my staff. Weygand was with the Hussars in the wood. I sent for him, and my first order was a farewell to the XXth Corps: 'General Balfourier will take command.' On the next day, the 28th, we left at noon for Vitry-le-François, where we reached General Headquarters. We crossed Nancy during a squall. Weygand took the opportunity to say good-bye to his wife, who had not yet left Lunéville. I had picked up on my way to Vitry, Majors Naulin and Tardieu. On the 29th they gave me Requin, a captain, and I had with me Ferrasson, my A.D.C.

"I fought the Marne with an incomplete staff."

It was thus that Marshal Foch in after years described the days of his advancement from the command of an Army Corps to that of an Army—at that time called simply a "detachment"—and under these conditions there began that association between Foch and Weygand which has become renowned as one of the strongest combinations between a great commander and a great Chief-of-Staff that military history records. So intimate did the association become in the course of years that in time Weygand rose from the position of Staff officer to what may almost be described as Foch's *alter ego,* but he always remained the ideal Staff officer, loyal to his chief and suppressing his own individuality to the end. Weygand's description of Foch's methods can here be introduced with advantage. He explained them most graphically to Major Bugnet. He told him that it was in the privacy of his office that Foch revealed himself most completely. His personality was indicated by the method adopted in his work. A man of action to the core, he retained a tremendous capacity for thought. His thoughts were busy from the moment when he rose from his bed. There was something new in his head every morning and he formed the habit of seeing Weygand first and passing the idea or proposal on to him with such an introduction as: "Here is the idea I had when I was shaving." Constant reflection and concentration of thought had thus given to Foch a very wide horizon of interest, and the decisions at which he arrived were the outcome of knowledge. Though based originally upon reflection, the mental processes that immediately preceded his decisions were not prolonged; they could better be described as vigorous, and action was decided upon quickly. He found incessant smoking a great aid to contemplation, and an outstanding feature of his line of thought was a determination not to lose grip of his opponent; constant tenacity and perseverance in this object could be described as the groundwork of his military strength.

For himself, Weygand claims no merit but that of having left his great Chief free to think at his leisure of the paramount problems without wasting his time over details—those twopenny-halfpenny rigmaroles for which someone or other, nevertheless, is compelled to find a solution. Weygand adds: "I took all responsibility in such matters." He himself, as events have subsequently proved, possessed a genius for command and leadership, but his suppression of all ideas of climbing the military ladder himself by transfer from the Staff to the limelight of high command, provided a model for all time for others similarly situated. "I will not have anyone thrusting ideas upon me!" is a saying by Foch to one of his officers who in the War brought a proposal before him. If Weygand even in later years took the initiative in the privacy of the office in any such matters, he has never confessed to such action even to the most intimate acquaintance.

The relationship between a Chief-of-Staff and his Chief has vitally affected the issue of so many campaigns that it will not be out of place for us to supplement the explanations of Foch and of Weygand by quoting the opinion of a senior officer of the British Army on the relationship between them:

"I have heard some people say that what Weygand thought to-day Foch thought to-morrow. Personally I don't agree. I think that what Weygand thought to-day, Foch also thought to-day—they suited each other exactly and they thought alike. Foch was undoubtedly the deeper thinker of the two. Of course he had infinitely greater experience, both practical and theoretical. Weygand must have absorbed most of his military knowledge from Foch. He may have had rather a quicker brain and arrived at conclusions a little before Foch. I don't know—it would be very hard to say. The fact remains that they were an extraordinarily good combination, and the reason was that their two brains and their two characters and personalities happened to fit each other exactly. It certainly was a pleasure to see them working together."

[151]

Weygand has further described how his Chief when in his office during the conduct of operations used to stride up and down smoking his pipe, moving sometimes in a cloud of smoke, but that most of their time together was spent on the roads in an automobile. Then the Marshal would talk freely, not about the operation actually in progress, the course of action that had already been determined and ordered, but rather about future developments following upon that operation. These they would discuss and about these they would argue. There were times when no conclusion had been arrived at when they parted, but the idea had taken root. "Think it over!" would be the final remark. Later on the subject would be further exploited.

We have the evidence of many others that Foch could not "suffer fools gladly," that he resented having to waste time in bringing himself down to the level of the less intelligent; that he was bored by those of lesser mental calibre. Sometimes he gave, by cryptic phrases, so little indication of his own decisions as to mystify those who were not so "quick in the uptake" as to be able to divine what was not expressed. Weygand tells me that his Chief sometimes returned to an idea of which the possibilities had not been apparent to Weygand at first sight, because he had not grasped the whole of the underlying thought. Then Foch would expound and continue the process. Sincerity enabled him to bring forward an idea in the first instance before it had fully matured in his brain. "We are present at the birth of his ideas, at their hatching. Little by little we see the idea develop and clarify. The Marshal hides nothing. There is only one thing that has importance with him—the result. Then he would turn over his ideas in every direction. They sorted themselves out while he talked. In the end he would

[152]

express them in a striking manner in two or three phrases. When I left him, I could get to work and finish my task in the right way."

Of Weygand it has been written by a colleague on the Staff that it was his utter forgetfulness of self which enabled him to rise nearer to the level of his Chief and thus render to him and to his country services of inestimable value. Once appointed to the Marshal's Staff he had no other ambition but to serve him with all his strength and with all his abilities. When once the Chief had spoken, his only concern was the execution of that decision, for which he knew that a complete abandonment of his own opinion was indispensable. Foch said of him: "With his astonishing intelligence, memory, and power of work, at the end of three months he knew all my views . . . and we were never apart. That is not the usual method of work for a Chief of the General Staff, but it is the best. He can express my views as well as I should have done myself." In later years (1922) he could tell the President to send Weygand to Poland to deal with the Russian invasion. "He will do what I should. I will go later, if necessary." Fortunate it was for Foch, as he has admitted, that Weygand was serving in a cavalry regiment in close proximity to Foch's headquarters when he was summoned by Joffre on August 27th, 1914, to deal with a critical situation, to fill up the yawning gap between the French Fifth and Fourth Armies, through which the German masses might otherwise have pressed and gained a decisive victory on the Marne, instead of a defeat which upset their whole plan of campaign.

Having studied such indications as we have been able to obtain on first-hand authority of the genesis of the Foch-*cum*-Weygand combination, we can now pass to the actual events. In order to grasp their meaning we must follow the example of Foch. Like few of the Army commanders of any nationality he considered the situation on the Western Front as a whole without allowing himself to be obsessed by local operations on however extensive a scale. There was, of course, a still wider aspect of the military problem in a world-wide theatre of war, but for the moment it will suffice to confine ourselves to the main events on the Front in France and Flanders up to the 29th of August.

By violating the neutrality of Belgium on the plea of military necessity—the Kaiser put it in his own handwriting in a cable addressed to the President of the United States on August 10th, that "Belgian neutrality had to be violated on strategical grounds" [1]—the Germans had gained a great initial advantage. While Foch was engaged with his XXth Corps, Lanrezac's Fifth Army on the French left found itself wedged into the sharp salient formed by the junction of the Sambre and the Meuse at Namur, with the German Second Army (Bülow) attacking in front and the Third Army (Hausen) established on its right flank, while on its left flank the small British Expeditionary Force (French) was confronting the whole of the First German Army (Kluck). On the enforced retirement of the left of the Allied line a dangerous gap was left between Lanrezac's Fifth Army and the Fourth (de Langle de Cary). The masses of the German Second and Third Armies (Bülow and Hausen), moving southward, were threatening to pour through this wide gap when Joffre decided to call upon Foch, with a detachment from the Fourth Army, to hold it at all costs, and it was in so doing that Foch has been credited with that historic message to his Commander-in-Chief:

[1] Reproduced in facsimile in *The Triangle of Terror in Belgium*, John Murray.

[154]

"Mon centre cède, ma droite recule, situation excellente. J'attaque!"

The significance of Foch's stand to stem the advance of an enemy in overwhelming strength can best be studied in the official histories, and it will suit our purpose better to refer to his own personal accounts of the experience, as given to us by his A.D.C. Starting with a few Staff officers, assembled haphazard to handle an army of several corps and extra divisions:

"I first had to find my troops. When on the 29th (August) I reached the Fourth Army, General de Langle cried out at the sight of me. 'It is Providence who has sent you!' 'All right! All right!' I replied, 'we shall see.'"

The troops whom Foch was to inspire with his own determination to hold the gap were worn out by several fights and days of retreat. They had been in contact with the enemy on the same morning, and the consequences of withdrawal before the oncoming hordes were beginning to show themselves in their morale. *Attaquez!,* as usual, was Foch's order here, as it was to be on future occasions when defending troops were sore pressed. By the 5th of September Foch's detachment, which had become the Ninth Army an hour before midnight, was holding a line north of Fère Champénoise, facing the left wing of Bülow's Second German Army, with the whole of Hausen's Third German Army coming down on Bülow's left flank. Foch was ready for action, and in touch, though only with a thin line, with the Fifth Army—now under Franchet d'Esperez—on his left and with the Fourth on his right. Beyond the Fifth Army was Maunoury's hastily organised Sixth Army, and above all Gallieni was commanding the garrison of Paris. It was through his initiative and representations that Joffre determined to arrest the retreat sooner than he had intended. Joffre accordingly ordered a general renewal of the offensive on September 6th and directed:

"The Ninth Army (General Foch) will cover the right of the Fifth Army, holding the Southern exits of the Marshes of St. Goud and sending a part of its forces on to the plateau north of Sezanne."

In carrying out his task Foch had to sustain a bitter and determined attack by von Bülow's Army and also one from Von Hausen's Army. We are told that after the anxious days of the continual retreat, the whole nation "shared as one man in the agony of suspense. Behind the battle-line emotions ran riot. The local inhabitants were asking whether the battle, whose violent cannonade they heard drawing nearer and nearer every day, was not going to an end in a reverse which would throw them at the mercy of the invaders." Foch's headquarters were at Plancey, with fighting headquarters forward at Pleurs. He described how the people with whom he was billeted in Pleurs were seized with fear and packed up ready for flight every morning when he left them. In the evening when he returned they unpacked again. This they did daily until September 15th when the danger was over and he moved his headquarters forward to Fère Champénoise.

The Fifth Army made progress on Foch's left on September 7th; the Fourth on his right could hardly hold its ground. On the 8th a gap was found on the right wing, and the XIth Corps was driven back. Fère Champénoise was lost and the situation was critical. The issue of the great battle hung in the balance. Foch, as usual, ordered an attack. Fère Champénoise was not retaken, but the enemy's advance was stemmed for the time. Foch moved a division (the 42nd) from the left to the right of his line, but on the morning of the 9th, while this critical move was in progress, the enemy launched a fresh attack, taking the Château of Mondement and threatening a ridge to the south which would give them artillery observation over the plain across which the movement was taking place. After having given the order for the important move of the 42nd division from one flank to the other, it is typical of Foch's power of detaching his mind when there was no immediate problem to be solved, that he went for a walk with his A.D.C. and talked about economics and metallurgy, while destiny was running its course (René Puaux: "Marshal Foch"). On the evening of the 9th a counter-attack was launched with the order that:

"The General Officer commanding the Ninth Army insists with the utmost urgency that the offensive which he has laid down shall be carried out in the most energetic manner."

The attack failed at the time, but on the 10th Fère Champénoise was re-occupied by the Ninth Army. Foch had not been obsessed by the dangers of the local situation. He had looked further afield. We are told on his own authority that he said to his troops:

" 'The Germans are at the extreme limits of their efforts; they are exhausted, and surprised at our resistance. Disorder reigns among them. Success will belong to the side which outlasts the other.' And I gave the order to attack, whatever happened."

As an example of Foch's methods of inspiring subordinates, we can cite his reply to the Commander of the XIth Corps who reported that his troops were so hard pressed that there was no longer any hope of their being able to retire in an orderly manner. "You report that you cannot hold on. You say that you cannot retreat. Then only one course is left to you. Attack to-morrow morning." And for a parallel we can go to the martial traditions of the old Zulu tribes embodied in their proverb: "To go forward is to die. To go back is to die. Let us go forward." Not a bad analogy for Foch's watchword *"Attaquez!"* which, as some thought, amounted to an obsession.

The incidents on the left of the Allied Line on September 9th, the attacks by the Fifth and Sixth French Armies on Kluck, and the advance of the British Army through the gap left in the German line are matters of common knowledge. They resulted in the retreat of the German Army and in the victory of the Marne gained under the leadership of Joffre. Concerning the question whether the credit was due to Joffre or to Gallieni, Foch had something illuminating to say which brings out clearly the principle of responsibility aptly described as "power to act, and liability to be called to account." This is Foch's opinion on the incident:

"Gallieni? He said that he thought that the moment to strike had come. Joffre, who wanted to retreat to the Seine, deferred to his opinion. But, all the same, it was Joffre who took the decision. If he had been beaten, no one else would have taken the blame for the defeat. . . . Let me add that if we had not had him in 1914, I don't know what would have become of us."

Four years later Foch was to prove that he also was great enough to defer to the opinion of a man fully cognisant of a local situation, and to take upon himself the responsibility for a decision thereon. Then it was said of Foch by a whole group of nations that "if we had not had him in 1918, we do not know what would have become of us."

[158]

The night following the victory was spent by Foch and Weygand in the town hall of Fère Champénoise, and the Marshal gave this typical description of their experience: "Weygand and I went to sleep on horrible mattresses. There was a terrific uproar. We could hear people going up and down the wooden staircase which was over our heads. There was no chance of sleep. At one o'clock in the morning they came and disturbed me to tell me that I had been appointed Grand Officer of the Legion of Honour. I replied: 'What do you suppose I care about that just now? Let me sleep!' At three o'clock in the morning an emissary from General Joffre came to bring us cigars. I said to him: 'Put them on the mantelpiece!' But he also brought some blankets. They were priceless. We each took one and rolled ourselves up in them. It was cold; it was in vain that we put on all our coats; we were frozen all the same. . . ."

That sleepless night of discomfort did not damp his ardour. He was exasperated at the slowness of the pursuit: "They ought to have pushed and pushed! They refused to believe in their success. That the men in the ranks should fail to understand it, I am not surprised, but those who led them? Intolerable!" Having sent a general officer ahead with a cavalry division, he followed not an uncommon practice of his and went forward himself to see how his order was carried out. He found the officer halted at the first bridge complaining that the enemy was in overwhelming strength and that he could not sabre them all. "That," said Foch, "is not what I ask you to do. You have guns. Why have you not used them?" And then, in exasperation, seeing there was no way of making him understand, "I put him out. 'Off with you! We shall never understand each other!'" The commander of a division who had halted before Châlons, where

"The Prince Royal of Saxe and his staff were having a final jollification and he might have wiped up the whole lot" got into similar trouble, and Foch was no respecter of persons. He complained that most of the generals after the Marne were so upset by the victory that they feared to do anything more. He complained bitterly of their reliance upon regulations. "Poor old regulations! They are all very well for drill, but in the hour of danger they are of no more use. You have to learn to think."

There we leave the leader, straining at the leash, following his enemy up across the Marne in the direction of the Aisne, putting into practice the knowledge that he had gained by many years of study, self-training, and peace practice, with no more experience of actual warfare than those whom he criticised, but with what he himself would scorn to call gifts or abilities:

"Gifts! Gifts! There is no such thing. There is nothing but hard work. . . . There is nothing but that, even for the artists. . . . Do not count upon gifts! Work!"

And again:

"Courage is based upon knowledge. . . . One must work to secure knowledge. . . . To work, it is not enough to learn up regulations. It is not a question of drill: Right turn! Quick march! . . . one must learn to think. . . ."

"Text-books encourage mental indolence. Something more is needed. Poor old regulations!"

CHAPTER XIV

"To Englishmen, Foch's character must have a special interest, for it was he alone among the more prominent of the French soldiers who ever attained any measure of understanding of the English mind or any real measure of sympathy with it." [1]

It has been said of Foch by one of his intimates that as the result of his experience in command of an army in the First Battle of the Marne, the grievous danger with which his troops were confronted in holding the gap between the French Fifth and Fourth Armies during the most critical days of the battle made his mind still more lucid, his intelligence more acute, and his soul more steadfast. It taught him to stand firm to the very end with the utmost tenacity. We can compare that with Colonel Henderson's very similar statement about "Stonewall" Jackson who found that battle "sharpened his faculties and made his self-control more perfect, his judgment clearer and more prompt," and there resulted a gain in self-confidence of the utmost value.

An apt comparison was made between Foch and trees on a bleak sea-shore which are bent more and more by each gust of wind but whose leaves nevertheless learn to cling to the twigs, the twigs to the branches, the branches to the trunk, while the roots burrow further into the sandy soil

[1] R. H. Beadon: *National Review*, May, 1929.

to grip the rocks buried beneath. The process of toughening the fibers is a long one. By his parents Foch had been endowed with a faith which his education increased and confirmed. His character was developed by his own systematic exercise of will, and he created his methods himself by hard work and by reflection. The result was what is inadequately called "a strong individual personality."—"Don't listen to him. What does the opinion of others matter? I pay no attention to it."

His object was to develop strength of will, but will based upon thought and reflection. "One must will, of course, but first one must know how to will." By work, by studying problems deeply, and by thought he improved his power of arriving at "a right judgment in all things." He developed an outstanding aptitude for concentration upon the definite problem to be solved for which he demanded "no stereotyped solutions! One must learn to reason." Then, when a definite decision has been formed, the will intervenes with implacable determination; and action, pursued to the very end, sweeping all impediments aside, becomes of supreme importance. Concentration upon a subject became a habit with him, more and more pronounced as the years went by. This became most marked in grave emergencies, and the worse things went the cooler and more quiet Foch became. If someone addressed him when he was concentrating upon the point at issue, he would put him off quietly, and if he bothered him again upon some other subject he became still more quiet, and, with his habitual shrug of the shoulders accompanied by a turn of the head and a quaint kindly glance into the eyes of the speaker he might remark: "Ah! But then *you* can think about and discuss two different subjects at the same time. . . . I cannot. *Moi pas!*"

It has been written of the human mind that man can control it, and so become the dictator of its course. "Rising thence to the highest pinnacle of possibility, he may become the arbiter of destiny itself." [2] All action has its origin in thought, which lends infinite importance to control over the mind. Appreciations of the great soldier's character have reached the author from a large proportion of the officers, British and foreign, who were most intimately acquainted with him during the fateful days of the Great War. The accounts vary in points of detail, largely on account of the temperament of the individual writers and of their power of appreciating different qualities. On one point—Foch's power of deep and concentrated thought—they all agree. One appreciation, which can be given verbatim, comes from a British general, pre-eminent in the eyes of the Army. He describes Foch thus: "In my humble opinion by far the biggest thinker and the biggest personality of them all."

During the autumn of 1914 and throughout the following year Foch was destined to be in constant personal communication with the British Army, so a favourable opportunity is now offered for quoting a few opinions of British officers beginning with those of an officer who in pre-war days had found him "a little man in elastic-sided boots and impossible clothes with a rather contemptuous and almost hostile attitude," but who subsequently became his warmest admirer. Foch's face struck observers as remarkable, with its long military moustache, high forehead, and piercing eyes; the features regular, the chin firm, the expression noble and severe when in repose. An officer who was for a long time in intimate contact with him accentuated his outstanding physical strength and activity, and added:

[2] *Right and Wrong Thinking*, A. M. Crane.

[163]

His whole bearing was martial, and he gave the impression of being a man of relentless energy and determination. In conversation he often employed gestures to emphasize his words; two blows in the air with his fists, followed by two kicks, used to show the fate which he reserved for his enemies. In any conversation of importance he began by saying *"De quoi s'agit-il?"* and he had a way of sweeping away any difficulties metaphorically with his hands; in explaining his own views he used to say: *"Ah si, Ah si"* in a firm and persuasive manner; or, if he disagreed, *"Ah non, Ah non"* in a very decided way. He also had a way of putting both hands on the shoulders of the man with whom he was talking, especially if he were taller than himself, in a manner that was both appealing and convincing. His voice was deep and he spoke in short, quick sentences, sometimes using rather colloquial language which at times made it difficult for a foreigner to understand him, but he used to add: *"Vous comprenez bien?"* and repeated his remarks if he felt that he had not been understood.

He always thought a great deal before answering, but, when once his mind was made up, he seldom or never changed his opinion, unless a new point of view persuaded him.

His written style was his own and not always quite classic. His secretary once told the writer that the Marshal asked him to criticise a document which he had written, and upon the latter saying timidly that some expression was not in perfect French, the Marshal replied, *"Je m'en f—; je suis de l'académie."*

In his habits the Marshal was quiet and unassuming; he used to ride or walk alone, or accompanied by one officer, and he was never difficult to see or in any way unapproachable.[3]

That gives us an admirable pen-picture of Foch as seen through average British eyes. Besides the impression of concentrated thought before forming a decision, the habit of

[3] Colonel C. J. C. Grant, in the *Army Quarterly* for January, 1921.

SHOWING THE CLEAR HANDWRITING OF FOCH

This letter was written to General Millet by Marshal Foch on the 20th of September, 1914.

gesticulation with the hands struck all British observers, and was described by one Staff officer as "more than an average wealth of gesticulation even for a Frenchman." With his special friend "Henri" (Field-Marshal Sir Henry Wilson) he unbent considerably. One observer who saw them constantly together describes them as "tremendous gossips. They spent hours together gossiping. They used to change caps and walk up and down the room talking and chaffing."

British Army officers who were in a position to know the facts are unanimous in their view that Foch had a great affection for the British Army as a whole and an intense admiration for the British regimental officer and soldier. The general upon whose opinion the author places the strongest reliance wrote: "This was evidently perfectly genuine, as he was not the sort of man to say anything that he did not mean." Others followed in the same strain. This genuine affection for the British soldier lasted until the end of Foch's life. Although to British observers he seemed to be failing in health, he went to the unveiling of the Marne War Memorial in October, 1928, and, inspecting the British Guard of Honour, one hundred strong, he showed great interest, pausing opposite to every man in the ranks and asking questions about many of them. An observer remarked: "You can see that he is really fond of the British soldier." Foch was popular with the British troops who knew of him, and he was loyally supported.

In the operations which we shall next follow, in October, 1914, an almost desperate situation developed. Complete disaster and a German break-through were only averted by coöperation between the British Army and the French whom Foch commanded. Of this period Foch himself said:

[165]

I had no right to command; nothing was put on paper. But I did not need it. That is all right for corporals. It is only necessary to be able to think of such a matter and then one goes ahead with it. I have never exercised such effective command as in 1914, when I was deputy to Joffre. I was in command [control?] of the Belgians and of General French, but I gave them no orders . . . nevertheless I gave them some hard tasks.

And here we can take note of the points that Sir John French had direct instructions from the British Government that he was not to be placed under the orders of any French general, and that only the King of the Belgians [4] could command the Belgian Army.

So far we have touched chiefly upon the average opinion of the typical British officers who were best acquainted with Foch, and have responded to the writer's appeal for such opinions. There remains the special friend who resembled him in some surface qualities, the late Field-Marshal Sir Henry Wilson, who was Commandant of the British Staff College at Camberley at the time when Foch held the same position at the *Ecole Supérieure de Guerre* from 1908 onwards. We can here recall a few points about their friendship. Wilson was appointed to relieve the late Lord Rawlinson as Commandant at Camberley at a time when the work that was being carried out on the German railways to facilitate the execution of the celebrated "Schlieffen Plan" —of which the full details have never been disclosed—gave a clear indication of the intention of Germany to violate the neutrality of Belgium in the event of war with France. Wilson used to spend part of his leave visiting the area con-

[4] On October 11th, 1914, King Albert loyally agreed to accept Foch's instructions. (Recouly.)

cerned on a bicycle, and the more that he saw and was told by other eye-witnesses the more determined he became to do his utmost to prepare the British Army to act in conjunction with the French and to afford effective military support if Britain should be compelled in honour to take up the sword. He knew all about the conversations between the British and the French General Staffs which had been authorised by members of the British Cabinet and are now a matter of history. He paid a personal visit to Paris, where he found Foch at first somewhat aloof and critical. There followed the entertainment by Wilson in England of his French colleague which resulted in a gradual thawing and finally in the genuine affection which developed between these two outstanding characters. Some time after the late Lord Haldane had formed the British Expeditionary Force Wilson asked Foch with what minimum number of troops he would be satisfied if the German menace developed and the British Government decided to come to the aid of France. "What would be the smallest number that we could usefully send to France?" Wilson always gave effect to a story by his mode of telling. At this point he used to gesticulate with his hands, hold up one finger, and give Foch's reply. "One soldier. I will see that he is killed at once, and then the whole British Empire will come to avenge him!" There are various versions of the story. That is the way in which it was told by Wilson to the author.

Henry Wilson, as is well known, kept very intimate private diaries, jotting down constantly the impressions of the moment—ideas in embryo before they had been matured by reflection. Voluminous extracts from those diaries were published after his death. It was with some, notably with one critic, a case of "Oh that mine enemy had written a book!"

and the occasion was seized for bitter attacks, tinged with spite, upon the reputation of the dead soldier. "No man is a hero to his valet." Few could afford to bare to others the thoughts which pass through their minds at moments when control over thought is relaxed. Wilson placed on record such thoughts, apparently using his diaries—unwisely, it may be—as a safety-valve. It is not the place here to discuss either the wisdom of their publication nor their contents as a whole, but some of the general opinions which he expresses of Foch, his personal friend, are too valuable to be ignored as historical material when writing of Foch as he appeared through English [5] eyes. To some we have already referred. From those not quoted elsewhere, we find Wilson describing Foch, when first met at the *Ecole Supérieure de Guerre* in December, 1909, as "increasingly nice as the day wore on," then "candid" and "interesting." Within a year we find him "one of the foremost authorities on the art of war in Europe." The meeting between Wilson and Foch in October, 1914, when their combined work to bring the British Army to the aid of France and Belgium had borne fruit, occurred at Foch's headquarters at Doullens. "Here a guard of honour and bugle, and Foch kissed me twice in front of the whole crowd! Foch absolutely full of fight."

Then, on the momentous 1st of November, "I believe Foch will save the situation. He is a splendid fellow." By December, the personal friendship between Foch and Wilson seems to have done much to reduce friction between French and British. They saw each other almost daily and they discussed debatable questions freely and without reservations. In chaff Foch is said to have been no match for

[5] Sir Henry Wilson was an Ulsterman from northern Ireland.

Wilson, and he once kicked Wilson round the room in an excess of excitement at the badinage. In the spring of 1915 we find the friendship as strong as ever at a critical time in Flanders, and Wilson a useful intermediary between Foch and French, but soon afterwards Wilson found Foch "perturbed" at the diversion of British troops from the Western Front.

It is not essential to our purpose to describe in detail the numerous meetings between Foch and Wilson during the long period that was to intervene before a serious difference arose between them during the closing stage of the War over the question of British man-power for the Western Front, the British Government having given up all hope of a decision being arrived at there and hoping to devise some easier road to victory involving fewer casualties. Then the friendship was perhaps a little strained, but the point brought out by the controversy, as affecting Foch, was his steadfastness in refusing, in the face of difficulties however formidable, to budge an inch from the original conclusions which the two friends had shared in 1915. This is the feature of Foch's character which is brought out most clearly in the Wilson diaries. Together with that steadfastness, there was what in some English eyes would seem an excess of surface effervescence, which only obscured the depth of his knowledge and of his determination.

While Foch had had the same training as the other French generals, his mental outlook was much broader. Being himself blunt in speech and sometimes abrupt in manner, he understood the same qualities in others, and he took no offence. He could realize that the English way of settling a question or of solving a problem differed widely from the logical process of the French. For that reason he did not, like so many others, quarrel with methods. All that he cared for was the final aim and the results.[6]

We can close our notes on "Foch through English eyes" with two quotations. Mr. Churchill wrote of the Marshal in the crisis of March, 1918, that "Foch, a week ago described as a 'dotard' [it would be interesting to know by whom] was the indispensable man. He alone possessed the size and combative energy to prevent the severance of the French and British armies."[7] And for the proper wording of a some-what deeper view of Foch's life and character, we will use a phrase employed by Sir Edward Grey,[8] perhaps the best of all exponents of matters about which the average Eng-lishman is inarticulate: "The strongest personalities are the outcome not so much of striving for personal success or fame as of patriotism and faith in an ideal." These words exactly express the average English opinion of the reason for Foch's strong influence over Englishmen.

To these reminiscences of Foch seen through English eyes we can add some seen through French eyes, which contain strong corroboration. Major Recouly jotted down various personal impressions of Foch as he appeared to him at vari-ous times in the War:

He is of medium height, neither tall nor short, and strongly built without any superfluous weight, seeming to be alert as well as powerful; his forehead is broad and well shaped, his nose straight and clean-cut; a grey moustache hides the lips which hold his perpetual cigar—a pipe was substituted dur-ing office work in later years. His eyes are his most striking feature; their look is at one moment abstracted, as if his thoughts

[6] R. H. Beadon, *National Review*, May, 1929.
[7] *World Crisis*, Pt. II, p. 425.
[8] Now Viscount Grey of Fallodon, in a tribute to Walter Hines Page.

are far away, and the next extraordinarily keen, darting suddenly from under somewhat heavy lids. His utterance is crisp and at times rather abrupt; his voice is that of one used to command. He gives the impression of being frank, loyal, and clear-sighted; if I had to choose a motto for the General I think this would suit him as well as another: "clear vision." [9]

So much for appearance. Major Recouly also noted that Foch gave him the impression of standing firmly face to face with realities, his disciplined brain enabling him to see a situation as a whole, while at the same time taking due account of its details. No preconceived ideas were ever allowed to obscure his vision or to warp his judgment, and nothing was permitted to come between him and men and things as realities. He did not underrate obstacles. He weighed them, and he made full allowance for them in his final decision.

Equilibrium between his intellect and his character was his strong point, between "the power to understand and the will to execute." The extreme rapidity of perception and the vivid imagination which he owed to his southern blood were tempered and dominated by thorough commonsense and by his judicial mind which he had accustomed to study conditions slowly and to weigh one point against another before definitely deciding. In Foch these qualities all balanced each other, were fused into a harmonious whole which is commonly called "genius."

At a later stage we shall see how these opinions fit in with those of Weygand, his chief Staff officer, who has just published his impressions of the great Marshal. Meanwhile a favourable opportunity is here offered for quoting one of the most discerning appreciations of Foch, from the human side,

[9] *Foch, His Character and Leadership*, Recouly, p. 16.

that has yet been published. It comes from the pen of Lady Sybil Grant, who wrote it in Paris on the day after the death of the Marshal. "Everyone," she wrote, "has heard of the Field Marshal's wonderful eyes, and the first impression you received was of an infinite horizon—he seemed to look beyond the common limits of human sight. When in the course of conversation he looked in your direction you felt the same helpless sense of inferiority as when, upon a night in deep summer, you look up at the stars. Nothing small, mean, or insincere could ever cloud that spirit, and the fierce impatience, almost horror, evinced at such a taint in anyone else found no source in pride, but came from the unexpectedness of discovering in others what was to him so impossible." Two other attributes are mentioned, a sense of humour which—swift and sudden—would illuminate and soften his whole face, and the amazing sympathy and understanding which must have caused the Field-Marshal infinite suffering during those terrible years.

CHAPTER XV

AFTER his manifold experiences of actual warfare Marshal Foch said, in a moment of exasperation: "Information? It is useless. It is nearly all false; it is only afterwards that you know the truth." He retained a special memory in that connexion of the Battle of the Marne. "One never knows anything," he said—"on the night of the Marne, when I was told that the Germans were no longer there . . . I did not understand!" After the battle he was exasperated by the tardiness of the pursuit. Military textbooks abound with maxims enjoining immediate and vigorous pursuit of a beaten enemy, but the pages of military history provide few examples of victorious armies overtaking and dispersing a retreating enemy by direct pursuit. The victors are usually as exhausted as the vanquished, and the problem of feeding a retreating force and supplying it with ammunition is simpler. It falls back upon its supplies. If a flank attack, threatening the rearward communications, can be delivered, it is another matter.

The troops of Foch's army had been tried hard, and even when inspired by so great a leader, there are limits to human endurance. Physical exhaustion can be repaired by a few hours sleep and nourishing food. Moral exhaustion requires a far longer time and different conditions for its cure. How-

[173]

ever that may have been with Foch's Ninth Army, the point was that in order to gather the fruits of victory it was necessary by a vigorous advance to hold the enemy's troops, overtaking and attacking them, thus pinning them to a position, and then manœuvring reserve forces round the outer flank. The German Army stood at bay on a line partly north and partly south of the Aisne. By the evening of the 15th of September, when Falkenhayn became Chief of the General Staff of the German Army in place of Moltke, the German right flank rested on the Oise. According to Falkenhayn's own account, it was in the air, with no reserves behind it, and then there came the attempts on each side to turn the flank of the other which goes in history by the name of the race for the sea; in those operations Foch was destined to play a dominating part. It has been said by a wise man that the only adequate reward for a good worker is to be given an opportunity to do better and wider work. We have seen how Foch received the decoration that was conferred upon him immediately after he had succeeded in preventing Bülow or Hausen from breaking through the gap in the French line, until the advance of the British Army across the Marne on September 9th through the gap between Kluck's and Bülow's armies had caused both those armies to retreat. Joffre's real reward to Foch was to select him for wider and for still more critical work.

During the period that covered the failure of the French to break through the German line and of the Germans to turn the left flank of the Allied Armies, the streams of advancing troops naturally pressed on towards gaps in their enemy's frontage. Outstanding features of the Battle of the Marne were the success of Foch in stopping the gap between the French Fifth and Fourth Armies, and the failure on the

German side to arrest the advance of the British Army through the gap between the German First and Second Armies. This is Foch's own description of his method of stopping gaps: "When one knows what one wills, everything becomes easy. To stop up gaps one fills them up with mud. It is incredible what one effects by this system." Joffre's first hope was to press through the wide gap between the German right and the sea, using all the available French troops, the British troops, and the Belgian Field Army which he hoped would have come out of Antwerp for the purpose. His plan was altered by political pressure and by representations by the British Government to induce the Belgian Army to remain in Antwerp, hoping that it could be relieved by British and French troops. It does not come within our province to speculate upon the results which Joffre's plan would have achieved if it had been carried out as it was designed. It is better to follow Foch's maxim: "The past? It is what it is; we can do nothing with it. Let it alone. One must look at the present. What is it to-day—in such-and-such a year, a month, a day?"

After various vicissitudes, Joffre decided to make a great effort on the northern flank with Castelnau's Second Army —with which we were first acquainted when Foch was commanding the XXth Corps in the early offensive from Nancy —and on the 26th of September,[1] 1914, he decided to appoint Foch as his deputy to take charge of the operations in that area. The best course that we can pursue will be to ask the question which Foch himself invariably asked: *"De quoi s'agit-il?"* What was the problem? By the 8th of October the northern flank of the French Second Army rested on the Somme. The Tenth French Army (Maud'huy) extended the

---

[1] *British Official History.*

[175]

line from thence to opposite to Lens. Beyond that was the XXIst French Corps with its left between Bethune and La Bassée. To the northward French cavalry filled the gap to a force of French Territorial troops covering St. Omer and facing Hazebrouck. Sir John French's British Army was being transferred secretly from its position on the Aisne to the left flank, and on October 8th a decision was arrived at to abandon Antwerp and withdraw the British Naval Division, which had been sent to reinforce the garrison, to England; the Belgian field army, "most of the units having ceased to exist as combatant formations and no longer in a state to offer resistance" [2] were to join the main Allied Army as originally intended by Joffre.

According to the evidence of Major Recouly [3] and others, a very important interview took place on October 16th between Foch and King Albert. The King is reported to have said that he did not think that his army, brave as it was, was capable of holding the line of the River Yser against the German advance. Many of his units had lost most of their officers, had been sorely shaken, and were in no condition for more fighting, so it would be more prudent to continue the retreat. Foch promised Allied support, and the King, won over to Foch's view, ordered his army to hold the line of the Yser to the last.

By the 26th of October the northern flanks of both armies rested on the sea near Nieuport. The depleted Belgians were holding the left of the line. A French Marine Brigade was holding Dixmude, and French Territorial troops spread from thence to the northern flank of the salient covering Ypres which was held by the British Army, now reinforced

[2] Deguise, p. 153, footnote.
[3] *Foch, His Character and Leadership*, p. 138.

by the remnants of the 7th Division and 3rd Cavalry Brigade which had been landed at Zeebrugge and Ostend, and
had tried to relieve Antwerp. The line held by the British
extended to a point facing La Bassée where it was in touch
with the left of the French XXIst Division on the La
Bassée Canal. Facing this line of about fifty-five miles, so
thinly held, were two whole German Armies. To the northward the Fourth Army, of five corps, north of Menin, and
the Sixth Army of three corps and four cavalry corps south
of that place. In the race to the sea, Joffre's attempt to turn
the German flank had failed, and the German plan now
was to burst through at all costs and to capture the Channel
ports: Dunkirk, and ultimately Calais—they already possessed Zeebrugge and Ostend, and they held them until the
end of the war. It would be impossible to exaggerate the
importance of the influence of Foch in averting so supreme
a disaster to the Allied cause.

Foch had been ubiquitous, and always at the critical point
at the right time. We read of his having received his orders
from Joffre by telephone, without any detailed instructions,
late on the afternoon of October 4th. By four A.M. on the
5th he was waking up Castelnau, his former chief, at his
headquarters of the IInd Army at Breteuil. For two hours
they talked, fortified by strong coffee, and by nine A.M. he
was with Maud'huy at the headquarters of the Xth Army at
Aubigny. Between October 1st and 6th the Germans attacked
the left flank heavily and Foch's words were: "Fight to the
last man, but hang on like lice. No retirement. Every man to
the attack!" On October 9th there was still a gap of thirty
miles between the Allied northern flank and the coast. On
that day the British Expeditionary Force began to detrain.
Foch speeded them to the front with motor transport for

[177]

10,000 men at a time. On October 10th he conferred with General French at Doullens, and they agreed to an advance —no defensive ideas as yet. On the 11th he was definitely appointed to command the *"Groupe des Armées du Nord,"* known shortly as the G.A.N.[4] On the 13th strong German columns began a confident advance against the Belgians, the force nearest the coast. By the 20th the yawning gap between Dixmude and Armentières was filled up, just in time, and a German bombardment by heavy guns began. On every day preceding that first crisis Foch had been everywhere, hurrying reserves forward and inspiring the commanders with his determination. As he was at times accused of using his constant *"Attaquez!! Attaquez!!"* as a parrot-cry, we can take note of the point that on October 15th he had suggested to Sir John French in writing to prepare a defensive line in case of need.

On the 21st of October (Trafalgar Day) a heavy German attack developed against the Belgian and French line on the River Yser and Dixmude. The forcing of the Yser had to be prevented at all costs. They telephoned to Foch who hastened to the spot. The main requirement was a rapid decision and orders easily understood as to what definite line to hold. A glance at his surroundings was enough for Foch. As he explained in later years: "I said: 'Hold the railway line.' I did not know the ground, but it was either an embankment or a cutting. In any case it was a line which would be well marked on the map, and it might provide some cover. They must stop and hold on there, that is simple! . . . It was an embankment, and we dug in on one side." According to Major Grasset's account Foch arrived at the moment when a retreat to Dunkirk was being discussed, and he just saved

[4] *British Official History*, Vol. II, p. 76, footnote.

the situation. Realizing that it was becoming more and more critical he also—according to the same authority—initiated the idea of letting in the sea-water to form an impenetrable obstacle to a further German advance against this sector. In his own description to his A.D.C.[5] after the War he took no credit for the flooding, but he rejoiced in it: "Then the floods came, and stopped the enemy on the other side [of the railway embankment]. After that we had some duck-shooting!"

On October 24th Foch moved his headquarters forward to Cassel. The IXth French Corps had come up on the 22nd and other French reinforcements were expected, and he used them, in his words, as "French cement"[6] to block up possible holes in the Allied line. The battles of Ypres, for the Ypres salient, had begun to develop on October 18th. On the 28th the floods further to the northward began to be effective, so there was little danger in that area, though the Germans tried another attack on the 30th. By the 30th the thin line of British troops covering the salient was at the point of being broken by constant and determined attacks of the German Fourth and Sixth Armies. Foch repaired to French's headquarters at St. Omer where he arrived at 1 A.M. The accounts of the interview vary. Some of them are highly dramatic, most of them probably apocryphal. M. André Tardieu was present as interpreter. Foch's own account runs thus: "Lord French at Ypres said to me: 'We are all in for it!' I replied, 'We shall see. In the meantime, hammer away, keep on hammering and you will get there. It is surprising the results you gain in that way.'" Other accounts say that Foch promised reinforcements at once. Later on the same day, October 31st, the situation of the British Army became

[5] Major Bugnet.   [6] René Puaux' account.

desperate. Gheluvelt on the Menin Road was captured, and Hooge threatened. Foch was at General D'Urbal's head-quarters at Vlamertinghe when General Dubois, command-ing the IXth French Corps on the British left arrived, and General French passed in a motor. The British were holding the southern half of the salient and their line was prolonged nearly to Armentières. The French held the northern half of the salient. If the British line was broken the IXth French Corps would be involved. There were no reserves. French's motor was halted, and he joined the conference of French generals.

We shall never know all that passed at that historic inter-view between French and Foch. The British Official His-tory [7] shows clearly that French knew already that the crisis at Gheluvelt had been solved by a magnificent counter-at-tack launched by a portion of the Worcestershire Regiment. Up to the close of the War neither French nor Foch told anyone what passed between them, but M. le Goffic stated: [8]

All we know is that the Field-Marshal (French) said to Foch, with his slight English accent and his British habit of pronouncing the French "u" like "ou," *Alors il ne reste qu'à nous t(o)uer?* and that Foch's reply was "We must stand firm first. We can die afterwards."

Commander Bugnet reported in later years, on Foch's authority, that French said: "All that remains for me to do is to get killed!" and that Foch replied: "You must not talk of dying, but of winning." [9] There is not much difference between the contemporary and the later account. That

[7] Vol. II, p. 327. [8] Puaux, p. 149.
[9] After further research, the author has come to the conclusion that Major Bugnet (*Foch Speaks,* p. 210) must have misunderstood the Marshal about the date of his statement to Marshal French. In the British Official History (*Military Operations,* Vol. II, p. 342) we read only that "General Foch, as ever, pro-

French derived encouragement and a great impetus from Foch when he was at the limit of his resources and almost of his endurance seems to be probable, and French needed all his strength before the acute danger to his army had passed. It is, however, to be noted that the tide had turned before any communication from French after he had seen Foch (the message is timed 3.45 P.M.) could have reached the British troops. The situation had been saved at Gheluvelt by 4 P.M. and counter-attacks there and elsewhere had followed the one by the Worcester Regiment. For the stand made by the British Army on that ominous day credit must be awarded to Haig and to the British regimental officer and man, for whom Foch from that time forward conceived so deep an admiration. Of the British troops engaged at Gheluvelt one battalion at the end of the action mustered only 50 men, another 70, another 105, another 204, another 260, and the remaining one only one officer and 35 other ranks, but the heavy attack was repulsed. The text of the memorandum given by Foch to French at 3.5 P.M. and sent on to General Haig, commanding the Ist Corps, later, ran:

It is absolutely imperative that no retirement is made, and to that end dig in on the ground on which you happen to be.

This does not prevent you from organizing a rear position which should connect with our IXth Corps at Zonnebeke.

But every movement rearwards made by a considerable body of troops ensures an advance of the enemy and certain disorder among the retiring troops. This must be absolutely prevented.

posed to remedy the situation by attacking." The legend of his actual words to French did not appear until after the *Second* battle of Ypres. The version given in Poincaré's *Neuf années de Souvenirs,* Vol. V, "L'Invasion," of what Foch said to him does not appear to the Author to be quite correct. The story seems, on the whole of the evidence available, to have been more likely to apply to the Second than to the First Battle of Ypres, although it has been repeated by so many French authorities.

On the 1st of November Foch accompanied the President and Joffre to meet Kitchener, Secretary of State for War, at Dunkirk, and it was on that occasion that the French military authorities accepted Kitchener's estimate of the probable duration of the War and his refusal to send untrained men into the fighting line. No important accessions to the British Army could be expected till the spring of 1915 and thenceforward there would be a ceaseless flow of reinforcements reaching a maximum in the summer of 1917. With that ruling in his mind Foch returned to the group of Armies of the North, and found that the offensives that he had directed could make no progress, but they had undoubtedly arrested the enemy's advance. The same applied to the next day, and on November 3rd Foch sent a Staff officer to reassure Haig with a message that it would only be necessary to hold out for a few more days. Between November 5th and 8th, 10th and 11th, the German Fourth and Sixth Armies continued to launch attacks, a fierce attack by the German Guards striking the British front astride the Menin Road on November 11th, and a lesser attack on November 14th, but the German plan to burst through to the Channel ports ended in failure.

Seen through English eyes, "although nominally Foch had no command over the Belgian and British Armies, and officially he could do no more than forward to them copies of the orders issued to his own troops, as a matter of fact his influence was considerable; and his proposals, so far as means allowed, were carried out by the Allied Armies without waste of time and without friction of any kind. French and Belgians, and French and British, as circumstances required —and as far as difference of training, war material and language permitted—fought side by side and sometimes as one Army." [10] Prolonged research through the pages of military history would be needed to find such an example of the influence of a great leader over troops of different nations. The troops had fought in the great struggle not only alongside each other but actually with units intermingled. Difficulties there had been, and were still, to be passed through, but the solid bond which was established in those days was never to be dangerously shaken, and Generals Foch and Haig were to work together with mutual understanding on many another field.[11]

Of Foch's methods in these operations it is difficult to write—one cannot analyse inspiration. He spoke often in enigmas and in parables, but we can draw some indications from his own description of those days. Personal influence seems to be the text. It is not enough to sit down issuing orders. The commander must inspire, must see to performance:

At the worst moment, when we no longer knew what to do, some more divisions were sent up. They thought that they had done all that was needed. And then? What? Not enough? What is wanted is the will to do something. One must say "Halt! We hold on here." One must decide on a line to hold . . . They send more divisions. And after that? They don't know what to do. Believe me, what is wanted above all is will power. What is most lacking is command. Nevertheless it is not difficult. But they give orders: "Send more troops." They regard that as sufficient. They issue orders and regulations. And again the orchestra has no conductor. One man plays one tune and the other another. No matter how well they play the noise is dreadful! That is not the way to get things done. One must know what one wills. One must will it, and then . . . and the divisions can come. The position will be held.

[10] British Official History, Vol. II, p. 127.
[11] Ibid.

We can close this chapter with a pen-picture of Foch at his headquarters at Cassel, a little office in the Town Hall. At night he would be found sitting with his elbows on a map and the telephone at hand. He has, it may be, sent off the last reserve of a couple of battalions in motor lorries to hasten them to the point of danger. He chews a cigar, and looks up from the map to the old Louis XVI clock on the mantelpiece. And back again to the map, waiting. Everything is quiet. All, in the little Flanders town on its eminence, have gone to bed early, but occasionally steps echo on the irregular cobbles of the deserted square: some Staff officer going home to bed. Then the sentry moves to warm himself. Then silence again. The minute hand of the clock moves slowly. The news takes long to arrive. Then a knock at the door and Weygand comes in with a paper in his hand. "There is a telephone message from the IXth Army to say, etc." "All right." His plan has succeeded; the reinforcements have arrived in time, and now he must go to bed. A last glance at the map, and then the eyeglasses at the end of their cord disappear into the breast pocket of his dolman. He puts on his black coat, rams the képi with the gold oak-leaves on the back of his head, and passes to the hall where the gendarme on duty rises hastily from a doze in his chair. A clatter outside of the arms of the sentry, and escorted by one of the officers working on the Staff the general walks to the lawyer's house where he is billeted, to return at an early hour to the office.[12]

On November 6th an interesting interview took place at those headquarters at Cassel, where Sir John French came to call upon General Foch to thank him for his attitude on November 1st, when Kitchener had proposed to the French

[12] René Puaux, *Marshal Foch.*

President and to Joffre at Dunkirk to remove French and to substitute Sir Ian Hamilton. Joffre would not agree, we read in the Wilson diaries that "Sir John thanked Foch personally and in the warmest terms for his comradeship and loyalty. They shook hands on it." [13]

[13] *Wilson Diaries*, Vol. I, p. 187.

Chapter XVI

THE ORDEAL IN FLANDERS: NOVEMBER, 1914

AGED 63 YEARS

In the preceding chapter mention was made of a conference that was held between Lord Kitchener, Secretary of State for War, representing the British Cabinet, and the President of the Republic accompanied by both Joffre and Foch. In the subsequent operations Foch had so much to do with the activities of the British Expeditionary Force that it will be desirable at this stage to pay some attention to the policy of the Government from which French, the commander of that force, received his orders. At the Dunkirk conference the French authorities accepted both Lord Kitchener's estimate of the length of the War and the programme which he unfolded to them of the military contributions which England was prepared to make to the Allied cause.

Great Britain had begun the War with no army on the scale understood in the Continental sense of the term. All the accessible documents, and their name is legion, give the impression that, as the result of the conversations between the French and British General Staffs which were authorized in 1906, no idea had been conveyed to the British Government of the scale upon which assistance by British armies was likely to be required by France. Only a portion of the British Cabinet seems to have studied the question at all, and Mr. Winston Churchill has explained clearly in his "World Crisis" how a strong section tried to prevent the Prime Minister (Mr. Asquith), Lord Haldane and Sir Edward Grey, the Foreign Minister, from "wandering into patriotic pastures." Lord Grey himself has since explained the situation in his "Twenty-five Years": that the object of his policy was to ensure that in any event the British nation should be governed, and British foreign policy be framed, by a united Cabinet. The official military advisers of the Cabinet in such matters were the members of the General Staff which had recently been established by Lord Haldane. From Lord Haldane's "Before the War," from the writings of Field-Marshal Sir William Robertson, who was one of the General Staff Directors at the War Office up to 1914, and from other authorities we can gather that the impression had been that the British Expeditionary Force of six divisions would suffice as a reinforcement for the French Army in the situation which materialized in August, 1914. Foch, as we have seen, placed the minimum at one soldier on the assumption that all the military resources in personnel and material would follow in course of time after that man was killed. Sir William Robertson explains the motives which caused the bulk of the General Staff officers at the War Office to be sent from their posts there to the Front, in anticipation of a short war. The writer of this biography who was with the late Sir Henry Wilson at the Staff College up to 1908 and a Brigadier-General on the General Staff up to 1912, can corroborate the view that up to that time there was no conception of the serious situation that was likely to develop over British aid on land in a Franco-German war if the country was committed to that policy.

Another point worthy of attention is the doubt whether

the French "Plan 17" was ever communicated in its entirety to the British military authorities.[1] To that plan, with its disastrous results, the urgent need by France for early military assistance from Great Britain on a colossal scale can directly be attributed. The plan, as we know, was severely criticised by some French authorities. General Lanrezac, commanding the French Fifth Army, wrote:

Cette combinaison me paraissait inquiétante: elle n'aurait été admissible selon moi q'avec des moyens actifs notablement supérieurs à ceux de l'ennemi: or, il fallait bien reconnaître que la situation serait tout contraire.[2]

In later years, Marshal Foch also expressed his disagreement with the French generals who were responsible for the plan. He considered that they were obsessed by their local knowledge of the terrain in the neighbourhood of Nancy. It is necessary for us to bear all these points in mind in connexion with the operations which followed and with Foch's part therein.

The situation on the 31st of October—when the British Expeditionary Force, helped, it may be, by his inspiration, had succeeded in holding out to the last in the position covering Ypres, which had been allotted to them by Foch, was that the equivalent of more than eight German army corps confronted a line held thinly by nine British and two Indian divisions, with eight German cavalry divisions, in addition, against three British. About the same time Sir John French reported his grave anxiety over the insufficiency of his ammunition. There were no British units available as reinforcements, though five German divisions were en route

[1] Apparently it was not. *Soldiers and Statesmen*, Sir William Robertson.
[2] *Le Plan de Campagne Francaise*, Lanrezac, p. 21.

for Flanders, and some of their five divisions opposite the Belgian line, defended by inundations, were becoming available for transfer to the southward. On the situation being reported to him, all the reinforcements that Kitchener could promise consisted of six selected battalions of Territorial troops.[3] Lord Kitchener had explained at Dunkirk, as we have already noted, that no important number of British soldiers could be expected before the late spring of 1915, that thenceforward there would be a ceaseless flow of reinforcements, and that the British Army would reach its high-water mark during the summer of 1917. As matters turned out, the total strength of the British Expeditionary Force in France, which stood at 230,000 in December, 1914, was gradually raised to 912,000 by December, 1915, and reached its maximum strength of 1,720,000 in August, 1917, so Kitchener fulfilled his promise. The strength at that date had been increased by Dominion and Indian troops to 2,045,000. The main point, however, was that France sorely lacked more military support during the year 1915. So urgent was the need that the French became very critical of their British Allies, thinking that they were not bearing their share of the sacrifice of life, and taking no account of British armies operating in the world-wide theatre of war which resulted from the accession of Turkey to the cause of the Central Powers in November, 1914. By May, 1915, when the next great ordeal was coming to a climax in front of Ypres, and the British Empire Army was pressed almost beyond endurance after their terrible experience in the trenches of the first winter of the War, a diversion of 126,000 troops—soon to be increased to nearly 390,000—had been made to the Mediterranean. The diversion of munitions to the same theatre

[3] *British Official History*, Vol. II, p. 344.

had been responsible for heavy casualties in Flanders from the gunfire of a better-supplied opponent and nearly for disaster to the Allied Armies in that area.

Views of "Foch through English eyes" during this period are to be found in the pages of the "British Official History" [4] which can now be supplemented by the impressions, supported by documentary evidence, of British officers who were in the most favourable position to know the true relationship between Foch and Sir John French during those critical months. Let us for a moment endeavour to picture the scene at Foch's headquarters, where the staff that came in due course to be known as the *"Famille Foch"* was gradually being formed. We are told that Foch himself showed every courtesy to delegates from foreign armies, receiving senior officers himself at all times if it were reasonably possible to do so. Work at his headquarters began at 8 A.M. daily, by which hour he was always in his office, and unless called upon to deal personally with some urgent local development he always stayed there until late at night. When they were not working at full pressure the members of his small staff left the office for about an hour's recreation every day, walking or riding, but with that exception they worked without ceasing. The strain told upon some of them in course of time as there was no relaxation. No ordinary gossip went on in the office, and there was no conversation on future military events. With them, as with their Chief, concentration upon the problem of the moment was the order of the day. Weygand's office was always next to his Chief's, and it contained a situation-map, which was cov-

[4] Vol. III, pp. 2, 12, 16, 67, 159, 160, 183, 201, 203, 207, 209, 211, 233, 254, 267, 271-2, 274, 276-9, 282-7, 292, 298-9, 303, 310, 354, 381, and a Memorandum by Foch on p. 404.

ered by a curtain or screen when anyone, however distinguished, not directly concerned in the operation in progress entered the room. Foch himself was not inclined to solitude and he often stood in Weygand's room contemplating the map and smoking, at this period, a light cigar; at a later stage he substituted a British pipe.

Time with Foch being priceless during some of the military operations ("Ask me for anything but time," was a saying of Napoleon's, and Foch had been steeped from childhood in Napoleon's maxims), he had what according to British ideas was rather a disconcerting habit of sending orders or instructions direct to subordinate commanders, and not through their superiors, whom he informed of the action he had taken. That time was saved by this method was undoubted.

Weygand, of whose relationship with Foch mention has already been made, was described by a British officer, whose duties brought him much into contact with the *Famille Foch,* as "a little active cavalryman, a consummate horseman, and a man of tireless energy." Warm tribute was paid by the same authority to his great military knowledge and exact memory. In work, Weygand was described as "the most precise and businesslike of human beings." He was always at the service of foreign officers. He could always find time to see them and to hear their opinions and explanations. He was tactful and sympathetic and his manners were excellent, but at the same time he was frank and open, saying exactly what he thought. One of his most conspicuous characteristics was his breadth of view, looking upon the situation as a whole and not being obsessed by the local aspect. "One must look at the whole front; it is only there that we see the situation as a whole." A point that struck the British was his inclination to centralize responsibility for Staff work in his own hands more than is considered desirable in the British Staff system. In loyalty to his master he was a model. "My opinion is as follows," he would say, at a later period, "but I have not yet discussed this with the Marshal." They were always together, however, and their opinions seldom differed. When Foch was too much engaged to see any-one himself he used to say, "Talk to General Weygand—*Weygand c'est moi*—we spend all day motoring together and I hide nothing from him." That was when Foch's responsibilities were spread over a far wider area, but the principle was the same when they were confined for such long periods in that office in Flanders.

Weygand never spared himself. His whole time was devoted to his duties, and he both expected and secured the same high standard of work from his subordinates. Possessing, as he did, great originality of mind, a fertile imagination, and an active brain, we cannot but believe that he may sometimes have suggested a plan to his Chief, but on no occasion was he ever known to have attributed any such credit to himself. "He was as modest as his master." He preferred outdoor life, was fond of horses and appreciated good pictures, old furniture and objects of art, and he was in all ways a delightful companion. If he held any personal ambition at all it was to hold a command himself in the War, but this was denied to him, greatly to the advantage of the France which he served so devotedly. With his future assistant, Desticker, we are not yet concerned. He was serving in Flanders at the time, and his good work there was constantly in evidence but he had not yet joined the *Famille*. All the members of Foch's Staff were capable, hard working, and devoted to their Chief. They worked together loyally and smoothly, without, it must be remembered, the same intimacy and familiarity that obtains in a British Staff. Distinctions of rank are more strictly observed in the relationship between French Staff officers. With this picture of Foch's headquarters in our minds we can pass to wider considerations. The work with which he was charged was the co-ordination, on behalf of Joffre, his Commander-in-Chief, of the efforts of the French, British, and Belgian troops to stem the advance of the enemy's masses towards the Channel ports.

To the commanders of French forces Foch would give orders. To those of foreign troops he could not. Nevertheless he said later that although he had nothing on paper he never exercised so effective a command as he did over the Allied troops at this period. We have his own explanation of his methods: "When important decisions were involved, I went to see them or I asked them to see me. We talked and discussed questions between ourselves and, without seeming to do so, I gradually won them over to my point of view. I provided them with a solution; I did not force it upon them." His view was that commanders can only carry out orders which they thoroughly understand, and that the ideal is that they should make the actual decisions themselves. He recognised that the process of convincing might be a lengthy one, but he judged the time well expended.

Sir John French, with whom he was dealing as the Commander of the strongest of the Allied Armies, had other instructions to consider when he was co-operating with Foch. He had been told by his Government that the "gravest consideration" would devolve upon him if he participated in forward movements in which large bodies of French troops were not engaged and where his force "might be unduly exposed to attack," and, owing to the difficulties that would be experienced in providing reinforcements, that "the greatest care must be exercised towards a minimum of casualties." On the 12th of November, after the tremendous stand made against overwhelming odds in stemming the German advance towards Ypres, the strength of Haig's first division had been reduced to less than 3000 in all. There was a shortage of ninety per cent in officers and of about eighty-three per cent in other ranks.[5] Wastage of personnel and paucity of gun ammunition caused great anxiety, and though a certain number of reinforcements were arriving they were of men reported by some units to be untrained, by others to have neither the will nor the physique to fight. The little "B.E.F.," that had stood in the path of Von Kluck and saved the French left flank by their stand at Mons and Le Cateau, had advanced into the gap between Kluck's and Bülow's Armies on the Marne on September 9th, had fought on the Aisne during the weeks which followed, and then had stemmed the enemy in the Ypres salient, was no longer in existence.

We have carried our narrative of Foch's activities in Flanders up to the end of October, 1914. The counter-attacks which he ordered for the French and Allied forces materialized on November 1st and 2nd but they made no progress. Between the 3rd and 5th there was a dying down both of French and of German offensives. Between the 6th and 10th the battles of Ypres were renewed. On the 6th Foch ordered attacks which made no progress as they were countered by a simultaneous German attack in great strength. On the 7th Foch had occasion to move one of his Corps Commanders. It is said that on the 8th, at a confer-

[5] *British Official History,* Vol. II, p. 449.

ence at his headquarters at Cassel, he confessed to be badly
served with information about the situation near the canal
where the British right connected with the French line, but
he took steps to deal with a critical situation. On the 9th
the Commander of the British forces told Lord Kitchener
that Foch had told him some days earlier the opinion of
Joffre that a withdrawal of enemy forces to the Eastern
theatre had already begun but that attacks must be expected
to cover the withdrawal. It was believed that these attacks
had already expended themselves, but in this belief Joffre
was to be sorely disillusioned. Foch drew the conclusion
that another attack on a great scale was developing and he
told French that the Germans intended to strike again between Ypres and the sea. He was right.

On the same day (November 10th) attacks were launched
against the French on the north face of the salient and
further to the northward, where Dixmude was lost. The
French view was that this would be pressed as the main attack, but on the 11th the full fury of the supreme effort
made by the Prussian Guards fell upon the British athwart
the Menin Road. On the 11th Foch promised to relieve Haig
with French troops transferred from Alsace. By the 12th
Haig's 1st division, which had beaten off attacks in overwhelming strength, was reduced to the plight already mentioned, and on the same day a surprise attack was launched
by the Germans against the French IXth Corps, on the
north-east of the salient. Lord Roberts on this day visited
Foch at Cassel, and was shown the situation of the forces
on Foch's own map.[6] On the 14th Foch again promised to
relieve Haig's sorely harassed troops, taking over their
trenches on the next day. On the same day the German

[6] *Wilson Diaries*, Vol. I, p. 187.

Guards launched a second attack which "failed even more thoroughly and decisively." [7] (It was on that day that Lord Roberts, who had tried in pre-war years to warn the Government and the nation what such a struggle would mean, passed away at St. Omer within the sound of the guns. Foch attended his funeral.) Joffre now suggested as a precaution the construction of an entrenched camp near Calais. The thin Allied line in the north seemed to have been tried beyond endurance. The weather had broken up on November 12th and terrible conditions prevailed—we read of cold and rain, of snow and frost, of frostbitten men standing in trenches half-full of water, some standing up fast asleep under fire, the enemy within 100 yards, unable to rest in peace anywhere for grenade-throwing and sniping; of ground a sea of mud, of paths through woods so soft that men sank to the knees, of the impossibility of bringing up rations and ammunition, of rifles jammed, and of an almost unbearable ordeal. Inspired by the soul of a great leader to hold on to the end, attacking as a last resort, the whole Allied line had held. On the 17th of November the Germans abandoned their supreme effort.

Between the 15th and 22nd of November many messages of congratulation, goodwill, and thanks for assistance rendered passed between the French and British commanders. Their troops had fought not only alongside each other but actually with units intermingled. There had been difficulties and more were to follow, but Foch and Haig were destined to work together with further mutual understanding in the future.

Foch's view was that the higher command was the principal thing; that in his own army there was a shortage of

[7] *British Official History*, Vol. II, p. 455.

real leaders; that they knew their profession, but nothing else. It was the fault of a general mental indolence. They did not work; they did not keep themselves up to the mark, and they did not dare to take responsibility. Instead of preparing themselves to hold important positions they did nothing and worked in a groove. They stuck in a rut, and realized it themselves, but it required an effort to get out of it, and mental indolence prevented them. Work was essential and lack of leaders was the trouble. The question really was one of discovering truths and then of applying them unconsciously and automatically, but in order to do that the truths must be so familiar, and one must be so steeped in them, that they became part of one's actual being. In Haig he had found a man who held similar views of an officer's responsibilities from his earliest years, and this formed between men differing so widely in temperament a constant bond of sympathy.

In the experiences of the late autumn of 1914 in Flanders, Foch plumbed the depths of endurance in action of the troops of three nations that he commanded or controlled. In the terrible winter spent in inadequate trenches which followed, he was to gain further experience of the utmost limit of human persistence, and thereby to base his own leadership upon the very bedrock of the truths which became still more deeply engrained in his actual being.

Chapter XVII

DISAPPOINTMENT: 1915

JANUARY-MARCH

AGED 63 YEARS

THE first group of battles of Ypres may be said to have died away on November 22nd, 1914, when the Germans, having definitely failed to break through to the Channel ports, turned their main attention to their Eastern Front. The opportunity was taken by Foch to sort out the British and French troops. The French VIIIth Corps took over the Ypres salient, with the British prolonging the line to the southward as far as the La Bassée Canal, near Givenchy, where they touched the French Tenth Army on their right. Between December 14th and 20th an offensive operation failed to achieve its purpose. Of those days on the British front in Flanders Sir William Robertson wrote:

Owing to the appalling shortage of ammunition, no effective artillery reply could be made to the enemy's guns, and the sorely tried infantry were thereby deprived of the essential support to which they were entitled, and without which the best troops in the world are apt to give themselves up to despair. Entrenchments were no sooner constructed than they were battered down and had to be remade; communications between the front and rear lines, and the conveyance of necessities across the shell-swept area, were carried out under the most trying condi-

[198]

tions; and, in general, life in the trenches during the first winter spent in Flanders was wellnigh intolerable.[1]

Joffre, Haig, and Foch continued to discuss their plans for 1915. The enemy obviously held the advantage of a central position. He was able to transfer his troops from one side of the European theatre of war to the other, and in order to help him in doing so Germany's network of strategic railways was of great value. This advantage, which goes by the name of "interior lines" in the textbooks, was employed with great skill by Napoleon when in 1814 Allied Armies moved by different routes converging on Paris. While the movements by road in those days were slow compared with those by railway in the Great War, the theatre of operations was more restricted. Although the time factor may have differed, the principles were much the same. Napoleon's idea was to use the facilities afforded by his central position to mass a big army under his own command, leaving small "containing" forces to "hold" for the time being his other opponents. Having defeated the enemy against whom he had massed, he left a small force to look after that opponent, and then turned his main strength against another. This process he repeated, striking out first in one direction and then in another, thereby keeping the Allied Armies away from Paris and separated from each other. He claimed afterwards that he could have carried on this process indefinitely and have won the war by such methods, but the nation behind him, having experienced over twenty years of warfare with only a short break, began to think more of the advantages of peace than it did of skill in the leadership of armies obliged to suffer heavy casualties in

[1] *Soldiers and Statesmen,* Vol. I, pp. 58-59.

the field. They were confirmed in their opinion by the gradual progress that was made by the Allied Armies towards Paris. These armies had discovered a slow though effective method of dealing with an opponent on "interior lines." They refused to engage in decisive battle against Napoleon himself, and his main force. They attacked the smaller bodies elsewhere, thus driving them nearer and nearer to Paris, hoping in the end to establish closer touch between the Allied Armies. Napoleon would then find his central position of no further value. If he was attacked from three sides by enemies in touch with each other, he would be at a disadvantage.

Whether or not he had this useful precedent in his mind, Joffre, enthusiastically supported by Foch whose firm belief in attacks was well known,[2] wanted to strike as heavy a blow as possible against the German Army on the Western Front as soon as the enemy faced eastward to strike at the Russians. As Joffre's deputy, charged with responsibility for coördinating the efforts of the Allied Armies north of the Oise, Foch had many communications with Sir John French, and he was anxious—in spite of the representations of unreadiness which had been made by Kitchener in November, 1914—not to lose a fleeting opportunity, and therefore to get the depleted British Expeditionary Force to take its part in the proposed offensive, and to do so in as great strength as possible. The will was there, but not the resources, especially in ammunition for guns, for a reason which will appear in due course.

[2] Foch had a great admiration for Joffre, to whom, as to all in authority over him, he was thoroughly loyal, but there is much truth in Sir J. Edmonds' summary: "Joffre, according to Foch's own judgment, originated nothing, sitting silent and calm as a judge to pass his verdicts on the plans submitted to him." R. U. S. I. Journal, May, 1929.

French, we must remember, had been told to bear constantly in mind that, while he was authorised to co-operate with the French Army, "the numerical strength of the British force and its contingent reinforcement was strictly limited," and "with this consideration in view it was obvious that the greatest care must be exercised towards a minimum of losses and wastage." It is necessary to bear these instructions in mind while we study the relationship between Foch and the British Army in the months which followed. As matters were to turn out, it became perhaps less a matter of the "strength of the British force" in the ordeals to which it was to be subjected than it was of its lack of gun ammunition, of which the result can only be adequately described as terrible. This was due partly to inadequate resources for manufacture, but also to the use that was made of the resources which were actually provided, and in justice to the British Government it is necessary to add in that connexion that the amounts actually received from contractors fell far short of the amounts promised. Taking the important field gun (18 pr.) ammunition as an example, about 1,800,000 rounds were promised between January and May by contractors; only about 800,000 rounds were delivered.[3]

Co-operation by the British Army in a French offensive in 1915 was affected by divided counsels in the political sphere in England, and by a prevalent impression that an attempt to secure a decision on the Western Front would lead only to further losses without any hope of success. From a communication sent by Kitchener to French we gather that the impossibility of breaking through the German lines was being accepted in principle. Those lines, therefore, represented a fortress that could neither be car-

[3] Sir William Robertson, *Soldiers and Statesmen*, Vol. I, p. 61.

[201]

ried by assault nor besieged. With Joffre and Foch, on the other hand—supported by French—breaking through was chiefly a question of having enough ammunition and suitable equipment. They thought that the operation should not be assumed to be impossible until it had at least been tried. An alternative proposal put forward by Mr. Churchill in October and again on the 7th of December, to turn the northern flank of the German Army by a descent upon the Belgian coast before allowing time for its fortification did not find favour either with Joffre or with the French Government.[4] Early in January another proposal that French should advance along the Belgian coast to Zeebrugge was also rejected for want of enough troops. A proposal to incorporate the Belgian Army with the British fell through by the 2nd of January.[5] In the absence of such alternatives, Kitchener's suggestion to French was that, in the circumstances described, the German Army in France and Flanders should be watched and "held" [6] by an investing force, "while operations proceed elsewhere."

We have noted how the influence of the British Government reversed the plan made by Joffre to get the Belgian field army out of Antwerp while it was still in a fit state to co-operate in the field with the British and the French Armies, and at this stage it is again necessary to refer to proceedings in the Council-chamber for the proper understanding of higher influences upon the relationship between Foch and the British Army. Without such references it would be as difficult to appreciate the operations of armies

[4] The opinion expressed in the *British Official History* is that with good luck in the weather such a landing might have succeeded. *Military Operations,* Vol. III, p. 15.

[5] *Wilson Diaries,* Vol. I, p. 199.

[6] Compare Napoleon in 1814, above.

as it would be to follow the procedure in a prize-ring by thinking only of men's fists and not of the guiding brains. Success in the contemplated offensive on the Western Front depended largely, in the opinion of the leaders of the armies, upon the supply of munitions, and this was destined to depend to a great extent upon the "operations elsewhere," to which Kitchener referred when writing to French on January 2nd, 1915.

Although there had been a strong objection in England to using the new armies in France, while they were still untrained and lacking in essentials of equipment, various proposals were now put forward for using these and more seasoned troops in the other theatres. The First Sea Lord of the Admiralty—Lord Fisher—wanted to land troops in the Baltic. The Secretary of the Committee of Imperial Defence, of which the activities were in abeyance, drew up at the instigation of the Prime Minister a plan to attack the Turks. One British Minister—Mr. Lloyd George—wished to remove the bulk of the British Expeditionary Force from France and Flanders for operations elsewhere, leaving the remnants in reserve near the Channel ports. Another scheme that received influential support was an offensive on a large scale against Austria, Germany's weaker ally, using either Ragusa on the Adriatic or Salonika as a base of operations for a large army. From neither place could a large army have operated at a range of more than a few miles from the coast, owing to the nature of the country inland and to lack of adequate communications.

The final decision was that the Western Front should be the "main theatre" for the activities of the British Army as long as the French required armed support. If, however, the next offensive indicated that no serious advance in that

[203]

theatre was possible, then the British troops were to be sent elsewhere. While that decision was still in force it was decided to launch the Dardanelles campaign, which was destined ultimately to absorb about 470,000 men, including 328,000 combatants with due proportions of guns and ammunition. Whether those who thought that the War could be won by offensives on a large scale in other theatres, rather than, as Foch thought, by defeating the German Army in France, were correct, is a question over which there has been much controversy. We are here concerned only with the effect which the diversion of fighting troops and ammunition to that distant area had upon the situation in Flanders where plans were being drawn up for attacks while the Germans were engaged upon the Russian front. Falkenhayn, Chief of the German General Staff, considered that a decisive victory in the War could only be obtained on the Western Front,[7] so the opportunity was fleeting.

It has been necessary to deal at some length with British policy both because of its effect upon the relationship between the French and the British commanders and also on account of its influence upon the French Army and nation. The French criticisms of the British at this time were outspoken, and they clamoured for more effective assistance in defending their country. Enemy propagandists made the most of the opportunity. Any nation in the same dire straits as the French, whose soldiers were defending their own homes, would have supported Foch in his determination to drive back the German armies, and attacks in other parts of the world seemed to entail unnecessary diversions of force. Foch therefore had the whole-hearted support both of his Government and of his nation. Sir John French had

[7] *British Official History,* Vol. III, p. 25.

not. There was a strong aversion to further expenditure of life in attacks unless there was a reasonable prospect of their being successful. The condition for success, as laid down by the leaders of the armies on the spot, was a sufficiency of gun ammunition, and this condition could not be fulfilled.

The impression in France that Britain was not taking her fair share in the military effort and sacrifice needed to clear the soil of France and Belgium of the invader lasted for a long period, although 5,400,000 British Empire Army personnel ultimately crossed the seas for the Western Front, while nearly 3,600,000 were sent to other theatres of war.[8] The difference in outlook between the two nations, largely due to the causes that we have examined, was a factor to be reckoned with in the relations between the commanders of the armies in the field almost to the end. Even in the long war in South Africa in 1899-1902 the British had looked upon warfare as the business of the Army and Navy, rather than of the whole nation—a view that perhaps had been encouraged by that speech early in the War about "business as usual" of which the echoes had a lasting effect in France. On the British side, confidence in French leadership may have been somewhat shaken by the failure of "Plan 17," which had been so costly in casualties.

Meanwhile Foch set himself steadfastly to the task of getting the maximum effort out of both armies on the Western Front to further the purpose to which he adhered rigidly to the end—the expulsion of the invaders from French territory, and across the Rhine. We have seen him at work at his headquarters at Cassel, well described as "an interesting little town, perched on a solitary peak from which it

[8] Statistics of the military effort of the British Empire, official, 1922, p. 744.

looks proudly over the wide and water-soaked Flemish plain, making a magnificent observatory." [9] A suggestion has since been made that in front of the old Town Hall in its picturesque little square there should be erected a record in marble that "From here the Battle of the Yser was won."

At this period Foch was described as always the same: sometimes abrupt in manner and yet very calm; sparing of words, his questions precise and to the point, going direct to the heart of what he wanted to know; his orders short and clear, leaving no uncertainty in the minds of those to whom they were addressed. Above all, no matter how grave a situation might be, as soon as anyone came under his influence he felt the indomitable confidence, atmosphere of security, and assurance of victory that seemed to surround the general and his staff. His headquarters might aptly have been described as a Temple of Faith, and those who entered disturbed and depressed came out cheered and strengthened. Some of Foch's interviews with Henry Wilson during the winter months are of special interest, especially one at Cassel on January 2nd, 1915, when Foch revealed his reliance upon the justice of the French cause as a factor in the certainty of success. He told Wilson that the French Army was better than it had been in August, 1914, owing to the effect upon French and upon German minds respectively of the events of 1870, the memory of which never left the mind of Foch himself. The result was a constant gain in the morale of the French armies and a deterioration on the German side as the campaign developed.[10] On February 2nd Wilson heard from a reliable source of the feeling that was arising in France against the British, partly because of apparent want of enterprise on the Western Front, partly on account

[9] Major Recouly.　　　　[10] *Wilson Diaries*, Vol. I, pp. 205-206.

of the British addiction to hunting and shooting, partly because conscription had not been introduced in Great Britain, and for other reasons. On February 3rd Wilson saw Foch, who said: "You English must not invite a long war by dilatory action. We French cannot go on for years, so send everyone you can as fast as you can." Wilson adds: "Can France be getting tired, as well as cross with us?" [11]

The first incident affecting Foch personally in 1915 which now requires our attention was an accident to the motor-car containing Joffre and himself on the road between Roobrugge and Dunkirk on the 17th of January, in which Joffre was seriously injured. The importance attached by Foch to the higher command is well known. Joffre, to whom he was intensely loyal, and of whom he had a high opinion, had by this time earned the nickname of "The Buoy," because he rode serenely in the stormiest seas, unaffected by their raging. Foch, anxious about the continuity of leadership and policy, at once wrote as deputy to Joffre to make inquiries of the Ministry of War about a substitute for the Commander-in-Chief if the need should arise. He received no reply for many weeks, and he was then told that General Gallieni, who had commanded the troops defending Paris at the time of the Battle of the Marne, had been in possession since August, 1914, of a letter of appointment as Joffre's successor. Foch did not approve of this arrangement, not, it need hardly be added, for any personal reason, but because Gallieni would not be in touch with the situation and would "have to grope his way." He looked upon the higher command as a delicate instrument, very sensitive, and likely to be thrown out of order if mishandled by an inexperienced hand.

[11] *Wilson Diaries*, Vol. I, pp. 205-206.

Up to the end of January, 1915, neither the British nor the French Government was committed to send troops to any destination other than the Western Front, and after some local operations on the Aisne and near Soissons the Germans were obliged by their commitments in the East to adopt a defensive attitude in France and in Belgium. They made the best of their time to fortify the line from the sea to Switzerland, and Foch in later years described that line as a "wall of earth, concrete, and steel." [12] While the War Councils in London and in Paris discussed operations elsewhere, elaborate plans for an offensive were drawn up by the high commands in France. In order to force the enemy to retire, blows at his lines of communication offered the best results. The alternative directions [13] for these blows were (1) an attack in Artois eastwards, north and south of Arras, cross the plain of Douai towards the centres of communication of the German forces in the Noyon salient, (2) an advance northward in Champagne from near Rheims to the Mézières-Hirson line and the railways in the gap between the Dutch frontier and the Ardennes, which supplied the German armies between the Belgian coast and Rheims, and (3) an advance northwards from the Verdun-Nancy front to cut communications and to carry the war into the enemy's country.

Joffre decided to carry out attacks in Champagne and to prepare further attacks by the other two routes (1) and (3), No. 1 to be delivered simultaneously with No. 2, and No. 3 to follow in order to threaten the German line of retreat. Sir John French wanted to co-operate as effectively as possible in this plan, and upon Foch lay the responsibility

[12] *Les deux Batailles de la Marne*, 1928.
[13] *British Official History*, Vol. III, p. 68.

for co-ordinating his efforts with those of the northern group of French armies.

Joffre's plan for 1915 not only formed the basis of the operations for that year; it contained the germ of Foch's greater plan which was to lead to final victory after three intervening years of disappointment, failure to "break through," and consequent "attrition."

In accordance with a decision arrived at on January 21st at Chantilly, the British extended their front to relieve two French Corps in the Ypres salient. Then, the co-ordination of a Franco-British effort for an advance having failed, partly through the diversion of the 29th British Division to the Dardanelles, the French, who had been badly impressed by the British "December Battle" (14th-20th December), seem to have gathered the impression that the British Commander was not in earnest about co-operating in their offensive. They thought that, while the British Army would be useful on the defensive, it would not be of much assistance in driving the invaders out of France. Sir John French, however, decided to launch an independent attack on March 10th, and the Battle of Neuve Chapelle (March 10th-13th) resulted. Shortage of gun ammunition brought the operations to a standstill. Though not undertaken in co-operation with the French the battle has been referred to briefly on account of its bearing upon further operations in 1915. The British casualties numbered about 13,000.

In making arrangements for co-operation with the French in further attacks, Sir John French could obtain no information from England about prospects of reinforcement. "A new theatre of war had been opened at the Dardanelles, and the original policy, the reconquest of Belgium and the defeat of the German armies in that theatre, seemed to be undergoing eclipse." [14] Preparations were nevertheless made for a combined offensive, but the Germans forestalled them and the Second Battle of Ypres (April 17th-May 25th) resulted. To the heavy fighting in that and in other battles in 1915 the next chapter will be devoted.

Foch's views upon the independent operation of the British Army at Neuve Chapelle have not been recorded.

[14] *British Official History*, Vol. III, p. 155.

CHAPTER XVIII

DISAPPOINTMENT: 1915 (*Continued*)

APRIL-DECEMBER

AGED 63-64 YEARS

ONLY by strict economy in January and February, 1915, had enough ammunition been collected for the Neuve Chapelle Battle, and a further period of accumulation was needed which caused a pause in the operations until the second week in May, when a Franco-British offensive was to open in the La Bassée-Arras area. The Second British Army on the Ypres front was only allowed the "miserable pittance" [1] of 2 rounds for each 18 pr. field gun, 3 for field howitzer, and 6 per medium (6 inch) howitzer, when, in April, they had to face the enemy's first gas attack which had such far-reaching results. To Joffre's spring offensive we can now turn our attention. The operation which affected Foch most directly was the first of the three mentioned in the previous chapter—the advance eastward from the Artois plateau, on a frontage extending north and south of La Bassée.

As a preliminary, the British Army extended its front to the northward so as to cover most of the Ypres salient, and the Belgian Army extended its frontage southward, two French territorial divisions filling the gap in the north of

[1] Sir William Robertson, *Soldiers and Statesmen*, Vol. I, p. 59.

[211]

the salient between the Belgians and the British. The British right rested as before on the La Bassée canal. The total length of the British line was thirty miles, compared with the nineteen miles held after the resorting of the troops at the end of November, 1914. It may be of interest in connexion with subsequent events to note that, on most of the French portion of the line which was taken over, the British found only very light entrenchments. Their Allies had depended for defense largely upon the fire of the celebrated "soixante-quinze" field-guns for which plenty of ammunition was available. These, of course, had been removed.

On April 17th the British launched an attack which resulted in the capture of "Hill 60." Five days later the Germans gave an entirely new complexion to the War by the use of poison gas. As early as April 14th they had given some warning of their intention by accusing the French of adopting the same course near Verdun, a feature of German propaganda which had not by that time been mastered by the Allies. Further warnings were received through intelligence reports, but these were not credited. They were regarded as a ruse adopted to prevent Allied troops from being withdrawn from Ypres to take part in the expected offensive in Artois.[2]

The first definite indication of an impending attack on the salient was given by a heavy bombardment of the town of Ypres, which reduced the place to ruins by April 21st. The official date for the opening by the Germans of the Second Battle of Ypres was April 22nd, and it continued until April 25th. Its main features were the driving back of the French Territorials as the result of the use by the Germans of poison gas against them, and the Canadians on

[2] *British Official History*, Vol. III, p. 165.

their right on April 22nd; an application on the same day from General Smith-Dorrien that Foch might be asked to put in enough French troops to restore the situation on the French front; an order from Foch to General Putz, during the night which followed, to hold on to the line that he actually occupied without further retirement, to organise a base of departure to regain the ground that he had lost, and to counter-attack. On April 23rd the French, having lost most of their guns, could barely hold their ground, and they could do little more. The British on their right carried out some counter-attacks.

On the same day (April 23rd) French visited Foch at Cassel and was told that Foch intended to make good the original line by sending reinforcements. The sharp salient into which their army had been crowded by the retirement of the French on their left put the British troops in a very dangerous situation. Sir John French agreed to co-operate in any counter-attack, but he added that, if the situation were not restored soon, he would be obliged to fall back out of the pocket which was only five miles deep and less than five miles across. Foch twice visited Putz during the day, but lack of reinforcements caused little to be done on the French front. The British counter-attacks, delivered at all costs, stopped a further German advance, the British battalions involved being reduced by their losses to mere *cadres*. During the night the situation became very critical for the British in the crowded salient. The evening's first local attack on the French was developing into a serious threat against the northern flank of the British Army and the whole British line.

Foch visited French on April 24th, promising in writing to reinforce the French line strongly, and to launch "a vigor-

[213]

ous offensive." By the night of April 25th—the day of the landing of a British Army in Gallipoli—the situation was no better. Foch and French both thought that the enemy's object was to stop the Allied offensive in Artois. On April 27th the British were still in the same exposed and dangerous position, and a vigorous offensive would have used up many troops and would so have played the enemy's game in the area further south. On April 28th Foch saw French again and also sent him a long memorandum requesting him not to consider any retirement and promising a French offensive on the 29th.[3] On the April 30th French warned Foch in writing that he would begin to withdraw from the sharp tip of the salient that night, if attacks had not restored the situation. Foch at once motored from Cassel to Hazebrouck and persuaded French again to postpone this measure for twenty-four hours.

On May 1st Foch came to see French again and told him that he (Foch) had been over-ridden by Joffre. French then issued orders for the withdrawal. Counter-attacks were ineffective for lack of resources and of co-ordination, and by May 4th the British and Canadians, who had been shelled day and night from three sides in their narrow salient, fell back at last to a semi-circular line of only three miles radius covering Ypres. Hill 60, now "a mere rubbish heap of shell and mine-torn earth, timber and dead bodies," had to be abandoned before a cloud of gas on May 5th.

As Foch had feared, the enforced withdrawal of the British from their exposed position encouraged the enemy to launch yet another determined effort against Ypres, "the most desperate fighting that ever took place in the salient." [4]

[3] The full text is given in the *British Official History*, Vol. III, p. 404.
[4] *British Official History*, Vol. III, p. 310.

No less than three corps of the German Fourth Army were massed against only two divisions astride the Menin Road. The battles of Frezenberg Ridge (May 8-13) Aubers Ridge (May 9), Festubert (May 15-27),[5] and Bellewaarde Ridge (May 24-25) saved Ypres, but made further offensive operations impossible. Sir John French reported to the War Office that they must cease until more ammunition was accumulated. The Germans also were exhausted by an effort lasting for a month. Divisions on both sides had fought again and again until practically annihilated. If fresh German divisions had arrived, as they had on November 11th, 1914, they would probably have turned the scale. Luckily the German reserves were in Russia. The British losses had amounted to nearly 60,000.

The only influence which Foch could bring to bear in this great defensive battle was by the small reinforcements that could be filtered through army, army corps, divisional and brigade commanders, to be used as best they might, and by constant urgings to counter-attacks, without any instructions about their delivery. "Second Ypres," which lasted for thirty-three days, was fought by brigadiers, regimental officers, and soldiers. It well deserves the designation of a "soldiers' battle." For Foch it must have been a nightmare experience. The main point, however, was that the main Allied offensive was launched in Artois on May 9th, as proposed.

It has been essential for us to dwell at some length upon the Second Battle of Ypres in order to bring out Foch's steadfast concentration upon the main Allied attack in Artois, north and south of La Bassée, and at the same time the difficulty that he must have experienced in adhering to his usual question, *De quoi s'agit-il?* with the problem of

[5] See below.

the British Army being shot to pieces in a narrow enclosure, with the probable loss of Ypres and the political results which would ensue, to distract his mind.

The Artois offensive was opened on May 9th by the British in the Battle of Aubers Ridge, north of La Bassée, of which the result was disappointing, and by the French in an offensive in Artois, fifteen miles to the southward, which made considerable progress at first. The Battle of Artois continued until June 18th, the British fighting the Battle of Festubert for ten days in that period (May 15th to 25th), after strong pressure had been put by Joffre and Foch upon Sir John French, who had been disappointed at the failure of promises of a French offensive to relieve the situation in the Ypres salient to materialise. Sir John French was in a very difficult position. The British Government's policy of "seeing too many things at a time" [6] had resulted in simultaneous failure in Gallipoli and in Flanders, and French did not know what to expect either in munitions or in men. There was serious friction between him and the French commander during this period. Foch's desire was that he should engage in an offensive north of La Bassée to prevent at all costs the Germans from reinforcing their front against Foch's main attack north of Arras. The British Army fulfilled Foch's wishes by advancing their line and drawing German reserves upon them in the Battle of Festubert; but they were sorely handicapped for lack of munitions against an enemy abundantly supplied with his requirements.

Operations by the French were resumed on June 7th, and a final general attack, the British co-operating in offensives near Givenchy and Bellevaarde, was launched on June 16th and brought to a conclusion on the 18th. The results were

[6] Napoleon's warning to the Austrian Generals at Leoben.

FOCH AND JOFFRE

In 1915 the generalissimo and the commandant of the group of armies of the North in the quarter of General de Warlus near Neuville-Saint-Vaast. This photograph is from the Duc d'Albufera.

indecisive, and no "break through" resulted from Joffre's spring offensives either in Artois or in Champagne. In conversation with Wilson on May 4th Joffre had hoped that Foch's attack would break the line past mending, that it might be the beginning of the end, that Namur might be reached, and the War be over in three months.[7]

As Foch judged others by performances, so he expected others to judge him, and there is no doubt that his status in the year 1915 began to be somewhat unsettled.

On June 23rd a conference was held at Chantilly at which Viviani, the Prime Minister, and Millerand, the War Minister, were present, as well as Joffre, Foch, Castelnau, and Dubail. Foch was then given the definite command of a group of armies,[8] his position up to that time having been somewhat anomalous. He held firmly to his conviction that ultimate victory was certain, but the result seemed to be more remote than he had anticipated, and it is said that to his intimates he appeared not to be unmoved, though no such impression was conveyed to others. Foch's prestige began for a time to suffer, and there were some murmurs against the heavy casualty lists in the Artois offensive in which the French casualties had considerably exceeded 100,000 of all ranks, including 35,000 killed.[9]

Perhaps some idea of Foch's estimate of the probable duration of the War as he saw it in the summer of 1915 can be gathered from the fact that he now took a furnished country house near Senlis, about thirty miles from Paris, in order that his family might be within visiting distance while he was commanding the northern group of armies.

[7] *Wilson Diaries*, Vol. I, p. 225.
[8] The "G. A. N." (*Groupe des Armées du Nord*).
[9] *British Official History*, Vol. IV, p. 80.

The people of Senlis had suffered severely from the invaders in 1914, and owing to their unhappy experience they still dreaded a return of the tide. The arrival of the Foch family caused a return of confidence. Foch liked Villemetrie where the house stood in an old park, and he went there on occasions to shake off his heavy responsibilities in the surroundings of a simple and quiet home. The people about got to know him well, but neither from him nor his family could any information be obtained in conversation. They were too discreet. Questions were firmly discouraged, and even a compliment upon a reported success would be met, perhaps a little impatiently, with the reply, "Wait, wait. The end is not yet in sight." With gloomy prophets Foch had little patience. To such he would say, "Civilians should not let any discouragement appear. Look back, and rejoice in the ground regained since September, 1914. Have patience. One or two more years of resolute waiting—less, if some unknown factor crops up. That is my firm belief, but it is not for me to foresee the future with certainty." He was satisfied himself with the 1915 offensives. "The bear has not gone to earth. He failed in his first leap, and he will not succeed. His teeth and claws are still intact, but we do not fear. He is in a cage."

The long periods of stagnation, during which the enemy strengthened his lines and the return of the German reserves from the East constantly became more probable, were not easy to bear. It is on record that Foch already foresaw something of the future. Pointing to a map, he said, "Near the coast, the way is too narrow, and cut by rivers. Further inland the mountains are impracticable. . . . So, no hesitation, we will force them back the way they came." [10]

[10] To M. Hanotaux.

He was perhaps consoled during the year of disappointment by further promotion in the Legion of Honour in October when "Foch, Ferdinand," was told that "as general of division, commander of a group of armies, he had shown in all circumstances since the opening of the campaign, in the defensive as in the offensive, unparalleled aptitude," and that "thanks to his undoubted authority and the soundness of his opinion he has contributed greatly to the perfect co-ordination of the efforts of the Allied Armies, and has thus rendered the most eminent services to his country."

Before that praise was earned, another heavy ordeal—the failure of the autumn offensive to produce decisive results—had to be faced. It was followed by a further loss of faith by the public in the Army commanders and by lack of confidence in the Government.

With that offensive we will deal but briefly. It could hardly, perhaps, have been avoided, on account of the need to draw the pressure away from the Russian front, where the Germans and Austrians gained great successes. "A series of fortunate events may dull the greatest minds, deprive them of their natural vigour, and level them with common beings; but adversity is a tonic capable of bringing back energy and elasticity to those who have lost it." [11] Whether Foch needed the spur of adversity or not, he was certainly subjected to the experience on many occasions during the years that preceded the final triumph.

At an inter-Allied military conference held at Chantilly on July 7th, with M. Millerand in the chair, Joffre pressed for a simultaneous offensive for all the Allied Armies, and French pledged himself to support the French armies to the utmost of his resources. (On the eve of the opening of the

[11] Jomini (Frederick the Great).

autumn offensive another inter-Allied conference was held at Calais, when a plan for diverting French troops, as well as British, to the Near East was accepted. On October 5th the Allied forces landed at Salonika and on the next day Austro-German forces invaded Serbia from the north. On the 11th the Bulgarians invaded from the east.)

On July 11th, at a meeting at St. Omer, Joffre disapproved of French's proposal, based on shortage of guns and ammunition disclosed at a meeting at Boulogne in June, to postpone the offensive until the spring of 1916, when the British Army would be stronger and better equipped. At another meeting at Frévent on July 27th between French and Foch a difference of opinion arose as to the best direction for a British attack; further meetings and arguments took place. Kitchener came to France on August 16th and accepted a new formula for the relationship between Joffre and French, conferring upon Joffre "the initiative in combined action of the French and British forces . . . notably as concerning the objectives [? objects] to be attained, and the dates fixed for the commencement of each operation." On August 21st, owing to the situation in Russia, Kitchener telegraphed to French telling him "to take the offensive and act vigorously." French on the next day promised Joffre to meet his wishes both as to the date and to the locality of the British attack, on which subject both he and Haig, who was to deliver the attack, disagreed with Joffre and Foch. As matters turned out, although the date was agreed upon, the zero hour was difficult to arrange because much depended upon the wind, the British having decided to use gas in the attack.

The Battle of Loos was launched on September 25th; the French Battles of Artois and of Champagne on the same day.

The best results were expected in the Artois Battle. The Battle of Champagne ended on October 7th, after an interval between September 30th and October 7th. The Battle of Loos continued until October 8th. The Battle of Artois closed on October 15th after an interval between September 28th and October 11th. Sir William Robertson provides a good summary of the intentions and the results,[12] as seen from the British point of view.

It may be said that although the operations were unproductive of decisive success, and were attended by tactical miscalculations which would have to be corrected before the enemy's lines could be breached, they nevertheless rendered valuable aid to an ally in distress, and provided useful experience in the handling of new troops and in the methods to be employed in the attack on continuous lines of field fortifications. They were, in fact, necessary stages in the preparation for the great battles that were subsequently fought. That the results might have been more immediately effective had greater resources and better-trained troops been available cannot of course be denied. . . .

The main point, from the aspect which concerns us, which emerges from the operations on the Western Front in 1915, is Foch's steadfast adherence to his convictions, arrived at after deep thought and by concentration upon his usual question, *"De quoi s'agit-il?"* that defeat of the German Army, however difficult it might prove, was the one and only road to victory; that diversions of force to other theatres and against other opponents must be judged solely by the influence which they would produce upon that policy. In England, and now in France, the terrible losses that were being sustained were beginning to affect public opinion and

[12] *Soldiers and Statesmen*, Vol. I, pp. 65-70.

therefore the security of the Governments concerned. These losses are naturally a subject of interest to the political authorities [13] whose natural tendency under such conditions is to provide the public with victories gained by some easier method.

Ludendorff has since confessed that "the German troops which were transferred from the East arrived only just in time to support the defenders of the Western Front who were holding out so gallantly, and to avert a serious defeat." The Allied attacks, as we have noted, were delayed, and their strength was reduced, by the diversion of men, of material, and of effort in general to the Dardanelles, which led inevitably to further and to greater diversions to other theatres. The enterprise was abandoned on December 8th.

The spring offensives of 1915 had been launched by Joffre and by Foch in high hope of a break through. The autumn offensive was partly intended to relieve the pressure on Russia and so to avoid the expected collapse of France's Eastern ally, if no such help were forthcoming. The casualties to the British, who would have preferred that the offensive should be postponed until 1916, resulted in a loss of over 12,000 officers and 273,000 other ranks.

Sir Henry Wilson's diaries contain fewer accounts than usual of interviews with Foch during this period. In the critical months between July and December he met him at Frévent on July 17th and 23rd, when Foch told him of a German overture for peace, made surreptitiously, and "his (Foch's) formula before talking about peace is excellent, because it is so simple and so appealing. 'Get behind the Rhine and then I will discuss terms—not otherwise.' "

[13] Viviani resigned the French Premiership on October 30th, and was succeeded by M. Briand.

He saw Foch again on July 27th, August 14th and 16th, and December 19th. The principal point with which the diaries deal at this time is the strong divergence in opinion between the soldiers in the field and the political authorities under whom they served. Sir William Robertson, on the other hand, maintains that "Mr. Asquith and Lord Kitchener . . . gave Sir John French all the support within their power." [14] The old question of "soldiers and politicians" is raised thereby, but Foch's main contention, in connexion therewith, was that committees and councils, whether of politicians or soldiers, were quite incapable of the rapid decisions and of the constant executive action that is needed either in the conduct of military operations, or in their control. The point being an important one, we cannot do better than to close this chapter with an extract from the considered conclusions arrived at by Sir Charles Oman, the Oxford military historian, after a lifetime devoted to such studies. He writes that he is fully aware of the perils of "amateur strategy" when a government interferes with or over-rules the decisions of the military authority to whom it has given responsibility, but military supreme authorities, like other human beings, are fallible. He provides a wealth of historical examples illustrating faults on both sides. His conclusion is that:

. . . interference, amounting to absolute negation of the commander's schemes, conducted by individuals not thoroughly versed in the practical affairs of war, is obviously deleterious. . . . So found the Austrian Generals opposed to Buonaparte in 1796-97, when the Aulic Council, not a military committee but a ministerial caucus, kept continually varying the objective prescribed to their commanders, and even interfering with the

[14] *Soldiers and Statesmen*, Vol. I, p. 71.

troops in the field. So found also certain British and French generals, if we are not mistaken, during the Great War.[5]

There is much to be said for that view in connexion with 1915, Foch's "year of disappointment," but whether the "wall of earth, concrete, and steel" could have been penetrated, with the resources that would have been available if the political authorities had not decided to undertake the expedition to the Dardanelles in the spring and to Salonika in the autumn, is a matter for conjecture, which cannot here be profitably discussed.

[5] *The Study of War for Statesmen and Citizens*, pp. 41-44.

Chapter XIX

THE SOMME, 1916

AGED 64-65 YEARS

IN 1916 Foch was destined again to be much in contact with the activities of the British Army, and to understand the nature and object of those activities we cannot do better than to refer to the summary which has been provided by Sir William Robertson.[1] He tells that, according to a decision arrived at on December 28th, 1915, France and Flanders were to be regarded as the "main theatre of the War on land" in the year 1916. He adds that this principle held good "nominally" for the next two years, but that:

Actually, . . . it never received complete ministerial approbation and support, even in 1916, whilst throughout the greater part of 1917, with the exception of a few brief intervals, the consistent aim of the Prime Minister, Mr. Lloyd George, was to replace it by a policy of another kind. Eventually, at the end of January, 1918, he achieved his object, the new policy being to undertake a decisive campaign against the Turks in Palestine, in preference to the fullest concentration in the West.

Robertson reports[2] that even by January 13th, 1916, British ministers were still indifferent to the necessity of adhering to a decision once taken, or did not understand the disadvantages, strategical, tactical, and administrative, that changes of plan always entail.

[1] *Soldiers and Statesmen*, Vol. I, pp. 254-255.　　[2] *Ibid.*, p. 260.

The same criticism was apparently applicable to the French Government. Two hundred thousand Anglo-French troops had been sent to Macedonia "and for this misfortune the French not the British Government was responsible." The British General Staff on June 1st, 1916, reported that "France is responsible for keeping a quarter of a million splendid fighting troops in the Balkans for what appears to be political reasons." The responsibility for the operations on the Western Front having less effect in shortening the War than was hoped must not therefore be attributed to the commanders in the field. The diversion of force to Salonika was apparently supported by Joffre as Commander-in-Chief, but there is no evidence that it had either support or concurrence from Foch, who was now to work with a different British Commander-in-Chief. Sir Douglas Haig had succeeded Sir John French in December, and we read [3] that Sir John visited Foch on December 19th to say good-bye, when on his way to Paris to bid farewell to Joffre. About ten days before French left, Joffre had discussed with him the plan for 1916, and an agreement had unanimously been arrived at that a decision could only be obtained in the principal theatres of war, defined as those which contained the bulk of the enemy's forces—the Russian, Franco-British and Italian fronts—where co-ordinated attacks made in the greatest possible strength were to be undertaken. This decision was in the hands of the Governments concerned on December 16th, 1915. The strength of the British Armies in France rose from 956,000 in January to 1,400,000 in July [4] but the British leaders, at the War Office and in the field, were anxious that the new British Armies should not be

[3] *Wilson Diaries*, Vol. I, p. 270.
[4] *Soldiers and Statesmen*, Vol. I, p. 261.

used for extended operations until they were fully trained and equipped. For reasons which will appear later their employment could not be postponed until a date later than July 1st, when they were launched into the Battle of the Somme, in conjunction with a French attack in which Foch took a prominent part. The nature of this offensive was determined at a further conference on February 14th. The plan was drawn up by Foch, and, as originally designed, it involved the use of forty French and twenty British divisions. The date was not then fixed, but the idea was that the attack should be made at the same time that Russian and Italian offensives were launched.

After the plans had been determined, Foch and his son-in-law, Fournier, were involved in May in a serious motor accident, from which he was fortunate to escape with his life. Resenting as he did all loss of time, he was credited with holding the view that his car could not be driven too fast. The accident occurred on the road from Amiens to Châlons, near a village, Plessis, not far from Meaux. The road was good and the car was travelling at high speed—Foch in his own account said, "We were not going too fast" —when a country cart stopped suddenly in front. The horse took fright and swerved across the road. The chauffeur in order to avoid it jammed on the brake and put the helm over so hard that the car skidded and crashed into a tree. Fournier collided with the door-frame and broke the bone of his nose. Foch went through the glass and sustained severe injuries with gashes all over his face, eyes, mouth, and head, but they were not as serious as at first supposed. He was at once taken in an ambulance to the hospital at Meaux where André, his medical officer, repaired immediately from Amiens and sewed up the cuts. Foch was soon afterwards visited by Poincaré, Briand, and Joffre. Great care was taken to keep his accident secret. It occurred on a Thursday, and as he described the affair himself, he was "off again on the Sunday, his head all bandaged up." What caused him most inconvenience was the injury to his mouth. He could not eat. Not a word was allowed to appear in the Press, lest the loss of so great a French leader should be suspected. Even if the losses and the failure to "break through" in the 1915 attacks may, for the time, have lowered his prestige with the political authorities and with the French public on account of the heavy losses which had been sustained, it stood as high as ever with the French and the British Armies. On the enemy's side, we now know on the authority of Ludendorff that in the "powerful offensive near Loos and Champagne [in 1915] . . . the [German] troops which had been transferred from the East arrived just in time to support the defenders of the Western Front, who were holding out so gallantly, and to avert a serious defeat," so it was obviously undesirable that the enemy should know about the disablement of a leader who had done so much to bring about such a situation.

Foch's hardy upbringing, fine constitution, and life spent in temperate living, were on his side and he made a rapid recovery. He was at work again within a few days.

The first important event in the 1916 campaign on the Western Front was the heavy attack by the German Army on the French front at Verdun. The battle there began on February 21st and it was not brought to a conclusion until August 31st. Before taking note of the situation on the Western Front and of the part taken by Foch therein, we must bear in mind that the Allied offensives in the other European fronts should, according to the original Allied plan, have been made simultaneously with that in France. The Italians attacked in the Trentino from June 17th to July 7th, this attack having been preceded by an Austrian attack between May 14th and June 3rd in the same area. They attacked again on the Isonzo between August 6th and 17th. On the Eastern Front Brusiloff's great and successful offensive began on June 4th. The Rumanians declared war upon Austria-Hungary on August 27th, and invaded Transylvania on the 28th.

Although, from the end of December, 1915, Sir Henry Wilson was no longer officially engaged in maintaining a liaison between the British and the French Armies, his position as Commander of the IVth British Corps allowed him several opportunities of visiting his friends, and his diaries contain certain entries which throw valuable light upon Foch's outlook during this period. We are also fortunate in having at our disposal Foch's own reminiscences of his views on the situation in 1915-16.[5] He described the enemy in 1915 as having sheltered behind armour which would hardly give before the attacks of the feeble Allied armaments. The Germans then made other armour, stronger and more modern in type, and so things went on for months. The Franco-British offensive against defences still formidable on the Somme resulted in some successes which, if not decisive, were at least quite appreciable, and those successes might have been more complete if the higher direction of the operations had been exercised continuously on the ground, and if at the same time they had ensured a proper timing of the work of the Allied Armies. Much time was lost for lack of some permanent form of higher command, when time was a factor vital to success.

[5] *Les deux Batailles de la Marne*, pp. 97-98.

Turning to Wilson's records, we find that he had a long talk with Joffre on April 7th, who "kept hinting and indicating that he thought that an early decision was necessary," which Wilson found rather disquieting as his information pointed to the impossibility of a move by Russia before August or September. On May 9th Wilson, then temporarily in command of the British First Army, again saw Foch, who pressed the point that the Allies ought to negotiate and organise their resources more fully, that infinitely more guns and ammunition ought to be turned out in France and in England, and that perhaps the victory could be gained in a year. Foch and Wilson were agreed that the balance of forces must be altered and that the Allies wanted a larger number of guns to ensure success. They had both changed their views since they had been intent on offensives on a big scale in 1915, but we can perhaps account for this by the difference in the general strategical situation. (In 1915 the German main army was facing East. In 1916 it was facing West in the Battle of Verdun.) Their relationship was evidently most cordial. It was at this time that they were constantly to be found closeted together for hours, gossiping, talking, and striding up and down the room, wearing each other's caps.

We find the first indication of the probable replacement of Joffre as Commander-in-Chief in a conversation between Wilson and Clemenceau on June 11th. The choice of a successor then lay between Castelnau, Foch, and Pétain. Clemenceau was reported to favour Foch himself, and in this he had Wilson's warm support.

The Battle of Jutland was fought on May 31st—June 1st, and Lord Kitchener lost his life on the *Hampshire* a few days later, being succeeded at the War Office by Lloyd

George. On June 22nd Wilson spent the night with Sir Henry Rawlinson, commanding the Fourth British Army with which Foch was to be associated in the Somme offensive. In order to relieve the pressure on Verdun, the date for this offensive had been fixed for July 1st. Foch had lunched with Rawlinson on March 9th at the Fourth Army Headquarters at Querrieu, near Amiens, and they had agreed about certain vulnerable spots where the French and British lines touched. Rawlinson at that time had already heard of Joffre's desire for the British to undertake an attack to relieve the pressure on the French, and he thought that "such a step taken in a hurry would be a fatal mistake" [6] In order to help the French to concentrate about Verdun the British took over a longer line of frontage, and a convenient opportunity is here offered for taking count of the length of line that was occupied by the British at various periods up to July 1st, 1916, when the Battle of the Somme began, bearing always in mind that the relative length of line in no way represented military effort. It was rather a question of the strength of the enemy's force confronting the line occupied, and of the activity, on one side or the other, at given dates.

On August 23rd, 1914, the date of the Battle of Mons, the British front extended for 25 miles (Condé—Mons—Biuche). On September 16th, after the first Battle of Ypres, the length was 20 miles (Soissons—Passey) and on November 20th in the same year 24 miles (N.E. of Kemmel—E. of Festubert). On April 20th, 1915, the length had been increased to 36 miles (Poelcapelle to Ypres Road—the La Bassée Road, Bethune). On the 25th of September when the Battle of Loos began, 70 miles were held; 40 (Boesinghe—

[6] *Life of Lord Rawlinson*, p. 158.

Grenay) and 30 (S. of Arras—Vermandovillers). On February 22nd, 1916, when the German attack was beginning against Verdun, the length was 67 miles; 42 (Boesinghe—S. of Loos) and 25 (Wailly—R. Somme). By the 30th of June the length was between 80 and 90 miles, from Boesinghe to Mariecourt.

The official dates for the beginning and ending of the Battle of the Somme were respectively July 1st and November 17th, 1916. The battle afforded the "baptism of fire" for the new British Armies, who bore the main share in the offensive. The battle took an entirely different form from that envisaged at the conferences in December and in February, at which the nature, but not the date, of the operation had been determined. The original intention had been for the French to provide about two-thirds of the attacking force, covering a far wider frontage. The effect of the Germans having taken the initiative on the 21st of February by launching their heavy attack against the French at Verdun had entailed the deflection to that area of the French forces which would otherwise have been used in the Somme offensive. Another result was to cause the British to launch their attack before the troops had undergone sufficient training. The final effect was to relieve the pressure at Verdun, where the French under Nivelle were able to launch a counter-stroke between the 24th of October and the 18th of November.

Although the numerous sources of information affecting the great Battle of the Somme in 1916 have not yet been co-ordinated in British official histories, plenty of material is available for considering the part that was played therein by Foch, and its influence upon his character and reputation. The British attacks were carried out in four phases, the

[232]

first continuing during the first half of July; the second
from thence to the second week in September; the third
from the middle of September to the last week in October,
and the Ancre phase from the 9th to the 18th of November,[7]
the total captures including 38,000 prisoners and 125 guns.
Sir Douglas Haig reported a steady deterioration in morale
of the German troops, and Ludendorff writes that they
could stand the loss of ground, but "the question of how
. . . the progressive falling off of fighting power of which it
was symptomatic was to be prevented was of immense importance," and "the troops were getting exhausted. . . .
The strain on our nerves in Pless was terrible."[8] A break
in the weather brought the battle to a conclusion in November.

Sir Henry Wilson[9] saw Foch at his Headquarters at Dury
on July 5th, and found him much pleased with the result of
the first French offensive, on the right of the British. Five
French divisions were engaged, the XXth corps north of
the Somme and the Colonial Corps south of it. Nine thousand prisoners and 60 guns had been taken with less than
8,000 French casualties, the Germans having expected and
prepared for the British but not for the French attack.
Joffre left the co-ordination with Haig to Foch. From all
accounts it appears that the relationship between Foch and
Rawlinson, commanding the Fourth British Army on his
left, was most cordial. Wilson saw Foch again at Villers-
Bretonneux in August, when Foch claimed[10] that since July
1st he had taken 42,000 prisoners with a loss of "only 58,000
men." Wilson adds, "He told me all about his methods of

[7] Sir Douglas Haig's dispatch of December 23rd.
[8] *My War Memories*, Ludendorff, pp. 266, 278.
[9] *Wilson Diaries*, Vol. I, p. 287.
[10] *Ibid.*, page 292.

attack and of how he worked his guns, infantry, and aeroplanes, and I got a lot of wrinkles for my Vimy attack, which I shall apply." Wilson regretted that the old system of liaison by a British General Officer, a post that he had previously filled, was no longer being maintained between Haig and Foch.

Wilson records an unfortunate incident of which account must be taken because of its lasting influence upon the conduct of the War on the Western Front by Foch and Haig respectively, each in his own sphere:

Foch told me of his long interview with Lloyd George, who came to see him yesterday. Lloyd George asked innumerable questions about why we took so few prisoners, why we took so little ground, why we had such heavy losses, all these in comparison with the French. Foch played up well as regards Haig. . . . He simply said he did not know, but that our divisions were green soldiers and his were veterans. Lloyd George said he gave Haig all the guns and ammunition and men he could use, and nothing happened. Foch said that Lloyd George was tres monté against Haig, and he did not think Haig's seat very secure.

As matters turned out, it was Foch's own seat that was destined to give way. Further information of considerable importance is contained in Rawlinson's records [11] after Lloyd George had paid his second visit to the front as Secretary of State for War in September:

L. G. visited Foch the other day, and invited criticism of Haig and our methods. Foch very loyally refused to do anything of the kind, and let Haig know what had passed. Methods of that kind are bound to make trouble. Now I hear that he

[11] *Life of Lord Rawlinson*, pp. 173-175.

[Lloyd George] has been criticising our heavy artillery, which is very hard on men who have been working like heroes. What is the reason for it? Is it the casualties? Is it our tactics, or just dislike of Haig?

From other reliable accounts of Lloyd George's visit to Foch at Villers Bretonneux it appears that the War Secretary was late for the meal and so created a record in causing Foch to be late for luncheon for the first and probably the only time in the War until March 26th, 1918. They met privately after lunch and Foch said afterwards that Lloyd George was foolish to believe that he (Foch) would "crab" Haig. Foch at once arranged for a meeting at 2.30 on the next day with Haig. On arrival Foch and Weygand found Haig on his doorstep, and Foch at once took Haig by the arm, walked him around the garden for half an hour, and told him what had happened.

In Rawlinson's army the "creeping barrage," the "most important artillery discovery of the War," had been developed during the battle, and on September 28th he wrote that "all prisoners captured speak of the effectiveness of our artillery, both by day and night," which gave him much pleasure. He was surprised to hear on the next day that "Mr. Lloyd George, on his return to England after his recent visit to France, has made the following statement to responsible officials at home: 'The garrison artillery in France is entirely untrained, it cannot shoot, and is quite unfitted to work the perfect weapons I have provided.'" Rawlinson wrote in his diary on the next day:

I am sure Lloyd George wants to win the War, and his splendid keenness and vitality can be a great asset to us. But he will only get himself into difficulties if he starts laying down the law on matters he knows nothing about. He has heard some silly gossip, and is using it to have a dig at Haig.

Foch's loyalty to his colleague seems to have secured Haig's position, for the time, and the incident evidently had its influence upon the intimate relationship between the two leaders without which the War could not have been won in 1918. For that reason it has been necessary to go into the matter in some detail.

Joffre and Haig met at Chantilly in an important military conference on November 15th, 1916, and they came to an agreement about their plans for 1917, but before the end of the year Joffre was superseded in the chief command, and Foch, his deputy, fell with him. Of the effect of that incident in the career of the great Marshal, Weygand has written [12] that it was necessary to have seen him in those sad moments to measure his greatness of soul. To those who expressed regret or even indignation he contented himself with the reply, *"Laissez-les faire,"* with a gesture which all those about him knew. Weygand adds that never, during the whole time when his great gifts were lying almost fallow, did a single word of discontent or recrimination escape Foch's lips. A contemporary British account says that "Foch took his being *limogé* marvelously well." On the same day he met two British officers on the steps of Joffre's Headquarters (Grand Condé) and stood arm in arm with them for "quite a few" minutes. He had a strong sense of the dramatic.

"One of the saddest things," said Lord Grey of Fallodon in 1923, as he looked back at the lost opportunities of 1919 and intervening years, "as one reflected upon the history of

[12] *Revue des deux Mondes,* May, 1920.

the world was the mischief that had been done and the opportunities that had been missed by men with great powers in great places being unable to forget themselves." In the great cause to which his life-time was devoted, Foch never allowed thoughts of self to interfere with what he conceived to be his allotted task. Weygand shows how the tragedy was accentuated by the fact that the year 1916 had been so "glorious for our arms that Germany asked for peace negotiations (*si glorieux pour nos armées que l'Allemagne demanda à traiter*)," and it was hoped to see the conflict end in victory in 1917, given a better direction of the War on the side of the Allies.

We can conclude with some intimate stories which have reached the author from British officers who were in close contact with Foch during the year 1916.

He showed his keen sense of the dramatic on one occasion during the Somme operations by asking Marchand, of Fashoda fame, to luncheon to meet General Ivor Maxse who had been entrusted by Kitchener directly after he had taken Khartoum, in 1898, to escort Marchand down the White Nile, on which after a heroic journey with a handful of Senegalese from the French Congo, he had anticipated the arrival of the British. (Somewhat heated diplomatic correspondence between France and Britain had followed the incident.) There had been much "jingoism" in England at the time of the original incidents, music-hall songs with a refrain "Marchand-marchez" and so on. The luncheon with Foch was a great success.

Another story shows him "one of the simplest of people" having no idea of his own unconscious gestures. An officer showed Foch an old photograph of the Marshal himself taken before the War, when, in a characteristic attitude, he

[237]

was addressing the *"Cours des Maréchaux"* at Châlons. Foch looked at the picture for some time, and then, waving his arm so as nearly to knock over a neighbour, he said, *"Ce n'est pas moi! Je n'ai pas de gestes!"*

On one occasion during the period of the Somme Foch showed himself to be "a little impatient." A liaison officer came to him from the Verdun front, arriving at the somewhat suggestive hour of 6.45 P.M., dinner being always served at 7:0, and was told to wait for the General. When Foch appeared, the officer presented his compliments. Foch asked him where he had come from, the officer replied, "I come, My General . . . er . . . er . . . I come . . . er—" Foch's reply was *"Bon, allez!"* and "the wretched man had to *aller* back to Verdun," as an observer who witnessed the incident adds. History does not relate whether Foch ever knew how far the officer had come.

One feature of Foch's character, which all British officers who knew him will report, was his absolute straightness and complete good faith. After a conference with one British General with whom he was co-operating, the orders resulting from an agreement arrived at were being drafted when a British officer who was present remarked that he thought by the wording that they misrepresented the agreement with the British General just a little. Foch said immediately, "Cross that out!" (*Annullez ça!*)

Foch told his A.D.C. in after years that he was represented as having said all sorts of things for which he would not be responsible. He would only take responsibility for what he had put in writing. An example of the sort occurred in 1916, when Foch said hastily about some General, "What is he doing? He's running away! (*il f— le camp!*)" Rather a junior British officer who was present said at once: "General—British Generals never run away." Foch—as an observer of the incident reported—"knew that he had been naughty and so said nothing."

While Foch cared little about other people's opinions he was sensitive in questions of honour, and on one occasion in July, 1916, he asked a British officer why Haig did not trust him. The officer made a tactful and somewhat evasive reply, and seized the first occasion to tell Haig the story. Haig at once invited Foch to luncheon, and all was well. There is a sequel to that tale. After the Armistice the same officer asked Foch whether he had not found Haig *"un Lieutenant loyal."* Foch rapped out: *"Le plus loyal!"*

Chapter XX

"SIDE-TRACKED": 1916-1917

AGED 65-66 YEARS

Foch reached the age limit of sixty-five years for his rank while the Battle of the Somme was still raging, at the end of September, 1916, but he was kept specially on the active list. The doctors who examined him after his motor accident in May had pronounced that he had the constitution of a man of thirty.

In the Somme offensive the attacks were on a scale far smaller than that originally intended and they had to be launched prematurely owing to the position at Verdun, when neither Russia nor Italy was ready for what should have been simultaneous operations. In a message which Foch sent to an Ulster newspaper on Armistice Day, 1928, he said that the task that was set to some of the troops had been an impossible one, but that there were moments in war when it was necessary to accept the impossible, for reasons that do not show on the surface. Those who gave their lives freely on that occasion made victory possible in the end.

The casualties on the Somme were very heavy, and it was natural that a public, encouraged, it may be, by the hope of the speedy termination of the War by a "break-through," should have thought more of the vast sacrifices than of the possibility of ultimate victory by such methods. According to some French authorities rumours were set afoot that

[240]

Foch had become too old to bear such great responsibility; that his health was impaired, and that unless he had a long rest he might involve the army in irreparable disaster. There is no doubt that his popularity began at this time to wane in the public estimation.

Such rumours were not confined to the public. The statements were circulated so widely that officers who visited his headquarters expressed openly their surprise at his mental and physical activity. Foch probably never knew how widely these rumours had spread, but he seems to have gathered the impression that attempts were being made to get rid of him. One French writer tells us that Joffre asked him whether he thought that Foch was really ill, and Foch remarked [1] in after years that it was necessary to find a scapegoat because the Battle of the Somme did not produce all the results that had been hoped for. "It was decided to side-track me and I was pronounced unfit for duty on medical grounds." The officer who notified this decision did not know what lay behind it; he was only acting under orders. Foch remarked that the officer in question did not know him, so how could he tell whether he was fit for duty? He told the officer that he might report him as suffering from fatigue which might well be the case. Everyone was fatigued, in such a life as they were living. That was a matter of opinion, "But," he added, "don't imagine that I am seriously ill." If the Government wished to remove him from his command he had no objection, but it must not be on the grounds of ill-health. "When one wants to kill a dog," he said, "one begins by saying that it is mad. It is a rule to which there are few exceptions." [2]

Joffre sent him to Senlis as head of a Board to investigate

[1] Bugnet, p. 213.   [2] Recouly.

inter-Allied questions and there he remained under the command of the French Commander-in-Chief. Amongst other matters he was entrusted with the duty of examining "Plan H," which had been drawn up to meet a possible violation of the neutrality of Switzerland by the Central Powers, and with a comprehensive study of the Allied position on the Western Front.

His natural desire was to remain with the fighting troops and if, for a time, he found his position somewhat irksome he soon obtained the mastery of himself and took a philosophical view of the situation. A friendly politician is said to have suggested some political subterfuge to save his dignity, but with such methods he would have nothing to do. Other men, who had refused work which had been offered, had not again made good. Some had been offered less important (divisional) commands, and they had refused them. Foch's comment was: "Mere pride! I would have accepted a division, rather than remain idle." One, who had been offered an Army Corps, had refused it because he wanted an Army. "An Army? Why an Army? . . . Your greatness does not depend upon the size of your command, but on the manner in which you exercise it." Foch himself would have accepted even a brigade in order to remain at the front, on the principle that: "It is never a downfall to command French soldiers." He visited Joffre at Chantilly when deprived of his active command. There is no historical evidence about the details of the interview beyond the fact that raised voices were heard outside the room. It was on that occasion that Joffre is reported to have said: "You are *limogé*.[3] I shall be *limogé*. We shall all be *limogés!*"

[3] Limoges was traditionally the place to which officers were sent when superseded in their commands.

Joffre was himself superseded on December 12th in favour of Nivelle, to whom Foch was always loyal and just,
giving full credit for his achievements. Nivelle had risen
rapidly to fame when he commanded the French offensive
from Verdun after the German reserves had been drawn
into the Battle of the Somme.

During his time at Senlis Foch naturally had more leisure
than he had when in active command, and there are various
tales of conversations with him at that period. He also could
visit his family occasionally and spend quiet hours working
in the library. His friend, Baron de Mariecourt, records a
conversation in which Foch said: "It is a war of which one
does not see the end. That end will certainly be victorious,
but we have to go down into the depths." The Germans at
the time were making peace overtures through the Crown
Prince and others, and Foch's view was that the hour had
not come for diplomacy, which would only make a mess of
the situation. It was necessary first to exhaust Germany and
to "cross the Rhine," otherwise the younger generation who
came after would have to do the work over again. After
successes he remarked: "Don't fuss; you are making a great
mistake if you think that Germany can be beaten in a
day."

Joffre and other senior officers used to visit Foch and to
spend a long time walking in the country roads, deep in
conversations which generally left Foch silent and preoccu-
pied for a time, probably with his favourite question: *"De
quoi s'agit-il?"*—What is the definite problem now to be
solved? His old friend and instructor Father Lacouture
came on a visit, and to him he said on parting: "I give you a
rendezvous at Metz; we shall go back there. We must." And
here we can recall the story, as Foch told it himself, of an

incident that had occurred in Metz in August, 1870. He had been engaged at St. Clément upon a thesis: "It is necessary that youth should prepare its faculties."[4] The next day was a Sunday, a holiday, with a feeling of calm brooding disaster in the air. Foch heard on that day that Napoleon III, after spending a night in Metz, had hurried off at the news of the twin disasters of Weissenberg and of Forbach. Government House, which the night before had been decked with flags and gleaming with lights, was closed and barred. A fresh poster was on the walls, which Foch could still quote from memory, so deeply had the experience cut into his consciousness. He remembered even a mistake in punctuation. The notice ran:

Marshal Macmahon has lost a battle [there should have been a stop there] upon the Sarre General Froisard has been obliged to retire . . .

The poster was signed "Napoleon." Foch added, when he recalled the incident: "On that day, before that poster, I felt that I should not be a tobacco importer, nor an engineer of bridges and roads, but a soldier." A poster, deficient in punctuation, seems a small matter to lead to so great results. As a further example of the experiences that prepared the future Generalissimo for his destiny we can note the months spent in quiet study of the problem of the Western Front as a whole, when Foch was not constantly distracted by having to deal with local situations. We must also take account of the undoubted benefit, to a man of sixty-five, of a period of comparative calm to enable him to recuperate after a motor accident which had followed nearly two strenuous years of hard fighting and constant responsibility.

[4] Kléber.

Foch had been described in many memoirs and writings as an "optimist." He was certainly not "optimistic" after the Somme battles to the extent of believing that victory would come rapidly and without sacrifices heavier even than those that had already been suffered. He might better be described as a man inspired by steadfast faith which gave him the staying power to remain calm until the end, confident in his certainty of ultimate victory. On the question of his bodily health, a British General who was associated intimately with him reported on a later occasion that "although everyone was unanimous in the selection of Foch for Allied Commander-in-Chief, there were still doubts in a good many people's minds whether the Foch of March, 1918, was the Foch of 1914 and 1915. I remember 'X' saying to me something to this effect: 'Well, do you think that we have done the right thing in selecting Foch, and will he be able to tackle the job? Can you suggest any possible alternative?'" Even after the advantage of comparative quietude at the end of 1916 and in 1917 it was considered by some British observers that Foch showed signs of strain which they attributed partly to his motor accident, but when the great work came, he was prepared for it both in mind and body. He was one of those who "find rest in labour."

Charles Kingsley's writings contain a passage which bears upon the effect of congenial work upon such temperaments. He was watching a sailing boat lying with her sails flapping and struggling, because they were not employed in their proper work:

Look at those spars, how they creak and groan with every heave of the long glassy swell. How those sails flap, thunder, and rage, with useless outcries and strugglings—only because they are idle.

[245]

Let the wind take them, and they will be steady, silent in an instant—that deafening dissonant grumbling exchanged for the soft victorious song of the breeze through the rigging, musical, self-contented, as of a bird on bough.

So it is through life; there is no rest but in labour. "No true misery," as Carlyle says, "but in that of not being able to work." Some may call it a pretty conceit, I call it a great world-wide law, which reaches from earth to heaven.

Kingsley evidently wrote from personal experience. Himself by nature a man of action, he longed at times to be in the Crimea and in the Indian Mutiny campaigns.

There was no "dissonant grumbling" from the future Marshal, as Weygand has assured us—and he was in the best position to know—but a competent British observer reported that during the months of absence from active command "Foch's attitude was rather interesting. He was very excitable and rather difficult to deal with; inclined to be rather autocratic. I put this down to two things. First that he had not quite recovered from his bad motor accident; and secondly that he was longing all the time to do some real soldiering. He hated being mixed up with politics and what were very largely academic studies of war. . . . I think that all this made him rather impatient and anxious to get to a command again."

At the end of 1916 Foch was awarded the high honour of the *Médaille Militaire,* as well as the *Croix de Guerre.* The former was accompanied by this citation (freely translated):

An unexampled tactician and accomplished Commander he has rendered the most eminent service to his country as commander of the covering forces before Nancy and of an Army during the Battle of the Marne. By his inflexible tenacity, undaunted energy, and remarkable aptitude for manoeuvre, he succeeded in checking the plans of the enemy and in breaking his efforts on the Yser. By the fortunate direction that he knew how to devise, he has since assured the success of operations which he has conducted as Commander of a group of Armies.

Weygand, recently promoted to the rank of general officer, went to Senlis with his Chief. Soon afterwards he was sent on a mission to Berne in connexion with plans to counter an enemy move through Switzerland, and this was the only occasion on which the two were separated. In such matters, as in more active employment, Foch trusted Weygand implicitly, and he is said to have felt the lack of his constant companionship very keenly. For such reasons this volume has been dedicated to General Weygand. In the original draft of the dedication, the words: *"Weygand c'est moi"*— an actual saying by Foch—were added. They were afterwards deleted in the belief that they would be displeasing to Weygand himself, who considered that Foch's generosity to those who served under him was almost unexampled in commanders, usually jealous of their own glory. Weygand was sure that without him Foch would always have been Foch, while, without Foch, he—Weygand—would not have reached the standard which he attained. Weygand's view was that anyone else would have served the Marshal as he served him. Foch was himself the force of victory, and it was necessary to do everything to make matters easier for him in so heavy a task. There was nothing, however small, that Weygand would not have done for him, for everything helped to the victory, and the better one knew him the more one loved him.

Weygand's views earned the universal support of the

whole group of British officers who had the good fortune to be associated intimately with the Marshal. Each one of them whom the author has consulted retains vivid memories of the great leader's every gesture, and especially of the atmosphere of peace and confidence which surrounded him even in the very gravest emergencies. Weygand, like Foch, can be acquitted of all trace of what Lord Grey called "one of the saddest things in the history of the world—the habit of men of great powers to miss opportunities by being unable to forget themselves." Weygand's self-abnegation—when others similarly employed sought chances to escape from Staff work for the limelight of command—did much to conserve the strength and energies of his great Chief for the performance of his final mission. When Foch became Chief of the General Staff in May, 1917, he was again accompanied by Weygand.

Chapter XXI

LOST OPPORTUNITIES: 1917

AGED 65-66 YEARS

THERE is abundant evidence, from the German side, that their army was worn out by the Battle of the Somme in 1916, coming, as it did, in the same year as their heavy losses in their unsuccessful attacks upon Verdun. Falkenhayn, the Chief of the General Staff, had been made a scapegoat in September, as Moltke was after the failure of the First Battle of the Marne, and his place had been taken by Ludendorff. The morale of the German Army had suffered severely, and on the Allied side further attacks were only rendered impossible by weather, not by lack of morale or of resources for their continuance. Joffre, Haig, and Foch had agreed on November 15th upon a plan for following up the offensive as early as possible in 1917 while the British Army was rising to its maximum strength and before the enemy had had time to recover, but the result of the heavy French losses without a definite break-through had so affected public opinion as to bring about the fall of the Government and the supersession of Joffre and of Foch, before the results of the heavy fighting of 1916 could be reaped.

On the British side, Robertson [1] assures us that throughout the year 1916 the General Staff were allowed suitable freedom of action in all matters lying within their sphere

[1] *Soldiers and Statesmen*, Vol. I, p. 286.

[249]

and that they received from the Government, as well as from individual ministers, the guidance and assistance to which they were entitled. To that fact may be attributed the military achievements of the year, which left the position in all theatres of war infinitely more satisfactory and hopeful than it had been twelve months before. In December, however, the Asquith ministry "fell to pieces under the weight of its own dissensions," and a new one was formed under the leadership of Mr. Lloyd George. "The same mutually helpful relations were not forthcoming in 1917," and "the operations suffered in a corresponding degree."

Foch remained in his employment upon more or less academic work until May, 1917, so he was not concerned with the conduct of the War on the Western Front until that date. It is only necessary for us, for the sake of continuity, to take note of the point that at a meeting at Calais on February 26th, 1917, when France was represented by M. Briand, General Lyautey, War Minister, and General Nivelle, commanding in chief in the field, and Great Britain by Mr. Lloyd George, Haig, and Robertson, Chief of the Imperial General Staff, General Nivelle produced a document which took Haig and Robertson completely by surprise. It was a plan for an offensive, in which Haig would be placed under Nivelle, designed to bring about a rapid decision on the Western Front by abandoning the approved plan for exploiting the successes on the Somme and by substituting a French offensive between Soissons and Rheims. It was disclosed that the War Cabinet had previously considered the problem without consulting or informing their Chief of the General Staff and official military adviser.

In the actual event the Germans anticipated the Nivelle attack. They fell back voluntarily to the Hindenburg line, thus upsetting the proposed offensive by the British Army to aid in the operations of the French. The abandonment of the Joffre-Haig plan of November, 1916, meant, as Rawlinson put it at the time, that "having won the initiative at great cost on the Somme, we had now to speculate what the German was going to do, instead of making him do what we wanted." [2] The initiative was lost. The British First and Third Armies launched a successful offensive, capturing the Vimy Ridge in the Battle of Arras which lasted from the 9th of April to the 4th of May.[3] The Nivelle offensive, after initial successes on April 17th, failed to attain its object and it was soon abandoned. On May 15th Nivelle was succeeded by Pétain, whose place as Chief of the General Staff was conferred upon Foch. From thenceforward he became the official adviser of the French Government in Army matters and Robertson's colleague.

Foch's view upon the change of command in the French Army was clearly expressed. He said that the change had followed the first battle of Army groups, the plea being that the progress had not been sufficiently rapid. The group principle had been sound, but there may have been faults

[2] *Life of Lord Rawlinson*, pp. 189-190.

[3] *Note.* Although such comparisons have only a limited value, local conditions having differed materially, the following statistics are of interest as indicating the advance in tactical handling of the new British armies as the result of experience and training since they had been used prematurely in 1916 to relieve the pressure upon the French at Verdun. The figures refer in each case to the first twenty-four days of the battle.

	Ground width	Taken depth	Casualties	Captures		German Division		British Guns in action
				Prisoners	Guns	Engaged	Withdrawn	
Somme, 1916	6m	3¼m	136,217	11,119	56	16	8	2090
Arras, 1917	20m	2-5m	83,970	18,128	230	32	16	3500 (app.)

Authority: *Official Statistics of British Military Effort*, pp. 640-1.

in its application. A good method, that of successive attacks, had, however, been established. The same method gained the victory later, but "they" refused to wait. They believed in the one who promised more speedy progress. This was unfortunate, because otherwise the Allies might have won the War at that time (1917). For the first time, after thirty months of warfare, unity of command was established on the Western Front, but the experiment did not succeed. The resources were available, but "they should not have changed horses. That is not done when one is going uphill. Joffre ought to have been allowed to use the resources which he had accumulated. The cart was given to Nivelle to pull. . . . Then another change, and the task had to be started all over again." Then everything was thrown into the melting-pot and the command fell into the hands of councils and committees. Foch was fond of quoting the passage from Machiavelli: "Never have more than one chief in war, because several wills enfeeble an army."

The result of the failure of the Nivelle offensive and of political intervention was that the morale of the French Army was severely shaken. The troops mutinied, and it was only by Pétain's influence that a complete collapse was averted. Thenceforward the British Empire was destined to bear the chief burden of the war on land, as it had in the naval, financial, and economic spheres from the commencement. The revolution in Russia was setting free enemy troops for employment in the west and the situation was becoming critical. The French mutinies were kept secret even from Army Commanders in the British Army. The Germans did not know of them until it was too late to take advantage of the opportunity, and by the time they did know, Haig's attacks were keeping them with too much on their hands.

Meanwhile the impaired morale was not confined to the French Army. It was spread right through the country by soldiers on leave from the front, until strikes, disorders, and defeatism were reported from many quarters.

On the enemy's side, the Germans were helped by the Russian revolution. "Had the Russians attacked in April and May," wrote Ludendorff,[4] "and met with even minor successes, we should then, as in the autumn of 1916, have had a desperate struggle . . . it was the Russian revolution that saved us from serious trouble."

At a meeting on the 25th of July at which Foch, Robertson his British colleague, and Pétain the French Commander-in-Chief were present, the effort which Germany, freed from the Russian menace, could make in 1918 was studied, and the two chiefs of the General Staff put forward a proposal to establish inter-Allied military machinery to study and to prepare for rapid movements of troops, as well as for the co-operation of the Allied Armies on the Western Front. Foch, in his description of the meeting, added: "Our suggestion achieved little success; it was judged to be pessimistic, and it was even discovered that soldiers were lacking in imagination."[5]

It was Lord Grey of Fallodon's considered opinion,[6] writing after the event, that in wartime it was the part of a civilian government to see that the highest professional posts in an Admiralty and War Office, and the chief commands in the Army and Navy, were filled by the soldiers and sailors best qualified for them; and that these were supported in the use of the armed forces. In the year 1917 the civilian governments, both in France and in Great Britain, fell far

[4] *My War Memories*, pp. 426-7. [5] *Les deux Batailles de la Marne*, p. 100.
[6] *Twenty-five Years*, Vol. II, pp. 71-72.

short of this ideal. In both countries there was a strong determination to maintain rigidly the principle that the commanders of the fighting forces and the war ministries should be under the control of the civilian governments, and apparently it was considered to be dangerous to depute to the commanders of the Allied Armies the responsibility for combined operations without first devising some combined civilian control over their plans. The first step must be to devise some such form of inter-Allied civilian control before establishing any inter-Allied military body such as that proposed by Foch, Robertson, and Pétain. It was in that direction that matters ultimately developed, but much valuable time was lost. The War was prolonged, and defeat nearly resulted from the delay in devising an efficient system under which the best use could be made of the two Allied Armies, acting in combination.

We can note in passing that, had the Nivelle attack succeeded, it would have been followed not only by the advance of the British Armies by land, but also by the embarkation and descent upon the Belgian coast of Rawlinson's Fourth Army—an operation for which careful preparations were made in July.[7]

The British offensive continued with the Battle of Messines (June 7th-14th) and the Battles of Ypres (July 31st-November 10th) culminating in the costly offensive at Passchendaele. The object of taking pressure off the French and other Allies was fulfilled as far as the conditions allowed. The ultimate object had been to clear the Belgian coast of German submarine bases and aerodromes at the urgent demand of the British Admiralty.

[7] For details of this interesting scheme, see the *Life of Lord Rawlinson*, pp. 190-200.

For considering "through English eyes" Foch's activities during this period, the diaries of his friend Henry Wilson and of his colleague, Robertson, contain some valuable material. Foch put his own view of the salient facts briefly in *"Les deux Batailles de la Marne,"* in his conversations at the time with M. Recouly and others, and, in later years, with the A.D.C., Commandant Bugnet. With the exception of a brief reference to his Chief's disappointment at the loss of opportunity in 1917 owing to political conditions and lack of co-ordinated control over the operations, Weygand passes lightly over this period in his recent article in the *Revue des deux Mondes.*

Recouly [8] impresses the point that, when Foch succeeded Pétain as Chief of the General Staff in May, no post could have suited him better. Installed in the Hotel des Invalides in Paris he became the technical adviser of the Government and "never had a broad and sane direction of the War, from a political as well as from a military point of view, been more necessary than at that moment. Never had it been more indispensable to grasp the situation on all the fronts, not only with the French and the British, but the Italian, Russian, Balkan, and even the Asiatic."

The Russian front crumbled in July. Many German divisions were set free for a blow elsewhere. America, it is true, had come into the War, but many months must pass before help in the field could arrive from across the Atlantic. The first problem was to divine where the first blow would fall. It was destined to fall upon Italy on the 25th of October, causing the disaster of Caporetto.

Passing to British authorities we find that Wilson contemplated resigning his post as liaison officer at the end of

[8] *Foch,* pp. 210-212.

May, having heard from Foch that Pétain did not want him. Foch was also opposed to Wilson going to Paris in a similar capacity. Towards the end of June, Wilson, on his way home, saw Foch again and dined with him and Madame Foch in their new flat in Paris. Foch then told Wilson that the British Army must relieve the French down to the Oise, or even as far as Soissons, and "if he did not do this, the present (French) Government would treat with the Boches for a peace, as both the Army and France are tired out." [9] Foch was entirely opposed to a force going down to Italy to help the Italians to crush the Austrians. On August 6th Foch told Wilson in London [10] that he was very anxious to make some progress with the plans for 1918, but that he found it very difficult to get any interest taken in the subject in England. He favoured the idea of sending an expedition to Alexandretta to cut the railway communications of the Turks operating in Mesopotamia and Palestine, and he wanted to get some French and British troops back from Salonika, though he did not favour the evacuation of that place. Foch spoke unfavourably of the inter-Allied meeting of statesmen on the next day, which he described as a fiasco. He saw Wilson again in London on September 4th and told him that he (Foch) wanted to send 100 guns to Cadorna in Italy. At another meeting in London on October 11th Foch was not in favour of a campaign in Syria so late in the year. He wanted the winter months to be devoted to making war material, in readiness for 1918. He was opposed to the idea that "the British could do all the fighting, and could win, in 1918." The two friends did not meet again until after the Italian disaster. Wilson, at that time, was holding a home

[9] *Wilson Diaries*, Vol. I, p. 363.
[10] *Ibid.*, Vol. II. pp. 8-9.

command and not in intimate touch with the conduct of the War.

Robertson, as Chief of the General Staff and Foch's colleague, also tells us of Foch's opposition to a Syrian campaign.[11] As affecting Salonika, he adds that Foch (also Joffre and Pétain) "showed in manner, if not in words, that they intensely disliked the project from the start and would be glad to see the end of it." Robertson also provides a valuable contribution to history in a statement that, before the Caporetto disaster occurred, Foch was opposed to sending Allied infantry to Italy, though he favoured giving the Italians help in artillery.[12] Read in conjunction with Wilson's report, this point may be taken as established.

Caporetto compelled the British and the French Governments to take stock of the situation. Through divided counsels and chaos in the major strategy of the War they had been heading for distaster to the Allied cause.

Foch, who had visited the Italian front early in the year while he was engaged in the academic study of inter-Allied military problems, was well acquainted with the local situation. His Staff had already worked out the problem of transport, and his immediate action was to offer troops to assist General Cadorna. Four of the best French fighting divisions began to leave on October 26th at the rate of forty trainloads a day, and the leading detachments arrived in Italy on November 1st. Divisions were also taken from Haig's army at a critical time for the same purpose.[13]

Foch repaired to Italy himself, "met the Italian leaders, inspired them with his confidence, and pointed out the grave

[11] *Soldiers and Statesmen*, Vol. II, pp. 176-177.

[12] *Ibid.*, p. 247.

[13] This weakening of Haig's army seriously affected the result of the Cambrai battle in November. (See below.)

danger of any further retreat." [14] According to the Wilson Diaries [15] there seems to have been a little friction at first between Foch and Diaz the new Italian Commander-in-Chief, but the matter was soon adjusted. The Italians held out on the Piave. The Caporetto disaster had far-reaching effects upon Foch's future. It led to the establishment of a "Supreme War Council" by a resolution passed at an Inter-Allied Conference at Rapallo, largely at the instigation of Lloyd George.[16] The decision to take this step had been arrived at by the British War Cabinet by October 31st, and French concurrence had been obtained by November 2nd.[15]

The Supreme War Council had as members the Prime Minister and one other minister of each of the principal Allied countries. The military side included four permanent military representatives of Great Britain, France, Italy and the United States, each with a staff of assistants. The Council was to sit at Versailles. Foch, as Chief of the French General Staff, was the military representative of France at first, but he soon arranged that Weygand, his loyal right-hand man, should take his place. Wilson was the British military representative, with an independent mission. The British Prime Minister thus had two responsible military advisers—Robertson, the Chief of the Imperial General Staff, to advise him in his capacity of British Prime Minister and head of the Imperial War Cabinet, representing the whole British Empire, and Wilson to advise him in his capacity as a member of the Supreme War Council. Both Wilson and Robertson

---

[14] Recouly, p. 2121.　　　　　　　[15] *Wilson Diaries*, Vol. II, pp. 20-26.
[16] Sir Charles Callwell has produced evidence to show that the setting up of the Supreme War Council was due to the initiative of Sir Henry Wilson before the British Prime Minister left England for Rapallo. *Wilson Diaries*, Vol. II, p. 11.

were of high military rank. They held divergent views upon the military strategy of the War, and an impossible situation was thus created. The system was altered soon after Wilson himself became Chief of the Imperial General Staff in 1918.

The creation of the Supreme War Council was a great step in the direction of a united command, as it facilitated agreement on general questions of policy—the business of statesmen—to which military strategy must be subordinated. The step was forced upon the governments concerned by the disaster to Italy, and it was taken none too soon in a year of grave disappointment which was due to divided counsels in high places both in France and in Great Britain.

At about this period, Foch described France as a country of last-minute recoveries. It was necessary that things should come to the worst, that the illness should reach an acute stage before the doctor or the surgeon was called in. There was no reason to be proud of such a situation. It was as if one began by setting fire to a house in order to have the pleasure of calling in the fire-brigade. Such experiences are too costly. They led to losses in human life and in financial resources, without taking account of the danger that, some day, the "last-minute recovery" would not be a recovery at all. The Army mutinies of 1917 were the result of an offensive not sufficiently prepared. "Pétain, with an infinity of intelligence, prudence, and decision, re-established discipline and strengthened the broken morale of the Army. That was his greatest merit. Few chiefs could have done so difficult a task so well." Foch added, however, that it would have been infinitely better if it had not been necessary to apply the cure. The cause was the thoroughly bad and unfortunate displacement of Marshal Joffre. All the trouble came from that. "If they had kept Joffre . . . the mutinies would have been avoided."

On Foch's work as Chief of the General Staff Painlevé wrote that there was never any difference of opinion between Foch, Pétain, and himself, or shade of dissension about the general conduct of the War between the 15th of May and the 13th of November when Painlevé left office. As technical adviser to the Government, Foch was a member of the War Committee and attended all the sittings. The whole policy of the War was that laid down by Foch and Pétain.

When the French Government fell in November, Clemenceau came into power. With Foch as military adviser, he soon became a dominant figure on the Supreme War Council, the advice given to him by Foch's lieutenant, Weygand, on that Council being naturally identical with that given to him by Foch himself, as Chief of the General Staff.

Between November 20th and December 7th, the British fought the Battle of Cambrai which began with great promise with a break through for a considerable distance, but German reserves restored the situation after November 30th. In the diary of the late Lord Rawlinson, perhaps the ablest of all Army leaders on the Western Front, we find the interesting entry on December 7th:

Just as we have a real chance of doing something good at Cambrai which will repay us for all our losses at Passchendaele, the Government orders off to Italy the divisions which would have made Cambrai a real victory. I said at the time that they could not arrive early enough to be of any real use in Italy, and now I hear that the Austro-Boche attack had come to a standstill before they got there. Haig told me that he had sent Kiggell over to London to see Lloyd George before Cambrai, and to beg that three of Plumer's divisions might be left for the battle, in which case he, Haig, was confident of a really big success. L. G. had answered that he had heard enough prophecies of big successes, and that the divisions were to go to Italy. The fact is that L. G. does not trust D. H. and it is hard to win a war when the Prime Minister and the Commander-in-Chief don't get on.

Pétain's policy had the support of his government. Haig's position, on the other hand, was insecure, and Lloyd George's policy, as representing the British Empire on the Supreme War Council, was sharply at variance with that of Robertson, Foch's colleague as Chief of the General Staff. The British Prime Minister was anxious to send away a considerable portion of Haig's Army from the Western Front. Haig, however, had survived when Joffre was superseded, and on this point Robertson wrote, on the occasion when Haig was put under Nivelle early in the year:

The agreement had in it much of the personal element, and should not be attributed, as it sometimes is, solely to a desire on the part of Mr. Lloyd George to unify the command. It was due in no small measure to his mistrust of Haig's qualifications for the post of Commander-in-Chief, and he probably derived quite as much satisfaction from seeing Haig's powers cut down as he did from seeing Nivelle's increased. More than once during 1917, when affairs on the Western Front were being discussed, he said to me that I would persist in always supporting what Haig did, and there is no doubt in my mind that a recommendation from me, as C. I. G. S., to appoint a new Commander-in-Chief would have met with instant approval . . . This personal matter is recalled because, unless it is borne in mind, neither the Calais agreement nor the treatment of other questions connected with the Western Front during 1917 can be properly understood.[17]

[17] *Soldiers and Statesmen*, Vol. II, pp. 215-216.

Robertson adds [18] that there is no doubt that, had Lloyd George's wishes prevailed at that period, the main British effort would have been transferred from France to Italy, and that the cessation of offensive operations on the Western Front in November, 1917, left the Entente without any comprehensive military plan for 1918. Owing to the supersession of Joffre, the task of co-ordinating the activities of the Allied Armies, which had been entrusted by common consent to French Headquarters, had gradually fallen out of French hands, and no adequate substitute had been provided. Robertson, after repeated applications, could get no guidance out of the Supreme War Council. The British General Staff were anxious to assemble as large a force as possible on the Western Front so as to be able not only to parry the blow which was threatened there by the movement of German divisions from the Russian front, but to hit back as soon as opportunity offered. Some 760,000 British troops were being retained in the East, and they could not be moved until some guidance was obtained from the supreme authority.

Late in the year 1917, officers at Pétain's headquarters were saying, *"Le père Foch veut se faire Généralissime."* Having heard this, a British officer called upon Foch during one of his visits to London, and found him at his hotel, sitting in an arm-chair after attending a conference. In reply to a question, *"Eh bien, mon Général, comment va la Conférence?"* Foch made one of his typical gestures. He drew circles in the air with his cigar, then in reply to a remark *"Il me semble, mon Général, qu'il nous faut un Généralissime. Pourquoi ne vous faites-vous pas nommer Généralissime?"* Foch's answer (verbatim) was:

"Parceque Monsieur Lloyd George ne veut rien en savior,

[18] *Soldiers and Statesmen*, Vol. II, p. 251.

et Monsieur Clemenceau et la Republic Française—jamais de la vie!"

On the 2nd of December hostilities ended between Russia and Germany. On the 6th Rumania followed, and by the 8th all hostilities on the Eastern Front had ceased. Germany was free to concentrate for a final bid for victory in the decisive area.

PART III

AFTER THE GREAT WAR

1918-1929

CHAPTER XXII

"SUPREME" CONTROL: DECEMBER, 1917-FEBRUARY, 1918

AGED 66 YEARS

IT was Robertson's considered opinion,[1] writing nearly ten years after the event, that one of the most praiseworthy features of the War was the solidarity with which the Allied countries, Russia excepted, continued to stand together through long years of difficulties and disappointments. In no previous war were the relations between allies more unselfish or mutually helpful than in the War of 1914-18. Between officers and men of the various armies a feeling of good comradeship everywhere prevailed, while in matters connected with concerted action the respective authorities invariably displayed every consideration towards each other —not an easy thing to do when dealing with people whose language, customs, and temperament are entirely different from one's own.

It is difficult, however, to contemplate with equanimity the terrible losses from wounds, poison-gas, sickness, and disease in the Allied armies, navies, and air forces during the interminable periods that were spent in discussions and in negotiations between the representatives of the Allied nations, discussions lasting for many months while action was urgently needed and time was of the utmost value. It may be that such conditions are an unavoidable feature in alli-

[1] *Soldiers and Statesmen*, Vol. II, p. 299.

ances between democratic countries in which those who are charged with the responsibility for government depend from day to day upon public opinion for their power. The difficulties are accentuated when that opinion is followed and not led by some outstanding personality.

Leadership in the political field doubtless offers a more difficult problem than it does in armies in which the tradition of discipline and of obedience prevails, but there again success depends less upon the office that is held than upon the personality of the holder. The most striking passage in Weygand's recent appreciation [2] of the life and character of Marshal Foch is the one in which he maintains that the master-key for a Chief in all departments of life is "authority." This, he holds, is indispensable to anyone who aspires to command troops, but if authority depends upon mere rank it is of no value. If it is the result of suppression ("*contrainte*") it will be of no avail in face of the terrible realities of war. If, on the other hand, authority bases its source and its strength upon personality, we then find a true leader of men, by which Weygand evidently meant one who leads, and does not follow, opinion. Such a man Weygand found in Foch, who possessed supremacy in leadership because of the strength and tremendous authority which his presence produced as a dominating impression upon others from the very first moment of meeting.

In Clemenceau and in Foch France now found two strong personalities accustomed to lead rather than to follow the opinions of others, and the only question that arose was whether two such strong men would work well together for the same objects, each in his own domain, Clemenceau

[2] *Revue des deux Mondes*, May, 1929.

in the political sphere of words, Foch in the military sphere of deeds.

For the doings of the Supreme War Council during December, 1917, and in January and part of February, 1918, we have the authority of the Wilson Diaries. For subsequent events we have the entries made in his diary by the late Lord Rawlinson, and published in his biography.

The first meeting of the Supreme War Council was held at Versailles on December 1st, 1917. Clemenceau, representing France, took the chair. Lloyd George and Milner represented the British Empire, Orlando Italy, and Colonel House the United States. The military representatives of the different countries were Weygand (France), Henry Wilson (British Empire), Cadorna (Italy), and General Bliss (U. S. A.). Foch was present at the meeting, and also Robertson, Sackville West (now Lord Sackville), Hankey (Sir Maurice, Secretary to the British War Cabinet), and M. Venizelos. Hankey, highly skilled in such work, drafted numerous resolutions. Lloyd George read them out, Clemenceau put them, and they were passed rapidly. On December 13th Wilson heard from Clemenceau that Pétain was asking for the British to take over from the French troops a line as far as Berry-au-Bac, near Rheims, and Clemenceau threatened to resign if they did not do so. Haig told Wilson the next day that he had already come to an agreement with Pétain to take over as far as the Oise, although the manpower position was getting acute. The British would be 200,000 short of their proper numbers in March, 400,000 in October.

It was decided by December 15th that the military representatives should meet as a body to study any subject referred to them by the Council, come to conclusions, draw

[269]

up notes, and send them up as proposed "Resolutions" to the Council secretariat. If passed, these resolutions were expected to carry executive authority with the Governments concerned. On the question of the relative length of line held, the French view was that they were holding too great a length in proportion to their strength, the British case being that they were holding by far the most important section. The machinery, it was obvious, was not likely to lead to rapid decisions. A conclusion as to the dividing front was not arrived at until January 10th, when it was fixed near the Laon-Soissons road, well on the French side of the Oise. Luckily this was not acted upon. The British ultimately extended as far as Barisis, short of the River Oise.

The military representatives met on December 22nd to consider papers by Wilson on Salonika and on Italy. Weygand opposed them, Foch having already sent orders to the Salonika force. Foch, as we know, was not enamoured of committees as organs for quick decisions and executive action. On December 30th Lord Milner told Wilson that it was proposed that he should supplant Robertson on the General Staff.

On January 2nd Wilson found Clemenceau out of humour as Lloyd George was suggesting a meeting of the Supreme War Council in London and discussion of terms of peace. On January 11th there came the most important departure. Wilson met Clemenceau and proposed a scheme for establishing a central reserve of troops under the Supreme War Council, or under Foch and Robertson. Wilson then heard of a project by Lloyd George to make Joffre Generalissimo, with Wilson as Chief of Staff. Wilson did not like this proposal, and told Milner of his own scheme for a Central Reserve "under Versailles."

On January 16th Wilson told General Smuts (member of the British War Cabinet) that he was coming round to the view that neither side would obtain a decision on the Western Front, and that "we ought to try to knock out the Turk." On January 23rd the Military Representatives passed a resolution that the creation of a Central Reserve was imperative, and on January 30th a meeting of the Supreme War Council was held to discuss the matter. Foch, who seems to have attended specially on this occasion, Robertson, Cadorna and Bliss supported the proposal to have a Reserve. At another meeting on February 1st Robertson pressed for the Reserve to be under Foch and himself. It was on this occasion that the Council passed a resolution, strongly supported by Lloyd George, that "a decisive offensive should be undertaken against Turkey, with a view to the annihilation of the Turkish armies and the collapse of the Turkish resistance." [3] Robertson expressed his disagreement with this policy—one which was not supported by Clemenceau, who opposed it, or by Foch, who remained silent.

Foch, at the same meeting, raised the question of British man-power, and Lloyd George protested against criticism by a foreign officer of the actions of the British Government.[4] At a further important meeting held on February 2nd an "Executive Board," presided over by Foch and including all the Versailles military representatives except Weygand, was set up to determine the strength of the Reserves and to control them. At a meeting of this Executive Board on the 3rd, Foch held out for a Reserve of 30 divisions—10 British, 13 French, and 7 Italian. On February 9th Wilson was summoned to London, and there followed "six days of chaos," ending, after many complications, in the substitution of Sir

[3] *Soldiers and Statesmen*, Vol. II, p. 286. [4] *Ibid.*, p. 289.

Henry Rawlinson, commanding the Fourth British Army, for Wilson at Versailles, and in the removal of Robertson from his post as Chief of the General Staff, his successor being Wilson. The result of this change was that from thenceforward Foch, as Chief of the General Staff in France, had his old friend Wilson, Chief of the General Staff in England, as his colleague. While their personal relationship seems to have been much the same as ever, there had developed by this time a strong divergence between their views on the general strategy of the War, Foch, supported by Clemenceau, holding to his original view that a decision could only be arrived at by one method—the defeat of the German Army on the Western Front. This view had been shared by Robertson who had thus lost his office, being unwilling to give way on a question of principle to the Prime Minister, Mr. Lloyd George.

Rawlinson, Wilson's successor at Versailles, is the best authority on what happened there after the 20th of February. He left England on that day after breakfasting privately ("to celebrate his 55th birthday") with the King and Queen and Princess Mary. He found them extremely kind and pleasant, and they gave him some whiting and marmalade for breakfast. "The King has not been too well since his accident, and has been ordered cream. He honoured me by giving me some. The Queen and Princess Mary were not allowed any. There are a good many messes in France where they have a better breakfast than the Royal Family has." (This incident is inserted to bring out the point that, owing to the destruction of shipping by German submarines, the people of England were suffering great hardship in order that sufficient shipping might be lent for the use of Allied armies and nations. British shipping was placed at the disposal of an Allied Board similar to the Supreme War Council at Versailles.)

On February 22nd, on his way to Versailles, Rawlinson studied at French headquarters the general plan that had been arranged between Haig and Pétain for the defence of the Western Front and he "fully agreed with it." After luncheon Pétain showed him the correspondence between Foch and himself about the divisions to be allotted to the Central Reserve. Haig could not agree to more than two divisions, which were to come back from Italy, and the Italian Government had protested against their being withdrawn. Pétain was to provide eight instead of the proposed thirteen. Rawlinson spent the 23rd in his Versailles office, noting that it would take all his tact to get the reserve question settled. "It ought never to have been raised." On the 25th, he and Wilson visited Haig. Wilson made the point that if he contributed eight divisions to the General Reserve, (then so called), he would get more help out of Pétain than he would in any other way if the Germans attacked him. Haig's reply was that if he sent any divisions away he could not be responsible for the safety of his front. He had barely sufficient troops even then to meet the attack which the Germans were preparing to make upon him. (That Haig was right, events were to prove.) If he did hand over his divisions to the control of the Executive Board at Versailles, they would not get information as early as Haig would; they would hold on to the Reserve until they knew for certain where the German attack was coming, and meanwhile Haig, who knew the situation, would have his line broken. Haig refused to budge. Wilson was "nonplussed, for D. H.'s arguments are unanswerable. He naturally does not place any reliance upon a committee acting promptly."

[273]

Foch shared these views throughout his life, but it is possible that on this occasion he thought that he himself, as President of the Executive Board, would have been in a strong enough position to take immediate action without the usual delays entailed by discussions. Haig told Rawlinson that he had seen Clemenceau who was quite in sympathy with his views.

Before proceeding with our narrative, it is necessary to take account that up to this date Haig had not received any written communication from Foch about providing divisions for the General Reserve. A letter to him on the subject from Wilson, as military representative at Versailles, was dated the 6th of February, but probably owing to Wilson's sudden summons to London it was not sent off (by Rawlinson) until the 28th. This disposes once for all of the accusation made against Haig of conspiracy against Foch.[5]

On February 27th Rawlinson and Wilson went to see Foch, to explain to him Haig's attitude about the General Reserve. Foch was not as disturbed as Rawlinson expected him to be, but he insisted on having the statement in writing. Foch's own comment on the incident in later years was that the *coup-de-grâce* was given to the General Reserve, to the Executive Board, and therefore to the unified Command, of which they contained the germ.[6] Rawlinson reported the result of the interview to Haig on the 28th, enclosing the above-mentioned letter of February 6th and adding that Foch would like a reply in writing (this reached Versailles on March 3rd) and Haig's scheme of defence for the British front. He already had had one from Pétain and from Diaz, now commanding in Italy. On the next day Rawlin-

[5] In *At the Supreme War Council*. For reply see the *Life of Lord Rawlinson*, p. 211. [6] *Les deux Batailles de la Marne*, p. 103.

son told Wilson that Haig's plan of defence and statement
of his arrangements with Pétain were being sent to Versailles with a request "to criticise them in any way we
like."

On March 3rd Rawlinson wrote that he had received
Haig's reply to lay before the Executive Board the next
day. He was opposed, himself, to the General Reserve, as he
did not think that it would serve any useful purpose. He was
quite satisfied to have the two Commanders-in-Chief to
fight their own battles in unison. Versailles could help them
by giving decisions if they got into trouble, and meanwhile
it was best to leave them as they were. The Executive Board
met on March 4th, with Foch in the chair, and considered
Haig's reply, which amounted to a refusal to earmark any
of his divisions for a General Reserve, so they sent a Resolution to the Supreme War Council reporting the situation.
Rawlinson then went to Clemenceau to tell him the result
of the meeting. Clemenceau replied that "he was quite glad,
though he knew that Foch would be annoyed. He said that
he.was better pleased with two generals conducting operations than four. Anyhow, he in no way resented the result
of our meeting."

On the evening of March 11th Rawlinson saw Clemenceau
again. Rawlinson's report of the interview gives so valuable
a clue to subsequent developments that it will be best to
quote it fully:

He [Clemenceau] was in good form, but was annoyed at
having to go over to England. He does not at all want to intervene in the discussion about Versailles, but I told him he would
have to whether he liked it or not; for the failure to create
the General Reserve had brought about an impasse which must
be settled one way or another. I told him that I did not see the

need of giving executive powers to the War Board, and that the military representatives could function quite well without executive authority, if he replaced Weygand by some senior French commander. He said he could not spare Fayolles, whom Pétain had specially asked should be recalled from Italy. He seemed rather bored with the whole question, saying that he was quite innocent in regard to the creation of the War Board, which had been carried through entirely by Lloyd George, and he did not see why the innocent should suffer with the guilty.

In connexion with the foregoing, it is well to remember that the only way in which a higher commander—apart from personal influence upon subordinates—can affect the issue of a great battle is through the use of the reserves which he keeps in his own hands. To entrust the Executive Board with the control of the reserves would have put that Board in the position of Generalissimo. Foch himself looked askance upon committees when decisions were required. The position early in March, 1918, was that no satisfactory substitute had been devised for French General Headquarters, which, in the time of Marshal Joffre, had co-ordinated the activities of the Allied Armies on the Western Front. Owing to the lack of such co-ordination in the year 1917, the chance of victory before the Russian collapse had been thrown away. Since then nothing effective had been done to substitute a unified command, which could be exercised only by an individual. The situation was menacing. Attacks in greater force than those hitherto encountered were obviously impending, and Foch, though always certain of ultimate victory, considered that the immediate outlook was disquieting.

Of Foch himself, many thought at the time that he was not the man that he had been in the early stages of the

War. It was said by some that he was ageing, by others that he was in failing health. One senior officer, who saw much of him during these months, found him "excitable and rather difficult to deal with." These impressions were probably caused by the fact that Foch, a man of action and a commander by nature, anxious only to "get things done," was chafing under the restraint imposed upon all whose functions are advisory with no power to do the things themselves. His star seemed to be setting, and in view of his age it seemed probable that the dream of his youth could not be fulfilled, and the labour of a lifetime would not be brought to fruition.

CHAPTER XXIII

In March, 1918, there came to Foch the call to action for which he had been waiting since the days of his adolescence at the College of St. Clément in Metz. Seldom has there been a more striking example of the saying: *"Post nubilia Phœbus."* The call came to him when recent happenings had apparently deprived him, after a lifetime of strenuous exertion, of all opportunity of helping his country when in dire peril. A difference of opinion with Clemenceau, who as Prime Minister and Minister of War was practically a Dictator, had left him deprived even of his advisory influence in his position of Chief of the General Staff. To the events in March which led up to this situation this chapter will be devoted.

March, 1918, marked a period when the fortunes of the Allies were at their lowest ebb. Not one of the diversions of military force to other theatres had in any way contributed to victory on the Western Front in France and Flanders where the issue was now finally to be determined. All of them, and the alliance with Italy, had absorbed French and British soldiers, munitions, and equipment. Only one, Allenby's brilliant offensive in Palestine, had provided a sop to public opinion, the Cerberus of all the Allied statesmen.

Russia, torn by internecine strife, had cast off her alliance, and on the 3rd of March the Bolsheviks signed a peace with the Central Powers. Rumania, another ally, decisively defeated in the field, followed suit on the 5th of the month, Finland on the 7th, and Rumania contracted a peace with Bolshevik Russia on the 9th. The arena was cleared, and Germany was free to throw her maximum strength against the French and British Armies in a final blow for victory. German aerodromes were near enough to England to bomb London from aeroplanes on moonless nights, and special German ordnance was within bombarding range of Paris. The Belgians stood at bay on their last narrow strip of territory.

In the far West, across the Atlantic, lay the potential force of a great American Army in the making, but the hammer-blow was ready to fall at any moment. Only three divisions of American troops were ready in France, and there was no prospect of an appreciable increase before the blow fell. Could the line be held for a long enough period to allow time for the new world to redress the balance of the old? And on what part of the long line would the blow fall? The British held one hundred and twenty-three miles; the French most of the remainder, but while the length of line held may have added to the uncertainty about where to place reserves to counter the blow, the real measure of military effort was the number of German divisions confronting the portion of the line that was held.

Germany, as we now know, had decided upon "England the Enemy!" as her war-cry, knowing the vast resources not only in armies, but also in fleets, in merchant vessels, and in the economic and financial spheres which the British Empire was contributing to the War. Haig had received information which pointed to the certainty of an impending

[279]

attack, but so, apparently, had Pétain. Britain, with Ireland almost in a state of revolution, and with a lingering fear of German invasion which now seems to us somewhat fantastic, still kept a considerable body of troops across the Channel. Pétain with a fear, now seemingly equally fantastic, of an advance of a German Army against his right flank through Switzerland, disposed a considerable proportion of his reserves accordingly.

For a long time it had been obvious that unless a greater measure of unity in command, or at least in direction, of the operations of the Allied Armies could be established, the Allied countries were heading for disaster. Foch had taken note [1] that on the Somme in 1916 the Franco-British operations had achieved more important results than those that were reached when the two armies were acting independently. He claimed considerable credit for the inter-Allied conferences which were organized by the French Army headquarters and attended by the respective commanders-in-chief or by their representatives, but however useful these meetings might have been, they could not take the place of the unity of command which was indispensable in the conduct and in the development of the operations. Towards the end of 1916, as the number of Allies increased, the idea of a stronger method of direction made some progress, but its application seemed so difficult that even its strongest partisans did not dare to give it practical form.

At the Calais Conference of February, 1917, Haig had been put under the command of Nivelle, just at the time when America was coming into the War and German troops were being transferred westward from the Eastern Front. "For the first time, after thirty months of indecisive warfare, the

[1] *Les deux Batailles de la Marne*, pp. 98-99.

united command of the two armies, British and French, was established officially on the Western Front." The experiment failed. Foch wrote that, on account of the position that he occupied, he was not free to express his opinions about the causes. There had been talk of differences between Haig and Nivelle. Foch knew nothing of such differences (*"Je n'en sais rien"*). He attached much importance to the failure of the 1917 attacks as a factor in the abandonment of a single command, and the lack of success came at a moment when unity of command seemed to be needed more than ever.

Towards the end of 1917 Foch and Robertson, the respective Chiefs of the General Staff, and Pétain, the French Commander-in-Chief, pointed out to the heads of the Governments the formidable effort which the Germans would be able to make against France in 1918 owing to the defection of Russia, and they proposed to establish an inter-Allied military organisation to study and to prepare for more speedy movements of troops as well as for their co-operation on the Western Front. Their suggestion was pooh-poohed on the score of pessimism and lack of imagination:

Nôtre suggestion eut peu de succès; elle fût jugée pessimiste et quelqu'on trouva même que les militaires manquaient d'imagination. Finalement, on se sépara sans avoir rien décidé.

Then in October, 1917, came the Caporetto disaster to the Italian Army, and, as a result, the Supreme War Council on November 7th, 1917, which might provide for co-ordination, it was true. It had, however, no means of directing, still less of commanding. All the Allied military representatives, British, Italian, French, and American, wanted something of the sort. General Bliss, directly he arrived in France in November, openly advocated a single military command,

He went so far as to express his view that the appointment of a Generalissimo ought to be made the first condition for the Americans to make the great military effort in which they were engaged, and he so informed his own War Department and President Wilson. Haig, with the memory of his unfortunate experience in 1917, assumed an attitude of prudent reserve. (*"Le Maréchal Haig, à qui la subordination temporaire de 1917 n'a laissé que de mauvais souvenirs, se maintient dans une réserve prudente."*) Robertson considered that the British Commander-in-Chief could not be placed under an Allied general.

The Versailles conferences went on. They met, they discussed, sometimes they agreed, but they had no power to act. At the end of January the military representatives proposed than an Allied General Reserve should be established, to be sent to the point of danger when required, and an "Executive Committee" (Military) was formed to decide how the Reserve should be composed, where it should be stationed, and to provide for its movement and concentration. Foch, as President of the Executive Committee, decided the composition of the Reserve.

There have been as many claimants in various countries for the origination of a unified command as there have been for "winning the War," so it seems best to confine ourselves to Foch's simple account of the preliminaries, which, in his usual style, makes no personal claims for anybody, if we except a short tribute to Mr. Lloyd George whose part will appear in due course.

In the actual event, the project for an inter-Allied Reserve fell flat, as no Allied commander-in-chief provided the quota of divisions stipulated. Haig, with his usual aversion to promising anything that he could not perform, stated definitely that he could not spare any troops for the purpose. He had already sent help to the Italians and he had taken over more line from the French quite recently. He expected, rightly as matters turned out, to have to meet the main German attack, and his force was all too small for the purpose. In the circumstances, the only solution would have been for the British quota to have been taken from troops kept in England, and the French from those watching for a German descent through Switzerland, but the anxiety to be strong everywhere which is always an attribute of a defensive attitude, was too potent a factor.

As an alternative Haig and Pétain came to an agreement for mutual support when the emergency actually arose. As there have been several renderings of this compact, we will take the one which has been furnished by Foch:

If the attack develops against the British front, the French army will send a strong army of five divisions of infantry, four divisions of cavalry, and three regiments of infantry. If it falls on the French group Marshal Haig will send to the support of General Pétain six to eight of his divisions with an equal number of groups of artillery.

Foch italicizes a condition that was attached to Haig's promise. The condition was that the troops could not be sent if the British front was actually being heavily attacked. ("*A condition toutefois que le front britannique ne soit pas lui-même englobé dans une offensive allemande de grand envergure.*")

At a meeting of the Supreme War Council in London on March 14th it was decided to give up the central inter-Allied Reserve. Clemenceau supported the British view and he had a difference of opinion with Foch, who registered a protest.

Foch probably did not know that his friend Henry Wilson had much to do with the decision, as shown by Wilson's diary:

March 14. Meeting of the Supreme War Council at 11.30 at 10 Downing Street. Two hours talk about General Reserve and no decision, then adjournment for lunch. I lunched with Lloyd George and Hankey, and at lunch we drafted a resolution, afterwards adopted, to the effect that, to begin with, no divisions in France should be put in the General Reserve . . .

Foch drew up a long protest, the substance of which he subsequently published.[2] He was staying at the Ritz Hotel, where Wilson saw him the next morning and persuaded him to be content to have his protest recorded. There is not much profit in speculating, in the light of later events, about what would have happened if Foch's executive committee had had the disposal of the proposed inter-Allied Reserve. Foch was not enamoured of committees when rapid decisions and their immediate execution were needed. The emergency occurred within a week, and it is just possible that some of Pétain's divisions on the far-away right of the French line might have been nearer to the danger-point than they were. When Pétain did move them, their proposed destination was in the hands of the enemy. The main effect upon Foch's prospects of the London Conference of March 14th was that it put him out of favour with Clemenceau and apparently deprived him of all further hope of being able to influence events.

On March 21st the main blow fell upon the British Fifth Army and upon the extreme right of the Third Army on its left. As Foch describes it:

[2] *Les deux Batailles de la Marne*, pp. 106-108.

[284]

The German soldiers were inspired by enthusiasm (*élan enthousiaste*) and by complete confidence. The British armies had to face the most formidable assault of the whole War.

The tale of that epic struggle, and of how, in spite of overwhelming odds, the great tidal wave was stemmed before it broke over Amiens, has been told by many pens. The details do not here concern us. The main point was that the British War Cabinet and the Supreme War Council, which had both been discussing sending troops and munitions to other theatres of war, were compelled by the logic of events to concentrate at last upon the fact that the Western Front was the "main theatre" where the War would be lost or won.

On Saturday, March 23rd, after various alarums and excursions in London and telephone calls from Versailles, Milner, in his house in Great College Street, Westminster, was rung up by Lloyd George from Walton Heath to say that someone must go over to France to find out what the position was, and to ask him if he as a member of the War Cabinet could go to Versailles on the next day. Milner started on Sunday morning (Palm Sunday) when the church-goers were dispersing,[3] and after many wanderings, missed rendezvous, and much lobbying with Henry Wilson,[4] Haig, and others, a few minutes after noon on the Tuesday, March 26th, found him arriving in a fast car at the Town Hall of Doullens which now bears the inscription:

In this town-hall, on the 26th of March, 1918, the "Allies" entrusted General Foch with the supreme command on the

[3] Considerable use has here been made of the judicial examination of the historical evidence by W. Basil Worsfold in *United Empire,* 1929.

[4] Before the meeting at Doullens Wilson had seen Foch and sounded him about a proposal to put Clemenceau in executive command of the Allied Armies, with Foch as his assistant.

Western Front. This decision saved France and the liberty of the world.

There is a smack of the eighteenth century both in the style and in the historical inaccuracy of that inscription, but it is well that the events of that day have been engraved in metal. Assembled in the large Council-Chamber were President Poincaré (in the chair), M. Loucheur, Foch, Haig, Wilson, and others. Milner had no authority to take any action, though the emergency was great. He had only been sent to report. The discussion disclosed that the best solution would be to give to Foch as an individual far greater powers than those which the Supreme War Council had given to the Executive Council, now impotent for lack of troops, and that such a selection would receive the support of the French Government through the President and Clemenceau, and of all present. It would have been possible for Milner to telephone to London for authority, but that would have caused delay where every minute was precious, and loss of the psychological moment. Pétain was already prepared to break away from the British to cover Paris. Haig could do no more with the force at his disposal.

In the critical time which preceded the First Battle of the Marne, called by some the turning-point in the War, certain suggestions were made to Marshal Joffre for the action to be taken. Joffre took the responsibility for adopting them, and so won the battle. To Milner suggestions had been made by Henry Wilson and others before the meeting. He now, on his own responsibility, committed the War Cabinet—now the "Imperial" War Cabinet, not only of Britain but of the whole British Empire—to stand behind Foch, trusting him to save the situation in the grave emergency. Foch accepted the charge, and at 2.30 P.M. the document which, as Foch put it, "will go down to history as the 'Doullens agreement'," was signed by Milner and Clemenceau as his authority. Haig and Foch shook each other warmly by both hands on parting.[5] Let us have the remainder of the tale in Foch's own rendering:

Foch tells us that after a quick luncheon he got to work at once. His plan had been ready for a long time. It was necessary to re-establish touch between the French and the British Armies without delay and to cover Amiens. For that to be done, two things were necessary. The troops must not fall back at all and the French divisions as they arrived must be thrown into the gap as quickly as possible. Foch carried those perfectly simple ideas himself to the different commanders,[6] either at their regular or at their fighting headquarters. During the evening of the same day everyone in touch with the enemy knew what was expected of him— resistance, always more resistance, resistance à outrance.

On the next day, the 27th of March, Foch went round again, constantly repeating that it was essential to organise on the actual ground held, and to stay there at all costs. He made sure that his instructions were carried out, if necessary going himself to the subordinate commanders to put things right and correct any mistakes.

Going round again on the 28th,[7] he sensed a gradual rebirth of hope and confidence, and a stiffening resistance. Still the enemy attacked with great violence; he took Mont-

[5] *Life of Lord Rawlinson*, p. 213.

[6] To Gough, commanding the Fifth British Army and chief of staff of the French (First and Third) Armies group, commanded by Fayolle, both at Dury. Then to Paris, to write to Pétain.

[7] To Clermont where he saw Fayolle and Humbert (Third Army); to Dury and Beauquesne, where he saw Gough and Byng (Third British Army).

didier, and at that moment Foch was given evidence of the solidarity of the Allies.

On the 28th of March, Foch was with the headquarters of the Third French Army which were installed in the little village of Clermont on the Oise. General Pershing arrived, came up to Foch and said: ("*Avec une générosité que je n'oublierai jamais*"):

There's no question at this moment but of fighting. Our infantry, our artillery, our air-force, everything that we have is yours, to dispose of as you like.

I have come to tell you that the people of America will be proud to take part in the greatest battle in history.

General Bliss added: "We're here to be killed. How do you want to use us?" Foch attached special value to this meeting as, owing to the urgent need for time, it had not been possible for the American representatives to be present at the Doullens conference, to which Pershing and Bliss thus gave full and complete force. Foch adds: "On my part, I could only reply to their perfect comradeship by at once putting the First American Division facing Mont-didier, in the very centre of the German attack."

On the 29th of March Foch saw Pétain and Fayolle; also Clemenceau, who promised to recall the Staff of the French Tenth Army from Italy; and Haig at Abbeville, there it was decided to "stop the enemy from Arras to the Oise . . . to assemble reserves behind the fighting troops as soon as possible." Meanwhile, Foch and his small Staff settled into two rooms at the Hotel de Ville at Beauvais. On the 30th Foch issued a general order to maintain connexion between the Allied Armies.[8]

[8] Brigadier Charles Grant, in the *Army Quarterly*, January, 1921.

MARSHAL FOCH

The German attacks gradually lost their force towards the end of March. The Allies succeeded in damming the flood, and by the 4th of April the enemy's advance had been definitely arrested, on the line from Arras to the Oise.

On the 5th of April, Foch received the French war correspondents. "Well, gentlemen," he said to them in the few minutes that he could spare, "affairs are not going so badly with us. The Boche (since we must call him so) has not advanced since the 27th of March. Look at the map—the wave is dying on the beach. We have stopped him—now we must try to do better. I think I have no more to say to you—go on with your task—work with your pens, and we will work with our arms." [9]

Foch was always the same, in small things as in great. "Greatness"—he said once—"does not depend upon the size of your command, but upon the way in which you exercise it." In driving others "to the battle" he was supreme. With a minute staff, little more than a personal one, he wielded great masses, appealing not to the troops, but only to the higher commanders, whom he trusted to pass on his spirit; he gave only general directions, and he never interfered in the slightest degree in details; [10] his favourite phrase was "a lost battle is one that one believes lost."

As well as the use that Foch made of an American division, inspired to share at once in the sacrifice that was needed to stem the tide of the enemy's apparently irresistible advance, we can take note also of the willing sacrifice in the British Empire armies. Foch got the last ounce of them in March and April. The casualties that they suffered reached a total of nearly 283,000 during those weeks.

[9] Lieutenant d'Entraygues, in the Paris *Temps.*
[10] Sir H. Edmonds, British Official Historian, *R. U. S. I. Journal.*

CHAPTER XXIV

DURING the months of April, May, June and part of July 1918, Foch was faced by a weight of responsibility which few human beings have been called upon to support. The test of character, determination and steadfast faith then reached its summit. During those momentous weeks the issue between the colossal armies engaged on a frontage extending from Switzerland to the sea was delicately balanced. A single hesitation, failure to secure the loyal co-operation of his French subordinates or of his Allied commanders, physical or mental weariness at a critical juncture, an error in judgment, or weakness in giving way to critics of his proposals—any of these causes might have tipped the balance in favour of the enemy and have caused ruin to himself (of which he took no account) or of the cause to which he had devoted a whole life of preparations.

De quoi s'agit-il? What, in his own accustomed phrase, was the definite problem to be solved? The initiative had passed to the enemy whose plans were unknown. He had massed his reserves in a position from which they could strike westward towards the British and the Channel ports, or once again near the point where the French and the British Armies touched near Amiens, or more to the southward towards the French-defended line and towards Paris which lay beyond. *Omne ignotum pro magnifico*—anxiety over the dangers of the unknown is unavoidable when an army, widely extended, is standing on the defensive. As an old seventeenth-century writer put it, the hostile armament can then at any moment go against one "like an arrow from a bow."

It gives no warning where it is to come. . . . It must wound, too, where it hits, if rightly pointed at a vulnerable part. . . . When this is done a new aim is directed. The enemy [the force on the defensive] in the meantime, like a man in the dark, labouring under an unwieldy shield, moves slowly to and fro, distracted and at a loss which way to go to guard against the stroke of the invisible hand.[1]

When the tremendous blow had fallen upon the British front covering Amiens in March, Pétain hesitated in sending the promised help to his colleague Haig, believing that the main attack was likely to fall upon his own line, and he even made up his mind to break away to cover Paris. The Versailles plan of forming a reserve under Foch had fallen through for want of troops, and the idea of depending upon voluntary co-operation between the Allied Army Commanders had proved abortive. Foch now held what has so often been called the "supreme command," in which he was anything but supreme—having to account for all his actions to Clemenceau—and he held no "command" over the "Commanders-in-Chief" of the Armies of the Allies.

What was the problem? "The major problems?" Foch

[1] *Conjunct Expeditions,* 1759.

said once—"I handle them as if they were minor. It is not difficult. The method is always the same." The method of "the deepest thinker of them all" was to simplify his problem by deep thinking until he got down to the bare essentials, then he made up his mind upon the necessary action to fulfil these essentials, and then he put all else out of his thoughts. He decided that there were two great dangers to be faced: the loss of the Channel ports upon which the British Army was based, and the separation of the French from the British Army. He resented being asked to waste time in explaining his reasons, and he did not intend to risk the chance of maintaining secrecy by stating his future intentions. The cryptic phrase that was most frequently on his lips was *"on fait ce qu'on peut."* Some, who did not understand him, saw futility and even weakness in this constantly repeated phrase. His intimates knew that what he meant was that, for the time, the enemy held the initiative to which it was necessary for him to conform, awaiting his opportunity to deliver an effective counter-stroke. Apart from the moral effect produced by his character and determination, the commander of an army on the defensive can affect the situation only in one way—by using, or by refusing to use, the reserves which he holds in his own hand. When he will use them, having lost the initiative, he does not know, but how he can use them will depend very much upon where he places them.

Foch was constantly asked, during these critical months, which he thought would be the most grievous risk—the loss of the Channel ports, or the separation of the Allied Armies? He always replied that he intended to prevent both these disasters, so "the question cannot arise until I am beaten." That was the spirit that governed his thought and decisions. Only on one occasion, at a meeting of the Supreme War Council at Abbéville on the 1st and 2nd of May, did he go so far as to say that he believed it to be more important to maintain touch between the two Armies than to retain possession of the Channel ports. He was reticent, even with those most intimately connected with him, and that is the only glimpse that we have into his mind on that subject. It was only through the influence of his old friend "Henri" upon the Council that he was forced to make any statement at all.

There is abundant evidence of Foch's opinion of the situation at this juncture in documents not yet published, and in the memories of those who knew Foch most intimately. His main object was to accumulate reserves, at his own disposal, whatever risks he might run by weakening the front line. It was really the old textbook idea that the weaker you are in comparison with your enemy the fewer troops you should put in the front line, and the more you should keep under your own control in reserve. It is one thing to know the maxims of textbooks and quite another to have the strength of character to apply them, refusing to respond to appeals for help by sorely harassed commanders whose troops have suffered almost beyond endurance. To them he used two set phrases, even in the gravest emergencies: "Never withdraw," and "Never relieve tired troops during a battle." He thought that a commander who even discussed the possibility of withdrawal was half-way to carrying it out, and his object being to accumulate reserves, he did not want these reserves to consist of tired troops. They would have to be capable of supreme effort when he did decide to use them.

In dealing with the British, when they had been so sorely

pressed in April, he proposed to establish a system of *"roule-ment"* under which the decimated and weary divisions should not be sent for their periodical rest behind the line in their own area, but to the front line in the quiet French sector, there relieving fresh French divisions which would reinforce Foch's own reserve. He meant to employ that reserve only to avert a grave disaster, or for a purpose which he already had in his mind—a strong counter-attack. The date of that decision is on record, but to disclose it at this stage would reduce the interest in the narrative of Foch's relations with Haig, with the Supreme War Council, and with the Prime Ministers who were the masters of both Commanders. One personal point must be touched upon in that connexion. Foch could look to Clemenceau for loyal and cordial support. In fact it has been said by a shrewd observer in high place that during the two or three weeks that followed the Doullens conference of March 26th, he thought that "Clemenceau, not Foch, was the dominating figure . . . Clemenceau was the driving force and Foch was his military adviser, until Clemenceau saw that Foch was safely in the saddle, when he began to drop out and leave Foch to run things on his own." But the general opinion was that, however it might have been in the political sphere, Foch needed no help in carrying through his military policy. Haig, as is well known, was not so fortunately situated in his relations with the British Prime Minister, of whose desire to depose him there are many reliable reports. Both commanders knew, as all generals who serve democracies know, the risks that they ran. Though the rewards for success, of which neither of them took account, were high, the treatment for failure would be ruthless. Responsibility has been defined as "power to act, and liability to be called to account." The "power to act" granted to Foch was limited. His "liability to be called to account," not always for his own errors, was unlimited. A recent example had been afforded in the treatment that was meted out to Sir Hubert Gough, the Commander of the British Fifth Army, with whose handling of his inadequate force against tremendous odds no fault could be found, and an earlier one on the French side, when General Mangin was made a scapegoat for the Nivelle disaster of 1917, until Clemenceau, above scapegoat making, reached down a strong hand when Foch proposed for him a corps, a decision to bear fruit in July, 1918.

Foch and Haig at one time did not see eye to eye on the step that was taken to fill up the gaps made by the losses suffered by the Fifth Army. Ten British divisions were reduced to mere *cadres,* and the men of those divisions were used to reinforce the remainder. It is difficult to know what other expedient could have been adopted in the circumstances. The estimate of reinforcements likely to arrive from England and the probability of continued fighting, which soon followed, convinced Haig of the futility of re-constituting these divisions. Foch's policy was threefold. The practice had crept in on both sides at this period of the War for the Intelligence Departments to estimate strengths by divisions, paying little heed to their strength, and the moral effect of any reduction in the number of divisions was therefore serious. Foch's views of the dominance of moral over all other factors in war are well known, so his policy was, first to maintain the number of British divisions in the field at as high a figure as possible, secondly to start the *"roulement"* to which we have referred, moving tired British divisions to quiet portions of the French front, and thirdly, to make the

[295]

earliest possible use of the American troops who were then beginning to arrive in large numbers.

Foch looked upon the great battle, while the Germans still held the initiative, as containing two aspects: the "Battle of the North," in which the enemy were trying to reach the Channel ports, and the "Battle of Arras, Amiens, Montdidier," which was intended to force the two Armies apart. His idea was only to feed (*nourrir*) the Army of the North, and to send there only the bare minimum of troops necessary to enable the sorely tried British to lose as little ground as possible (*"Jamais reculer!"*). He determined to accumulate as strong a fresh reserve as possible farther to the southward (astride of the Somme) to prevent the Allied Armies being forced apart, and this affords us a suitable opportunity to draw our own deduction from the fact that Foch had inscribed in one of his books Napoleon's saying: "It is not a guiding spirit (*"Génie"*) that reveals to me secretly in a flash what I must say or do, but thought and reflection." When once he had made up his mind he was adamant, and against even the most desperate appeals by tired troops for relief.

To this we can add the personal impressions formed of Foch at this period by a British officer who knew him well and gradually conceived an increasing admiration for his character and for his outstanding qualities as a commander. Like many others this officer found it difficult to understand Foch's methods of explaining himself. Certain phrases were repeated constantly without explanation. The French Army was referred to as "we" but not the British, which brought out the point that Haig could still only be dealt with as an ally, not as a subordinate. Only those accustomed to

Foch's methods for some considerable time and taken completely into his confidence—Foch did not trust easily, but when he did he trusted thoroughly—were able to interpret his ideas readily. In spite of his age Foch was exceptionally alert, both in mind and in body, and his character was masterful and determined. He knew what he wanted, and he got it accomplished. He was "inspired by soldierly ideas in a marked degree, and a fighter" animated "by no thought other than the successful conduct of the campaign." Another point was that Foch's habit of intervention by dealing with subordinate commanders direct and not through their superiors seems to have become even more accentuated than it was in the days of the Ypres battles of 1914 and 1915. The procedure certainly saved time, but it might have led to difficulties. In the actual event no serious friction arose from this cause. Weygand, for whom Foch could never find high enough praise, seems to have been at his best at this critical time, thoroughly justifying Foch's description some years later: "Weygand! He is a paragon." By his thorough understanding of his Chief he performed great service in getting Foch's wishes carried out both smoothly and quickly—a difficult matter when dealing with Allied Armies. In his "Principles of War" Foch had written a note that Napoleon used to put "Activity! Activity! Speed!" at the bottom of his orders. Foch said *"Without delay* I would add to mine. Weygand declares that that is the expression that I used most during the War." Nevertheless there was none of the "busyness" which R. L. Stevenson once described as "a sign of deficient vitality." He got things done, which "busy" men seldom do. He did not think it sufficient to make a suggestion or to give an order. If it was a case of persuasion, he

stuck to his point to the end, never changing his opinion—
as we shall see later. If it was an order, he saw that it was
carried out.

To summarize: Foch was determined to hold the line
then occupied to the last, sanctioning no retirement, and
doing his best to prevent its being even discussed, on account
of the moral effect which such discussions produce upon a
commander and through him on his troops. His object was
to accumulate reserves, and to keep the bulk of them astride
the Somme to prevent the formation of a gap between the
French and the British Armies, and to be ready for eventualities, which as early as April 3rd included an offensive in
the French zone.

The German reserves were by no means exhausted by the
beginning of the month. Another attack was obviously impending. The British, forecasting correctly, expected that
attack to fall upon them. Pétain, on the other hand, expected
it to be delivered on his front. Foch had only limited powers.
Disclosure of the text of his instructions kills the prevalent
illusion that they enabled him to take rapid action to relieve
the highly critical situation in March. He had no such
powers. He had to waste time travelling between Pétain
and Haig, persuading them to do what he had no power to
order. His personality did what no paper authority could
have achieved, but things were going from bad to worse,
so he applied for further powers at a conference which was
held at Beauvais on April 3rd and attended by Clemenceau,
Lloyd George, Pétain, Haig, and Henry Wilson, and also
by Pershing and Bliss representing the American Army. At
the Doullens conference Foch had been given no power of
"co-ordinating the action" of the "Associated" American
Army with the "Allied" Armies of France, the British Em-

pire, and Belgium. America had not been represented at Doullens.

It was Foch's old friend "Henri," according to Wilson's own diaries, who prevented him from obtaining all the powers for which he asked:

April 3rd.—Tiger [Clemenceau] said position of C. in C.'s wanted more definition. Foch said Doullens [Conference] only "co-ordinated" action, but that if there were no action there would be no co-ordination; hence "direction" should be added in order to bring about "preparation," to be followed by action. I replied that Doullens already gave Foch that power . . . and I was afraid the new definition would raise the question of what was strategy and what was tactics . . .

I drafted a part of Tiger's new declaration into the middle of the Doullens agreement, and added at the end a paragraph of right of appeal of each C.-in-C. to his government if he received from Foch any instructions which he thought would endanger the army.

Introduction of the power of appeal, not at Foch's suggestion, is the interesting point. On one occasion Haig very nearly resorted to this procedure, but he finally abstained from doing so. On other occasions members of the Government which he served wished Haig to adopt this form of protest, but he loyally supported Foch and complied with what appeared, in some British eyes, to be Foch's excessive demands. The actual wording of the decision of the Beauvais conference ran:

General Foch is charged by the British, French, and American Governments with the duty of co-ordinating the action of the Allied Armies on the Western Front; and with this object in view there is conferred upon him all the powers necessary for its effective accomplishment. For this purpose the British, French, and American Governments entrust to General Foch the strategic direction, so Foch succeeded in getting that requirement of military operations. The Commanders-in-Chief of the British, French, and American Armies shall exercise in full the tactical conduct of their Armies. Each Commander-in-Chief shall have the right to appeal to his Government if, in his opinion, his Army finds itself placed in danger by any instructions received by General Foch.

That kills, once for all, the illusion that Foch was made "Generalissimo" in the sense that he was authorized to give any orders he liked to the Allied generals. According to his instructions he could not even order them to attack, which comes within the province of tactics, but Foch could do such things by inspiration better than others could do them by the medium of orders, and, in the French Army, he had the advantage of being able to choose subordinate commanders in sympathy with his ideas. Sometimes it was a little unfortunate that "Foch's men" were not always those with whom the British Army found it easiest to work, but that, perhaps, was unavoidable.

Public opinion in France had been unsympathetic and somewhat cruel towards the British Army in the days that followed the great German attack of March 21st, from which the British succeeded in saving Amiens; and on the British side there was an undoubted feeling of soreness, the impression that Pétain had been disloyal in leaving his Allies in the lurch when the publicly proclaimed object of the Germans at this time was to knock out the British Army once for all. These feelings formed an important factor in the situation with which Foch had to deal. He dealt with them successfully, and it is sufficient to add that the relations gradually improved, especially when the French were faced by a similar ordeal and, by the request of Foch and the loyalty of Haig, British divisions shared with them in that ordeal. The immediate blows, however, from the 9th of April onwards, were again delivered in the British zone, and by the 12th the situation in Flanders caused grave anxiety.

Chapter XXV

THE SUPREME TEST: APRIL–JULY, 1918

THE FIRST STAGE: APRIL (CONTINUED)

AGED 66 YEARS

"ONE must *do* something. That is understood. But with an aim, a plan, a method. At first reflect, study the problems . . . but do not start off at that stage without knowing what you are going to do. Know what it is you *will,* and do it. . . . In action one does not study; one simply does what one can to apply what one knows." So Foch had written in the old days of his academic teaching, and he had also written that in action it became a question of applying truths unconsciously and automatically—"we must be steeped in them." As a veracious reader in his youth and an admirer of Clausewitz as a deep thinker ("Clausewitz—there's a man for you!") one of the truths with which Foch's knowledge was stored must have been the truth about what Clausewitz calls the "culminating point of victory," [1] when the attacker has come to the end of his resources and has reached the summit of his success. If he cannot then take full advantage of his gains, woe betide him if he cannot at once enforce a favourable peace. The tide is turning. If he fails to seize that moment he will be immersed in the flood of reaction. For that culminating point Foch was patiently waiting, running the

[1] *On War,* Bk. VII, Ch. XXII.

[302]

grave risk that the British Army would be engulfed by the rising flood.

On April 9th the blow fell upon the British front. A heavy bombardment from the La Bassée Canal to Armentières, followed by strong attacks, forced back the Portuguese division (due for relief on that day) and then the British to the line of the Lys at Estaires. Neuve Chapelle was lost. Hangard was lost and retaken. Elsewhere attacks were repulsed. On the 10th the battle extended northwards, and the enemy reached the left bank of the Lys. North of Armentières the line was forced back to Wytschaete, Messines Ridge, and Ploegstreete. Armentières was abandoned. On the 11th fighting became general on the whole front, the British line being bent back to south of Neuve Eglise and Bailleul. Merville was lost. Minor attacks south of Arras were repulsed. The Germans claimed 20,000 prisoners up to date. On the 12th strong enemy pressure was continued. Neuve Eglise and Messines were penetrated. It was estimated that one hundred and ten German divisions had been engaged, and this was the day of Haig's great "Backs to the Wall" appeal.

First words of praise and encouragement:

Words fail me to express the admiration which I feel for the splendid resistance offered by all ranks in our Army.

Not "my" Army—the Army of all of us. And then the sympathy of a comrade, exposed to the same ordeal:

Many of us are now tired. To those I would say that victory will belong to the side which holds out the longest.

And then the final appeal for a last great effort:

There is no course open to us but to fight it out. Every position must be held to the last man. There must be no retirement. With our backs to the wall and believing in the justice of our cause, each one of us must fight on to the end.

That historic appeal combined the body of the brief *"jamais reculer"* of Foch with the soul of Haig the Commander in intimate touch with his sorely harassed troops, some of whom had already met the hammer-blow of the great "Kaiser Battle" for Amiens and had been sent northward for rest and recuperation in what was then a quiet part of the line. Foch's forecast—gamble if the term is preferred—on the steadfastness of British troops in the defence had been justified in the event. So far, the great German attack had failed, and Foch's object, to accumulate reserves astride the Somme, had suffered no serious set-back; but there were still more anxious days to come. It is on record, on first-hand evidence, that on the 13th of April Foch thought that the enemy's attacks were dying down. He had been fully warned by Haig of the impending attack. On April 6th Haig had told him in writing that information pointed to the enemy's intention to continue his efforts to destroy the British Army, and Haig had appealed either for a vigorous offensive by the French on a big scale to draw away the enemy's reserves, or for four French divisions to relieve British troops south of the Somme, or for a group of the same number of divisions to be sent somewhere near St. Pol as a reserve for the British front.

Foch had the unwavering support of Clemenceau, but on the 8th of April the question of recalling Haig was discussed in the British War Cabinet. Foch on the 7th had refused to respond to Haig's appeal of the 6th, and the War Cabinet authorized Sir Henry Wilson, in whose diaries these things are recorded, to cross over to Flanders with full powers to do what he thought best. Wilson saw Foch for two hours on the 10th and records that "Foch would not hear of relieving us either up at Ypres or at Amiens." On the same day Wilson saw Clemenceau "who began by saying that never, never, never, would he make peace," and they discussed what Haig should do if forced back. Clemenceau advocated a swing-back of the British left, uncovering the Channel ports, to join the French on the Somme. Wilson would not hear of this and said that the British right must fall back, swinging back towards the sea and covering the ports (Foch strongly objected to all such discussions, and claimed that he must be judged by results. There was no object in meeting disaster half-way. He could not say how he would deal with a situation until it actually arose. His main object was to accumulate reserves, upon which all would depend).

On the same date (April 10th) apparently on the advice of Wilson, Haig wrote a protest to Foch, reporting the gravity of the situation, stating that in his opinion the steps decided upon by Foch would not deal with the situation adequately, and adding that it was of vital importance that the French should relieve some part of the British line immediately, and take an active share in the battle. These steps were necessary in the combined interest of the Allied Armies. On the 11th Haig reported further to Foch that all his divisions had been engaged, the fighting was still severe, the enemy was still pressing towards Hazebrouck and Calais, and it was urgently important to concentrate at once at least four French divisions between St. Omer and Dunkirk, ready to support the British Army. The next day (April 12th) was the day of Haig's great appeal to his Army "with our backs to the wall." On the 13th Foch thought that the situation had been relieved and that the battle was dying down, as it did for a very short time. On the 10th Wilson had recorded in his diary "Foch wants a title [apparently meaning a designation giving him greater authority] for himself." [2] Clemenceau suggested "Commander-in-Chief of the Allied Forces" but the Doullens and Beauvais agreement only referred to France, so "Commander-in-Chief of Allied Forces in France" was suggested and this title was conferred upon him on April 14th. The Belgian Army remained, however, under King Albert as its constitutional Commander-in-Chief.

On the 13th Clemenceau telegraphed to ask Lloyd George to come over to see him, and Sir William Furse, a member of the Army Council, had an amusing story, published with the Wilson diaries, of how Wilson prevented his going over, as told to him by Wilson at the time:

W. Furse: Well, did you dissuade him?

H. Wilson: We are not going, but it was the devil to get it home to him. After much talk I said [very slowly, with many pauses and in his deepest tones]: "There are times—and seasons —when a Prime Minister's presence is worth—his weight—in diamonds— There are other times—and seasons—especially when a decisive battle is in the fighting—when a Prime Minister's presence—is nothing but—an infernal nuisance."

W. Furse: Did that settle it?

H. Wilson: Yes! Arthur Balfour was the only other present, and when I said that he exploded with laughter, put his hand on my shoulder with a clap, and said "Quite right. Quite right."

And Foch was thereby saved from sore embarrassment in the midst of a grave crisis. We can now pass to his attitude up to April 14th, on which date an important conference was held between Foch and Haig at which Milner, repre-

[2] Up to this time he had been addressed simply as "General Foch" with no indication of his position.

senting the British Government, was present. Haig pressed the point that the British Army had borne the brunt of the fighting since the 21st of March, thus exhausting its reserves. He did not, so far, ask for French troops in the front line, or even in the actual battle zone, but that the small reserve under Maistre, north of the Somme, should be moved further northward in readiness. Foch held to his original position again embodied in the words: *"On fait ce qu'on peut"*—*"Jamais reculer"*—*"Jamais la relève pendant la bataille."* The proceedings were lightened by one of Haig's remarks. During the discussion, Foch constantly interpolated the exclamation *"Bon!"* Haig retorted, *"Ce n'est pas bon du tout!"*—which seems to have relieved the tension.

The situation was worse than Foch had imagined, as the Germans soon returned to the attack. We have followed the narrative up to the 12th of April. On the 13th the British re-captured Neuve Eglise, and stood fast elsewhere against continuous attacks. On the 14th Neuve Eglise was lost again and the British line was temporarily penetrated near Bailleul. On the 15th Bailleul and Wulverghem were lost. On the 16th very heavy attacks developed against the British. It was on that day that an important meeting at Abbeville was attended by Milner, Foch, Weygand, Haig, Lawrence (Chief Staff Officer) and Wilson, who had come over at Milner's request.

The meeting of April 16th seems to have been rather a difficult one. Foch and his friend "Henri" no longer saw eye to eye. Wilson had recommended salt-water inundations to stop the German progress on the Dunkirk line. Haig produced data showing that it would take thirty-five to forty days to make such inundations effective, so if they were to be of use, they would have to be started at once. Foch would have nothing to do with the idea. On April 12th he had given orders for a small inundation ("*barrage*") of fresh water, and that was as far as he would go. Even this had to be much restricted as it flooded the roads. Plumer, commanding the Second Army, wanted reinforcements. Foch thought that the two French infantry and three cavalry divisions already sent (on the "*nourrir*" principle) were enough, and finally "nothing was settled," though much valuable time seems to have been expended. On April 17th Wilson was present when Foch gave Plumer his instructions which consisted of holding his present ground and "tidying up."

Afterwards Wilson had a long talk with Foch alone, telling him that there were two courses: to accept battle, or to retire with the left resting on inundations. (The account reminds one of Foch's saying in earlier days, to the effect that he had no use for other people's suggestions.) Wilson added that if Foch accepted battle he must call up more troops. Foch replied that he intended to accept battle without more troops, and he then left to visit General Plumer and the Belgians.

The result of the fighting on the 16th of April was that Wytschaete and Meteren were lost and retaken, and attacks elsewhere repulsed, but Passchendaele had to be abandoned on account of German progress on the river Lys. There was also heavy fighting south of Arras. On April 17th a heavy bombardment had been followed by infantry attacks on the whole line. Wytschaete and Meteren were lost again.

Foch's attitude at this date in private conversation has been recorded. He wanted to discourage all discussion of withdrawals and to insist upon a step-by-step defence.

Why lower the *moral* of your troops by such a retirement and let the enemy advance half-way to Calais without a fight?

If you fight, how many weeks, if not months, will it take the enemy to get to St. Omer, and how many fresh divisions will be used in the process? Make him a present of nothing.

On April 18th Haig again made strong representations to Foch about the need for more troops to reinforce Plumer's Second Army which was in a sorry plight owing to heavy casualties sustained. It was understood that five French infantry divisions and three cavalry divisions would soon be at Plumer's disposal, but three more divisions were needed to enable the British Army to continue to play its part. This representation was strongly backed up in writing by Henry Wilson, adding that Haig would carry out Foch's wishes in the most loyal manner. Foch's reply was to ask Haig for four divisions to relieve French troops—on a quiet portion of the front—the original *"roulement"* proposal. Haig at once promised to do so without any considerable delay, and proposed to send a Corps Headquarters with them (19th of April).

On the 23rd of April Haig informed Foch that one of these divisions would be ready to entrain on the 25th, the remainder as soon as tired divisions could be relieved by French troops on the spot. At the same time he reminded Foch that, after the heavy losses that the British Army had suffered, he had been obliged to disband five divisions, owing to shortage of reinforcements from England, and he was giving orders for the disbandment of four more. He strongly recommended on about April 27th the French taking over seventeen kilometres of front line from the British.

Between the 17th and 27th of April, an intense bombardment, followed by an infantry attack, had been held up on the 17th in the British sector. Further heavy attacks followed on the 18th; the enemy made a slight advance about Givenchy. There was sharp fighting on the 19th, in which the British took some prisoners. Minor operations occurred on the 20th, 21st, and 22nd. Then violent enemy artillery fire and heavy infantry attacks at Albert and between the Somme and Aisne. During this battle one hundred and two German divisions had been identified as having attacked the British front alone up to date. On the 24th further violent attacks occurred on the junction between the British and French in the Amiens sector, south of the Somme. On the 25th there were further violent attacks, but the Allies retook Villers-Bretonneux, lost on the day before; on this day Mount Kemmel, held by the French, was lost. On the 26th there were further violent attacks in the Ypres area and elsewhere, and on the 27th further attacks about Ypres.

The 27th of April was to prove a critical day. Milner and Wilson came over for a conference at Abbeville, attended also by Clemenceau, Foch, Weygand, Haig, Lawrence, and Du Cane (liaison officer between Foch and Haig). Wilson arrived at the conference upset by the fact that Foch had not sanctioned the salt-water inundations, in spite of Wilson's urgent representations ten days before. He records in his diary:

I raised the subject of *roulement* and punishment. I pointed out that our 60 divisions had had 300,0000 loss and their (French) 100 divisions had had 60,000-70,000 losses. I pointed out that if this went on, and we started a *roulement,* the British Army would disappear and we should lose the War; and then I proposed that the French should take some of the punishment. Foch said he would not relieve during a battle, and there was no good relieving when there was no fighting.

[310]

An important point elicited at this conference was Clemenceau's proposal to send two French officers to England to study the question of British man-power, the idea being to discover whether reinforcements could be sent to Haig and so ease the situation and enable the British to stand still further punishment. Wilson went from Abbeville to Versailles where he was told by his liaison officer that there was a dangerous campaign on foot in France to depreciate the British Army and to exalt the French. The *Matin* and Clemenceau's paper the *Homme Libre* had published dangerous articles. This was not very helpful to Foch, who knew the true circumstances, which were these:

His anticipation that the German attacks in the Battle of the Lys would die down were being fulfilled, though a fortnight later than he expected. On the 28th further attacks were repulsed. On this date it was announced that American troops were now on the northern battle front. On the 29th the Battle of the Lys was over.

Foch had won the first round, but he had been obliged to increase his French D.A.N. (*Détachement de l'Armée du Nord*) to nine divisions and three cavalry divisions. The Germans had lost very heavily. They had gained no important advantage, and their line now formed a salient which was a death trap to their troops, who were shelled out of it by the British guns.

Foch had clearly not known how supreme the effort and how great the losses of the British would be, but they did all that he had required of them, with a bare minimum of "nourishment" from the reserves which Foch was bent upon accumulating for an object which was disclosed at a later date.

By the time when he again was summoned to attend a

full-dress conference—this time of the Supreme War Council
—his policy had been justified by events. The Council met
on the 1st and 2nd of May at Versailles, and the divergence
between Foch and Wilson became more pronounced.

We can conclude this chapter with Foch's own version of
his policy as he described it to Major Bugnet, his A.D.C., in
after years:

Q: They said to me: "There are the Channel ports and Paris.
Which are you going to defend—the ports or Paris?"
Foch: "Both."
Q: "But if you have to let one or the other go?"
Foch: "I shall let nothing go."
Q: "But if you really have to?"
Foch: "I shall hold on and defend both: nothing shall be
let go."
There is nothing to let go . . . I did not let anything go.

Then he tells what, at the time, was his method and his
intention. This was not "wisdom after the event" or *"esprit
d'escalier."* The evidence of British officers who were near
him at the time and of many contemporary documents,
support his claim fully:

What was to be done? We could not afford to lose a yard
of ground, and, above all, it was necessary to maintain liaison
with the Allies. To do that, the first thing to do was to hold
the enemy and to stand fast. There was only one way to do
this—to reorganize, cost what it might, in the positions we held
and with our feeble resources. Only after that could we think
of relief.

Then we must also counter-attack to break down offensives.

But even this is insufficient; we must conquer, that is to say,
attack. To do that we must have reserves. After that to build
them up.

Looking back at those days eleven years later, now that passing misunderstandings and propaganda have died down, we can see clearly that it was not the choice of Foch, but of the Germans, which in those critical days caused the British to be tried almost beyond endurance under Foch's "directives." If the blows in April had fallen upon the French portion of the line, as Pétain constantly expected, there is no reason to suppose that Foch would have parted with his reserves, which were covering the point of junction between the Armies, in order to help Pétain to any greater extent than he helped Haig. The policy of *"nourrir"* would then have been applied to a *Bataille de l'Est* just as it was actually applied to the *Bataille du Nord*. To anticipate for a moment, we can note that this view is supported by the action that Foch took on the 8th of June, when a German attack on the British front appeared to him to be imminent. He sent instructions to Pétain to be prepared to send reserves to the British front in the same way that he had required Haig to hold British reserves ready to go to the French front on a previous occasion. On June 17th Pétain was arranging to send six divisions and a corps of cavalry to the British front if seriously attacked.

Nevertheless there is no doubt that at the time the inter-Allied relationship passed through a critical stage, and full advantage was taken of every such opportunity by enemy propagandists. Of this the writer can supply evidence. During the period mentioned he was serving in the Secretariat of the War Cabinet in Whitehall and the study of all propaganda and its influence upon the situation came within his province. It was reported one morning that in society and on the Boulevards of Paris a rumour was being spread that the British had sent only 400,000 men to the aid of the

French whom they were leaving to their fate, not taking upon themselves a proper share in the fighting.[3]

In considering the military operations one had constantly to bear in mind their effect upon public opinion, and of that upon the governments concerned. The tall wireless stations on both sides were continually shouting at each other, and those on the German side were naturally making the most of any opportunity of driving a wedge between the French and British nations, while Foch was expecting attempts to drive a wedge between the Armies. The reply to the Paris gossip was "The Boche says that there are only 400,000 British soldiers in France. They must be fine men to have stopped over 1,000,000 Germans from reaching Amiens in March." The shrieks of those high-power wireless stations vibrating in circumambient space were compared by an imaginative writer to the screams of women echoing above the combatants in a street-fight in a London slum.

Propaganda certainly was a force to be counted on by Foch as by other commanders, but it seems to the writer to be inconceivable that the French press could have played the enemy's game by trying to force the hands of the British Government in the matter of sending stronger reinforcements to Haig, and he retains no memory of any such incident. The subject of the reconstruction of Haig's depleted divisions and its effect is dealt with elsewhere.

[3] Even after this long interval, it may be interesting to quote these figures. On April 1st, 1918, the British Expeditionary forces abroad, excluding native labour corps, numbered about 2,800,000, of whom nearly 1,850,000 were serving in France.

Chapter XXVI

THE SUPREME TEST: APRIL-JULY, 1918

THE SECOND STAGE: MAY

AGED 66 YEARS

So far we have concentrated our attention upon the influences that were brought to bear upon Foch during this critical stage of the struggle on the Western Front, rather than upon the action which he took in reply to various appeals, as disclosed in the orders or the directives which he issued. His policy, while based continually and unswervingly upon his original views of the best solution, was constantly affected by the actual events, sometimes foreseen, but usually unexpected—the "unexpected" which "always happens" in war, and against which provision must be made. For this reason it will be more convenient to reserve our consideration of Foch's actual orders until the close of what we can call the defensive period which lasted until July. We can then review his action in a continuous statement, unbroken by diversions to consider the other authorities that were affected.

The Versailles Conference of May 1st and 2nd marked a crisis, and the whole question of unity of command then hung in the balance. The Supreme War Council had originally been established as a device for securing, by direct discussion between the principals, a more efficient and a more rapid combined control over the conduct of the War by the Allied Governments concerned than the previous method of diplomatic correspondence had afforded. It introduced the principle of diplomacy by conference. It unified political control, as a step towards unifying military control, which was exercised on its behalf by an Executive Board, even as the Doullens and the Beauvais agreements unified military control in so far as the Western Front was concerned. This Versailles Conference was attended by Clemenceau, Foch, Pétain on behalf of France; Pershing, Bliss, and Frazier (Counsellor of Embassy) on behalf of the United States; Orlando on the part of Italy; Milner, Wemyss (First Sea Lord), Henry Wilson, Lawrence, Sackville West [1] and others, and one of the first steps taken was to abolish the Executive Board for which there was no further use if the governments concerned were consistent in their wish that Foch should be in control. Another discussion referred to the American troops and their distribution on arrival. To this we shall revert later.

Wilson gives this account of the discussion of May 2nd in his diary:

I at once raised the question of the Channel ports and the Somme. Foch said if retirement was necessary he would conduct all along the line. I said that this was no answer to my question, and I asked my question again. Haig said that it was vital to hold on to the French. In his opinion to get separated from the French meant absolute disaster, as both Armies and ports would be lost. Foch said that such a retirement as we were considering would never occur, but, if it did, he would fall back to the South and base himself on France. Wemyss

[1] British Military Representative with the Supreme War Council. Now (1929) Lord Sackville, Governor of the Channel Islands.

and the French Admiral both seemed to think that if we lost the ports we lost everything. Foch asked for more labour. Pétain underlined my question and Foch's final answer, and that it had now been decided that for the British to hold on to the French came first, and the ports second. This was unanimously agreed to.

Before proceeding further, it is interesting to note that we find in Wilson's diary nine days later that he advised Lloyd George and Milner to bring Haig home to succeed French in Ireland, where serious trouble seemed to be brewing.

Except for local fighting there was comparative quiet on the British front in Flanders from the beginning of May, and Haig's Army was given an opportunity to recuperate and to reorganize for three months, which was to cost the enemy dear. A point to be noted is that in his estimates of requirements in reinforcements when he determined to reduce the number of his divisions, Haig had expected that the heavy casualties would continue. As matters turned out he not only was able to respond to Foch's appeal for troops to reinforce Pétain, but, by the first week in August, he was ready to launch Rawlinson's Fourth Army in the Battle of Amiens which surprised not only the enemy but Foch himself in the progress made towards decisive victory. We have noted Haig's agreement, as stated by Wilson, with Foch's appreciation of the importance of not allowing the Allied Armies to be forced apart by the enemy. There was still some divergence of opinion on the question of reducing the number of British divisions, but the situation being easier, Haig was able to meet Foch half-way by the 11th of May, by which date Foch expected the crisis of the defensive campaign to come within the next few weeks.

Clemenceau's proposal to send French officers to England

to examine the position in British man-power which at first somewhat startled the British authorities, as was natural, ultimately bore fruit, the result being that neither Foch nor Weygand could find any criticism to make, excepting that our Class B men, trained but physically unfit for service overseas, led to some comment. Then also, in connexion with reducing the divisions, Foch wanted the number of battalions in each to be reduced from twelve to nine, and the number of men in a battalion from nine hundred—some stood at one thousand—to eight hundred—a measure that the French had been obliged to introduce under the pressure of the Army in the days of the Somme (1916). What Foch was constantly pressing for was a strong reserve under his own control. The main point, however, was to secure more reinforcements from England, and in this Wilson supported Foch and Haig most loyally, starting a rigorous "comb-out," and proposing to use Class B men for reconstructing some of Haig's *cadre* divisions. On May 16th Haig met Foch at Montreuil, and agreed to this proposal, though he doubted the value of "B" men. He gave way to Foch on the question of raising the divisions to a strength of twelve battalions and agreed to the nine-battalion organization, but he could not accept the proposal for weak battalions of eight hundred men. A start was thus made in the direction which Foch wanted, and we must bear in mind, as affecting Haig, that it was still widely believed that one of the principal objects of German strategy was to destroy the British Army. The French Army had not been really seriously engaged, so there was much to lend colour to this view, but their ordeal was yet to come. No one at that time, neither Foch nor Haig, imagined that the Germans would leave the British front comparatively quiet for three invaluable months.

Foch's policy of the *roulement*—sending worn-out British divisions to the French front to relieve fresh French divisions which passed into the reserve—was the next to be developed. Haig, as we saw, sent one more division in April in response to Foch's appeal, and three more were being prepared. The Supreme War Council on the 2nd of May endorsed this policy, and the despatch of Corps Headquarters of the IXth Corps and these three divisions was approved, to be followed by two more, six in all. These four divisions were actually sent, making five in all, the "quiet" area chosen for them by Pétain being the Chemin des Dames.

Pétain, needless to say, chose in good faith this area for the tired British divisions to rest and to reorganize. Unluckily the Germans again succeeded in achieving a complete surprise, as will appear in due course. The result as far as the British tired divisions was concerned was that in spite of their weakness in numbers and the heavy losses that they had faced, they "comported themselves admirably under trying and difficult circumstances," and the French commanders, Foch included, recognised their services to the full. The five divisions of the British IXth Corps were opposed by eleven German divisions. It is a good tribute to the effectiveness of enemy propaganda, which would doubtless be pleaded in excuse, that the villagers showed hostility to the British troops who had endured so much for the defence of French soil.

The time has now arrived for us to take count of a factor which affected the military situation above all others, especially in its moral effect, at this stage in the War. The Germans, in ignoring the ethical factor—the "soul which exists in nations" [2]—had in 1917 thrown the whole of the mili-

[2] Sir Edward Grey—now Viscount Grey of Fallodon—in defining "militarism."

tary man-power of the United States of America into the balance against them. Largely through the instrument of British sea-power, of which so little account was taken by Foch, Joffre, and Henry Wilson in the pre-war interview that we have described, American troops were beginning to pour across the Atlantic. For a time German propaganda ignored their existence, and it was not until they were met with in the front line that the true facts became known in Germany. Much depended upon the time factor. If whole units were sent, divisions complete with their artillery, engineers, transport, and subsidiary services in addition to the infantry, the time that must pass before they could take part in the actual fighting would be indefinitely prolonged. Much training and experience in handling large units were needed before such a measure could be contemplated. The smaller and simpler the unit, the sooner it would be fit to take its place alongside the veterans of previous experience in the ordeal of modern battle. Foch's first demand now was for men, the second for men, and the third for men. Man-power was failing on both sides of the long line of battle in France and Flanders, and the quickest way to render American man-power available to take an active part in the conflict was to send the infantry over first. Mr. Lloyd George had asked President Wilson to do this at the time when the great "Kaiser-Battle" in March had taken the German troops within gun-range of Amiens, and the response was immediate.

A question was now arising about the best use to which the masses of American infantry could be put now that they were actually arriving. The British Government, the Army Council, and Haig were all particularly anxious to make use of large numbers with the British Army. Not much was known of the standard of training which had been reached, but it was obvious that they could render the best service, for the time, if they were embodied in the experienced formations, and everything pointed to the British Empire troops for the purpose, on account of the language problem which would interfere with a proper understanding if they were embodied in French formations.

Foch agreed. When, however, details were discussed difficulties arose, and it was not easy to discover the best solution. Foch, as usual, simplified the problem as far as circumstances allowed. He laid special stress on two points in his communications with Haig. "Maintain the number of your divisions, and make use of the American troops as soon as possible. If they are not fit for the battle-front, put them on quiet portions of the front line."

Four proposals were put forward: either to make the British divisions up to twelve battalions by adding a regiment of American infantry; or to make up the British *cadre* divisions to nine battalions, mixing British and American troops, or to make up the *cadre* British divisions entirely with American infantry; or to train the American troops with the British in small bodies gradually increasing their size up to the regiment which would then take its place in an American division. A compromise was ultimately made which answered well, but only after prolonged discussion. The arrangement was that the infantry of ten American divisions should be trained with the British Army, but there were never more than five in the British zone at the same time, and only two remained until the end of the War.

Pershing during the discussions referred constantly to the effect upon the American public which would want a separate American Army, fighting under its own commanders, at the earliest possible date. It seems that everyone saw the strength of his point, but if it were pressed too far the American Army might not be in the field in time to avert defeat, of which the Americans would be mere spectators. Foch constantly repeated *"Il faut se servir des Américains le plus tôt possible."* By the 12th of June Pershing had decided not to send any more American troops to be trained either with the British or with the French Army, and in that connexion we must bear in mind the prevalent impression that the War would still be going on in 1919. When the decision was made the situation had become acute again from the end of May, on account of the successful blow struck by the Germans at the French Army; but, in view of Pershing's opinion, Foch accepted the American decision.

It was the blow on the 27th of May that killed, once for all, Foch's policy of *roulement,* of sending tired Allied divisions to quiet portions of the French line. Foch's reason for it—the accumulation of a reserve of fresh French divisions—had disappeared. The French Army was so heavily engaged that it had plenty of tired troops of its own for purposes of *roulement,* and thenceforward British tired troops were in the main rested behind their own front line. Questions of the disposal of reserves of fresh British divisions still arose, and these will be dealt with in due course. We can now revert to Foch's policy, which he urged upon Haig and upon the British Government, to reconstitute the British divisions which had been reduced to mere *cadres.*

The conference between Foch and Haig on the 16th of May resulted as we have seen in an agreement, Haig agreeing to take Class B men from England, and to the nine-battalion organisation, which he hoped to increase to twelve battalions with American troops, but not giving way on the subject of the weak eight-hundred-men battalions. A start was made at once to carry out Foch's wishes, and they bore fruit in due season. Full use was made of the three months of comparative quiet on the British front. The impression made upon independent observers in close touch with Foch was that while the credit must be given primarily to Haig and to the British Government, Foch's influence and the impetus that he had given had a most beneficial effect. He placed a high value upon the British Army and he contemplated with dismay all ideas of allowing it to dwindle. These opinions he expressed constantly. With our usual British inconsistency we protested that we could not meet his wishes and in the end we did far more than he expected. It is, perhaps, better in the end to perform without promising than it is to promise without performing, and Foch in his academic days had always said that his standard of judgment rested upon action, not upon words.

Bearing in mind the forces behind the lines—the influence of discussions in high circles and of propaganda in low places—we can now deal briefly with the events on the Western Front in May, 1918. It is unavoidable that in a book on Foch as seen through English eyes, it is necessary to devote more space to his activities in connexion with the "English" than with the French, American, or Belgian Armies. Historical evidence bearing on the British relationship is abundant, and it will be almost overwhelming when the celebrated Haig diaries are released for researchers. On the other hand very little contemporary first-hand evidence on Foch from the French point of view in 1918 is as yet accessible.[3] General Weygand's authority on such matters is

[3] Since these words were written General Weygand's article on his Chief appeared in the *Revue des deux Mondes*. This will be dealt with later. (Author.)

indisputable, but it is understood that he considers that any such publication would be premature. We will therefore adhere to our brief, and touch upon the operations of May, 1918, chiefly from the British point of view.

Excepting for a strong local attack on the 8th of May when the Germans entered the front line near Morlancourt, there were no serious operations until the 15th, when heavy artillery fire with local infantry attacks opened on the whole front. Air forces were active on both sides with bombing machines, and only local "ground" attacks occurred on either side up to the 26th of May. On the 27th a storm followed the calm. The British had constantly expected a renewal of the German attacks, and, according to their intelligence reports, they thought that an attack with sixty to eighty divisions might be expected to develop between the Lys and the Somme. Foch did not agree. His idea was that the failure in Flanders had crippled the Germans and that they had not enough troops available to make an attack on so large a scale. He expected the calm to last longer, while the enemy was hesitating about the direction of his next blow. Meanwhile Foch was continuing his policy of accumulating reserves for a counter-stroke, especially on preparations for a French attack on the Noyon-Montdidier front. He wanted to free the vulnerable railway lines passing through Amiens. On the 21st he issued a directive with this purpose in view, the British to co-operate with the French. There were various discussions between Foch and Haig about this and alternative policies, the Allied intelligence departments differing in their information. It was not until the 25th of May that any special attention was drawn in the French area to the Chemin des Dames, and not until the 26th that anything definite seems to have been reported. On that evening

Foch was asked whether he thought that a great attack was pending, and he replied that he did not think so. Similar reports had reached him from all parts of the line every day.

The storm burst on the next day, and before nightfall the enemy penetrated fifteen kilometres into the French line. The "Third Battle of the Aisne" came as a complete surprise. On the 28th the enemy crossed the Aisne on an eighteen-mile front. On the 29th they took Soissons. On the 30th they reached the Marne, and by the 31st held the river from Château-Thierry to Dormans. By the 1st and 2nd of June a violent battle developed on the River Ourcq but the tide was stemmed, French and American troops driving the enemy back across the Marne on the 3rd of June.

Never was Foch so much admired by British observers as he was in that great battle. His command, his reputation, the success of his plans, were all at stake. He had the enemy in front of him, and the Supreme War Council behind him. They assembled on May 31st and they met on June 1st and 2nd, when feeling ran very high. First Clemenceau, Foch, Weygand, Lloyd George, Milner, Haig, Lawrence, and Wilson met and discussed the prospects of American arrivals, and Foch again pressed hard for keeping up the number of British divisions. Wilson backed Foch, and Lloyd George offered Clemenceau to send a man over to England to "see if he could find any men." [4] Then came a mass meeting of the Supreme War Council. Then, at 7 P.M. a small meeting—Milner, Foch, Pershing and Wilson—discussed the American contingents. There were further long meetings on the afternoon of June 2nd and an argument took place between Wilson and Foch on the relative strength of the armies in divisions.

[4] *Wilson Diaries,* Vol. II, p. 103.

The strain on Foch during these and the preceding days must have been very heavy. He had recently changed his headquarters twice, first to Monchy, then to about fifteen kilometres south of Beauvais, and then again to Bom Bon, near Melun, where he was within forty minutes by car from Pétain's headquarters at Provins. He was with Pétain in the morning, then at the Supreme War Council, and then he had an hour and a quarter's run to get back to his headquarters. In addition to the physical effort there was the mental strain of the acrimonious discussions at Versailles where all were critical and no one made things easier for him. The Versailles atmosphere was full of apprehension. Discussions were going on between individuals about what was to be done "when Paris had fallen," and it was a case of "taking counsel of their fears," or what Nelson used so much to deride as "painting pictures." We cannot do better than take verbatim an account by a British observer who was at Versailles at the time:

Foch was calm and confident. He drew a little diagram of a modern battle, which, simple as it was, did much to make others share his confidence as the days went by and the line was not penetrated. The diagram [see opposite page], he explained, illustrated the waves of the attack, which tended to diminish as its energy was consumed. To all who asked him how things were going he replied: *"Pas mal. Les vagues diminuent."*

There we will leave him, "calm and confident," for the time being. At the same time we must bear in mind the inevitable British soreness at the use to which—through the misleading intelligence collected by Pétain's intelligence bureau or through some other cause—the British IXth Corps of tired divisions, sent for rest, recuperation, and reorgan-

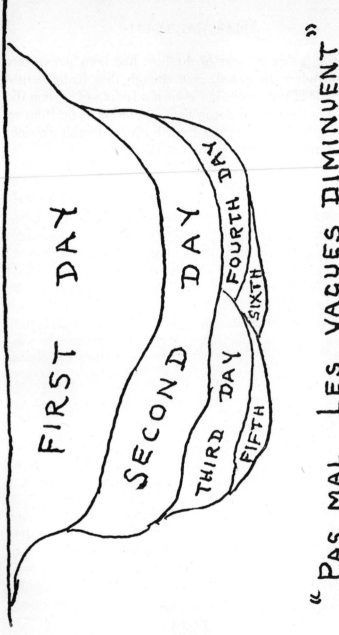

FIRST DAY

SECOND DAY

THIRD DAY

FOURTH DAY

FIFTH

SIXTH

"PAS MAL LES VAGUES DIMINUENT"
(FOCH)

ization in a "quiet" part of the line, had been put to face so tremendous an ordeal, even though they had emerged with honour and credit. But even if a feeling of tension did exist for a time, it did not in the end prevent Haig from responding to further appeals from Foch for British divisions to reinforce the eastern portion of the line.

Chapter XXVII

THE SUPREME TEST: APRIL-JULY, 1918

THE FIRST AND SECOND STAGES: APRIL AND MAY

AGED 66 YEARS

Foch, in the closing years of his life, described clearly to Major Bugnet the methods which he adopted of dealing with Allied commanders at this eventful period. His view was that "unified command" was nothing but a word. It had been tried under Nivelle in 1917 and it failed. It was necessary to learn to *lead* Allied Commanders-in-Chief—it was not possible to *command* them. Much depended upon their personality and upon their national characteristics. "The English are English, [here he missed the point that Sir John French was Irish and Sir Douglas Haig a Lowland Scot] the Americans are another matter, and similarly with the Belgians and with the Italians." It would have been useless to attempt to deal with Allied generals as he did with his own French commanders. "They were also brave men who were representing the interests of their country. They saw things from a different light from ourselves." This is a statement of special interest. Both during and after the Great War, the French had been widely criticised for their alleged inability to see the "other man's point of view," and similar remarks about the English are doubtless current in France. Add misunderstandings due to difference of language, to national temperament, and to "war aims," and it seems surprising that the solidarity between the British and French Armies under Foch's guidance was maintained throughout this period of "supreme test" between April and July, 1918, in spite of the political divergences which the Versailles and the other conferences and councils disclosed. Foch learned in due course to see the other man's point of view, and therein lay his true greatness when his responsibilities were extended far beyond the confines of his own national army.

Foch further explained to Bugnet that he could not give orders "in an imperative manner" to Allied commanders. "One cannot work to a system, especially with them! Anything might have happened. It was necessary to hear their views, otherwise they might have kicked." The most successful results were obtained by personal interviews. Foch's method was to talk over questions and to discuss them and usually "without seeming to do so" he gradually got others to see his point of view. The best British evidence supports this statement. Foch was considered to be not very approachable at first. He judged by deeds, rather than by appearances and protestations, but with a man with actual performances to his credit Foch thawed more easily. Even then it was not always possible to follow so nimble a brain, especially one addicted to parables and to colloquialisms difficult to follow for those not possessing a complete mastery of the French language. When the ideas at the bottom of Foch's mind were clearly grasped, his influence at once became complete.

In further explanations of his procedure, Foch said that by such methods he gradually won the Allied commanders over to his point of view. He was really a far greater man than that. He did not claim omniscience, and when he found a commander whose own ideas would fit in with, and perhaps be an improvement upon, his own intentions, he was quite content to accept suggestions, as we shall see later. According to his own showing Foch satisfied others in the end. He did his best to convince them. This may have been a lengthy process, but "we always got there." He would have a talk in the morning and another in the evening, and if necessary this would go on for several days. When he was sure that they understood his point he left them, leaving behind him a written note which had been drawn up with the assistance of Weygand, handing it over without appearing to attach much importance to it, explaining that it was a summary of his ideas. "It agrees with your own in principle. Perhaps you will glance through it. Come and see me again and we will go into it together." The result usually was that they made the decision their own (compare his "People only carry out . . . decisions which they have made themselves") and that they were keen upon making it a success. "If handled differently they would have strained at their chain if I had made them aware of it!"

Such, according to Foch, was the true spirit of the unified command as he employed it with all Allied commanders, and in that connexion he paid a warm tribute to Weygand on whom he placed a high value in such negotiations. Weygand was patient, Foch said—Foch himself sometimes was inclined to be hasty and impulsive when faced by opposition —and he used to return, go into the subject again, interpret Foch's point of view, and in the end persuade. Such, in Foch's opinion, was the true principle of an Allied command.

There is another aspect of his procedure upon which it would be advisable to dwell. Like other great commanders he has "suffered from his friends," somewhat grievously on occasions, as he did in the fables of the early days of the

War, when it was spread abroad that it was his impulsive spirit which led to his XXth Corps being taken in flank and driven back, thus occasioning the retirement of the whole of Castelnau's Army. Foch, for once in his life, was moved to take up his pen and write to the *Revue des deux Mondes,* not to defend his own reputation but that of his troops, and to point out that he advanced and retired by order, not on his own initiative. Then again there was the legend, which still persists, that he won the First Battle of the Marne by driving the Prussian Guard, which had disappeared long before the counter-attack which he ordered took shape,[1] into the Marshes of St. Goud. In such examples it has certainly been a case with Foch of "Save me from my friends," but the effect of such things is evanescent, and in course of time they are given short shrift by competent historians. With Foch's reputation it is likely to be a case also of "Good wine needs no bush."

We come therefore to a current impression that Foch solved all problems by constantly exclaiming, *"Attaquez! Attaquez!"* Such procedure would have disclosed neither the possession nor the use of a logical brain, so it will be well at this stage to examine the procedure which he adopted when, in April and May, 1918, he was co-ordinating the action of inadequate forces, "with their backs to the wall," and when according to his view they must stand and fight, whatever the odds, on the ground which they held. His detailed suggestions for procedure in such circumstances throw quite a different light upon his character. The initiative still lay with the enemy. Foch meant to attack in due course, but it was no occasion for staging brainless attacks upon a large scale. It may be "sweet and decorous" to die

[1] Sir J. Edmonds, *R. V. S. I. Journal,* May, 1929.

for one's native land, but logic teaches that one's native land will be better off if one can arrange that its enemies shall die first. Foch not only told Allied troops his desire that they should stand and fight where they were; he also told them how, in his opinion, they would have the best chance of succeeding. Interest in the details may, perhaps, be confined to the professional reader, to the so-called "expert," but no appreciation of Foch's methods could be possible without a brief summary of the instructions that he issued on the 19th of April and on the 3rd and 5th of May for using the resources for defence to the best purpose.

He began by giving the definite reasons why no ground could be given up under the conditions that existed in April. No further advance of the enemy could be permitted on the road to Calais, in the direction of the mining area, towards the railway-centre at Amiens, or the line of the Paris-Amiens railway. The defence must be based upon a series of defensive positions covering these vital spots, and the maximum number of powerful guns must be established in position. The defence must be full of energy. At least two positions must be embodied in the defence system, the second one being prepared and held in readiness for an extreme emergency in the event of the troops occupying the first one being driven back. The troops intended for holding the second position must constantly be in readiness, close to their positions [2] which must be allotted to them beforehand (artillery and infantry), and they must occupy the line at the required moment.

Counter-attacks to recover lost ground were absolutely necessary to stop the enemy's advance, the nature of the

---

[2] Subsequent experience of German successes showed that, in order to be in time, the troops had actually to be in the second position. [Author.]

counter-attack to depend upon local features of the ground, which must be studied for the purpose, and the reserves from which to draw them, must all be clearly understood from the first. They must not just be thrown into the line where the attack happened to have taken place. If this is done they are likely only to melt away. They must be properly organized for counter-attack, with their jumping-off ground determined in advance. Artillery support must be arranged, and definite enemy formations must be selected for attack. The two uses of the reserves must therefore be to occupy the second line as speedily as possible, making sure that the retirement from the front line was stopped there, and to counter-attack, using the main body of the reserve.

Every inch of the ground must be defended. No ground whatever was to be surrendered voluntarily. Even if the enemy did succeed in breaking through at some point in the first line, even if he did so on an extended front, no commanding officer was authorised to order his troops to retire, even on the plea of straightening the line or of occupying a new position. It was necessary not only to dig lines parallel to the front, but to split up the defence into compartments by arranging switch-lines. These were indispensable for two reasons: if properly used they would protect the sections bordering the scene of an enemy's break-through, and they would provide cover from which to launch counter-attacks. Personal reference to Foch himself was requested before any extended withdrawal was considered.

It is important to note the weight that Foch attached to field defences under conditions that arose at the time, because it has been stated that it was only by way of concession to British views that he sanctioned this method of "defence in depth" at all. He pressed constantly for the rapid development of the positions actually held, of fire effect—artillery and infantry combined—and of careful and detailed preparation for counter-attacks. At that period he was strongly opposed to "advanced observation lines" with "lines of resistance" behind them. He thought that the distinction had been justified by former conditions when a few hundred yards could be given to the enemy without serious inconvenience, but under these conditions the smallest withdrawal would be playing the enemy's game.

Foch considered it to be essential that there should be no voluntary withdrawals whatever, even on the plea that bodies on the flank had been driven back. Whatever the conditions might be every body of troops was to defend its position to the last. Certain strong points in the line were held by special garrisons. If one of these points fell, its garrison must attack to re-capture it, and commanders who failed to do so would be held guilty of culpable negligence. Retiring troops are the ones who become most disorganized and lose most heavily.

These tactics would save the troops the most and they were deemed by Foch to be the only ones which, under the conditions which obtained, would prevent the enemy from gaining ground that was indispensable at this juncture to the Allies.

In connexion with some of the above instructions, we know, of course, the effective use made by Gouraud at a later date—when he stopped the great German attack east of Rheims in July—of a thinly held line of observation to lure the enemy to attack, and a strong line of resistance behind, against which he comes unexpectedly; but circumstances altered cases. Another point to note is that Foch found by later experience, obtained by the middle of June, that there was no time to occupy the second line after a heavy attack developed with distant objectives for the attackers, so the only reserves which were of any use were those which had been already in the second position.

Foch's strong objection to relieve troops in the middle of a battle was that it involved the commitment of twice the number of divisions if the enemy's attack continued during the relief. (A definite example was to be afforded on the German side in front of Amiens in August, 1918.)

These notes on the written instructions which Foch issued between the dates mentioned, which perhaps have been of a somewhat technical nature, will suffice to establish the point that *"Attaquez! Attaquez!"* was not his invariable cry. We must, however, bear in mind his determination to attack as soon as he had reserves enough to do so decisively. Without further preliminaries we can now pass to the month of June, 1918, after the conclusion of the Third Battle of the Aisne where the French Army and the British IXth Corps of tired divisions had faced an experience similar to that which confronted the British Army covering Amiens in March.

So far, excepting to the most far-seeing and stout-hearted, Foch did not appear to have achieved much success, and there were those who said that after all there was not much virtue in "unity of command." Foch remained calm and confident.

CHAPTER XXVIII

THE SUPREME TEST: APRIL-JULY, 1918

THE FINAL STAGE: JUNE 2ND TO JULY 17TH, 1918

AGED 66 YEARS

WHEN the German advance across the Aisne on May 27th bent the Allied line back to the Marne and the gloom of Versailles spread to the nations there represented, Foch did not lose heart for a moment. He held fast to his determination to accumulate reserves for the counter-stroke which he kept steadily in view. Obviously, however, the first step must be to stem the flood which had already cut the line from Paris to Nancy. "On June 5th," he said in later years, "the tidal wave had spent its force on the embankment." The British were right in expecting an attack on the Noyon-Montdidier front, but not about the date upon which it was to be delivered. Foch collected troops from all quarters to consolidate his front and he asked the British and the Belgians to release French troops. Between the morning of the 27th and the evening of the 28th of June, ten divisions and a cavalry corps moved to the battle-front; three divisions from the east and two from the west were under orders to move at once. Foch travelled from one of his commanders to the other, demanding of them more energy, more activity, and more vigilance. Supported as he was by Clemenceau and encouraged by the faith reposed in him, he "stiffened his muscles, summoned all his will-power, and resisted the attack. Equilibrium was regained."

On the 3rd of June Foch telegraphed to tell Haig that he had been obliged to take away the French reserves from the Montdidier front and asked him to place three British divisions astride the Somme in their place. Haig responded to the demand at once, and at the same time he asked Foch to send back the British IXth Corps, which had been sent to the French front to rest and recuperate and had been in the thick of the fighting for seven days. Wilson records in his diary that on the 3rd of June he had visited Franchet d'Esperez's headquarters at Provins, and Gordon, the Commander of the IXth Corps, had reported that:

He had only the 19th Division on its legs. The 8th and 50th were quite knocked out, and the 21st and 25th much used up. All the same, his impression was that, if his troops were removed and replaced by French, the whole line would go back. Franchet praised Gordon and his Corps warmly.

The British IXth Corps was not sent back to Haig until later. Before that time relationships had become somewhat strained. Wilson, as Chief of the Imperial General Staff, continued to press for the salt-water inundations in the Dunkirk area to shorten the line in the north, and to that policy Foch was strongly opposed. Wilson returned to England on June 4th with Milner and the others from Versailles, and, when he heard of Foch's request to Haig and of his withdrawal of the French reserves from his area, he seems to have thought that Haig's report of the incident amounted to an appeal under the Beauvais agreement against Foch's authority. Disapproving, as he did, of Foch's strategy as affecting the British Army, he reported the matter to the

War Cabinet, who decided that Milner and Wilson should cross over again at once to make serious representations to Foch and to Clemenceau. They spent the night of the 6th at Montreuil, discussing the situation with Haig and Lawrence. On the next day (June 7th) they met again at the Crillon Hotel, Du Cane, the liaison officer with Foch, also being present. Then they went on to the Ministry of War to meet Clemenceau, Foch, and Weygand. At one time there seemed to be a danger of appeal to the Beauvais agreement, which provided that Haig might appeal to his government if Foch's instructions endangered the safety of the British Army. That would probably have killed unity of command. In spite of the strength of the force put by the Germans into the blow which forced the Allied line back to Château Thierry, Prince Rupprecht's reserve of about twenty-five divisions was believed to be intact and that the enemy contemplated a blow which the British Army, depleted by Foch's withdrawals, would not be strong enough to withstand. A good deal of steam was blown off on both sides, but unity of command was ultimately saved, largely through the conciliatory attitudes of Milner and of Clemenceau. The details of rather an acrimonious discussion are of no permanent interest.[1] The main points were that Foch said at last that he was only asking Haig to make plans to send more divisions away in certain eventualities which had not arisen. Haig agreed, and said that he was already at work on his plans. Foch then said that he was sure that in future Haig would not protest unless Foch committed *"des imprudences,"* and that in that case he (Foch) would agree with Haig. After useful interventions by Milner and Clemenceau all was well. The fact that Foch, in the emergency

[1] A full account appears in the *Wilson Diaries,* Vol. II, pp. 106-107.

of the Battle of the Aisne, had withdrawn French and American divisions from Haig's area without telling Haig himself was smoothed over. Wilson, however, still pressed his points about shortening the line and about the directions of retirement of the British and French Armies if forced back, and we find in his diary:

Foch replied that the continuous touch was of primary importance but he also said that he would not uncover the ports. After a pause he asked Haig if he agreed to touch being maintained [between the British and French Armies] and Haig said "Certainly."

The general opinion was that the meeting did much good and that Foch's position had been strengthened. Clemenceau thought that these meetings could be avoided in future if Foch and Haig met more frequently. The liaison officers' work had been excellent, but nothing can take the place of meetings between Principals, as had been proved in the political sphere after the establishment of the Supreme War Council at Versailles. All went well until the Supreme War Council itself met again early in July, and meanwhile Foch had a better chance of maturing his plans without feeling constantly called upon by higher authorities to explain them. These discussions have been described at some length in order to give an idea of the constant mental and physical strain to which Foch was subjected at a time when all his energies and powers of concentration were needed to prepare to take full advantage of the expected "culminating point" of the German offensives. He began to work hard at his plans as soon as the Battle of the Aisne died down.

On the 16th of June Haig addressed a long letter to Foch stating the exact position about the state of every division of the British Army, and other letters about relieving the

THE BEDROOM OF FOCH IN HIS HOTEL AT THE RUE DE GRENELLE

Note at the head of the bed are the colours of the flags of all the allied armies.

"D.A.N." (*Détachement de l'Armée du Nord*) which had helped in the strenuous time in April and May, and about other matters. On the 21st Haig wrote again agreeing with Foch's proposal to sort out the armies under their own commanders, the British IXth Corps to come back, and the "D.A.N." to rejoin the French Army.

On the 9th of June there began the expected German attack on the Noyon-Montdidier front which has been called the Battle of Massigny or of the Matz, and between that date and the 14th the enemy gained some ground on the Noyon-Montdidier line, but his advance was arrested. Foch expected further German attacks to follow. He was not sure of their direction, but he instructed Haig and Pétain to organise reserves behind their inner flanks for mutual support and for securing the junction of the two Armies. On the whole he thought that Paris and Abbeville would be the enemy's most probable objectives and he wanted the reserves distributed to cover them.

Foch pointed out on the 16th of June the advantage to be gained by a limited attack eastward to bring the Soisson railway junction under artillery fire. This idea gradually grew in his mind into a more important project which was to have momentous results. The distribution of the reserves which he had arranged—between Château-Thierry and Lens with the bulk of them behind the French left and the British right—favoured the secret concentration of troops for this proposed attack.

On June 28th and again on July 3rd Mangin succeeded in some minor operations to improve the point of assembly of the reserves for such a blow, and Foch expected the Germans to launch an attack in Champagne on July 14th. He made up his mind that Mangin should lie in wait to deliver

[341]

a counter-stroke against the flank of such an advance, but he kept his own counsel, informing neither the political chiefs, nor the British Commander-in-Chief. The British expected the first blow to fall on their own front, proving their case by detailed information of the arrangements that had been made by Rupprecht's force to attack them. (Their information was really correct, but they did not know that Rupprecht's blow was to be delayed until the issue of a previous attack on the French line had been determined. This has since been ascertained on Ludendorff's authority.)

As usual, Foch was compelled to look behind him, to the Supreme War Council, at a moment when he hoped to use all his energies to mature his preparations for the great blow. Wilson had gone to Italy on June 21st. On the 29th he arrived in Paris and waited there to attend a meeting of the Supreme War Council to be held at Versailles on the 2nd to the 4th of July. There the discussion covered the conduct of the War in many theatres, the impression that was made upon some of the leading British representatives being that Clemenceau and Foch were "attempting to confine the conduct of the War in the interests of France alone." Wilson calls the meeting "the angriest we have ever had," but he was "anxious that we should give the French clearly to understand that they were not going to take us over, body and bones, and take charge of every theatre. We have done this plainly—if a little, and not unnecessarily, roughly." Of the portion of the discussion which bore on Foch's plans, which Foch was careful to keep secret, Wilson writes that "Foch and the Tiger tried to get the Belgian Army under them," that "Foch wanted to know when our 'B' [2] divisions would be out, and urged adding another division to

[2] Composed of men in the "B" medical category.

our 59, making 60," also that "Lloyd George said he wanted
to make it quite clear that we could not promise always to
keep up 59 divisions, because either our man-power would
not allow it, or we might require to send some divisions to
the near East.[3] This greatly incensed Foch. . . . I was astonished at Foch's attitude. He never referred to the pros-
pective and enormous increase in American troops. I did."

Foch remained unmoved, and he went on working secretly
upon his plan for a counter-stroke.

On the 13th of July Lloyd George, on behalf of the
Imperial War Cabinet, wrote a very strong and comprehensive letter to Clemenceau pointing out the weak and
exposed position of the British Army in France which was
causing great anxiety in all the members of the War Cabinet,
adding that they had instructed Wilson to communicate
with Foch on the subject, and asking for Clemenceau's support. Wilson wrote a very strong private letter to Foch to the
same effect, from "Ever your friend, Henri." From 9 P.M. till
midnight on July 14th Wilson was with Lloyd George and
others at Hassocks; he wrote:

Lloyd George began by saying he would not allow 4 of our
divisions to go south unless Haig could give a guarantee that

[3] *Author's note:* The root of the divergence between the points of view of
the British and French Governments lay in the change, since 1915, of the British
political view of the general strategy of the War. The French opinion had remained unaltered. Clemenceau and Foch held that, the German Army being the
chief factor in the problem (Foch's *"De quoi s'agit-il?"*), the issue of defeating
the main German Army must necessarily be faced, however costly in casualties
the task might prove. The British political view, now for the first time receiving
the support of a responsible military adviser in Whitehall, was that experience
had proved that the impossibility of gaining a decisive victory over the German
Army by Foch's methods had been abundantly proved by experience, and that
in any event the limit of its costliness in casualties had been reached. It was
therefore necessary to obtain a decision by striking in some other theatre against
Germany's Allies. These views were irreconcilable.

Rupprecht would not attack him . . . Milner was quite sensible, and in the end he got Lloyd George to agree to send Haig a wire to say that if he thought that his force was being put in danger . . . he [Haig] was to appeal to the Beauvais agreement.

Sir Charles Callwell, Editor of the Wilson Diaries, adds:

The Field-Marshal [Haig] understood his position perfectly. He was quite aware that he could appeal to his Government if he thought it necessary. He did not think it necessary. He accepted the responsibility of reducing the numbers on his front so as to meet the wishes of the Generalissimo, realising that this was imperative in the common interest.

General Smuts and General Radcliffe [4] were sent across the Channel to impress the Prime Minister's views upon Haig. Smuts explained his mission as an envoy of the War Cabinet to Haig and offered him the support of the British Government, if he thought that he was being unduly pressed by Foch. Haig replied: "I will take the risk. I accept the responsibility. I have acted in the Allied cause."

Then, in case the British Government should not find a verbal undertaking sufficient to relieve their anxiety, he handed to Smuts a written memorandum:

I take the risk; and I fully realise that, if the dispositions [of Foch] prove to be wrong, the blame will rest on me. On the other hand, if they prove to be right, the credit will lie with Foch. With this the Government should be well satisfied.[5]

Foch, on the other hand, had the full support of "The Tiger" behind him. We have a clue to Clemenceau's

[4] Director of Military Operations.
[5] World Crisis, Part II, p. 499.

remark to Harry Wilson on July 22nd, "Your politicians are fools, but you are a good boy.[6]"

So far the men of words and their influence upon Foch and upon Haig, the man of action. They lead us on to a great climax. On July 3rd and 8th Haig had written to Foch (who does not seem to have taken him into his full confidence yet), reporting the arrangements that he had made for distributing British troops. Foch's plans were working out exactly as he hoped. From Mangin's easy successes on June 28th and July 3rd he deduced that the Germans were sacrificing their divisions in the front line to form a mass in reserve, and there were indications that the blow would be struck southwards, both east and west of Rheims.[7] Rupprecht's reserves, threatening the British Army, had not moved. Haig being in England on July 12th, Lawrence went to see Foch on that day, and he was told verbally that Foch wanted Haig to send two divisions south of the Somme. On the next day (July 13th) Foch asked Haig to send four divisions and a Corps Headquarters to the French front at once, the entrainment to begin at 2 P.M. on the 14th. Four more divisions were to be held ready. Haig complied, and he wrote on the same day a long letter to Foch asking the reasons for Foch's change of view about the situation. Foch was still waiting for the great German attack in Champagne which his Intelligence Department had told him to expect on July 14th. It did not take place.

Then Foch on the 14th arranged for a meeting with Haig at Monchy on the 15th, adding that if things went badly he might not be able to go, but there would be time to stop

[6] *Wilson Diaries,* Vol. II, p. 117.

[7] The British Air-Force (night-bombers) deserved great credit for the information which they supplied to Foch during this period. They noticed every night a movement southward of a long line of German bivouac-fires.

Haig in the morning. If the enemy attacked and all went well, Foch would keep the appointment.

The Germans attacked early the next morning, (15th) exactly as had been expected. On his way to see Haig, Foch visited Fayolles at Noailles.[8] There he learned that Pétain had postponed the preparations for Mangin's great counter-stroke and had ordered all available reserves to be ready to go to Rheims. From Ludendorff's writings we now know that this was exactly what he had expected his opponent to do. Foch cancelled Pétain's orders at once, and directed that the preparations for Mangin's great counter-attack on the western face of the Château-Thierry salient should be pressed on as fast as possible. He wanted it to be launched on July 17th, but, very reluctantly, he allowed the date to be postponed until July 18th. To Haig he then gave some inkling of his plan, and Haig, though he expected to be attacked by Rupprecht, who, as we now know, would have attacked a fortnight later if the Champagne attack had succeeded, conceded to Foch's wish that all the four divisions of the British XXIInd Corps should be sent to the French front. On the morning of the 17th of July, Foch sent a verbal message to Haig to tell him the secret that, at 8 A.M. on the 18th, Mangin would attack the Germans with a force of twenty divisions. When the German blow fell Gouraud had held up the attack east of Rheims. Southwest of Rheims the enemy had crossed the Marne and by the 18th he had made some advance southward. Then Mangin struck from the westward.

"The culminating point" had arrived, and Foch had

---

[8] The actual circumstances were that Foch arrived at Monchy half an hour early for his meeting with Haig, and spent the time in visiting Fayolle. The momentous result reminds us of the value of Foch's lifetime habit of punctuality, and of Napoleon's: "In war, ask me for anything but *time*."

timed his blow exactly at the right moment. His patient preparatory reticence, his staying power, and his determination not to be diverted from his purpose had its reward. He had had much to endure, and he had stood the supreme tests of apparent failure and of ruthless criticism.

Nelson, who like Foch faced long periods of adversity and of disparagement before his efforts were crowned with success, used to take as his motto *Post nubilia Phœbus*—"After the clouds the Sun." The sun, for Foch, rose in a stormy sky. No one, at the time, realised that for the Germans the tide of victory had turned once for all, but there was to be much hard fighting before the success of Mangin's attack of July 18th could be exploited.

It may happen that some historians, when searching the archives of the Great War, will find that Haig, under pressure from above and from his surroundings, was compelled to write again to Foch to point out the danger in which the British Army lay, with its weak and widely extended line, from attack by Rupprecht's force of twenty-three divisions in reserve and of eight in the line obviously preparing to strike; and it may be that our historian will also discover that Haig, in the same letter of July 17th, had requested Foch to send back the British XXIInd Corps. Let us hope that he and all historians will also discover that Haig sent with the letter a verbal message to Foch to say that "if the British troops were wanted to exploit a success, they would, of course, be available." [9]

So ended an acute crisis in the unified command and in the relations between Foch and the British Government. Haig had taken upon himself the whole responsibility for

[9] Lieut.-General Sir John Du Cane carried the message.

refusing to take advantage of the "Beauvais agreement." When appealed to personally by Foch, he gave a soldier's answer, and to the result, in added credit to the troops that he commanded, we will turn in due course.

Foch had run great risks, even of the estrangement of Haig, by the strict secrecy that he had maintained, but he believed it to be essential to success.

Few people who did not know the facts at the time can have realised how critical Foch's position was during the six or seven weeks that preceded Mangin's attack of the 18th of July. We have referred—perhaps *ad nauseam*—to the pressure that was put upon him by the highest British authorities—even by his old friend *"Henri"*—to turn him from his unswerving purpose. So far we have not touched upon the attitude of his own fellow countrymen. The defeat on the Aisne and to the southward between May 27th and June 2nd, leading, as it did, to so close an approach of the enemy to Paris, which was actually being bombarded by long-range guns at this time, caused some bitter French criticism both of Foch and of Clemenceau. Another reverse in July, if it had happened on the French front, would have led to the fall of both. Democracies, as we know, are pitiless when dominated by fear. A reverse on the British front, if we can judge by the evidence which we have examined, would have caused the British Government to look askance upon the principle of unified command, certainly as it was embodied in Foch.

Anything might have turned the scales. Gouraud's magnificent defence east of Rheims alone made Mangin's attack possible. Pétain's order which would have stopped that attack might not have reached the ears of Foch in time. His plans might have leaked out, when their success depended entirely upon the surprise which was actually effected. Foch had determined not to allow a soul to be told anything which it was not essential to him to know his plans. In the light of events, it may be that he would have been wiser to have taken Haig more into his confidence. In the course of a conversation at Monchy on the 29th of June Foch did talk generally of his offensive plans, but without indicating their nature.

Foch's considered opinion when he was talking over his plans at a later date (September 7th) was that if the Germans had decided to continue their blows upon the British Army, then they might have succeeded in effecting a separation. There must always be "ifs" in wars, they cannot be won without taking risks. We have dwelt, of set purpose, upon these long weeks of staunch determination and of quiet confidence as the true test of Foch's genius and leadership, rather than the limelight triumph of the months which followed, when his reputation rose to a pinnacle and he rode upon a great wave of public acclamation.

The inspiration which Foch conveyed to others in the time of trouble and depression lay not in his written words [10] but in himself, and in a personality proof against adversity. By one who knew him well and saw him constantly in the quiet spot which he chose to think deeply over the problems which he faced, he was said to be "always approachable and always charming." Others said that they found strength in the steady gaze of his eyes which on occasion became the windows of a soul fortified by complete faith in victory. In later years Foch was asked whether, in spite of the confidence that he always felt and expressed, he had not been surprised at the extent and at the completeness of his own

[10] A *précis* of the substance of his "directions" is given in an Appendix.

success. He answered that he had been, and he added: "I was not the Foch that I knew."

He spoke, as we know, in parables, and the individual reader will interpret that one as he will, knowing of the "robust faith" in which Foch resembled Charles Kingsley, who, in the darkest days of the Indian Mutiny, had said: [11]

An officer in wartime has work to do; a heavy, dangerous, almost hopeless task . . . He finds himself weak, when he expected to be strong; puzzled, when he thought himself cunning. He is not sure whether he is doing right. He is afraid of responsibility . . . His own honour and good name depend upon a single word which he speaks. The comfort, the fortune, the lives of human beings may depend upon his making up his mind at an hour's notice to do exactly the right thing at the right time. . . . He tries to fancy himself strong enough for anything. He feeds himself up with the thought of what people will say of him. . . .

People round him are mistaking him, slandering him, plotting against him, even when he is trying to do all the good that he can. Little comfort does he then get from what people may say of him. . . .

He is set in a snare, and he cannot find his way out. He is at his own wits' ends; and from whence shall he gain fresh wits? Who will give him a right judgment in all things?

Many who, like Foch, have been faced with similar conditions have agreed with Charles Kingsley's answer.

[11] *Heroes and Heroines.*

Chapter XXIX

LEST it should be inferred that Foch and his Staff and liaison officers were always at "concert-pitch," not sharing the weaknesses of humanity and having no relief whatever from constant strain, perhaps it would be as well for us at this stage to mention a few details of the life led at his quiet headquarters at off moments during the weeks when he was handling the great crisis of the War. "Approachable and charming" are epithets used of him by British officers who knew him best, and all those who were round him used to conspire in order to save him as much as possible from all interviews that were not essential.

At one time he was visited by great artists, once by the late Solomon J. Solomon, who did so much for the Army in connexion with *"camouflage."* Solomon claimed not only to be able to hide our own troops, but to be able to see through the enemy's wiles in the same direction, to detect his methods, and to identify, in what appeared to be harmless hamlets or other common features of the landscape, the positions where large bodies of hostile troops lay concealed. He claimed, it is said, to have acquired such skill in this art that, had he been called in in time, he would have been able to save the Allies from some of the surprises which were so regrettable a feature of the spring and sum-

[351]

mer months of 1918. When Foch was told of Solomon's arrival to give the benefit of his knowledge to teach the Generalissimo his business, an audience was of course politely arranged for the distinguished artist. Foch's time was very valuable at the moment, and the device for saving it was for Foch to pose as being very highly impressed, but at the same time so ignorant of art and photography as to be incapable of doing full justice to Mr. Solomon's valuable information. Having said all that by way of preliminary, Foch sent his visitor on with a special recommendation to the head of the French Army Photographic Section, to whom it was seen that Mr. Solomon was conveyed with the maximum of comfort and in the minimum of time. The Generalissimo then returned to his strenuous work, knowing how much he was likely to hear from the photographic department.

At another time Sir William Orpen came to paint a picture of Foch in such spare moments as he could find to sit. Sir William stayed with the British liaison officers for the purpose, and the question arose whether very early rising would be necessary in order to find Foch at leisure, the idea being that Orpen was not at his best in the early hours of the day. He was recommended not to trouble about that, and told that if he was with Foch by about 9 A.M. he would be in plenty of time. Much reassured, he went at that hour, and put in a good morning's work.[1] When he returned and was asked about his experiences, he commended Foch as an excellent sitter, and added: "But he asked me to be there at *eight* to-morrow morning!"

A little personal touch about Foch that is interesting at

[1] The Orpen portrait, besides being a good likeness, possesses a valuable feature in showing so well the "expressive hands" for which Foch was famed.

MARSHAL FOCH

this stage affects the question of the need or otherwise for good horsemanship—for which Foch was famed in his earlier life—for high commanders. The point has constantly been stressed that he used at one time to be fond of horses and very keen on riding. At this period he never seems to have ridden, certainly not as a recreation, and it seems that for a good many years before the War he rode from a sense of duty rather than for pleasure. He is, in fact, reported to have said that for as many as forty years he rode "less from conviction than from a sense of duty," because before the War it was an article of the military creed in France that war must be made on horseback:

I forced myself to ride every morning, winter and summer, in every sort of weather, and to ride for two hours, from 7.30 to 9.30. And see the irony of it! War breaks out, lasts for four years, and not once during those four years, except on parade, did I ever have occasion to show my riding powers. In fact I ceased to ride at all from the day when I actually began to make war. Ridiculous![2]

For actual movements in war-time he left the details entirely to his Staff, whether he went by motor-car, as he usually did, or by train. He called himself "a mere parcel" and added: "I let them pack me up, and then put me into store again."[3] The Staff were devoted to him, and took care to do their best to expedite the "parcel."

Another point well worth noting is Foch's habit, which he shared with Kitchener, of resting his mind from war subjects for an hour in every day, when he took care to think of other matters in which he was interested and not of the problems with which he was perpetually being con-

[2] Said to M. Charles le Goffic.   [3] Said to Major Bugnet.

fronted. Kitchener was a great collector of curios, especially old china, which offers a sufficient contrast to warfare, but we find that on one occasion at least Foch spent his leisure hours reading Zola's *La Debâcle,* which can hardly have provided a marked change of mental occupation.

It is interesting to note how Foch, in common with most great men, gloried in his work, but needed rest from it at times. We are reminded of Lord Grey of Fallodon's "If work be worthy or noble the greatest satisfaction in life is to be found in doing it well; the exercise of his highest qualities is the glory of man's being" and then "not all work is of this kind, and in most if not all of it there is much drudgery, so that we are tormented from time to time by a strong desire to get away from it." [4] To Foch that desire seems to have come but seldom in 1918, and the hour a day sufficed to keep his faculties at their best.

There is one other point to be mentioned about a source, lightly touched upon in the preceding chapter, from which Foch constantly derived comfort and a serene outlook. He sometimes spent his leisure moments in a wayside church, and a tale of that custom is told by an officer who was with him in this final stage of the War. Foch was thinking over one of his most important "Directives" at a critical time and he issued a message that, if possible, he wanted to be left undisturbed for an hour. They thought that he wanted to sleep, but when a very urgent telegram arrived they decided that he must see it. They found him in a little chapel, kneeling in prayer before the Holy Sacrament.

He was never articulate about such matters, doing them as a matter of course, and the incident reminds us of the discovery by a flag-lieutenant of Nelson similarly occupied

[4] *Flyfishing,* Sir Edward Grey.

in his cabin when the *Victory* was just going into action; of "Chinese Gordon" tying a handkerchief to his tent-pole when he wanted to be left alone to read his Bible; of John Nicholson of Indian Mutiny fame; and of many other fighters in causes in which they believed whole-heartedly.

The time has come, before we leave Foch's headquarters, to introduce the name of another member of his Staff, Colonel Desticker, of whom Foch thought very highly. On the numerous occasions on which Foch had occasion to be absent visiting the commanders and the troops and attending the various critical conferences, some of which led to heated discussions, Desticker was in charge, in the absence of Foch and Weygand. Like them he was an indefatigable worker. He was highly competent, and the first after Weygand to be taken into the confidence of their Chief. Desticker, at this period, sat in the same room with Weygand, next to Foch's own room. The British liaison officers walked in and out of this room as they liked, and Desticker, like Weygand, was always ready to lay work aside to attend to them. Foch often would stroll in when he heard them talking and join in the conversation. It was all quite informal.

Desticker, like Weygand, remained with Foch almost continuously until the end of his life.[5] He had been Chief of Staff to General Putz in Flanders in the early months of the War, and he had held an artillery command and several other Staff appointments. He has been described as having been in Foch's confidence and able to give decisions in his absence, as well informed with opinions eminently sensible and clear. He had patience, good manners, and consideration for others which enabled him to understand the

[5] Desticker died a few months before his Chief.

[355]

difficulties with which from time to time they were confronted. It was easy to work with him, and he was always helpful.[6]

Of the remainder of Foch's small Staff, all we need add is that all accounts agree in describing the *Famille* Foch as a "happy family."

We have taken our narrative as far as the close of the period (April-July 18th, 1918) during which Foch was subjected to the supreme test. Writing from the British point of view it may be as well to mention that all the four divisions (XXIInd Corps) sent by Haig to Foch on July 17th took a prominent part in the operations which began with Mangin's attack of July 18th and ended with the complete reduction of the Château-Thierry salient and the withdrawal of the Germans beyond the Aisne. On this occasion there were none of the difficulties which occurred with the British IXth Corps in the previous battle (May 27th to June 6th). All the British commanders and the troops worked on most friendly terms with the French, and in the end they left the French area with most cordial feelings of mutual goodwill. A shrewd observer of this and of other examples of joint operations between the Allies said that "whether they throw flowers or mud at each other depends more upon success or failure than it does upon anything else." It was during the long period of comparative failure that Foch's capacity for ensuring combined action under a unified so-called "command" had been put most severely to the test.

According to British nomenclature, the "Fourth Battle of Champagne" which began on July 15th with the German attack came to an end on July 18th with Mangin's counter-

[6] Colonel C. J. C. Grant in the *Army Quarterly* for January, 1921.

[356]

stroke, which opened the "Second Battle of the Marne" that lasted until the 4th of August, French, British, and American troops sharing in the captures of territory and of prisoners. These numbered 20,000, with 400 guns by August 20th when the Germans re-crossed the Marne. The general retirement north of the Marne was in full swing by the 27th. The French took Soissons on August 2nd. The Germans reached the Vesle on the 3rd, and the battle ended on the 4th of August, the fourth anniversary of the German invasion of Belgium, with the Allies on the right bank of the Vesle, and there we can leave them and transfer our attention to Haig. He had made good use of the respite on the British front since about the 8th of May.

The victory which forced the enemy back to the Vesle caused Ludendorff to abandon altogether the attack in Flanders, of which the probability had been correctly foreseen at Haig's headquarters. The German losses had been heavy, 30,000 prisoners, 800 guns, 6,000 machine-guns, and so forth. The Allied line had been shortened by thirty miles by a method far more effective than the suggested salt-water inundations at Dunkirk. Ludendorff was now faced by what he had constantly feared—a defensive on a colossal scale. The main line of railway from Paris to Châlons had been freed. An end had been put to the threat to Paris, and the initiative had passed definitely to the Allies. Foch in achieving these results had given an example of the truth of his contention in old days that victory is not a question of numbers but of leadership, of will-power, and of spirit. On the 19th of July the Allies were weaker than the Germans were in this theatre of war. The Allies had 144 divisions in the line, and 46 in reserve. The enemy had 145 divisions in the line and 60 in reserve, according to a perhaps somewhat favourable estimate.[7] It will be interesting to check these figures when the German *data* are available.

On July 12th Foch told Haig that he was anxious to free the Bruay mining district by an advance by the British on a front Festubert-Robecq—a proposal which he had already put forward on the 20th of May. When the late Lord Rawlinson, then Sir Henry, commanding the Fourth British Army heard on the 16th of July that the German attack on each side of Rheims had failed, he at once went to Sir Douglas Haig to tell him that the German morale in front of the Fourth Army was very poor and the defences weak, so all the factors on the Amiens front were favourable to an attack, which Rawlinson strongly recommended. Haig had also had his eye upon the Amiens front. He told Rawlinson to carry on at once with his preparations, and on July 17th he wrote to Foch to say that instead of the comparatively small operation suggested, he wanted to attack on the Amiens front, to secure the junction between the British and the French Armies once for all and to clear the railways. On the same day (July 17th) Haig received from Rawlinson a detailed plan of attack, which was the attack that was actually carried out, excepting in one important particular. Rawlinson proposed that the attack from Amiens should be entirely British, on the front Moreuil-Morlancourt, his chief reason being that experience had proved the difficulty in keeping Allied attacks secret, and secrecy was now vital to success. He hoped that a French attack would be made from the south from Montdidier, immediately the British attack had shaken the German defence. (It was ultimately launched on August 10th, after the German reserves had had time to get up.) Rawlinson told his corps commanders the secret

[7] Colonel Grant, *Army Review*, January, 1921, p. 281, footnote.

on July 21st but no divisional commanders knew till the 30th, so the news did not reach the brigade and battalion commanders until a day and a half to two days before the attack was launched.[8]

Meanwhile, on the 24th of July, Haig, Pétain, and Pershing met at Foch's headquarters, and Foch read to them a memorandum giving his opinion that bringing the German offensive to a standstill had turned the enemy's previous victories into a defeat. (We are here reminded of the warning by Clausewitz to his countrymen about the "culminating point" of victory). The moment had therefore arrived for the Allies to pass to the offensive, which, without seeking a decision, might in Foch's opinion produce useful results. The objects of the proposed operations were to clear the Paris-Metz railway on the Marne, and to clear the Paris-Amiens line and the Paris-Metz railway near St. Mihiel. It was not possible to forecast the results, but if these objects were obtained before the season was too far advanced, they would look forward to an important Allied offensive in the autumn.

On the 26th of July the plan put forward by Haig and Rawlinson for an attack on the Amiens front was discussed at Foch's headquarters and after some argument it was finally determined that British and French attacks should be made in the first instance from the same direction, Debeney, commanding the First French Army, to be under Haig's orders for the battle, and the French attack to be made by the XXXIst French Corps on the British right, the date to be the 10th of August. On the 1st of August Foch met Haig,

---

[8] The account by Lt.-General Sir A. Montgomery-Massinberd in the *Journal of the Royal Artillery Institution* for May, 1929, has in the main been followed here. He was Chief Staff Officer to Rawlinson in the Fourth Army. (Author.)

Rawlinson, and Debeney at Monchy, when Foch advanced the date to the 8th of August, and extended the proposed destinations of the Fourth British Army to Nesle and Hain if the Amiens defences and railways were successfully cleared.

Thus it was that, on August 8th, 1918, the great Allied offensive was opened by the British Fourth Army and the XXXIst French Corps. It was destined to end with the total defeat of the German Armies in the great battle of the "Hundred Days." In the first phase, the operations, known in the British despatches as the Battles of Amiens, Bapaume, and the Scarpe, lasting for nearly one month, the Germans received a blow from which they never recovered. Ludendorff called that fateful 8th of August "the Black Day" or "day of mourning" of the German Army. He attributed to it the defection of Bulgaria and the discouragement of Germany's other Allies. Hindenburg called it "our first great misfortune." We are told that when on August 7th Foch heard that after the recapture of Château-Thierry and Soissons he had been made a Marshal of France, he said:

It is not a wreath of flowers on a grave. If it had been, I should not have wanted it. We must at once exploit the change in the military situation . . . We must strike harder than ever.[9]

Foch's idea was to make a deep penetration from the Somme front, north of Villers-Bretonneaux towards Roye.

"Go as far as you can the first day," he is credited with having said. "Go on again on the second day and again on the third, before the enemy can concentrate his reserves. After that you will certainly have to pause, but you may

[9] Bugnet, p. 239.

succeed in going so far that the enemy will have to clear out of the Amiens salient. Renew the attack as soon as you can and you may force him over the Somme."

He persisted in his opposition to an attack by Debeney on the Montdidier front as he was afraid that neither of the attacks would be sufficiently strong to make a deep enough penetration. However that may be, from the outset when complete surprise was effected and the Australians and Canadians, aided by tanks, carried all before them in the first rush, the triumphant advance lasted for three days. On August 11th the attacks were closed down by common consent, and Haig issued orders to his Third Army, on the left of the Fourth, for a fresh attack further north.

A glimpse at the records on the other side show that at 10.15 on the 9th of August Ludendorff sent a somewhat discouraging telegram to say that a big French attack on the retreating troops was to be expected from the south, and at about 1 P.M. another one to say that although he hoped to strike the attackers west of the Somme, he thought that preparations ought to be made for a retirement to the line Bapaume-Peronne-Hain (the line of the Somme). At 6.30 P.M. the situation seemed to Marwitz to be desperate and he thought that the Second Army should shelter behind the Somme. This would have placed the German Eighteenth Army, to which the panic spread, in a desperate position. It was only the timely intervention of Prince Rupprecht which prevented the disaster being made still more decisive by the retirement of the Second and Nineteenth Armies in confusion across the Somme. He proved the truth of Foch's maxim that the fact that a Commander has made up his mind and is prepared to give definite orders changes the whole aspect of a situation. His firmness spreads downwards, as it will do whatever may be the size of the force which he commands.

There was talk of re-capturing Mount Kemmel next, but of this Foch would not hear. "If you go on with these operations," he said, "and they succeed as I expect, Kemmel will very likely fall without a fight. Give the enemy no rest. If you find his resistance stiffening at one point owing to the arrival of fresh reserves, attack him somewhere else. He cannot have reserves to meet you everywhere."

The plan which Foch now formed was to make a series of deep penetrations in different parts of the German front and then to attack at points from which the reserves had been withdrawn and thus make a series of sharp salients in the enemy's line from which he would be forced to withdraw. Constant repetition of these manœuvres would compel a retirement along the whole front, and the enemy would lose all initiative.

Haig had already discussed an attack with Byng, commanding the Third Army, and Foch wanted the blow to be struck between Arras and the Somme. Mangin's Tenth French Army attacked at Noyon on August 21st; Byng's Third British Army attacked south of Arras on the 22nd, and the First British Army further north on the 26th. All the attacks succeeded admirably. The Fourth Army then advanced again and by the end of August the Germans had been obliged to retire across the Somme. On August 30th Mangin advanced again in the Soissons area, enabling Berthelot's Fifth and Degoutte's Sixth French Army to gain ground. The debâcle had begun.

Foch was ungrudging in applauding the work of the British Army. After Byng's blow had followed Rawlinson's, he wrote to Haig:

Things are going well. I cannot help applauding the resolute manner in which you pursue the enemy without allowing him any respite, and at the same time increasing the scale of your operations. It is such an offensive, ever increasing in extent, fed from the rear and strongly pressed on from the front, with no objective, with no regard for alignment or for too close *liaison,* which will yield the best results with the smallest losses, as you have already perfectly understood.

And Haig, in an eloquent despatch to England, said:

Our troops felt that at last their opportunity had come . . . and that they could now press forward resolutely to reap the reward of their patient, dauntless and successful defence in March and April.

The fame of the British Army owed much to the constant and patient appeals made by Foch and Clemenceau to the British Government to provide Haig at any cost with the men to fill up the depleted divisions which otherwise would have been broken up.

On the 1st of August the total strength of the British Army on the Western Front stood at nearly 1,900,000. On the 1st of September, in spite of the casualties sustained, the numbers had increased, largely through the efforts made by Foch earlier in the year to impress the point that the decision must be obtained against the main German Army.

Turning to the Wilson Diaries, however, we find these entries, showing the opinions held in the British War Cabinet:

July 31st. Milner is clear that we shall never thrash the Boches and he suggests holding them in the West . . . Hughes [Australia] thought he must thrash the Germans in France. Borden

[Canada] favoured aeroplanes . . . Smuts agreed with Milner that we could not beat the Boches in the West next year.

August 1st. Practically all the Prime Ministers, i.e. Lloyd George, Borden, Hughes (but not so much), Smuts, Massey [New Zealand] and Milner, are of opinion that we cannot beat the Boches on the Western Front, so they go wandering about looking for laurels. Hughes sees clearer than the others, and sees that we must beat the Boche if we want a lasting peace.

Callwell, editor of the diaries, adds that in justice to the political heads it must be admitted that even the Allied military authorities, Foch, Haig, and Wilson himself had not realized to the full how critical had grown the position of the hosts under Ludendorff, or how bright had suddenly become the prospects of the Entente.

On August 11th Wilson met Foch at Sarcus, and told him that the British Army might soon be reduced to forty to forty-three divisions. Foch pressed for fifty-nine to sixty-one and took a very strong line, threatening resignation and adding that England would thus prolong the War for two years. Then ensued what ended as a storm in a tea-cup between two old friends, thus described, and here quoted as illustrating their relationship:

He said we did not send our wounded back to the front. I jumped in at once. I said he totally ignored our efforts in other theatres, [it was to those that Foch objected] our Navy, mercantile marine, coal, industries, etc. and that his observations about our wounded were untrue.

I pretended to be much more annoyed than I really was, and it did him good. I told him that if he wanted more divisions all he had to do was to put his boys of 18½ in, as we were doing. . . . It was nice and breezy while it lasted, and we were as good friends as ever after it.

[364]

Du Cane came to the train for lunch and told me Foch's plans for this year and next.[10]

The plans, which there is no need to give in detail, showed clearly that at this stage Foch had no conception of the grandeur of his success, or of the rapid approach of the fulfilment of his life's purpose.

[10] *Wilson Diaries*, Vol. II, p. 121.

Chapter XXX

THE DEBACLE: SEPTEMBER, 1918

AGED NEARLY 67 YEARS

BEFORE proceeding further it is desirable to clear up one point which affects the part taken by Foch in the successful advance of the British Fourth Army in the Battle of Amiens of August 8th-12th. It is clearly established, and proved by Foch's memorandum to the Allied Commanders-in-Chief, that he had definitely made up his mind by the meeting on July 24th that German morale was weakening and that the moment had arrived for a general offensive. It is also clear that the proposal for the actual offensive which took shape in the Battle of Amiens was initiated by Rawlinson. This is shown in the previous chapter, to which we can add a valuable entry in Wilson's diary for July 22nd:

Met Rawly at Abbéville at 8 A.M., he does not believe that Rupprecht will attack anywhere, nor that he will do much good if he does. He wants Douglas Haig to give him 5 or 6 divisions and tanks, and let him push out from Villers-Bretonneux; and this is certainly worth thinking about . . .

Drove Johnnie Du Cane on to Bom Bon where I arrived at 3 o'clock. Foch delighted to see me and as nice as ever. Long talk . . . He is already contemplating an attack from our lines, and I told him of Rawly's proposal, which we discussed and which pleased him.[1]

[1] *Wilson Diaries*, Vol. II, p. 117.

Partly on account of his pre-war sayings and writings, Foch has been credited with objecting to other people's ideas, and never changing his own. These accounts do him a grave injustice. He was greater than that. There is a great difference between advocating an operation of war and bearing the whole responsibility for success or failure. Foch's greatness lay in his readiness to bear the responsibility not only for a single operation on one portion of the front, but for those along the whole front in France and in Flanders, making the best use of the vast horde of troops assembled for the greatest battle in the world's history. As long as a commander would secure the object that Foch intended he might do so in his own way. To him should be applied the verdict that he gave himself upon the issue raised between Joffre and Gallieni, about credit for the victory in the First Battle of the Marne in September, 1914. "It was Gallieni's idea. Joffre bore the responsibility. The credit is Joffre's." By allotting more distant objectives Foch also increased the effectiveness of the blow struck by the Fourth Army. A good story, illustrative of Foch's character, referred to a similar occasion. He was told that Haig had changed a decision to meet his wishes, and he said at once: "The finest thing a man can do is to change his mind *if he thinks it right*. God alone is never wrong."

Commanders of armies in the field being necessarily the subordinates of governments which represent the nations whom they serve, and of prime ministers who have the power both to dismiss them and to interfere in the details of their operations, Foch also showed great tact and discretion in wording his answers to inquiries from Mr. Lloyd George on August 1st and 3rd about the operations which he was contemplating on the British front, when both the

British Government and a large section of military opinion in France were nervous about the safety of the British front in view of the strength of Rupprecht's reserves. Foch's answers, drafted by his own hand, were non-committal but at the same time sufficiently satisfying to stave off the danger of political intervention. They did, however, have the effect of straining the relations between Foch and his friend Henry Wilson for a time. Wilson came over himself to see Foch who had said that he would discuss any subject with him personally but not in writing. There was rather an unlucky contretemps over that meeting. Wilson arrived late, so they were only together for ten minutes, when the King of the Belgians arrived and Wilson had to go, but no permanent harm was done according to subsequent entries in Wilson's diaries.

We have already taken note of the objects which Foch had in view when he met all the Allied commanders, for the only time in the War, on July 23rd and submitted a memorandum of his objects to them on the 24th. The first of these objects—the straightening out of the Château-Thierry salient—was achieved or in process of certain achievement. The second, the straightening out of the Amiens salient, was completed by the arrival of the British on the Somme opposite to Peronne on the 29th of August.

Confidence was now spreading widely in the Allied Armies, and it was caused by two main factors: the arrival of the masses of American troops with their great potential though not immediate value, now that man-power in Europe was failing on both sides; and the alteration and improvement in tactical methods in the attack, which dated from the Cambrai battle (1917) and from Von Hutier's attack at Riga. The political heads in England had been told such things before and the prophecies had been falsified by events. Foch only hoped to convince the sceptics by results, and he deprecated the British Government's proposals at this stage to postpone the decisive battle until July, 1919. At the same time even he could not foresee the suddenness of the German collapse and he thought that the early spring of 1919 would mark the final stage.

Events in August enabled Foch to form his plans for the second stage of the great battle. After some preliminaries and special communications with General Pershing on September 1st and 2nd, to be considered in due course, he issued instructions on September 3rd for further operations without waiting for the third of the original objects: the clearing of the St. Mihiel salient by the American Army. (That was effected successfully on September 12th, when the Americans, aided by the French, caught the German and the Austrian troops in the act of withdrawing from their exposed position.)

Foch's next plans were:

(1) For the British Army, supported on its right by the left of the French Armies, to attack in the direction of St. Quentin-Cambrai.

(2) The centre of the French Armies to continue to drive the enemy back beyond the Aisne and the Aislette.

(3) The American Army to carry out forthwith the St. Mihiel attack in the Woeuvre as far as the line Vigneulles-Thiacourt-Règneville, to clear the Paris-Metz railway.

(4) The American Army then to carry out as strong and violent an attack as possible in the direction of Mezières, with their right on the Meuse and their left supported by an attack of the French Fourth Army. These two American attacks to take place on the 10th and 25th of September.

On the question which has arisen whether Foch at first directed an American attack from St. Mihiel towards Metz, a divergent direction, and whether Haig persuaded him to alter this to a more effective convergent attack "from St. Briey to the Meuse-Argonne," Lord Haig stated subsequently that he did not know whether it was he who "persuaded"— Foch to alter the direction of the American attack, but that when Foch advanced his plan for an American attack northeast towards Metz, he (Haig) at once wrote to Foch a personal letter pointing out the urgent need of the attack being concentric for all the Allied Armies, including the Americans. As Foch then changed the direction of the American attack, Haig thought that the presumption was that his letter had something to do with the change of plan.[2]

Documents which the author has since been able to consult show that the plan for the Americans to strike in the direction of Metz, was General Pershing's, and that when Haig's letter reached Foch, the Generalissimo had already been discussing for some days the idea of changing Pershing's direction to one more convergent. The point is of interest in its bearing upon the difficult task with which Foch was confronted in co-ordinating the independent views of the commanders of the Allied Armies in order to form one coherent Allied plan. Only by such means could he make the most effective use of all the Allied forces, the efforts of which he was endeavouring to co-ordinate with the help of the limited powers that had been conferred upon him at Doullens and at Beauvais.

Foch's intention was to combine the French and the Americans in two attacks, to be delivered east and west of the Argonne, but Pershing preferred that the American

[2] Letter from Lord Haig to the author, July 27th, 1923.

[370]

Army should be trusted to undertake a separate task of its own,[3] so it was arranged that the Americans should attack with their right on the Meuse and their left on the Argonne, the French with their right on the Argonne. The American task was the more difficult. The country was wooded, with few roads, while the Champagne country confronting the French was easier. Foch would have preferred that they should exchange rôles, on account of the inexperience of the American troops. In the actual event, the American Army was confronted by great difficulties which rendered forward movement impossible for some weeks after the first successful attack of September 26th. The choice of the area east of the Argonne may have been forced upon Pershing by the situation of his advanced bases and the railways.

Having made his arrangements to the eastward of the Scarpe, Foch turned his attention to the left of the line, and to Flanders, where the fighting had already been so heavy. On the 8th of September he prepared a memorandum which he showed to King Albert at La Panne on the 9th. Foch's idea was to take advantage of the absorption of the German reserves in the more southerly battles to reconquer the country north of the Lys by gaining certain commanding positions, and then to press on to Bruges, cutting off the Germans on the coast and the reinforcements coming to them from the south. The operation was to be under King Albert; the British, French, and Belgian Armies to co-operate, starting on September 20th and 25th.

Last but not least, Foch on the 8th of September called upon Haig for the British Armies to undertake the most important operation—an attack upon "the most formidable line

[3] There had been a parallel to this with the reservation of the British new armies in 1915-1916 until they could be used in large formations. (Author.)

[371]

of resistance of all." In an interview with Foch that lasted only for a few minutes Haig undertook to attack the famous Hindenburg Line, considered by the Germans to be impregnable after their years of work upon dug-outs, obstacles, and shelters. This was all that was said: "After a few words Marshal Foch said: 'You will do it. There is nothing that the British Army cannot do,' and Sir Douglas Haig agreed." [4]

We can now recall the events from the close of the Battle of Amiens on August 12th. From the British point of view, the main events were the German retreat from the Ancre, which began on August 14th; the Battle of Bapaume, when the 3rd and 4th Armies advanced on August 21st; Albert being taken on the 22nd and the advance continuing, the Battle of the Scarpe beginning with the advance of Horne's First Army on the 26th, and the evacuation by the Germans of Mount Kemmel, as Foch had anticipated, on the 31st. On September 2nd the British First Army broke through the "Drocourt-Quéant Switch Line" south of the Scarpe, the British Armies continuing to advance, the Germans falling back on September 7th towards the Hindenburg Line. An advance in the Cambrai area began on September 12th, and on the 18th the British attacked in strength on a sixteen-mile front northwest of St. Quentin, and captured the outer defences of the Hindenburg Line.

On September 27th a strong British attack was made on the Cambrai front; the Second Battle of Cambrai and the Battle of St. Quentin began, and the great Hindenburg Line was pierced. On the 28th the Anglo-Belgian advance in the north under King Albert began. On the 29th, in the Cambrai battle, the British Empire troops and Americans work-

[4] Brigadier Charles Grant, *The Household Brigade Magazine*, Spring, 1929.

ing with them broke the Hindenburg Line on a six-mile front, having taken 22,000 prisoners in three days. "It is immortally true that there is more in defenders than in defences," was a principle that was learned from Foch by one of his intimates.

By the end of September, 1918, the *Famille* Foch were convinced that there were definite signs of the breaking-up of the enemy. The successive attacks of the Allies were producing greater results almost every day, and Foch told his Staff that he thought that the enemy's situation had become "infernal."[5] In those days his favourite expression was "Everyone to the battle!" He would not hear of fatigue, of exhaustion, or of the many other reasons which made it difficult for some of the Allied Armies to continue to fight with neither rest nor relief. The moment had arrived. *La Debâcle* had come.

Mention has already been made of the desire of the Americans, as interpreted by General Pershing, to fight as one army as soon as possible. Reference has been made to various proposals on the part of the British and French for training the American troops—especially the infantry who came over in large numbers before the remainder—with the British and the French experienced troops so that they should gain knowledge of the tactical methods found most effective, before they were collected in large formations when the Commanders and Staff would learn to handle them. There has also been disclosed, especially by the Wilson Diaries and similar documents, a hope on the British side that, as British man-power was failing, the thousands of American infantry who were arriving would help to bear the burden of casualties and wastage at an earlier date than would be possible

[5] Brigadier Charles Grant, *The Household Brigade Magazine*, Spring, 1929.

if they waited until the larger American units were trained to participate in a large operation as a separate army. Such matters did not come within the province of Foch to arrange. In the "nice and breezy" meeting between him and Wilson on August 11th, from which extracts have already been given, we find Wilson suggesting to Foch to do what he had already been obliged to do with the French Army and to some extent with the British—to raise the number of divisions by reducing their establishment. When Wilson asked why Foch did not "turn the American divisions from 12 battalions of 1000 men to 9 battalions of 900," Foch naturally replied that he did not command the American Army, and that summed up the situation.

In connexion with the preceding narrative, however, account should be taken of the point that at one time five American divisions were training with the British Army and two of them shared in the triumphant advance. Further details of the part taken ultimately by the American troops in other areas, or of the relationship between Pershing and Foch would be out of place in a volume devoted to the subject of Foch "through English eyes," but before we leave the subject a few words on the American troops "through Foch's eyes" will not be out of place. He expressed the highest admiration for the way in which they captured the St. Mihiel salient, reaching all their destinations in two days in an irresistible advance, and taking more than 13,000 prisoners and 450 guns. For a first blow by a new army he described it as a master-stroke, which had a far-reaching moral effect upon the German Staff and rank and file. He also accentuated the difficulties with which the American Army was confronted in the subsequent advance towards Mezières. (*Les deux Batailles de la Marne,* 1928.)

Before turning to the momentous events of October and November in the last year of the War we will now return for the moment to the quiet headquarters where the Generalissimo was thinking out the problem of the next move and drawing up the Directives for the Allied Armies which were invariably reinforced by personal visits, and usually by previous discussion.

Soon after the events of July and August, Foch had dined with the British mission of liaison officers at his headquarters, and he then told them for the first time what he thought that the enemy should have done in March. He considered that they ought to have gone on with their attacks upon the British east of Amiens. It was by no means impossible for them to have reached Abbeville. Had they done so, all the most important road and railway communications from the north of France would have been cut and the French and British Armies would have been separated:

Oh ho! Oh ho! They renewed their attacks, but in the north, where they expected to gain an easy success.

Where we made a single command, they made two, that of the Crown Prince and of Prince Rupprecht of Bavaria; I wonder whether Ludendorff knows his business; I do not believe that he does.[6]

Foch, as we know, had studied German psychology from his early youth, and this gives us an example of his method of constantly learning by recent experience to add to his store of knowledge. As a rule, however, current operations were never referred to at the twelve o'clock meal at Foch's quiet headquarters, usually established in a small village, if possible away from a main road, and before returning to

[6] Brigadier Charles Grant, *Household Brigade Magazine*, 1929.

[375]

more serious matters we will take another short glimpse of the life there.

Meals were always punctual—luncheon at midday and dinner at 7 P.M. It was an unforgivable crime to be one minute late, and even Weygand, his Chief-of-Staff, would wait and have his lunch afterwards rather than disturb the Marshal at table. Foch's A.D.C., a retired cavalry officer, was often in a kindly way the butt of little family jokes, such as that he arranged a weekly menu to save himself trouble. As a matter of fact the food was simple and excellent.

Once when some British officers were lunching there was a distinct pause after all were seated. The Marshal began to become impatient and asked why luncheon was late. Boutal, the A.D.C., with many apologies, said that a special dish was being cooked for the English guests, and it would take exactly two minutes. There was a general laugh when it appeared and was discovered to be—boiled eggs, half raw in the (supposed) "English way."

There is another story—of Foch's cigars. Being very frugal in his habits he smoked the cheapest, and in extravagant British opinion the least attractive, brands. An English officer on a later occasion gave him one early in the day. Foch examined the band round it, noticed that it was a good Havana, apologized to the donor and put it in his pocket, saying that it was such a superior one that he hoped that he might be allowed to smoke one of his own and keep the good one until after his dinner. To another British officer, at his war headquarters, he once offered a cigar which the recipient felt that he really could not face. He saved the situation by saying how excellent a cigar it was, but "not to my taste."

These little incidents are worth recording because they

show how, by complete detachment at times from the tremendous responsibilities which he was shouldering, Foch, whose sixty-seventh birthday fell in October, 1918, was able at that age to "stay the course" without ever being tired. A point not mentioned elsewhere is that he always began the day by attending early Mass, hardly ever missing his attendance; and another point is important: he only spent two nights out of bed throughout the whole duration of the War, one when he slept under conditions that we described on the floor of the Town Hall of Fère Champenoise after the Marne, the other on the night preceding the Armistice. That says much for the care taken by Weygand, Desticker, and the other members of the *Famille* Foch, of whom their Chief said that they packed him up like a parcel when he had to go from one place to another.

It was written of Foch at this time that it was impossible to be near him without seeing that he had one single aim—to drive the enemy out of the country he loved so well. He was never tired, and as determined as he was infinitely patient—that patience which, as had been said about that of the great Duke of Marlborough, "appears God-like."

Chapter XXXI

THE HARVEST: OCTOBER, 1918

AGED 67 YEARS

In Mr. Churchill's words: [1] "By the night of the 30th of September the Hindenburg Line on a front of 25 miles was blasted and pierced to an average depth of seven miles, and 36,500 prisoners and 380 guns were reported to Sir Douglas Haig." On September 29th, when the line was broken, a conference, convened at Spa on Ludendorff's initiative, decided to approach President Wilson with proposals for an armistice; on the 1st of October Hindenburg demanded that the request for an armistice should be made by the next morning.

The convergent blows which Foch had co-ordinated and inspired were producing more rapid and more decisive results than even he had anticipated. A few days earlier he had thus summed up the situation: "The battle begins on one part of the front and the enemy is compelled to send there all his available reserves—Hardly has this been done when it begins again elsewhere and then again in a third place. The situation of the enemy is infernal." He seemed to himself to be fighting the Battle of the Marne again, with the circumstances far more favourable. The opinion of the *Famille* was that the American attacks might succeed; that much was not to be expected at that stage from the French advance in Champagne; that there would be some opposi-

[1] *World Crisis,* Part II, p. 536.

[378]

tion to the Anglo-Belgian advance under King Albert, the effect of which, if unopposed, would cause disaster to the German troops on the coast, cutting off their retreat. That the British attacks would succeed was looked upon as a certainty.

It is not quite clear at what exact period the idea that the War would be brought to an end in 1918 by a decisive victory began to dawn on the mind of Foch, but judging by the Directives that he issued in October and the destinations which he allotted to the Allied Armies the probability of a decision seems to have been in his mind during nearly the whole month. In Britain, and in the British Army, hope deferred seems to have "made the heart sick," not, however, in any way reducing the dogged determination to see the thing through, once for all, regardless of the date of completion. Amongst the more junior ranks of the Army were to be found the most hopeful prophets, especially amongst those nearest to the enemy and best able to judge of his morale. The original impetus for the decisive attack at Amiens on August 8th came, as we saw, from the front line, and there was now no need of inspiration from above to make the regimental officer and man, upon whom so much depended, keener than he was already to continue his triumphant advance.

Foch's solution was to arrange what has been aptly called a constant crescendo of attack, and his views are shown clearly by his Directives to Allied Armies. Of one feature of those Directives it is desirable to take note. When addressing Allies they nearly always contained a tactful little phrase —"If you share my opinions." Foch's method, when once his process of deep thought had led him to a definite decision, was if possible to arrange a conference with the Allied commander most directly concerned, to propound the idea, and to persuade, rather than to order, its execution. It is well to bear this point in mind when studying the substance of the Directives themselves, some of which as we know produced protests, but almost invariably the action asked for was taken at the same time that the protest was put forward, and with Foch action was the alpha and omega of his creed.

The point is on record that by the 4th of October, after the British had pierced the vaunted Hindenburg Line, Weygand, inspired, it may be, by Foch, thought that the climax had arrived, and that very great results might be expected if the Allies kept up the pressure for a few days. This they undoubtedly did. The Germans fell back on October 2nd on a wide front north and south of the La Bassée Canal; Armentières fell to the British. The French took St. Quentin. Lille was soon to be abandoned by the enemy, and an incident there is worth recording as an example of national psychology as illustrated by propaganda. British troops happened to be nearest to Lille when the entry of the victors into the town was imminent. The British Commander, thinking that after the long years of hostile occupation the French folk in Lille would like to see their own troops first, waited until a French unit, about eight miles away, could arrive to head the British delivering army. German wireless propaganda then announced that for the sake of the safety of the women of Lille the French had insisted that their own troops should precede the English. Propaganda is rather a dirty trade, from which the subject of straightforward fighting provides a welcome relief.

On October 3rd the Germans fell back from the line Lens-Armentières past La Bassée, and the British, attacking

on an eight-mile front, took Le Catelet. The British took
Gheluwe and French and Belgians reached Hooglede. Fifty-
five German aeroplanes were brought down on this day in
trying to cover the retreat. A brutal order about the treatment of all French prisoners captured was found on a dead
German officer, and during the retreat devastations were
carried out which Foch did not consider to be justified by the
military situation.

On October 4th some stiffening in the resistance on the
St. Quentin-Cambrai front was encountered by British and
French. German heavy guns were now being removed from
the Belgian coast. On the 4th the German retreat continued
between Le Catelet and Crèvecœur, and Douai was burned.
During the whole of this period the French and Americans
in the Argonne country, away to the southward, were pressing forward. On October 8th a three-mile advance was made
in an attack by the Third and Fourth British Armies, the
30th American Division, and the French on St. Quentin-
Cambrai on a twenty-mile front. Cambrai fell to the British
on October 9th, and Le Cateau on the 10th. Foch described
the Cambrai battle on the 9th as a "hammer-blow."

Lest it should be gleaned that the long Cambrai-St. Quentin battle and breaking through the Hindenburg Line was
a "walk-over," it is necessary to mention that in September
and up to October 9th, 6500 British officers and 133,700
other ranks had fallen, but the pressure was sustained.
There was a great response to the Generalissimo's appeal.
Between noon on September 28th and noon on the 29th
a million British shells of three to fifteen inches calibre
(costing nearly £4,000,000) fell in the German lines.

On October 9th Haig wrote to Foch recording an agreement that the boundary with the French on the British

right should run northeast to Wassigny, and adding that he now learned that the boundary should thence be continued east to Etreux. He strongly recommended, in order to obtain important results as quickly as possible, that the British should move northeast between the Sambre and the Scheldt towards the line Valenciennes-Maubeuge, thus cutting the German principal lateral line Valenciennes-Hirson-Mézières. A move northeast would also enable Haig to co-operate with the force further northward under the King of the Belgians.

For an offensive movement to be possible Haig reported that it was essential that his right should not extend beyond the Somme. As progress on the Rheims-Verdun front appeared to be unlikely within a reasonable time, he asked for American troops to be diverted to his front as soon as possible to exploit the offensive that he proposed, and he offered to arrange for the supply requirements of six large American divisions.

No record of Foch's reply to Haig on this point is available. We know, however, that Milner went to Paris on October 24th to propose that the American divisions should be distributed along the British and the French front, in order that better advantage might be taken of their fine fighting qualities than was possible as long as they remained massed in an American Army. The struggle was becoming a war of movement, and in the forward movement of masses in the difficult country that had been selected for the American Army, only a highly experienced Staff could have coped with the problem of transport and supply. The proposed step was not taken. The end was approaching. [Wilson Diaries II, p. 143.]

On October 10th, Foch summed up the situation clearly.

[382]

Three great convergent attacks were then in progress: the first the one in Belgium which we have been studying; then one by the French on the front Solesmes-Wassigny; and the third the Franco-American advance on the Aisne-Meuse front. Of these the second seemed to Foch to offer the best chance of being exploited owing to the successes that had been gained by the British armies.[2]

Foch directed that the Solesmes-Wassigny attack should be continued towards the line Mons-Avesnes, and at the same time the British Armies, acting in combination with the Belgian attack, should strike northeast between the Scheldt and the Sambre to clear the Lille area. One of Foch's objects, the clearance of the mining areas, had now been fulfilled.

The rapid advance in the northern area threatened the safety of the mass of German troops that were still in the salient between St. Quentin and Rheims. These had to come tumbling back, and the French on the Aisne front made big advances on the 11th and 12th of October.

The next important Directive was issued by Foch on October 19th. The Flanders group of armies was to move on Brussels; the First, Third, Fourth and Fifth (now reconstituted) British Armies south of the line Pecq-Hal with their right just north of Givet. To them was to fall the task of driving the enemy into the inhospitable Ardennes country. This advance also tended to help the forward movement of the Flanders Armies. The First, Tenth, Fifth and Fourth French Armies and the First American [3] were to support the

---

[2] *"Grâce aux succès des armées Britanniques."* (Foch.)

[3] In Sir Henry Wilson's diary (Vol. II, pp. 140-1) for October 21st we read that in the evening of that day Mr. Lloyd George sent for him "to try to persuade the Tiger that Foch should force Pershing to spread out the American army over the French and over ours, as no one was getting full value of it now."

British attack in the direction Capelle-Chimay-Givet, to out-
flank the Germans on the line Serre-Sissonne, to reach the
area Metz-Sedan and the Upper Meuse, and to turn the line
of the Aisne by working on the left in the directions Chau-
mont-Porcien and on the right (Fourth French Army and
American Army) in the direction of Buzancy-Le Chesne.

In the execution of these proposed movements the destinations allotted to the Armies were not always reached,
largely because of the continuous strain upon men and
horses, the state of roads and railways, difficulties of supply,
and the resistance in places of some of the enemy forces
who fought with the energy of despair. The German accounts show that Foch was right in his view that his enemy's
situation must be "infernal," and he and the *Famille* around
him now expected a military collapse within a few weeks.
The whole of the enemy edifice was tottering on its foundations.

After October 10th the Allied line continued to advance.
October 14th was marked by a strong attack by the northern
force under King Albert and an advance of five miles, with
further progress on the 15th, when the British took Menin
and closed on Courtrai. On the 16th the Germans fell back
from the Douai-Lille front pursued by the British. Part of
Courtrai was taken. On the 17th of October came the Battle
of the Selle, the river being crossed by British and Americans
south of Le Cateau. The British took Douai and occupied
Lille.[4] The King and Queen of the Belgians entered Ostend,
the Germans rapidly falling back. The advance of all Allied forces in Flanders continued. On the 19th the Belgians
were in Zeebrugge and Bruges. On the 20th the British were
over the Selle after hard fighting and within two miles of

[4] *Vide supra.*

[384]

Tournai. On the 22nd they were in Valenciennes and on the 23rd they launched a violent attack between Valenciennes and Le Cateau, advancing on that day and the next and taking many prisoners. October 25th found British and French troops ten miles east of Courtrai, and they advanced still further there and at Valenciennes on the 26th of October.

Ludendorff then resigned, or was dismissed, on October 27th.

From the date of the opening of the great convergent offensives by the French and Americans on September 26th, the British on the 27th, and King Albert's force on the 28th, and more especially from the British success in breaking through the Hindenburg Line, the Allied Armies had reaped continuously the fruits of Foch's strategy. Hardly a day had passed without some signal success being reported from some part of the front, which compelled the enemy to fall back somewhere else in order to form a united front. Nevertheless, however successful the attacks might be, they perforce resembled the enemy's successive waves, decreasing in intensity, about which Foch, "calm and confident," had said to the anxious statesmen assembled at Versailles in the early days of June—"*Les vagues diminuent.*" There was neither calm nor confidence now at the headquarters of the German Armies. No great reserves were massed for a counterstroke. Only intervals of exhaustion and difficulties of supply on the part of the attackers left their enemy short periods to readjust his front and to keep it intact to stave off a complete break-through.

By the middle of October there was a strong feeling at Haig's headquarters that the British Armies, great as their efforts and generous as the credit allotted to them had been, were bearing more than their fair share of the burden and of the sacrifice involved. The Germans, looking upon the British menace as the most pressing, had taken more formidable steps to hold up an advance by the British than on any other portion of the line. This point cannot pass without mention, as it affected, for a time, the cordial relationship between Foch and Haig, luckily only temporarily. Difficulties came to a head at a meeting between the two Marshals at Noyon, headquarters of Debeney's Army, on October 24th, when Haig pressed for the return to his command of his Second Army, which was operating under the King of the Belgians. Foch would not give way, on the plea that the move would interfere with operations still in progress that should be carried on continuously. An agreement was arrived at that Haig should put his protest in writing, and that Foch would refer the question to the British Government. Haig wrote accordingly on October 25th. Foch replied on the 26th, adhering to his position, and the debate was transferred to the higher authorities. The result is described in the Wilson Diaries.[5]

Lord Derby came to Versailles to propose that he should see Clemenceau and suggest to him that Foch ought to let the Second Army come back to Haig:

Then Derby came out again to lunch and told Milner and me that he had seen the Tiger, who entirely agreed with him that the Second Army should be given back to Haig, and that he should go out to Senlis to see Foch, but that, in the event of there being a difficulty, he gladly accepted a proposal made by Derby that he [Derby] should go and see Foch and try to persuade him . . .

Derby went off at 6 o'clock to see Clemenceau after his return from Foch, and he reported that the Tiger had been quite unable

[5] Vol. II, pp. 143-144.

to persuade Foch, and even that he [Tiger] has greatly weakened in his opinion that the Second Army should come back to Haig.

It was then agreed that Wilson should go to see Foch on the next day (October 28th). Wilson writes:

October 27th—If I can't persuade Foch to give up his position I shall have to order him. But this, of course, is the last thing I want to do.

October 28th—I went to Crillon at 10 A.M., saw Haig and had a talk, and he gave me a letter, which he read to me, to Foch, restating his reasons for wanting the Second Army back. I then went up with this to Senlis, and saw Foch and Weygand, who have moved there from Bom-Bon. I had rather a stormy meeting with Foch, but I think I was able to put my case strongly, but quietly. We parted excellent friends.

Then back to the Embassy for lunch. Douglas Haig also there, and as he had to go to see Foch at 4 P.M. I told him I was sure the old boy would meet him half way now, and I suggested asking for the Second Army to be given back when it reached the Scheldt. This he did, and both he and Du Cane telephoned to-night to say that everything had gone splendidly at the meeting, and flowers, and tea, and delights! So that corner is turned.

To anticipate for the moment, Foch ordered on November 4th the return of the British Second Army to Haig's command.

In order to bring the narrative to the end of October we can take note, on the enemy side of the lines, that von Lossberg took Ludendorff's place on October 28th. The Allied successes continued without a break. On the 28th the British made a further advance south of Valenciennes. On the 29th a successful French attack developed on a seven and a half mile front northwest of Château-Porcien, near Rethel. On the 30th the region about Valenciennes was flooded by the enemy. On the 31st a British attack south of Audenarde achieved all its objects.

Turning now to the other theatres of war, the loss of prestige from which the German Army suffered from defeats in the field, which could no longer be concealed, caused her Allies to desert the cause of the Central Powers—the only possible course that they could adopt in a struggle in which all hope of success had been lost with the collapse of the German Army. Bulgaria had been the first to give in, and an armistice had been granted to her on the 30th of September when the Hindenburg Line was pierced. On October 27th an armistice was asked for by Austria-Hungary, to be conceded on November 3rd. On October 31st hostilities ceased with Turkey. It has frequently been advanced that desertion by their Allies had caused the weakening of the Germans before Foch's constantly repeated blows, but there is no evidence in support of that view. With the exception of a few Austrians, Germany's Allies had never supplied and were not likely to supply her with any fighting troops to fill the gaps in the ranks and to restore the shaken morale of the German commanders and their armies. It was spirit rather than material that had achieved the triumph, and Foch's spirit remained calm, confident, and steadfast throughout, rejoicing in the success of a mission for which nearly half a century of training and experience had fitted him. With him there was no trace of self-glorification in the approaching triumph—it was solely *"Non nobis, Domine. . . ."*

The conditions of an armistice were discussed between Foch and Haig at their meeting at Noyon on October 24th. For the sake of continuity in describing the closing scene in the great world-drama, that subject can best be considered later, and we cannot do better than use here Marshal Foch's own summary [6] of the operations which he directed in September and October.

At the end of August the Allies had reached the general line Arras-Péronne-Noyon-Soissons, and by the middle of September the enemy had fallen back to the celebrated Hindenburg Line, which he had quitted six months before for his great attack upon Amiens. The Allied Armies had thus more than fulfilled the first part of Foch's programme, the clearing of the Amiens front. His second object—to free the mining area—had needed no great attack. The enemy had fallen back on August 7th from the line of the Lys. There remained the third item in the programme—clearing the St. Mihiel salient which Foch entrusted to the American Army. The result was that on September 12th "the advance of the Americans was irresistible; in less than two hours all their destinations were reached. . . . More than 13,000 prisoners and 450 guns remained in their hands. For the first effort of a new army it was a master-stroke (*coup-de-maître*). The moral effect of the victory of Saint-Mihiel was considerable."

The next object was to enlarge the sphere of operations and to allow the enemy no respite. For that purpose the frontage of attack had been extended, and conditions were good for a general offensive *from the North Sea all the way to the Meuse*. (Foch's italics.) Pétain had been told to prepare a Franco-American offensive on a frontage between the Meuse and Rheims, in the direction of Mezières. At the same time Haig was to carry on and develop his attacks on Valenciennes, St. Quentin, and Cambrai. The King of the

[6] *Les deux Batailles de la Marne.* 1928.

Belgians was asked to take the command of a group of armies composed of some Belgian divisions, the Second British Army, and some French divisions. Their object was to clear the enemy out of the Ypres position and press on towards Bruges and Courtrai.

Between the 26th and 28th of September the Allied Armies attacked in convergent directions on a frontage of three hundred and fifty kilometres. The enemy gave way everywhere before the heavy blow, but the obstacles were formidable. (*Le choc est rude, l'ennemi cède partout; mais que d'obstacles à surmonter!*)

In the southeast, on the American front, the broken and wooded country of the Argonne caused great difficulties. In the centre the Franco-British Armies—it is notable that Foch did not write "French and British." He now looked upon them as one—and several American divisions faced the formidable defences of the Hindenburg Line which had been made in the winter of 1916-1917 on the front Cambrai-Saint Quentin-La Fère.

To the north, where King Albert's group of armies was to operate, was the low and marshy Flanders country with its water-logged soil, starred all over with shell-holes, and almost impassable for heavy guns.

Nevertheless, by the influence of the leaders and the zeal and ardour of the troops all the difficulties due to natural obstacles and to the enemy were overcome. By the 15th of October the Hindenburg Line had been crossed and the "Franco-British" Armies were on the line Douai-Cambrai-Saint Quentin-Laon-Rethel-Vouziers. On their right the First American Army (General Liggett) was occupying the Argonne after hard fighting and strong efforts. The Sedan-Mézières railway line was threatened. On the left the

Franco-British forces and the Flanders group of armies was near Bruges and on the outskirts of Courtrai. The difficult *terrain* had been passed. On ahead stretched a comparatively easy country. It was then only necessary for all to press forward.

All that was then required (October 19th) was to allot destinations to the Armies: Brussels for the Armies of Flanders; the Meuse from Givet to Mézières for the "British and French" Armies; Sedan for the American Army. During the last days of October and the early days of November the Armies continued to push forward towards these destinations, while the enemy, protected by groups of guns and machine-guns, gave up more and more ground, leaving behind him devastation, "not always justified by the necessities of warfare."

Foch's own summary has been given almost *in extenso* as an example of his clear-thinking and lucid exposition of his intentions and the achievements of the Armies which he inspired.

Chapter XXXII

THE REAPING: OCTOBER-NOVEMBER, 1918

AGED 67 YEARS

On the 1st of November the American and French Armies advanced further in the Argonne between the Aisne and the Meuse. A great battle of the Sambre began, the British reaching the outskirts of Valenciennes. Further advances were made in both areas on the 2nd. By the 3rd the enemy was clear of the Argonne Forest, and in Flanders he was driven back into Ghent. On the 4th the British First, Third, and Fourth Armies under Haig struck another hammer-blow on a thirty-mile front extending from east of the Scheldt near Valenciennes to beyond the Sambre-Oise Canal. The Belgians approached the suburbs of Ghent. On the 4th of November the Allied advance continued on all fronts, inspired by Foch's messages hounding on all the forces to the pursuit, and dealing specially with the effect of the withdrawal of the Austrian troops in accordance with the armistice granted to their country. The last message of November 9th proclaimed that the enemy was giving way along the whole front, disorganized by the repeated attacks, and it was necessary to speed up the movements. Foch made a personal appeal to the energy and initiative of all the commanders to ensure a decisive result: *"Il importe d'entretenir et de précipiter nos actions. Je fais appel à l'energie et à l'initiative des Commandants en Chef et de leurs Armées pour rendre décisifs les résultats obtenus."* With him, now reaching the summit of the labour of a lifetime, there were to be no half-measures. The task must be accomplished once for all.

On November 5th further successes were reported from all parts of the line. The British took Le Quesnoy and the Mormal Forest with its memories of the anxious days of the retreat from Mons in August, 1914. On Pétain's front French troops were in Château Porcien on the Aisne and Guise on the Oise, and they crossed the Ardennes Canal between the Aisne and the Meuse; the Americans crossed the Meuse and took Beaumont.

On November 6th German armistice-delegates left Berlin for their enemy's lines, the retreat becoming general. The British advanced towards Mons of historic memories, Maubeuge and Avesnes. The French between the Oise and Aisne took Vervins and Rethel. The Americans entered Sedan, and the main German line of communication running along their front was severed. The new world was redressing the balance in the old. Further advances were accomplished on November 7th, and on the 9th Marshal Foch received the German delegates at Réthondes, four miles from Compiègne, refused abruptly a request for a provisional armistice, and prescribed the terms upon which an armistice would be allowed if the terms were accepted by 11.00 A.M. on November 11th—the eleventh hour of the eleventh day of the eleventh month—the end of the "Battle of a Hundred Days" that had opened with the great eastward thrust from Amiens early in August. While Foch and the delegates were meeting, the Allied Armies pressed forward relentlessly. The French reached the outskirts of Hirson and Mézières on the 8th. French and Americans cleared the high ground east of the Meuse. The British took Avesnes and crowned their efforts

[393]

by the capture of Maubeuge, taking Condé by crossing the Scheldt Canal, and by reaching the outskirts of Tournai, which fell to them on the next day (November 9th), when the French were in Hirson and surrounding Mézières. On the 10th French and Americans were pushing on towards Montmédy, and before dawn on November 11th the British, or rather Canadian, troops were in Mons, the scene of the first clash of arms between Kluck's great army and the original little British Expeditionary Force on the 23rd of August, 1914.

On the 7th of November Bavaria had become a republic, on the 9th a revolution had broken out in Berlin, and on the 10th the Kaiser had fled into Holland.

With Foch, victory was measured in terms of spirit to which all else must bow, but with most people ocular demonstration of results is needed. "Prisoners and guns" were selected by Clausewitz, the exponent of German military psychology, as the best of such demonstrations, and of these the captures had thus been divided:

British Armies,	200,000 prisoners,	2,540 guns
French Armies,	135,720 prisoners,	1,880 guns
American Armies,	43,300 prisoners,	1,421 guns
Belgian Armies,	14,500 prisoners,	474 guns

This forms a total of nearly 400,000 prisoners and over 6300 guns between July 18th, 1918, when Mangin's attack was delivered on the right flank of Ludendorff's last great bid for victory, and the 11th of November.[1] The commencing date, as will be noted, was July 18th. In connexion with the

[1] Statistics of the Military Effort of the British Empire 1914-1920 (official). The total British casualties on the Western Front in 1918 numbered about 880,000. (*Chronology of the War*, Vol. III, p. 193.)

feeling, at one time prevalent, that Foch had thrown upon the British, compared with the French Army, too heavy a share of the sacrifice after they had borne the brunt of the attacks in March and April, it is necessary to mention that between July 15th and November 11th the French suffered 300,000 casualties to 310,000 British.

Such, then, was the magnitude of the great Armageddon in which Foch had triumphed, and in which he had remained calm and confident throughout. The best account of his motives and of his guidance of the tremendous forces which he handled, is his own, which we shall take up at the point where we left it in the last chapter, when the victorious advance of the Allies was beginning in the early days of November.

He tells us [2] that his first object was to press the pursuit so as not to allow the enemy time to form a new front in a strong position such as the line of the Meuse. It was for that reason that he issued orders to Pétain on the 20th of October to prepare for an attack in Lorraine, east of the Moselle, in the direction of Metz and the Sarre. That attack was to be carried out by two French Armies and the Second American Army, under General Bullard, everything to be ready for striking this blow on the 15th of November. Meanwhile the enemy was to be pressed, day and night, the object being to press forward to the Rhine, when Germany would be at the mercy of the Allies. *"En avant! Au Rhin!"* was now to be the watchword. If necessary, the victorious battle which began on the 18th of July was to be carried on right through the winter, with a frontage extended to the Moselle and to the Vosges. Events marched quickly. A debâcle appeared to be a certainty. The German leaders

[2] *Les deux Batailles de la Marne,* p. 131.

were menaced by revolution, the inevitable consequence of military defeat.

Great efforts have been made to attribute the military defeat to the attitude of the Government and the civil population whose loyal and patriotic endurance of endless sufferings had presented a model to all.[3]

By the 5th of November the German Army was retreating on a frontage of three hundred and twenty kilometres, Ludendorff *"demissionné"*, and the Emperor on the eve of flight. On the 6th General Pershing wrote that an American division, pushed forward forty kilometres from its base, was on the bank of the Meuse, facing Sedan, and the strategic object had been attained. The principal enemy's line had been cut and only capitulation or an armistice could save his army from complete disaster.

On November 8th the plenipotentiaries of the German Empire came to beg for an armistice. On the 9th when the Americans were in Sedan, the French occupied Mézières and pushed on into Belgian territory towards Chimay. The English occupied Maubeuge and Mons,[4] and the Belgians were in Ghent.

There was yet another blow to be struck. On November 9th Foch issued an appeal to the Allied commanders-in-chief, pointing out that the enemy was giving way along the whole front to the constant attacks, and calling for energy and initiative to make the results conclusive. "And they, feeling their flags stirring to the breeze of victory, answered: 'Count upon us' . . . The splendid spirit (*élan*)

---

[3] "Despite Ludendorff's frantic protests in his series of exculpatory books, it is an undeniable fact that it was the disintegration of the Front which led to the revolution, and not the revolution which caused the Front to crumble." *The Path to Peace*, p. 350.

[4] See above—Mons was not taken until November 11th. (Author.)

paid for all the past sufferings and the anguish of the early days of the year seemed far away! . . . Before sunrise on the 11th of November Germany . . . submitted to the conditions imposed by the Entente as the price of ceasing hostilities."

From Foch's own account of the final battle we can now revert to the negotiations by the Germans for the respite which they so sorely needed.

When the military situation became desperate on September 30th after the Hindenburg Line had been pierced, Count Hertling the Chancellor and all the German Secretaries of State resigned. On the 4th of October Prince Max of Baden became Chancellor and on the same day Germany and Austria-Hungary appealed to President Wilson, proposing an armistice. President Wilson replied on October 8th demanding as a preliminary the evacuation of occupied territories. On the 12th the German Government accepted these conditions. On October 14th the President attached further conditions, warning against further breaches of the laws of war, and insisting upon dealing only with a "democratic" government. On the 20th the Germans agreed to these proposals, and on the 23rd President Wilson agreed to submit the matter to the Allied and associated governments. The process of establishing communication through President Wilson therefore occupied no less than nineteen days of unnecessary fighting, resulting in disintegration of the German Army, which might possibly have been saved by a direct appeal to the Supreme War Council, representing the combined political power, or to Foch the Generalissimo, representing the Allied Armies with whom the German Army was in close contact.

The subject of the terms of an armistice, should one be

granted, was a live question in the British War Cabinet with whom, however, we are not concerned excepting in so far as they influenced Haig in his conference with Foch near Noyon on October 24th.

We find [5] that on October 5th Clemenceau had told Lloyd George and Orlando at Versailles that Germany, Austria, and Turkey had notified President Wilson that they were ready to treat on his Fourteen Points and asking for an armistice pending discussion. Sir Henry Wilson's comment was: "Pretty piece of impertinence. As I have always said, let the Boches get behind the Rhine and then we can discuss." We are not concerned with the discussions in the political sphere excepting with one on October 7th at Versailles which Foch and Weygand attended and where Wilson was directed to consider the steps that were necessary. That his views coincided with those of Foch we know from the previous entry. Discussions continued, and on October 18th Haig went to London. He saw Henry Wilson and afterwards Lloyd George, Milner, A. J. Balfour, and others, and told them that he, for his part, would be satisfied if the Germans went back to the 1870 frontier and if we occupied at once all Alsace and Lorraine and particularly Metz and Strasbourg. He thought that although the Germans had been roughly handled they were not yet reduced to accepting either Foch's or Henry Wilson's terms. Wilson opposed this view. Lloyd George and Milner rather agreed with it, and this discussion seems to have had a strong influence on Haig in the outspoken discussions on October 24th. Foch held strongly to the view that the Germans must withdraw across the Rhine and that the Allies must establish bridgeheads across the river. Haig's view was that, if hostili-

[5] *Wilson Diaries,* Vol. II, pp. 133-138.

ties were renewed, he would sooner have the German Armies west of the Rhine, with the river behind them than have Allied troops in exposed positions in the bridgeheads east of the river. Their views were not reconciled, and this is no place to discuss the general question whether the "strategic frontier" idea of security by obstacles, regardless of the sympathy and original nationality or race of the population on your own side of the obstacle is likely to make for permanent peace and security. The issue between the Marshals seems to have hinged upon different estimates of the German *moral,* rather than upon such considerations, but the point that is brought out is that the armistice terms were ultimately based upon military rather than upon political considerations, upon the immediate military security of French territory.

We know how Foch described the final battle; of his thoughts during the last stage we have no certain knowledge, but from what we have learned of his life-mission, of his motives, and of the source upon which he relied for strength it may be permissible to imagine them; and this might be the issue of our imagining.

As a clue to his outlook on such subjects we know of his scorn of the Ems telegram forgery whereby Bismarck had let loose the great war-machine, relentless in its force, which Moltke and Roon had designed and perfected. Bismarck's pencil-strokes had caused the methodical advance of those long columns of perfectly organized armies which had smitten France and humbled her to the dust in the days when Foch, in his ardent youth, had witnessed the results in Metz, at Nancy, and in Paris.

We know that, in the very depths of his consciousness, there lurked a conviction that there is an ethical law for

[399]

the conduct of States in their relationship with other States, even as there is one for individual men in their relationship with their fellow-men. We know too that it was by their conduct, by their actions rather than by their protestations, that he judged his colleagues and others in the field of warfare, and it is not unreasonable to assume that he judged nations by the same standard.

He knew that, by the withdrawal of her troops six miles from her frontiers in those critical days of 1914, France had acquitted herself in the eyes of the world from all trace of aggression. The enemy's accusations were afterwards confessed to have been false by Ludendorff himself. As a student of national psychology Foch also knew of the influence upon German thought of philosophers who held that a State, in its relations with others, is bound by self-interest alone and by no ethical standard whatever. As a careful reader of Clausewitz, the apostle of the German military creed, he cannot have missed the passage on the use of words in war which runs:

These [words] which are very inexpensive are chiefly the means with which the wily one takes in those upon whom he practises.[6]

Foch knew of the words in which the Chancellor of the German Empire reassured the Belgian Minister in Berlin in 1911, telling him that Germany had no intention of violating Belgian neutrality. He knew that, two years later, a German Secretary of State had said in the Reichstag that "Belgian neutrality is provided for in international conventions, and Germany is determined to respect those conventions," and he knew also that on July 31st, 1914, the Ger-

[6] *On War*, Bk. III, Chap. XI.

man Representative in Brussels—who actually had in his possession (in a sealed envelope, it is true) the ultimatum that was presented three days later—had told the Belgian Foreign Office that he knew of the assurance that had been given by the Chancellor in 1911, and that he was "certain that the sentiments expressed at that time had not changed."

We know of Foch's firm and steadfast belief in an almighty force, an instrument of justice in human affairs which, like the grain of mustard-seed, was capable of infinite growth and development, and we know of his habit of deep and concentrated thought, often in a wayside chapel, usually in the simple surroundings of his village headquarters, sometimes in a great cathedral. Is it then too much for us to assume that his memory took his thoughts back to those clouds of dust raised by the tramping columns that violated the soil of Belgium on the 4th of August, 1914, magnificent in pomp and circumstance, perfect in organisation and equipment, irresistible in their relentless advance? He may then have thought how other clouds of dust had descended in later years upon the soil of France and of Flanders in the form of millions of soldiers of the British Empire; of their part in his great Battle of the Hundred Days, carrying all before them from the early days of August, and smashing through the vaunted Hindenburg Line at the end of September, when clouds of Belgian dust again arose—from the explosion of nearly a million British shells in twenty-four hours.

Then he may have recalled another early triumph of material force, also followed in the appointed time by a sequel of retribution. He may have remembered the rising of a column of Atlantic waters mingled with explosive gas which tore a hole in the bottom of the *Lusitania* and left

[401]

American women and children at the mercy of a seething whirlpool strewn with the wreckage from that great Atlantic liner. He knew well the sequel, long delayed but inevitable, of that outrage—the stream of millions of American citizens crossing those same Atlantic waters to help him to hurl the invaders back from French and Belgian soil and, it might be, further than that, across the Rhine, an object to which nearly half a century of his life had been devoted. The first of the American legions to arrive had already cleared the St. Mihiel salient and the difficult Argonne country, and some had borne a fine part, shoulder to shoulder with British Empire troops, in the breaking of the Hindenburg Line.

These may have been the thoughts of Foch, as a steadfast believer in ideals, while others spoke of economic development, of the power of dynasties, of political "gestures," of national self-interest, of personal advancement, or of worldly success; these thoughts may have been with him when he was summoned on the 8th of November to meet the German delegates in that quiet spot in the fifth year of the Great War. Here are some extracts from his own account:

When I saw them at the other side of the table, I said to myself: "There is the German Empire." I thought: "We will be polite, but we must show them who we are." I asked them: "Who are you?" They gave me their names. "Have you any papers? We must examine them." Then I asked them:

"What do you want?"

"We wish to know your proposals?"

"I have no proposals to make."

"We should like to know on what conditions an armistice would be granted?"

"I have no conditions to give you."

Erzberger wished to read me a paper—President Wilson's note—but I stopped him.

"Do you wish to ask for an armistice? If so, say so."

"We ask for an armistice."

"Good. We will read you the conditions drawn up by the Allied Governments."

They were weary, tired out, like hunted animals ... Erzberger made me a long speech in order to secure concessions, explaining that revolution had broken out at home, that their soldiers would no longer obey orders, that the country was in a state of famine, that all authority had disappeared. I stopped him.

"You are suffering from a loser's malady, not a conqueror's. I am not afraid of it. I refuse everything."

And, as you know, I should have adhered to my decision. Immediately afterwards, I wrote to the Chiefs of the Allied Armies: "Redouble your energy in order to consolidate the results attained by your victories." I only stopped because we should get the Rhine. Without the Rhine we should have gained nothing. Holding the Rhine, our minds would be at ease.

Foch always used to say that one did not fight for the sake of fighting, but to obtain results. Having secured these results no one has the right to go on fighting. The Allies had to have the Rhine, and under the terms offered they would have it. They could therefore sign the peace that they wanted. "We had no right to continue shedding blood." A short respite was given to the delegates to bring back their answer. The tale of the final meeting must be deferred to the next chapter.

Chapter XXXIII

VICTORY: NOVEMBER, 1918

AGED 67 YEARS

AT about 7 P.M. on·Friday, November 8th, 1918, a train made up of several *wagons-lits,* a private saloon, a dining saloon, and various saloon-cars fitted as offices and typing and telephone compartments, slowly drew up in an empty siding in the Compiègne Forest near Rethondes. The train contained Marshal Foch, Weygand, and a few selected members of the *"Famille",* representing the Allied Armies engaged in the greatest battle in history which had been raging since March 21st; Admiral Wemyss,[1] First Sea Lord of the British Admiralty, and two or three colleagues, representing the Sea Power which had rendered possible the victory of those great armies which were advancing continuously in spite of exhaustion and difficulties, urged on up to the very last by the Marshal with all his energy and power.

The surroundings were peaceful and quiet, a clearing in the woods made originally for heavy artillery, surrounded by sentries and cut off from the outside world except by telephone communication with Foch's headquarters in the field and with Paris and Versailles. The road from Compiègne to Soissons ran close to the clearing, and the River Aisne was not far away. Darkness reigned in the forest, ex-

[1] Then Sir Rosslyn, now Admiral of the Fleet Lord Wester Wemyss.

cept where a shaft of light from saloon door or window
shone occasionally upon the tree-trunks. About a hundred
yards from the Marshal's train was another siding, empty.
A similar train containing the German mission was expected to arrive there at midnight. A simple dinner was
soon served in the dining saloon of Foch's train, and afterwards the Marshal with Weygand and others met the British naval delegates who found them "all as charming as
possible." In an atmosphere of quiet expectancy the party
all retired to rest before the historic meeting that was to
set the seal upon what seemed to be certain and decisive
victory, news having been received that the train containing
the German delegates had been delayed.

At 7 A.M. on Saturday the 9th, a dark November morning,
their train came to rest in its special siding in the forest
all white with the hoar-frost. Weygand at once boarded
the saloon containing the German mission, conveying a
message that if they wished to see the Marshal he would
be disposed to receive them exactly at nine o'clock. At that
hour they crossed to Foch's train in single file: Erzberger,
the Catholic Deputy and Secretary of State, Count Obendorff representing diplomacy, Major-General von Winterfeldt[2] representing the Army and Captain Vanselow the
Navy, two officer-interpreters following. It was clear from
the composition of the delegation that the desire was to
give a civilian, rather than a military atmosphere to the
meeting, and this is said to have caused much annoyance
to the French army officers. An armistice on the field of
battle should be negotiated between the combatants, not

[2] Winterfeldt's father was one of those who made out the terms of surrender
in 1870. There was some speculation over the reasons why he should have been
chosen to represent the German Army on this occasion.

between civilian representatives of the Governments concerned. Their work should come later.

On entering the saloon in single file the German delegates, "uncomfortable and rather nervous," were received "stiffly but courteously" by Weygand representing the Allied Armies and by Sir George Hope representing the Navies. Weygand, saying that he would announce the arrival, went at once to the Marshal's saloon and then Foch entered, accompanied by Wemyss. After exchanging salutes they all lined up facing each other across the long narrow table in this order:

Obendorff	Erzberger	Winterfeldt	Vanselow
			Interpreters
Hope	Wemyss	Foch	Weygand

Foch having asked for the reason of the visit, there followed the conversation that we have already recorded in Foch's own words. When Erzberger had said definitely that the German delegates had come to ask for an armistice Foch asked to see their credentials. When these had been produced Foch and Wemyss retired to examine them. On their return Foch requested Erzberger to introduce the German delegates and then he introduced the members of his own mission. Then the Marshal announced the terms on which he was authorised by the Allied Governments to grant an armistice. Winterfeldt asked for a suspension of hostilities in order to save further loss of life. This was refused. The Germans then asked for copies of the terms, for facilities to send a radio message to their Government, and also for leave to send a courier with a copy of the text. These points were conceded, and the Germans retired to their saloon. Erzberger seemed to British observers to be nervous and speaking with difficulty, Obendorff very alert, Winterfeldt sad, and Vanselow sullen.

Immediately after the meeting, Foch issued what was destined to be his last general operation order during the War:

The enemy, disorganized by our repeated attacks, is giving ground on all the front. It is necessary to keep up and to quicken our action. I call upon the energy and initiative of the Commanders-in-chief and of their armies to render decisive the results that have been obtained.

The afternoon of that Saturday (November 9th) was spent in various discussions about details of the terms [3] between the German and British naval officers and between Winterfeldt and Weygand. In these the crushing effect of the naval "blockade" [4] and the danger of Bolshevism, needing machine guns for its suppression, was much emphasised on the German side. It was obvious that the Army was badly shaken and the Staff upset, and the German delegates suffered from delay thereby caused; their courier had great difficulty in crossing their own lines, and his car was shot at on one occasion, when he was forced to turn back. Changes in the German Government caused doubt to prevail about the issue and so matters rested on the Saturday.

The Allied delegates formed a small and happy party but they only assembled together for meals described as "plain and good" in the restaurant car of their train. There is mention of a gift by some admirer to Foch of an old bottle of 1778 brandy (Louis XVI) which appeared at din-

[3] See appendix.
[4] Technically, there was no "blockade" by the Allies, as recognized in diplomacy.

[407]

ner-time. The Marshal was kind and amiable to all, excepting when the Germans were present, and then his manner was described as "stern and dignified." He was only seen to leave his train once, and that was to attend Mass on the Sunday morning. The British delegates naturally did most of their business with Weygand, whom they found "always charming."

After a fairly quiet morning and an afternoon more occupied by meetings between the naval and the military groups, the Sunday passed without incident until the evening. Hostilities were to be continued relentlessly unless the German delegates signed by 11.00 A.M. on Monday morning, so not many hours remained. On Sunday evening the Germans received a telegram from their Government. Negotiations were then resumed, and here we can recall a remark that was made by Foch to Colonel House on October 31st: "I do not make war for the sake of making war, but for results. If the enemy signs an Armistice which gives to the Allied Governments the means of obtaining the results which they desire, there is no reason for continuing the bloodshed." [5]

The night of that Sunday (November 10th-11th) was only the second which Foch had spent out of bed during the whole four and a half years of the War. The first, it will be recalled, was the night of September 10th-11th at Fère-Champenoise, after the first battle of the Marne. We have his own account of this later occasion:[6] "We slept but little. During the evening we had resumed our discussions. I lay down from 11 P.M. to 1.30 A.M. Then we started arguing again until 5.15 in the morning. At last they

[5] *Revue des deux Mondes*, May, 1929 (Weygand), p. 18.
[6] As told to Commandant Bugnet.

signed." And again: "On November 11th they gave us what we asked for. The interview at Rethondes, was not that a deed? It marked the disintegration of the German Empire, and I saw Erzberger brandish his pen and grind his teeth when he signed the document. I was then glad that I had exerted my will, and employed the means of exerting it, for the business was settled."

After the signature a pile of papers had to be dealt with, and Weygand took charge of everything while Foch had a short hour's rest. The following order was issued:

Marshal Foch à Commandants-en-chef.
du 11 *Novembre* 1918.

1. Les hostilités seront arrêtées sur tout le front à partie du 11 novembre, à 11 heures, heure français.

2. Les troupes alliées ne dépasseront pas, jusqu'à nouvelle ordre, la ligne atteinte à cette date et à cette heure; rendre compte exactement de cette ligne.

3. Toute communication avec l'ennemi est interdite jusqu'à reception des instructions envoyées aux Commandants d'Armée.

Signé, F. Foch.

Desticker at Senlis and three Staff officers were employed in getting this order to all concerned as rapidly as possible. The first copy was despatched at 5.40 A.M. to the fighting forces, the last, to Versailles, at 9.40; at 11.00 the persistent gunfire ceased in the long battle-line and there followed a "silence that could be felt."

At seven o'clock Foch's train had left for Paris, and he said afterwards: "I had the Armistice in my pocket. It was a foggy morning, but the sun came out later! I called on M. Clemenceau and M. Poincaré. Then I went home." When he handed the acceptance of the Armistice terms, signed by the German plenipotentiaries, to the President, Foch said to Clemenceau who was present: "My work is finished. Your work begins."

Weygand has since told us exactly what was in the Marshal's mind. His sole object was security for France. He, above all others, had made a study of previous invasions, and in common with all Frenchmen he embarked upon the War determined to win, whatever the cost might be, and to safeguard French soil from all chance of future violation. In order to ensure that he believed that it was essential to the safety of the peoples of Western Europe that the Rhine should form a barrier to bind the German Empire in the West. He used to pronounce the word "Rhin" hoarsely and with emphasis "as if he wanted to lay stress upon the depth of this great obstacle (*fossé de sécurité*)." The Armistice had given this, although hostilities were stopped before it was actually conquered. Foch wanted to keep it, not, as has been wrongly said, as the frontier of France, but as a line on which to stop Germany. He left to the plenipotentiaries the task of devising the nature of the new State which would thus have been created between the two countries. He advocated that policy directly the Armistice was signed.

After leaving M. Poincaré, Foch went at once to his Paris home in the Avenue de Saxe to tell his family the good news. A street-market is held there twice a week, Monday being one of the days. The crowd saw Foch's car standing outside his house and a popular demonstration began outside in the road while he was having his luncheon. In his description of the incident Foch remarked simply: "So I went off." He was recognized as he passed the Place de l'Opéra, where there was a still more enthusiastic demonstration and the people raised cheers for him. "It seemed likely that they would drag me out of my car. But I wanted to get away." He accordingly gave the crowd the slip in the Rue Lafayette and "took cover" at Army Headquarters. As he left Paris he met crowds in the suburbs converging on the capital, full of joy over their delivery. He put it more strongly than that himself. "It was Victory—I repeat, Victory. We could do what we liked with it." On the day following, Foch told those who had helped him in gaining the victory:

You have won the greatest battle in history, and have saved the most sacred of causes, the liberty of the world. Be proud. You have adorned your colours with an immortal glory. Posterity reserves its gratitude for you.[7]

With most of them, however, there was a consciousness of reaction rather than of elation, and the British view has been well summarised by Mr. Churchill in prose which few modern writers can excel:

Is this the end? Is it to be merely a chapter in a cruel and senseless story? Will a new generation in their turn be immolated to square the black accounts of Teuton and Gaul? Will our children bleed and gasp again in devastated lands? Or will there spring from the very fires of conflict that reconciliation of the three giant combatants, which would unite their genius and secure to each in safety and freedom a share in the rebuilding of the glory of Europe?[8]

The only criticism to be offered on that extract is the use of the word "glory"—a sentiment that counts for little in English eyes.

[7] *World Crisis,* 1916-18, Part II, last page.
[8] Bugnet, p. 248.

[411]

Of Foch himself it has been well written[9] that that
Monday in November, 1918, marked for him the result of
method applied by character. He then reached the culminating point of a life of hard work, devoted to his
country. After weeks of struggle, nights of misery, days of
gloom, mornings of vision, evenings of hope, thousands
of hours so full of events grave in their consequences, moments of vivid divination resulting in a decision, instants
in which fate has lain in one's hands, no one who has lived
through such times and has wrested from them a final victory can have wasted his lifetime. He deserves the supreme
recompense.

To that we can add the view, well expressed from the
British side,[10] that in the moment of victory, when a word
from Foch would have postponed the granting of an Armistice and would undoubtedly have associated his name for
all time with a crushing defeat of the Germans in the open
field, he showed the moderation of a really great mind.
The conditions which the enemy had accepted had achieved
the purpose of the Allies and he maintained that he had
no right to shed one drop more blood. For him it was sufficient reward that he had restored France to the place which
she had held before 1870.

A British general officer who saw Foch late in the evening
of November 11th found him all alone, as he had sent
Weygand to bed after his strenuous and continuous work
of the preceding thirty-six hours. The Marshal was in his
chair, smoking, and in answer to his visitor's congratulations
he said: *"Ce n'est pas moi—c'est nous,"* which naturally
pleased his hearer. Foch's account, in a conversation which

[9] Bugnet, p. 248.
[10] Sir H. Edmonds, in the *Journal of the R. U. S. Institution* 1929.

lasted more than an hour, of his reception of the German delegates, described his attitude and that of his officers as *"très propre, mais sec!"* He was quite sure that, had he launched the attack in Lorraine by twenty American and French divisions under Mangin (that he had prepared for the 14th of November), the result would probably have been such confusion on the German railways that veritable disaster would have ensued. He was quite satisfied, however, with the Armistice. After it had been concluded, he said to his British visitor, as he had to Colonel House at the end of October, that he was quite satisfied with the terms. The object being to clear the enemy out of France and Belgium, that object could be achieved more rapidly under the Armistice than it could be by further fighting. "And what is more, without any further sacrifice of life. No, I am quite satisfied"—"And well he might be," is the narrator's comment.

Looking back at the Marshal's own achievements, we find that in March, 1918, he had been entrusted with his limited powers during a grave crisis in the fortunes of the Allies, during the course of what appeared to be a lost battle. In 1914, 1915, and 1916 he had borne much of the credit and responsibility for averting defeat when on the defensive, and he had also taken a leading part in the offensive operations which followed. Those attacks did not produce any decisive results at the time, but that was largely on account of the lack of the necessary equipment for attack.

In March, Foch's policy had been to send help to the British when Pétain was just about to break away from them, drawing back his left to cover Paris. What would have followed upon the separation between the Allied Armies we do not know—certainly not victory in the field.

His policy in April had been to maintain the British front at a time when many British experts, including his friend Henry Wilson, spoke of shortening the line of defence, of retiring, of flooding the country with sea water, and even of abandoning the Channel ports to the enemy. Foch's next severe test came in May and June, but his nerve never failed for a moment. He constantly prepared for a counter-stroke when others did not believe that a general offensive would be possible before the spring of 1919. In August, the Supreme War Council, representing the Allied Governments, gave instructions to their military representatives to consider that proposed campaign. These experts went to see Foch at Bom Bon in the middle of September, and they put forward the view that it would not be justifiable, for lack of sufficient superiority in force, to seek a decision by attack before the spring. They were received with ceremony, and Foch addressed them thus:

Gentlemen,
    If you ask me what I am going to do to-morrow I will tell you, but if you ask me what I am going to do the day after to-morrow, I shall have to request you to come back to-morrow morning because to-day it is too soon.

On many other occasions Foch proved his capacity for terse and definite expression, the result of knowledge and thought, but his genius as a leader of armies lay in his character, and in the effect of that character upon those around him, whether he was talking or silent.

It was through his personal energy and inspiration that the French Army during the closing period recovered its lost *moral*. He got more out of them, as he did out of others, than they thought themselves capable of facing. His position was delicate and difficult. Determination, combined with great tact, were the qualities required to achieve any results at all. Though masterful by nature, he knew when to yield. Impatient of all opposition, he maintained a strong control over himself, acquired by long and determined training. He obtained his own way in the end because he inspired confidence. One who knew him best wrote: "Confidence simply exuded from him, and it was impossible to doubt long in his company." His own saying on the subject of co-operation between Allies was: "A rigid command delays and divides efforts. Confidence unites and strengthens them." [11] He could not stand large conferences, with their endless talk and decisions which were seldom correct. He had only two general conferences of Allied Commanders-in-Chief in 1918, one on July 24th when the programme for the summer offensive was disclosed, the other on October 25th, about the terms on which an armistice would be granted. Since we have taken note of the differences that arose on that occasion, a suitable opportunity is here offered for telling the story of the way in which Foch overcame the opposition to his claims for bridgeheads on the far side of the Rhine. He produced a book out of his pocket and he read an extract to the effect that in order to invade Germany it was necessary to have bridgeheads at Cologne, Coblenz, and Mayence. When it was discovered that Moltke was the author, Foch gained his point, from which it would appear that there was an idea in the minds of those present that before a satisfactory peace could be secured operations might have to be carried beyond the Rhine. The origin of the bridgeheads, which are still occupied (1929), is important.

[11] *Les deux Batailles de la Marne*, p. 134.

Separate conferences between Foch and individual Commanders-in-Chief were held frequently, every four or five days, and they were either preceded or followed by a letter or by a Directive which served either as a basis for discussion or as the conclusion arrived at with his *"excellents collaborateurs."* The result on the whole was cordial agreement which greatly simplified the task.[12]

Foch concluded his observations on his experiences of 1918 by expressing "to all whom he had had the honour to command, whatever their rank and under whatever flag they served," his deep acknowledgement of their help. In peace, as in war, he never forgot them. They had been "the true workers of the combined Victory (*Les vrais artisans de nôtre Victoire commune*)."

When the victorious armies had reached the Rhine, Foch and Weygand went to Metz. They arrived at 11 P.M. on November 25th and they were received in the "Emperor's waiting-room" before being conducted to the waiting motorcars. Though snow lay on the ground, Foch preferred a walk through the streets, thinking of his youthful experiences and the achievement of his purpose.

I was so happy that I said to Weygand: "Here, have a good cigar, and let us go for a stroll." I took him round Metz for an hour. The weather was atrocious. The streets were covered with snow, and there was no one about . . . I shall never forget it.

In the course of that walk they noticed German statues which had been thrown down from their plinths. On the next day a review was held, and to see French troops march past on the Place de l'Hotel de Ville of Metz was to Foch an "ample reward" for his life's work. After the march-past

[12] *Les deux Batailles de la Marne*, p. 134.

he said that the troops might be dismissed. For himself, he was going to thank the Lord of Hosts for granting him the victory:

> Everyone followed me. I have never seen such a crowd as there was at the Cathedral for this *Te Deum*.
> Yes I have: at Malines, when we went there with M. Poincaré to hand the Croix de Guerre to Cardinal Mercier.
> It was extraordinary. When it was all over, the crowd sang the Marseillaise in the Cathedral.[13]

Forty-seven years had passed since the day when the young Ferdinand Foch, student at the College of St. Clément, had heard a thundering salvo from the guns of the forts, followed by the knowledge that Metz had been lost to France, and he had then mentioned to a fellow student the need to regain the lost territory, and his own determination to become one of her liberators.[14] No one who studies his career can fail to be struck by the way in which all his experiences, his apparent failures no less than his obvious successes, contributed to his training for the final achievement. Dismissal from the *Ecole Supérieure de Guerre* where, as a lecturer, he had established a school of thought in the French Army, gave him the practical experience with troops which was highly necessary to him after so much academic work, and being *"limogé"* in 1916 and deprived of active command gave him time for recuperation after his motor accident and two years of great strain. The work with which he was then charged, though perhaps it was distasteful to him at the time—the study of the Western Front and its problems as a whole—was exactly the work best suited to improve his fitness for the mission with which he

[13] *Vide supra,* Chap. III.   [14] Bugnet, pp. 250-251.

was finally charged—the co-ordination of the Allied effort on that same frontage.

Of Foch's sense of humour a good story is told by an officer of the Brigade of Guards who presented him in the summer of 1918 with a tobacco-pouch of the Brigade colours with the words *"Blague* (pouch) *de la victoire dans les couleurs de la Garde."* Some time after the Armistice the same officer came to see the Marshal, bearing a message. Foch was sitting at a table covered with a litter of papers amongst which he began to search. The officer tried several times to deliver his message but each time the Marshal waved him aside saying, *"Attendez! Attendez!"* The puzzle was solved when the lost object was discovered and the Marshal held up the tobacco-pouch saying, *"Voici la blague de la victoire, mais cette victoire n'est pas une blague* (a sell)!"

Chapter XXXIV

THE AFTERMATH: 1918-1922

AGED 67-70 YEARS

It fell to the lot of Marshal Foch, as it did to that of Nelson, to come upon the scene at a moment when a great tendency in historical progress (the defeat of "militarism") was nearing its culmination, and of him we can write, as Admiral Mahan did of Nelson, that "specially gifted with qualities needed to realize the fulness of its possibilities," he so identified himself with it by his deeds that he thenceforward personified to the world the movement which brought him forth and of which his own achievements were the climax and the culmination. Few amongst such men, deemed by Mahan to be the happiest of all, are those who do not survive their instant of perfected success, but "pass from our ken in a blaze of glory which thenceforth for ever encircles their names . . . and their sun goes down with a lustre which the lapse of time is powerless to dim."

For lasting fame the great Marshal needed no such dramatic exit from the scene of his labours and achievements. The secret of his enduring reputation, after descending from a pinnacle of power as a man of action to the subordinate position of an adviser whose advice was often ignored, lay undoubtedly in his banishment of all selfish motives. "Nothing seems more certain in human life," said a great divine in an address to schoolboys, "than the law that it is only in unselfish use that the gifts of intellect and feeling reach their full development and go on from strength to strength, from light to light." He added that one can see it happening again and again, and one may know it with humiliating distinctness in one's own self, that any such faculty quite certainly deteriorates, and swiftly loses all its purity and worth, when it is used for selfish ends—for display, for ambition, for popularity, or for pride. "Often this change is felt immediately; in many cases simply to detain with pleasure the thought that one is doing a thing effectively is to begin at once to do it less well. Sooner or later the deterioration always comes; there is no escaping the Nemesis of misuse." [1]

While many have survived periods of adversity such as those which Foch experienced in the course of his career, few great characters in history have passed through successes so consummate without deterioration. Through self-abnegation and acceptance of any work, however subordinate, that was allotted to him by the rulers of his country, Foch retained during his ten remaining years of comparative obscurity the universal respect that had been his portion in the days when his name was on all men's lips. The principal accessible sources of information "through English eyes" about his thoughts and his activities up to the month of June, 1922,[2] lie in the diaries of his great friend, the late Field-Marshal Sir Henry Wilson, who, as Chief of the Imperial General Staff acted in an advisory position towards the British Government similar to that occupied by Foch towards the Peace Conference and subsequently towards the Council of Ambassadors. For events after June, 1922, Wey-

[1] *The Hallowing of Work*, Dean Paget's addresses at Eton.
[2] The date of Sir Henry Wilson's assassination.

gand's article in the *Revue des deux Mondes* is of great value, while Foch's aide-de-camp Commandant Bugnet has drawn for us in his little book of reminiscences [3] an intimate picture of the closing years spent by the veteran Field-Marshal in his office in Paris.

On December 1st, 1918, Clemenceau and Foch came to London. During their procession from Charing Cross station to Claridge's Hotel the streets were lined with troops and "the visitors, and especially Foch, were accorded a stirring reception by the crowd."

At Claridge's, H.R.H. the Duke of Connaught spent some time with the Marshal, who "said very nice things" to him about the British Army and about Haig. In a subsequent conversation with Wilson Foch gave a clear account of his proposals for ensuring the future security of France. Wilson wrote:

He [Foch] proposes to throw all the Rhenish Provinces into the Western group, to consist of France, England, Belgium, Luxembourg, and an autonomous Palatinate, but under the eyes of France and England. He does not see by what other means he can guard his left flank . . .

At a more formal meeting at No. 10 Downing Street, held on the same evening, Foch gave further information about his views to Lloyd George and Bonar Law:

At this meeting Foch developed his proposals that, in order to face 65 to 76 million Boches over the Rhine he wanted to combine all the French, Belgian, Luxembourg and Rhenish Provinces in one confederation, amounting to 54,000,000, which, with the help of the British, might hope to cope with the Boches. Both Lloyd George and Bonar Law were opposed to this, as

[3] *En écoutant le Maréchal Foch.*

making of the Rhenish Provinces another Alsace-Lorraine. I think that Foch is going too far, but at the same time it is clear to me that neutrals like the Luxembourgs and the Belgians unduly expose the flank of the poor French, and that therefore some precaution must be taken . . .

Both Foch and Clemenceau encountered "the most tremendous receptions everywhere," until they returned to France on December 4th. On the 22nd Wilson saw Foch at Senlis, finding him "as nice as ever," but unhappy at the precipitancy displayed in demobilising the Allied Armies, and insisting upon the need to hold the line of the Rhine until the danger had passed. Late in January, 1919, further discussions took place on the strength of the British Army of Occupation, and on proposals to limit the strength of the German Army. Wilson wrote of a meeting with Foch and Weygand on January 26th:

We discussed the possibility of limiting the enemy's number of trained men, and we were both agreed that it was quite impossible . . . As Foch put it, we can no more limit the number of men trained to arms in Germany than the Germans could limit the output of coal in England. Then we discussed the possibility of checking and limiting guns, rifles, lorries, etc., and again we came to the conclusion that it would be quite impossible. Foch is determined to stick to the line of the Rhine, and I agree that it is much the wisest, and in fact the only, plan until we have secured the fruits of victory.

Early in February Wilson found Foch very anxious about the general situation and about the "total inability of the Peace Conference to come to any decision upon any subject." He feared that the French soldiers would not stand it for much longer and that they would demobilise themselves.

MARSHAL FOCH, H. M. KING GEORGE V, AND SIR DOUGLAS HAIG

At 4th Army Headquarters: Flixecourt, August, 1918.

At the end of February, after calling M. Clemenceau a "wonderful old boy" and receiving the reply: "Why old?", Wilson saw Foch again and found him convinced that the line of the Rhine must be held "for good," as the cheapest form of insurance. From any but the purely military point of view "this is impossible," Wilson adds. At a Plenary meeting of the Peace Conference on March 7th, Foch contended for a limit of 100,000 for the German Army, and for its being based upon conscription. At another meeting held on March 19th, when the frontiers of Poland were being discussed, President Wilson objected to the views of soldiers upon frontiers being heard at all, on the plea that "frontiers have nothing to do with soldiers." At the end of March proposals by Foch to deal forthwith by military action with Bolshevism in Hungary were discussed, the decision arrived at being that military action was not the answer to Bolshevism. At a subsequent discussion on the Danzig problem on March 29th when a conference between Foch and the German authorities at Spa was proposed, President Wilson said at the conclusion: "And I would affectionately ask General (*sic*) Foch to act more as a diplomat than as a soldier." Sir Henry Wilson adds in his diary that "the old boy's face was a study, and he put his hand up to his mouth and said in an audible whisper (I was sitting beside him): *'Ce n'est pas commode, Henri!'* "

On March 31st Foch read two papers to the members of the Peace Conference, insisting in both of them upon the vital necessity to the French of holding the left bank of the Rhine. Thenceforward, from April onwards, Wilson reports a growing disposition on the part of the "Big Four" (Clemenceau, Lloyd George, President Wilson, and Orlando) to ignore Foch. On April 6th, the Marshal told

[423]

Wilson that the Germans had agreed to all his terms at Spa, but that they were "crying out about Bolshevism." On the 11th Foch expressed to Wilson his opinion that proceedings in the French Senate were only the opening of troubles for Clemenceau, and that "France will never agree to come back from the Rhine."

Weeks passed by in long discussions in a world seething with unsettlement and craving for clear leadership. Foch told Wilson on May 1st that he was kept in complete ignorance of all that was going on, and on the next day that he would not attend the meeting with the German delegates, due during the following week, unless he had first been told, and had approved, the military clauses in the Peace Treaty. (The Germans had been waiting since April 30th.) Wilson records in his diary that Lloyd George told him on May 6th that Clemenceau was "watching for an opportunity to remove Foch and to put in Pétain," and that he (Lloyd George) had impressed upon Clemenceau and upon President Wilson that Foch ought to be given a copy of the Peace Terms and to be "treated with the greatest consideration." At the last Plenary Conference that was held before the Peace Treaty was handed to the Germans, Foch made his final appeal for the line of the Rhine. Lloyd George, Mr. Arthur Balfour and others said that he did so clearly and with dignity.

On May 7th, at 3 p.m., the peace terms were handed to the German plenipotentiaries at Versailles, "never having been read by any of us in their entirety" (Wilson). Wilson was upset by the power that was given to the Germans to write their objections, but Foch's comment to him on the telephone after the meeting was *"Soyez tranquille, Henri, c'est une affaire de wagons."* The question of the strength

[424]

of the contingents on the Rhine was then referred, not to Foch, but to the military advisers to the Supreme War Council. Foch bided his time, but on May 17th there occurred an incident in his relationship with Clemenceau which had best be described in his own words: [4]

I have had frequent squabbles with Clemenceau. The most serious arose out of the incident of May 17th, when he wanted me to send for the German plenipotentiaries before the treaty was signed. I refused to send the message. I said:

Foch—"No, I do not understand."

Clemenceau—"You do not need to understand."

Foch—"Yes I do, or I shall wire 'By order of M. Clemenceau.'"

He would not agree to that, of course. He wanted me to sign the message. In his eyes, discipline is like that described in De Vigny's *Canne de Jonc* . . . No! I sign nothing which I do not understand. Eventually he sent the telegram himself.

On May 19th, Foch was instructed to be ready to march into Germany on the 27th, as it seemed likely that the Germans would not sign. On the 23rd Foch told Wilson that he did not think that the Germans would sign. On June 16th Foch, recalled from a visit to Luxembourg and summoned hastily to President Wilson's house by the "Big Four"— now three, in the absence of Orlando—was kept waiting which "was too much for him, and he went off." [5] Sir Henry Wilson, who was consulted, explained that Foch was ready to advance ninety kilometres to the Weser, but that he did not like going to Berlin, and that he had received no instructions. Wilson was then told that clear instructions, including going to Berlin, had been given. If Foch would not carry out their wishes they could get someone else. Wilson comments:

[4] See Bugnet, pp. 254-255.
[5] *Wilson Diaries*, Vol. II, p. 198.

"I wonder. And what a way to get the Boches to sign—to unload Foch!"

The next step appears to have been to try to induce Pétain to undertake what Foch considered impracticable or undesirable. On June 18th Clemenceau told Wilson that Pétain agreed with Foch that an advance far into Germany would be most difficult to carry out. On June 19th Clemenceau added that "he had had a most satisfactory discussion with Foch, and that the difficulties between the two were happily at an end."

On June 28th the German plenipotentiaries signed the Treaty of Versailles. Foch absented himself from the ceremony, which was thus described by Wilson:

I have never seen a less impressive ceremony. The room was much too full, a crowd of smart ladies, a buzz of conversation, the whole thing unreal, shoddy, and poor to a degree. The fountains played and some guns fired, and we went away.

There was to be no question with Foch of "sulking in his tent." The treaty once signed, he was ready to undertake the task to which he was appointed, which was to see to the execution of the military clauses. In January, 1920, he became president of the Allied Military Committee of Versailles which was set up for that purpose, and the former Generalissimo became the subordinate of the Ambassadors' Conference. He served them loyally, with the remark: "I uphold the Versailles Treaty. It is a minimum." [6]

Meanwhile he had paid two more visits to London, where he had met with a rousing reception. He arrived first on July 18th, 1919, the first anniversary of the great counter-stroke on the Château-Thierry salient which had turned

[6] Bugnet, p. 258.

MARSHAL FOCH AND GENERAL WEYGAND

the fortunes of the Allies, and on the 19th he rode at the head of the contingent of French troops past the King's dais in front of Buckingham Palace. On the 21st, he "went off beaming, after a wonderfully successful visit."

The Victory March in London was arranged to take place a few days after that in Paris, and Haig had invited Foch to come to London to take part in the procession.

The French contingent consisted of one hundred and four officers and eight hundred and ninety-seven other ranks with fifty-five flags and two bands. Fifteen regiments of infantry were represented, together with most of the more famous regiments—the Chasseurs d'Afrique, Chasseurs de Cheval, Foreign Legion, Moroccans, Algerians, Zouaves, and the Tirailleurs. Foch landed at Folkestone where he inspected the troops, received by a Guard of Honour of the Middlesex Regiment. Afterwards he came to Victoria where a huge crowd was gathered to receive him.

Haig was on the platform. He seized Foch's hands before the Marshal alighted, and the two men were still clasping hands when Foch stepped out of the train, to be greeted by a gathering of distinguished representatives of the Army, Navy, and Air Forces. A fine floral arch had been erected, and through this the Marshal passed to the Royal waiting room. In the courtyard there was awaiting him a Guard of Honour of the Welsh Guards, and the band of the Irish Guards greeted him with the "Marseillaise."

Foch inspected the Guard of Honour, and then with Haig, Weygand, and Henry Wilson, took his place in the first of the three royal carriages sent to meet him. He was to stay at the Carlton with his Staff, and on the way there the crowd gave him a most enthusiastic welcome. At the hotel itself an immense crowd had gathered to greet him as he drove up. Even after he had disappeared into the building they refused to disperse, but with that persistence which characterises an English crowd when it really does break through its reserve, they shouted again and again for the great Marshal to show himself. Foch appeared on a little balcony, and acknowledged their welcome which seemed to surprise him. He looked tired and a little wondering, though he was at pains to indicate that he appreciated their attentions. He had known too much of the fickleness of public opinion to be overmuch exalted or cast down by its manifestations.

The route chosen for the Victory March, which started at Albert Gate, took in South London as well as the western districts, crossing Vauxhall Bridge, and returning via Westminster Bridge, and so to Whitehall; the Cenotaph which had been unveiled for the occasion, being the second saluting point, the first being the Royal Pavilion outside Buckingham Palace.

It was a marvelous spectacle, and even the English papers seemed to agree that Foch was its central figure. His aloof, modest, dignified, almost impassive bearing, seemed to impress the crowd who cheered him again and again, evoking occasionally one of the Marshal's rare smiles. So Foch passed through London which yelled its welcome; women throwing red roses under his feet, the crowds recognising him with shouts of "There he is!" as baton in hand, he rode quietly past. Behind him came the Poilus, singing their favourite "Madelon"—the "Tipperary" of the French troops—to which had been added the new victory chorus:

"C'est pour fêter la Victoire!
Joffre, Foch, et Clemenceau!"

[428]

For most of the time Foch rode with his gaze fixed straight ahead, looking neither to the right nor the left, but outside Chelsea Hospital he paid marked attention to the veteran pensioners. There was a poignant moment when he gravely saluted the Cenotaph to the British Empire's million dead, of whom so many lay buried in the soil of France and Flanders. Carrying the gold and blue baton of his high rank he rode on unperturbed in the hour of his triumph as he had been in moments of disaster.

When the procession reached the saluting point at Buckingham Palace, Foch dismounted at the request of the King and Queen to stand at their Majesties' right hand in the pavilion, where Haig and Pershing joined him later.

The next day being Sunday, Foch attended High Mass at Westminster Cathedral, wearing his undress uniform of light blue, and accompanied only by two young officers. He looked grave and rather strained, as if unable in all the triumph of victory to forget the cost, or perhaps to dismiss from his mind the disappointments that he had recently experienced over the peace treaty. He was received by Cardinal Bourne in crimson robes, and given a chair and a footstool at the top of the nave, close to the chancel. There, a solitary conspicuous figure, he stayed throughout the service, which was brought to a close by the "Marseillaise" and the British National Anthem, played by the band of the Welsh Guards.

As he left the Cathedral, the Marshal paused before the shrine of Joan of Arc, which was blazing with votive candles surmounted by the Tricolor and the Union Jack. Before he passed on he made a deep genuflection to the figure of the Maid, for whom he had always entertained a profound reverence. A few minutes later there occurred one of those little incidents which serve to show his human side. As he stood on the steps of the Archbishop's house, the Cathedral choir boys came thronging round him with open autograph books. With his keen blue eyes twinkling, Foch stood patiently signing his name until he was sure that no single lad was disappointed.

On the evening of the 20th the Prince of Wales presided at a dinner that was given at the Carlton in honour of the Generalissimo. Foch had been to Windsor Castle in the afternoon, and he arrived in London only just in time for the dinner, to which all the Allied Commanders and their Staffs had been invited. The room had been magnificently decorated with red, white, and blue flowers, and the guests were in full uniform. Foch sat on the right of the Prince, who had Pershing on his left.

The Prince made an excellent speech, in which he said, "It is a great honour to be presiding here to-night, and that it should fall to my lot to propose such a wonderful toast." He summed up the events of war and Foch's services to the world, and before proposing the final toast he gave a *précis* of the speech in French, which greatly pleased the French guests. He then gave the toast of "The Allied Generals, coupled with the name of Marshal Foch."

In reply Foch made a brief and telling speech, in which he thanked the Prince for his words, and said that he saluted most of all the splendid comradeship, by which they had been so greatly illumined.

Next day Foch left for Paris, and Sir Henry Wilson saw him off. During the visit Foch and Wilson had returned to their boyish pranks when they were alone together. Changing headgear was one of them, and they were sitting, Foch in uniform and Wilson in plain clothes, in Foch's private room in the Carlton Hotel, Foch wearing Wilson's "billycock" hat, which was too big for him, over his ears, and Wilson with Foch's képi balanced on his head, when there came a knock at the door:

In response to the summons to enter, a stalwart Grenadier Guardsman marched in and presented a letter from Buckingham Palace to Foch . . . He accepted the letter, and the Grenadier, with the imperturbable stolidity that was to be expected in a representative of the Brigade of Guards, saluted and marched out again. He probably found something to tell his comrades in the barrack-room when he got back.[7]

Foch crossed the Channel again on the evening of July 19th to receive his baton as a Field-Marshal in the British Army from the hands of H. M. the King. Next morning he and Wilson went to the Palace where the King made a "charming little speech" and handed the baton to Foch, who in reply recalled Wilson's first visit to him at the *Ecole Supérieure de Guerre* in 1908 and added that neither Brigadier-General Wilson nor General of Division Foch would in those days have believed that, at the end of the greatest war in the world, they would both stand in front of the King as British Field-Marshals. Foch then drove to the Guildhall in one of the royal carriages, receiving an ovation on his way. Speeches and a luncheon at the Mansion House followed. The City Fathers had invited a crowd of distinguished people to do him honour, including Prince Arthur of Connaught and all the Generals. It was noticed at once by experts that instead of the baton of a Marshal of France Foch carried a British Field Marshal's baton which he had just received from the King. In his speech on the War he hardly mentioned his own part but praised the other Gen-

[7] *Wilson Diaries*, Vol. II, p. 205.

[431]

erals and paid a special tribute to Haig: "In spite of the
distance between us, and the fatigues and difficulties, we
sought each other out constantly like two big brothers of a
family working for the good of the rest." He made a moving reference to the British dead, whose graves would be
cared for by his countrymen. He attended a state banquet
at the Mansion House in the evening and left for Paris the
same night, the giant airship R.34 hovering over Victoria
Station to give him a farewell salute.

The Marshal wrote a letter to Lloyd George, that was
published in the *Times* of August 30th, about handsome
tributes which had been paid to him in speeches in both
Houses of Parliament:

The French Ambassador in London has sent me the text of
the words that you were kind enough to say about me in the
House of Commons, as well as the substance of those Lord
Curzon spoke in the House of Lords; he also informed me of
the reception given to those speeches by the two houses.

I do not forget, however, that if I was appointed to be Chief
of the Allied Armies, it was on your initiative and thanks to
your confidence. If I was able equally to bring the war to a
speedy conclusion, it was thanks to the sustained determination
of the British Government to reinforce and keep up, in 1918,
sufficient reinforcements for the Army in France, and also to
give powerful assistance to the transport of troops from America
to Europe.

In the face of such confidence and such serious efforts, I employed on my part all the activity of which I was capable, in
order to achieve victory, making the best use of the means which
had been confided to me. To-day it is an honour and one most
highly appreciated to see my services so received, and in such
flattering terms, and in a particularly moving way by the Government and Parliament of Great Britain, and I am profoundly

grateful to you, the Prime Minister, for having taken the initiative in this token of satisfaction on their part, and I ask you to receive the assurance of my respectful devotion.

In February, 1920, the Marshal was received at the *Académie Française* with a valedictory speech from President Poincaré. In January, 1921, he and Weygand had luncheon with Lloyd George at Chequers, the time after luncheon being chiefly occupied in submitting to the attentions of "fifteen photographers and cinema-men," who followed the party everywhere. Foch refused an offer of a bed at Chequers and returned to London in the evening. In March Foch attended a meeting of the Supreme War Council in London when the question of German violation of the peace terms was discussed. The occasion was marked by a dinner-party at the Wilsons' house in Eaton Place when Foch spoke most feelingly to Lady Edwina Lewin, Lord Roberts's daughter, about her father, and Wilson comments: "His (Foch's) love and admiration for Lord Bobs is very touching and very curious, since they knew each other very little and always spoke through an interpreter." The news-placards on that evening coupled the names of Foch and Wilson, who wrote in his diary: "What an honour to be coupled with the great Marshal."

A critical situation, owing to a miners' strike and to the sympathy with them of the railwaymen and transport workers, developed in England in April, and there was talk of having to withdraw British troops from the Rhine and from Silesia. Wilson sent a message about it to Foch who replied at once that, as "Henri was in danger," whatever troops he wanted could be withdrawn, and he (Foch) would hold the gate until the troops could be sent back again, adding that Wilson had only to ask and "any mortal thing" would be done by Foch to help him. "What a splendid old man he is, and what a loyal comrade," was Wilson's comment in his diary. Foch went further, and in reply to another verbal message in April, asking that, if the eight British battalions at Cologne were replaced by French ones, General Morland would still remain in command there, the "old Marshal" replied that, if Wilson so wished, he would certainly agree.

In May 1921 the Supreme War Council met in London to consider the delay in paying off the war indemnity by Germany, and Foch laid before them his scheme for occupying the Ruhr, using only French troops, on account of the disturbed industrial situation in England. Foch's own views on a temporary occupation of the Ruhr were afterwards clearly expressed. "We will go to the Ruhr. Right. What next? Are we to stay there? No. Well then, what is the good of that? What advantage will it be to us?" An ultimatum was subsequently sent to Berlin. On the 21st the centenary of Napoleon I was celebrated at the Invalides, when Foch said in his address:

Truly, duty remains common to all. Of greater importance than leading armies to victory is the need of serving the Motherland for its greater happiness as each understands it. There is justice to be expected everywhere. Above War comes Peace.

In October Wilson discussed with Foch, who was going to America to visit every State in the Union, the critical situation in India, Mesopotamia, Egypt, Palestine, Syria, and Constantinople. On the subject of Asia Minor, where the Allies had sent the Greeks to Smyrna, Foch agreed with Wilson that the Greeks, who had advanced far inland, would have to go back to Smyrna, and possibly even to clear out, but he was not as certain as Wilson was that they would also be obliged to clear out of Thrace and of Adrianople. The Marshal kept on repeating *"Pauvre Angleterre, pauvre Angleterre,"* and he added his poignant regrets at the pass to which England had been brought. He thought that France would pull through, partly because of her peasant proprietors, and "partly because, as no one pays taxes and as everyone has served in the War, everyone invested in *rentes* and so no one wants a revolution." [8]

The Marshal's visit to the United States in 1921 was undertaken in response to an invitation from old soldiers. He attended the annual convention of the American Legion at Kansas City and he travelled for two months over the huge territory of the United States, winning the hearts of his audiences everywhere by the simplicity of "the greatest Chief of the greatest Army in the world." He was touched by the admiration shown for him, which he freely reciprocated. Sometimes, it may be, smiling at the exuberance of his hearers, he thought highly of them all as constructive folk, who "get things done . . . if they do not know, they learn, they work, they get their way." [9]

In May, 1922, Foch met King George, who was visiting the first-line cemeteries, at Notre Dame de Lorette. They went to Vimy Ridge where the ground was still pitted with shell-holes and one stumbled over rusty iron and over tree stumps. His Majesty in passing shook the hand of the Marshal who said: "Always friends, Sire, for the same reasons and for the same cause." In October of the same year Foch went to Rumania, to attend the coronation ceremony

[8] *Wilson Diaries,* Vol. II, p. 310.
[9] Bugnet, pp. 269-271.

and returned to Bucharest with the King and Queen on the same day.

In 1922 a correspondent in New Zealand sent a message which ran *"M. le Maréchal—à Berlin!"* On that Foch simply commented, "To Berlin? Yes . . . and what then? . . . go to Berlin? How? . . . Supposing that we do go there. We shall have to come back again. And what then?" He knew the ultimate futility of force as a remedy.

At this period Foch made a prediction that in five years' time the position would still be unchanged and its problems would not be much nearer to a solution. The chief thing was to be on the Rhine. "We had to go there; I went. After that we can hold the position while they argue."

In March, 1922, Wilson went to Paris to receive a present of five pieces of Sèvres from the French Government. Foch was at the presentation and Wilson referred in his speech of thanks to "the old Marshal as one who held all my admiration and all my friendship, and for whom I entertained a reverence." [10] That was their last meeting. Wilson was assassinated on the doorstep of his house in Eaton Place on the 22nd of June. When he was laid to rest in St. Paul's Cathedral four days later, it was his friend, the "Old Marshal," who escorted his widow from the Cathedral.

With the passing away of his most intimate friend in England our knowledge of Marshal Foch "through English eyes" becomes less intimate, so the seven closing years of his life will be touched upon but lightly in the next chapter.

[10] *Wilson Diaries*, Vol. II, p. 330.

On his birthday in October, 1921, the Marshal had reached the "allotted span" of human life. For the sake of the happiness of his closing years, he was more fortunate than his friend Henry Wilson, in that, when offered a seat as Senator—first by the Department of the Moselle and afterwards by Finisterre—he declined to take any part in politics. He had been brought up in a school of officers of the French Army who were forbidden by tradition, as they were by law, to intervene in any way in such matters, and he had no thought of changing his views. Of those who took part in politics he used to say: "They can do nothing but talk. They are wonderfully clever at saying what should be done, and then they don't do it." Action was the standard by which he measured both others and himself, and the action which concerned his life-study and experience was that of armies. Having failed to get his way about a buffer state, he advocated fortifying the frontier strongly, to make up for the smaller numbers of the French population.

Amongst his other activities he was a member of the "Forty" at the *Académie* and he was there known as an opponent of proposals to admit women to membership.

The year 1923 was perhaps the most important to Foch since the signing of the Peace Treaty in 1919. The Reparations Commission then reported that Germany was voluntarily in default over coal deliveries. This, in the opinion of the French Government, justified the application of "sanctions" specified in the terms of the Treaty. It is doubtful whether Foch shared their views.[1] Relations between France and Germany became strained, the French decided to seize the principal German coal field, and in this policy France acted alone. The Allied Military Committee nearly broke up, but largely through Foch's moderating influence it continued to meet weekly throughout the year. Weygand was sent, with the Minister of Public Works, and he reported to Foch on his return that within two days two railways would be available for the use of French troops, thus rendering their position secure. Weygand was duly thanked by the Government, but he is said to have found such work rather tedious till Foch persuaded him to carry on. Foch was ready to be recalled "if things went wrong." He was constantly consulted by the French Government at this period and he wielded considerable influence.

A Reuter telegram that was sent from Paris two days after the death of the Marshal in 1929 reported that M. Herriot had recalled in the *Ere Nouvelle* that in subsequent negotiations in London over the Dawes Plan of reparations the British and Americans had "demanded" the evacuation of the Ruhr, that Marshal Foch had sent General Desticker to London, and that when the situation gave ground for serious anxiety Herriot asked Desticker to visit him. Desticker reported that operations on the Ruhr were of no value from the military point of view, and that Foch's opinion was that they could only be dangerous. Herriot added: "Then I had to justify before the Chamber what had been

[1] See below.

done. General Desticker then came of his own accord and confirmed the Marshal's opinion." *"Pertinax"* wrote at the same time in the *Echo de Paris* that Britain remained loyal to Foch from the beginning of the War.

In October of the same year (1923) the bankruptcy of Germany seemed to be a possibility, and then the Marshal recalled his own saying when the question was raised in 1918 whether to give up Paris or the Channel ports. He had then said that he would defend both, and would let nothing go. Now again he said that both security and reparations must be obtained. German bankruptcy might give security. It would certainly not provide reparations, without which Foch believed that France would be ruined, and his conviction was that if the British troops were withdrawn from the occupied territory no more reparation would be paid.

Various war-panics followed, and with them abuse of France's Allies who had sacrificed so much for her in the War. Uneasiness was widely spread, even amongst sensible folk, and to these the Marshal, knowing as he did from war experience the danger of panics started by "rumours" which are seldom in accordance with facts, asked the simple question: "War? What war? With whom?" To which there was no reply. He added that one should not always accuse others if things went wrong. It was not the fault of others.[2] The maintenance of the Entente in spite of divergent policies is said to have been largely due to his readiness to accept British amendments, when coming within his province.

During the same year, Foch visited both Poland and Czecho-Slovakia. In 1918, he had looked upon Poland as a "myth" and could not then believe in its continued existence.

[2] Bugnet, p. 265.

He left the country much impressed by its possibilities. "They have children, swarms of children. Soon they will be as numerous as ourselves." He was made a Marshal in the Polish Army.

In June, 1923, he met Lord Cavan, who had succeeded Sir Henry Wilson as Chief of the General Staff, at the unveiling of a war memorial at Abbeville, where Haig's headquarters had been established in 1918. The events of the year had caused some strain in the relationship between France and Great Britain, and after the speeches were over the Marshal led Lord Cavan by the arm to the monument, saying: "Let us show our dead that we remain united." It was his dearest wish that France should keep her friends. In the days of the Locarno Treaties, Foch thought that something might be done in that direction. He did not want France and Germany to be looking at each other "like china dogs," and he was on the side of the "peacemakers, not of the pacifists." He did not believe that this generation would see another great war. "No one wants any longer this abominable thing that war was. . . . It was to prevent that that we made the Treaty of Versailles. No. No more wars. It is too dreadful." [3]

Weygand, who of all others is the most reliable authority on the thoughts and on the policy of the Marshal, tells us that in Foch's capacity of adviser to the Council of Ambassadors he took care to keep constantly in touch with representatives of the Allied countries, and that he made a point, as intermediary, of maintaining close relations with his military colleagues and with their Staff officers; that he always used his position to maintain the traditions of friendship—

[3] *Ibid.*, p. 269.

FOCH IN HIS GARDEN

in spite of inevitable differences of opinion—and of the trust and collaboration to which he had himself contributed so much during the course of the War. His object was to keep up the cohesion of all the nations to whom the maintenance of the treaties of 1919 formed a vital interest. Weygand adds that his Chief's wide views, diplomatic skill, strength, and moderation enabled him to wield an unrivalled authority. To the last day of his life, his outstanding personality helped to guard the solidarity which had been the source of victory.[4] "It was the union between all the Allies which saved us," was his frequent saying.

We find the same idea running as a *motif* through all the speeches and public actions of the great Marshal during the closing years. When he attended the funeral of Cardinal Mercier in Brussels in January, 1926, he headed the foreign representatives who received the coffin on its arrival at the Gare du Nord from Malines. King Albert then sent for him, to thank him for attending. The Marshal said in reply to the King's thanks that two men might be taken as representing the resistance of Belgium, Cardinal Mercier and King Albert himself. He (Foch) had come to testify his respect and his admiration for the one of those two who had passed away. "When it comes to the turn of the other," he added, "I shall not be there." "One never knows," said the King. "I do," was the reply. Thenceforward there came to him, as to most of us as the years advance, many thoughts of the past.

Foch paid a visit to Morocco, and he is reported [5] to have said on his return that if he were twenty again he would go to that country. "There is something to work for there."

---

[4] *Revue des deux Mondes*, May, 1929, pp. 44-45.   [5] Bugnet, p. 281.

He looked sadly upon those in his own land who "trample on each other and are jostled without forging ahead. . . . If I had my life to live all over again, I should not trouble about words, I should go where deeds are done."

He also visited the old Pyrenee country of his youth, showing the homing instinct which is felt by so many men of action as the end of their human activities approaches. There again he was incited to impress the need for definite action, rather than for incessant talk. He wished, for instance, to use the water-power near Saint-Gaudens and to turn it to electric power to improve the amenities of his former neighbours. Then again, he was anxious to develop the little seminary of Polignan. He was faithful to all his friends and to all those whose influence had helped him, even in his early youth, and when they had passed away he turned his attention to the institutions where he had known them. It was at Polignan that he had first become acquainted with a religious community, and it was there that he had been so impressed by the devotion of the priests to their vocation [6] of teaching. As the last years passed peacefully by, the Marshal devoted some of his latest energies to writing, as an inspiration to patriotism like his own, the tale of the life-history of Joan of Arc. These, the last pages that came from his pen, have been described by Weygand as giving a fine lesson in that idealism which nowadays is more needed than ever.

Duty was the watchword of the Marshal's closing years, as it had been of his whole lifetime. To do one's duty in whatever position one might be placed, and to do it to the utmost possible degree, seemed perfectly natural to him, and not a subject either for pride or for vanity. From his

[6] *Vide supra,* Chap. II.

sense of duty sprang his perfect simplicity. He realized, of course, the greatness of his achievements. When he spoke of them, which he seldom did, there was never the least trace of boasting. He went no farther than: "We have not done too badly," or, maybe, "We have done some business." And he never, on any occasion, took upon himself the credit for success. He shared it with others—his lieutenants and his collaborators; [7] and to Providence, above all, he gave acknowledgement.

He hoped that the War would not be forgotten. He unveiled many memorials, even in the smaller towns and villages, hoping that they would remind future generations of his countrymen of those who "stood firm and remained devoted unto death," and on such occasions he usually expressed the intense patriotism which had been his life-motive. At the unveiling late in 1928 of his own statue at Cassel he contracted a severe chill from which he was said never to have completely recovered. He had no fear of death. He described it as the only thing of which we can be certain, something to be faced in due course. The chief thing was to be prepared, and the thought of it should not cause alarm.

The veteran Marshal never forgot his old friends. Early in 1928 he came to England to attend the funeral of Lord Haig, his old comrade, and, for the first time, he was tired. The wonderful spirit which, throughout the War, had dominated the internal trouble from which he had suffered for years and had never allowed the body to tire, was at last beginning to weary, now that the work had been completed. When he attended the unveiling of the Marne Memorial in November, 1928, a British general, whom he had known well in Flanders, attended the ceremony. He was the last

[7] *"Et avec quelle générosité!"* Weygand adds, with feeling.

[443]

senior general officer of the British Army to see Foch alive, and this is his account of the meeting:

He was always pleased to see one and never forgot old friends. I was very touched when I went over to the unveiling of the Marne Memorial last November. It was the last time I ever saw the Marshal, and at the time I thought him in very failing health. He inspected the Guard of Honour of a hundred British soldiers with the very greatest interest, stopping opposite every man and asking questions about a good many of them.

You could see he was really fond of the British soldier. After the unveiling, when we were all waiting to go away . . . he caught sight of me standing and immediately came up and shook me warmly by both hands and said how delighted he was to see me again. This was the sort of friendly act that was bound to endear him with anyone who had dealings with him . . .

He was by far the most attractive personality . . . by far the most genuine friend of the British, and in my humble opinion by far the biggest thinker and the greatest personality of them all.

Commander Bugnet has provided us with an intimate picture of the Marshal at work in his Paris office during the last years. Foch arranged the room himself, with everything as simple as possible. The curtains were always looped back, to throw as much light as possible on the tables. His own large writing table was well lighted; another table, close to a window, with the maps and the large atlas constantly to be consulted. The room was very large and high. Maps of Europe and of Germany were fixed to the wall by drawing-pins. By the work-table there was an armchair with swivel-seat and a telephone close at hand. There was a low bookcase on which a barometer stood and a few chairs and armchairs which the orderlies carefully placed in line round the carpet every day, and there was plenty of empty floor-

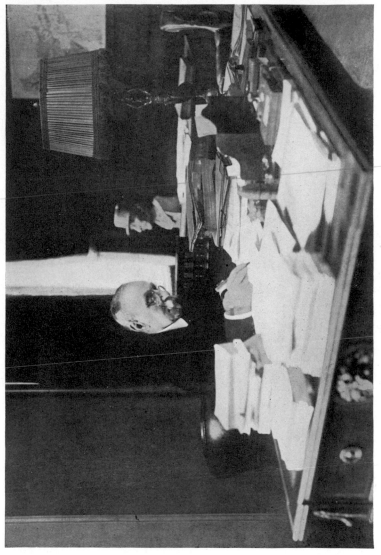

FOCH IN HIS STUDY

space. Before him stood a plain glass inkpot, filled to the brim, and a number of ordinary wooden penholders, on one of which he had cut a notch. It was fitted with a golden nib, which he always used. There were pencils, india-rubber, a packet of tobacco in grey paper wrapping, some pipes, and a brass pipe-scraper presented by Mr. Lloyd George during the War. Such were the simple surroundings in which he received visits from many of the great folk of the earth.

Weygand tells us that many of his visitors, French and foreign, were rather shy at finding themselves in the presence of the Chief who had commanded millions of men, and whose name for eight months had embodied all the trust and all the hopes of the Allied nations, the victor in the greatest battle in history. They left his presence impressed by the greatness of his intellect and of his soul, and fascinated by his simplicity. "They made no mistake; they had been in the presence of true greatness, with which there is always simplicity." (*La vraie grandeur, qui ne vas jamais sans la simplicité.*) [8]

The Marshal worked, as usual, to a routine. To the A.D.C. the daily walks with him to and from the office were "the best moment of the day." On the way back the two trusty Staff officers, Weygand and Desticker,[9] saw the Marshal to the gate where they turned to the right, down the Avenue de Tourville, while Foch and Bugnet turned to the left, up the Boulevard des Invalides. He wore plain clothes when walking, with the ribbon of the *Medaille Militaire* in his buttonhole. If he was in uniform, he went home by car. At

[8] *Revue des deux Mondes*, May, 1929.
[9] Desticker died some months before his great chief, who insisted upon reading the funeral oration which he himself had written, but he only had strength to read one page. Weygand read out the remainder.

the office he always saw the faithful Weygand first, and was closeted with him for some time before going on with the business of the day. Some of the conversations, in the office and during the daily walks, are interesting and revealing, but the accounts come through French, not "through English eyes," so quotations would be out of place, but one of his remarks is so revealing of his inmost thoughts about the recognition of his services which he would have valued that it would be well to place its substance on record.[10]

The Rumanian Chamber, by unanimous vote, granted an estate of two hundred acres with a château and farms to General Berthelot, in recognition of his services. When he heard of it the old Marshal said: "A gift like that, a country's recognition of services done: that is worth all the titles of nobility in a family. One leaves one's children something to bear witness. . . . An estate, or no matter what—something given in national gratitude, I should have liked that . . . a house—some sort of hut, even, a national gift!" When grants were voted in the British Parliament to admirals and generals, Lloyd George sent a message to the Marshal by General Du Cane that he (Lloyd George) had suggested making a grant to Foch himself, but he had been told that that was the business of the French Government. The Americans then thought of making him a General in the United States Army, with pay, but the precedent of refusal of the British offer prevented acceptance. The story is told simply, and without complaint, but Bugnet adds that Foch did say, good humouredly: "They turned to us in desperate straits . . . and now?"

There is no doubt that he felt the office employment less congenial than the work, with all its human interest, of

[10] Bugnet, pp. 92-93.

FOCH WITH HIS GRANDCHILDREN

Taken in his garden at Traoufeunteniou.

throwing the whole force of his character and personality into the conduct of his great triumphant battle, but his intellect was as keen and his powers of concentration as great to his last days in his office at the end of the year 1928. He seems seldom to have rested from his work, and the old home in Brittany with its surroundings does not seem to have attracted him quite to the same extent after the death of his only son and of one of his sons-in-law, though he went there sometimes and took the same interest as ever in village life. One of his visits there in 1926 was described by M. Recouly,[11] who tells us how keen the Marshal was to get to work with a *secateur* on his trees, directly he arrived, and how he walked in the neighbouring villages as a simple, smiling, and charming friend to all. There is a picture of him, surrounded by folk in Breton costume, the centre of attraction in a small crowd during a village fête at Huelgoat. He always kept his love of trees, as reminding him of those of the Breton woods where he had spent his early married life and to which he had retired for deep thought and guidance in the crisis of his career, when he was chosen to teach others and determined to arrive at bedrock truth before he took the responsibility of spreading doctrine which might have a lasting influence upon the future of France. There was a tree in the courtyard by his office in Paris, which gave him pleasure.

Judging by the evidence of the later portraits, his expression became more grave and rather sad as the years went by, but it still remained peaceful. Early in the New Year of 1929 his physical strength began to fail and he was stricken with a heart attack that caused much anxiety to his family and to his friends. At the end of January other organs were

[11] *L'Illustration*, April 6th, 1929.

[447]

involved and slight congestion of the lungs was reported in the bulletin. He recovered for a time, and it is touching to learn that some of his last energies were devoted to drafting a message to accompany General Gouraud and a party of French soldiers who were coming to London to pay homage at the Cenotaph in Whitehall. The message, which was left incomplete, ran thus:

It is with regret that I find that I cannot join in the tribute to the British dead which French pilgrims are making, but I shall be with you in spirit when the British dead are honoured on behalf of the French nation and army.

I recall with pride the achievements of the British troops who fought under my command, and it would have given me the greatest pleasure to have identified myself in person with this tribute.

This pleasure is not for me now, but that does not prevent my saluting your glorious dead in spirit.

No one in France is likely to forget what our nation owes to the British Comrades-in-arms who laid down their lives so freely for the common cause.

He rallied over and over again, and there was talk, at one time, of a move to the south of France, but it was not to be. When sitting in his chair by the window on the evening of Wednesday, the 20th of March, he was seized with a heart attack just before they were about to move him to his bed. Extreme unction according to the rites of his Church was administered by a priest from the neighbouring church of St. Clotilde before he passed away, unconscious at the last, and Madame Foch was with him at the end. The closing of the shutters of his window told the outside world that all was over. Within half an hour there arrived tokens of sympathy, flowers and messages from the President, from members of the Government, and from the British Ambassador.

The Chamber of Deputies was sitting at the time, and M. Poincaré, the Prime Minister, announced the death of the great Marshal, adding with emotion: "Marshal Foch was not only a great soldier, he was a great citizen. I know that the Chamber will associate itself with the national mourning." M. Flanderi, the Vice-President of the Chamber, said: "To try to make any eulogy of Marshal Foch would be to dim the glory which surrounds his memory in the thoughts of all his grateful countrymen. I am sure that I shall be interpreting Parliament's wishes in addressing our supreme homage to his memory and in sending our condolences to his family." Members of the Chamber were visibly moved as they filed out quietly. Within a few hours there arrived condolences and tributes to his memory from all parts of France and from the rulers and the peoples of foreign countries. It is said that the Marshal's last words were: "*Allons-y*"—Let us go. He was ready.

Chapter XXXVI

IN MEMORIAM, IN SPEM

MARCH, 1929

THROUGHOUT the night of Wednesday, the 20th of March, the remains of the great "soldier and Christian" lay in the bedroom on the first floor of the house in the Rue de Grenelle which the French nation had lent to him for his lifetime. He had been dressed in his field service uniform, the cloak that he had worn in the War over his feet. On the wall behind the bed were the colours, embroidered in silk, of the forty-seven Allied nations who owed so much to the still, silent figure below. Officers stood on guard in the room throughout the night, while respectful crowds gathered in their hundreds to pay tribute to the memory of the saviour of France from the invader. As the news spread throughout Paris, through France, and over the whole world, messages or regret and condolence poured in constantly on the 21st to Madame la Maréchale and to the French Government.

King George wrote to the President of the Republic:

With heartfelt sorrow I offer to you, M. le Président, and to the French nation my deep sympathy in the death of Marshal Foch. France mourns her greatest soldier, my country the loss of one whose name honoured the roll of British Field-Marshals. For all time he will be remembered as the distinguished chief

[450]

who led the Allied armies to victory, while his memory will be cherished by all ranks of the Empire's forces who served in the world war.

The British Government's message to the French Government contained the words: "His impressive personality and knightly character have endeared him to the people of this country, and his loss will be mourned in every English home." To this the British Prime Minister added in a message to the President of the Council that "the British people will sincerely mourn one whose services to the Allied cause are fresh in every memory, and whose distinguished and inspiring personality has won the affection and profound esteem both of every British soldier that served under him and of the British nation as a whole."

During the forenoon and later in the day representatives of the French and of many other nations passed through the house to pay homage to the illustrious champion of the Allied cause. M. Clemenceau, then approaching his nine-tieth year, was amongst them, and he stood for a long time by the bedside in meditation. Then he turned to Weygand. They talked together for a time about those eventful years when the balance trembled between victory and defeat; and the veteran statesman said as he turned away:

How could we have lost the War with such collaborators? It seems unjust that I, who am older than he, should come to salute him on his death-bed.

The President of the Republic was an early visitor, and there came also Marshal Joffre (lame from an injured knee and helped up the steps), many general officers, members of the *Académie,* representatives of the associations of veterans, Cabinet ministers, ambassadors and others. In spite of bitter memories, this German tribute came from General von Seeckt:

Death, which knows no nationality, allows an old enemy to lower his sword before Marshal Foch, who was a great soldier and a great Frenchman.

King Albert of the Belgians came specially to Paris for two hours to pay respect to one who bore so large a part in Belgium's deliverance. Meanwhile the crowd outside increased constantly in numbers, so later in the day the Marshal's remains were moved to a *chapelle ardente* on the ground floor where they lay in state until the Sunday morning. The Marshal's baton, sword, and képi of scarlet and gold lay by his side, the sash of his high rank across his breast on which the hands lay clasping a crucifix. The Parisians passed in their thousands to do homage to their deliverer. It was estimated that 20,000 had passed before the doors were closed in the evening. Flags throughout Paris hung at half-mast. The brother to whom Foch had written so constantly in the fullness of his life's work—Father Germain Foch, the Jesuit priest—prayed long beside the elder brother. He had been in Paris two days, having come there ill, and he had to undergo an operation.[1] On that day the death-mask was taken by a famous sculptor, Michelet. Two days before his death, Foch had cut short his moustache, because it caused him inconvenience when he coughed, so the death-mask shows the lips set in a smile of ineffable contentment and sweetness. The eyes through which so many had drawn inspiration from the spirit of the great commander are closed as if in peaceful sleep.

On the Thursday afternoon the French Senate met to

[1] Father Foch passed away three months later. [Author.]

THE EXPRESSION OF FOCH ON THE 16TH OF MARCH, 1929

hear from M. Painlevé, the War Minister, a eulogy of the dead Marshal, and they then adjourned, as a token of respect. That date, the 21st of March, was the eleventh anniversary of the day when the heaviest attack in the history of land warfare had been made by the enemy's legions in their thrust towards Amiens which, if successful, might have made a yawning gap between the French and the British Armies and have so caused irreparable disaster. The still figure with the peaceful smiling face reminded many in that long procession of mourners of the indomitable spirit of the man who saved the situation. Of the art of command on that occasion Foch wrote to one of the British officers who knew him best and admired him the most:

Mon cher ami,

. . . Vous avez parfaitement compris que la grande force de notre guerre fut le patriotisme absolu de tous, et que l'art de commander consista à l'exploiter, sans réserve, dans une union de pensées, comme aussi d'efforts.

The wife of that officer, Lady Sybil Grant—the late Lord Rosebery's daughter—who was passing through Paris, wrote a wonderful pen-picture of the passing of "The Tired Heart" [2] and of Paris and its people on that day of mourning.

Sitting in the sun on that radiant spring morning, she opened the paper and she read: *"Le Maréchal Foch est mort,"* and below, a sketch of the Field-Marshal upon his death-bed. "At once the noisy passing of the traffic took on a dull, distant sound, as though the sudden enveloping sadness fell like some heavy curtain, shutting out the world outside." Lady Sybil had met the Marshal several times quietly in

[2] *The Scotsman*, March 22nd, 1929.

[453]

their home, and from the first meeting she had been struck, as many others were, "with the rare certainty that here was someone even greater than you had hoped, that the reality came up to the high ideal you had formed, the glorious dual personality, soldier and visionary, which alone used to make—that alone can still make—the Crusader." With him it was sympathy with others which caused a strain much more severe, much harder to endure, but which also made him worshipped by all those who had the honour to serve under him; which makes his death a bitter grief to those who knew him intimately and saw him continually during every day for many months. Of how many other great men can it be said that such daily intercourse and close contact increase the devotion they inspired at the beginning? Yet these very qualities that so endeared him to his fellow-men were those which reacted most upon his strength.

There are soldiers—fortunately few—who are blind to the horrors of war. There are visionaries who remain deaf to the agony of those who are sacrificed to the cause. Not so with this crusader.

Then Lady Sybil tells us of the reception of the news in France, as she saw it: "Only a few hours have passed since the announcement of his death, and yet you are already aware how well the people over here in France understood this—the psychological side, so much more powerful than the physical—in determining the issues of life and death. For instance, an old workman:

Yes, it is indeed a tragedy. But I am the friend of one who was once his servant, and so I can tell you how little the Maréchal used to sleep. It was his heart that was tired.

"And then later on when I went among hundreds of others to sign the simple little book at the house which the country had given [3] him: 'You see,' explained my taxi-driver, 'it was his heart—after those years of suffering, his heart was tired—tired out.' You hear and read everywhere of his victories—but there was that other side. The sufferings which no glory, no gratitude, could ever make that heart forget."

On the morning of Palm Sunday, March 24th, a company of infantry with colours and band, under the command of a Colonel, was drawn up in the courtyard of the house in the Rue de Grenelle to do honour to the cortège which was then to move, escorted by ministers, generals, and Staff officers, by way of the Invalides and the Champs Elysées to the Arc de Triomphe for the lying in state near the Tomb of the Unknown Warrior of France. There the coffin was laid on a simple gun-carriage. Over the coffin was spread the French Tricolour and the Marshal's cloak. Surrounding it were giant candlesticks surmounted throughout the night with great flares. An officer carrying the Marshal's personal flag as Generalissimo of the Allied Armies, draped in black, stood on guard with four officers with drawn swords, and boy scouts. During that sunny Palm Sunday it was estimated that in the daytime 350,000 people filed past the bier and 750,000 were unable to approach the gun-carriage. The night passed in solemn pageantry, the flares illuminating the great Arc de Triomphe, the gun-carriage and its burden, the Unknown Warrior's tomb and the silent watchers, until in the dark hours the coffin was transferred from the gun-carriage to a motor-hearse and moved to the Cathedral of Notre Dame. A crowd of many thousands who had waited in hope

---

[3] The house was lent for his lifetime. [Author]

of being able to file past witnessed the transfer. An escort of cavalry bearing torches preceded the hearse, which moved to the sound of distant guns, booming in salute. "Paris knew how to mourn with dignity and simplicity." The procession to Notre Dame on that Sunday night passed through silent streets under a starry firmament. The hearse was followed by a long line of mourners extending across Paris to the Cathedral. On its arrival at the square opposite to the façade of Notre Dame two priests in vestments appeared in the western doorway in response to the harsh notes of a trumpet call. The troops formed a hollow square outside while the coffin was borne past the dark empty nave to a chapel draped in black and silver. The entrance was lighted by high candles from which shafts of light flickered upon a silver cross, and there the mourners left the bier, covered with the Tricolour and guarded by boy scouts and by the officer bearing the Marshal's personal flag.

Soon after the dawn of the Monday shone through the stained glass of the eastern windows, Madame Foch returned, followed later by soldiers, statesmen, high dignitaries and others. The original intention had been to allow only these personal mourners to enter, and then to close the Cathedral until the obsequies on the Tuesday, March 26th—the anniversary of the day at Doullens when the Allied statesmen in their extremity had entrusted the great soldier with the championship of what seemed to many to be a cause already lost. Soon, however, the throng outside the Cathedral, who had been disappointed at the Arc de Triomphe, formed itself quietly into a long patient queue until, at half-past ten, the Door of Sainte Anne was opened to admit a thin stream anxious to convey the silent gratitude of fellow-citizenship—officers, deputies, workmen and girls,

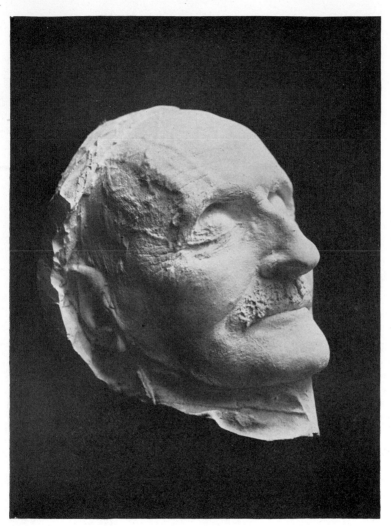

FOCH DEATH MASK

business folk, market-women, all that goes to contribute to the work-a-day life of Paris. They passed out continuously by the centre western portal, the Porte de Jugement, with a break between noon and three o'clock, until late in the evening the doors were closed for the night.

A great multitude waited throughout the night in the silent streets. As day dawned on the Tuesday morning, street vendors appeared to sell food and drink to the patient watchers of whom many had come from afar. The weather was dull and the sky overcast. No rain fell, but an atmosphere of mourning hung heavily over the expectant city. By seven o'clock the great square by Notre Dame was closed to the public while the various delegations were marshalled there in order of entrance to the Cathedral. In one corner of the square waited the gun-carriage—of the celebrated *soix-ante-quinze*—with a team of black horses in readiness to convey the Marshal to his last resting-place. His charger, caparisoned in black and in silver, stood quietly in the square. The weather gradually improved, shafts of sunshine breaking occasionally through the cloud-banks and shining on the façade draped in black and silver and on a great letter "F" surrounded by a silver wreath of laurel.

The bells of Notre Dame rang a muffled peal as the great folk of France and other lands, who came in hundreds to attend the service, arrived and were directed to various entrances to the great Cathedral. The Prince of Wales and Prince Charles of Belgium arrived at nine o'clock. They were received at the threshold by Cardinal Dubois, Archbishop of Paris, surrounded by clergy and by all the members of the Government. M. Doumergue, President of the Republic, passed into the Cathedral with the Princes, where the seats, covered with black, were packed with people.

Heavy black hangings, bordered in silver, were draped from the summits of the great pillars and crowned with Tricolour flags. The coffin lay high upon a black catafalque, surrounded by six great candles. The silence was broken only by the low murmuring of the priest—curate of the Marshal's old parish—celebrating the Low Mass so suited to the simple nature of the departed. The day fell in Holy Week, so the ritual of the customary Solemn Requiem High Mass was not followed. In the Requiem music of Faure, in Beethoven's Funeral March, and in the Heroic Symphony of Saint-Saens the notes of the great organ blended with those of the orchestral instruments of the Paris Conservatoire.

After the Mass the Abbé Verdrie moved to the steps of the Altar and recited the *De Profundis ad te clamavi,* with responses from all the assembled clergy headed by the Papal Nuncio. Then Cardinal Lucon, the octogenarian Prelate of the Cathedral of Rheims which had been battered by enemy shell, walked in cope and mitre to the head of the coffin and pronounced the Final Absolution. The service closed with a fervent Amen. The great doors of the Cathedral were then thrown open showing bright uniforms in the daylight beyond.

Of that great funeral procession from Notre Dame to the Invalides, where Foch was to be laid to rest beneath the golden dome which covers the resting-place of Napoleon, much has been written. Surrounding Napoleon's tomb there are small chapels containing the remains of his brothers Joseph and Jerome, of Vauban the great military engineer, of Turenne; and the heart of Latour Dauvergue. During the service in Notre Dame the sun had shone for a time, but a sombre grey pall of mist veiled the sunlight while the

[458]

procession was being formed and during its progress by the Rue de Rivoli, past the Louvre to the Place de la Concorde and thence up the Champs Elysées to the Arc de Triomphe, where the Marshal had ridden at the head of the troops in the Victory March of July, 1919, and thence across the Alexandre III bridge to the Invalides.

The clergy, heading the cortège, were followed by the charger caparisoned in black and silver and the officer bearing the Marshal's personal flag in front of the gun-carriage with its black team. Amongst the pall-bearers were all the Marshals of France excepting Marshal Joffre, lamed by a twisted knee-cap and unable to undertake the long, slow march. Of Foch's British brother Field-Marshals five were present: Lord Plumer and Sir George Milner representing the British Army, Lords Methuen [4] and Allenby and Sir Claud Jacob. The widows of Lord Haig, his loyal colleague, and of Sir Henry Wilson, his closest friend, also attended the funeral. Behind the gun-carriage walked the nearest relatives and then the French and Allied officers most closely connected personally with the work of that great Generalissimo—beyond them the President of the Republic, the Royal Princes, and an endless procession of statesmen, troops, and delegations.

At the Invalides M. Poincaré delivered the funeral oration [5] from a black rostrum set in a wide open space. It contained some fine passages:

The flame that had just been extinguished was one of the most ardent and pure that had ever shed its brilliance upon earth. He had all the qualities which Bossuet enumerated as the

[4] Also representing H.R.H. the Duke of Connaught, the senior of British Field-Marshals.
[5] Reproduced almost *in extenso* in *The Times* of March 27th, 1929.

characteristic traits of the hero—bravery, magnanimity, natural goodness, vivacity, penetration and greatness, and the sublimity of genius. He had no other ambition but to serve. He desired no other recompense than the feeling of duty accomplished. That is the reason why the mourning in which we are plunged to-day is the mourning of France, and of a great portion of civilized humanity.

A simple service accompanied the laying of the remains on the threshold of a vault in the Invalides on a high catafalque surrounded by fourteen tall candles. The red and gold cap of a Marshal of France and the drawn sword and scabbard rested on the coffin with the Marshal's baton on back velvet bordered with silver at the head, decorations of the Legion of Honour and the *Médaille Militaire* below. The batons of British and Polish Field-Marshals were on each side and numerous foreign ribbons and decorations were grouped downwards to the second of the steps of approach. That was the sight that met the gaze of thousands of veteran soldiers who passed by in procession for eight hours on the following day—March 27th, the anniversary of the occasion on which the great Christian warrior had inspired the sorely harassed troops covering the point of cohesion between the British and French Armies to hold to the very end the ground on which they stood. There we "leave him alone in his glory."

On the Saturday, March 23rd, a Solemn Requiem Mass had been celebrated in London in Westminster Cathedral and attended by the Prince of Wales representing the King, by the Prime Minister (Mr. Baldwin) and many of his colleagues, and by a vast congregation representing every class of society and every walk of life in England. The senior British Field-Marshal, the Duke of Connaught, was represented by his son, Prince Arthur. Many representatives of foreign powers attended. It was said that "no international bereavement has ever brought together such an assembly as that which filled the great church." Cardinal Archbishop Bourne in red robes occupied his throne by the Sanctuary. Bishop Butt was the celebrant of a service of great beauty and solemnity. The singing of the *"Dies Irae"* and the inspired words which seem majestically to bring together the living and the dead, and sweet solo voice of a choir-boy, singing the *"Motet"* Justorum Animæ during the offertory was followed by the solemn moment when the Cardinal, in cope and mitre, left his throne for the final ritual at the representative bier, and then in the *Requiescat in Pace* the soul simply of "Thy servant Ferdinand" was commended to the Divine mercy.

Far away in Washington a gun-salute was fired, and all over the world services were held—so many of them that it would be impossible to provide an appropriate record. We will take one only, from another London, a small place in Ontario, Canada, where the Thames is a tiny stream, "Cheapside" a residential quarter, and another "St. Paul's Cathedral" stands in more rural surroundings. In that Cathedral a special service was held in April to honour the memories both of Foch and of Haig, the comrade Field-Marshals who had passed away at so short an interval. Hundreds of war-veterans attended the service. The Church was filled to its full capacity and crowds thronged outside to catch a few words of the service through the open doors. Dean Tucker, who preached the memorial sermon, referred to Marshal Foch as "above all reproach in all his relations of life, personal, domestic, and public. In him all the elements were so mixed that nature could stand up and say 'This is a man.'

He did not believe that victory perched on the banners of large battalions." Then the preacher drew a picture of the Marshal praying for victory in the little rustic churches of France, so it was appropriate that the victory in which he played so large a part should be recalled in his name in that St. Paul's Church upon a Sunday.[6]

On a special occasion a few years ago an eminent Canadian brought to the attention of the late Marshal Foch a fine translation from a certain address—dating from the fourth century before Christ—by Pericles, the great Athenian statesman and at one time sole ruler of Athens. Foch gave the words a warm commendation. He proposed to make use of them for some opportunity which offered itself. Whether he eventually did so we do not know, but as a conclusion to his own Life, it would be difficult to discover a more appropriate quotation:

The Tribute

But each one, man by man, has won imperishable praise, each has gained a glorious grave—not the sepulchre of earth wherein they lie, but the living tomb of everlasting remembrance wherein their glory is enshrined, remembrance that will live on the lips, that will blossom in the deeds of their countrymen the world over. For the whole earth is the sepulchre of heroes; monuments may rise and tablets be set up to them in their own land, but on far-off shores there is an abiding memorial that no pen or chisel has traced; it is graven, not on stone or brass, but on the living heart of humanity.

Take these men, then, for your examples. Like them, remember that prosperity can be only for the free, that freedom is the sure possession of those alone who have courage to defend it.

[6] *London Advertiser*, Ontario, April 22nd, 1929.

L'Envoi

It may be that students of the life-history of Foch in some future age, thinking as he did in parables and judging others by their actions, will ponder over the results of three little deeds through which material forces triumphed for the time being—Bismarck's pencil-stroke on the Ems telegram; the tramp of the first German soldier's boot on the soil of Belgium; and the touch by one Emil Schweiger on a firing-key in a submarine to blow up the *Lusitania*.

Further imaginings may follow about the "imponderables" which in the appointed time incited the armies of France, Belgium, the British Empire, and the United States of America to free the soil of France and Flanders of so powerful an invader, employing Ferdinand Foch as the predestined instrument, not of "vengeance" but of inevitable consequence.

APPENDIX

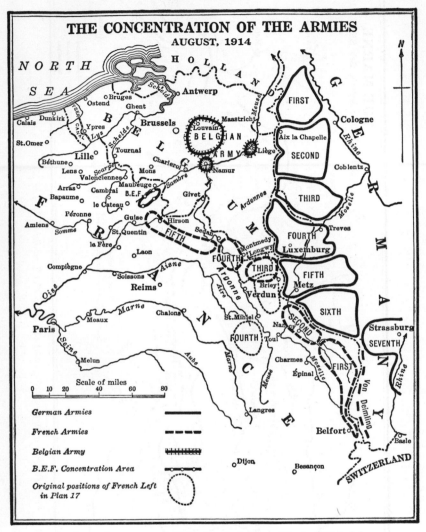

THE CONCENTRATION OF THE ARMIES
AUGUST, 1914

Redrawn from a map in "History of the Great War," published by
The Macmillan Company.

[467]

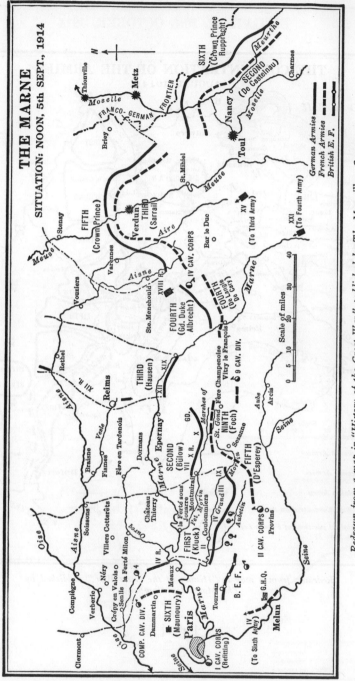

THE MARNE

SITUATION: NOON, 5th SEPT., 1914

Redrawn from a map in "History of the Great War," published by The Macmillan Company.

German Armies

French Armies

British E.F.

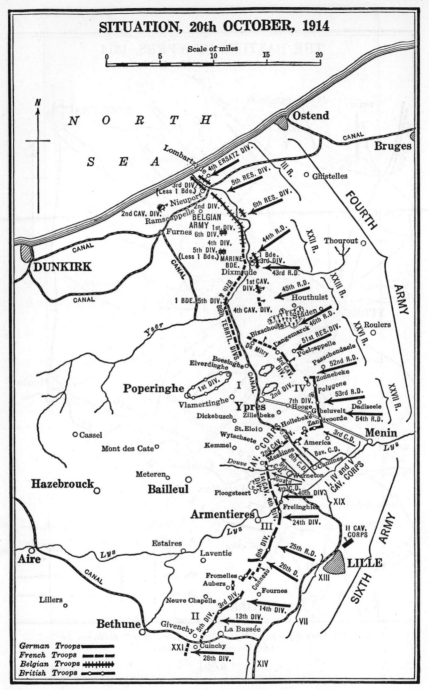

SITUATION, 20th OCTOBER, 1914

Redrawn from a map in "History of the Great War," published by
The Macmillan Company.

[469]

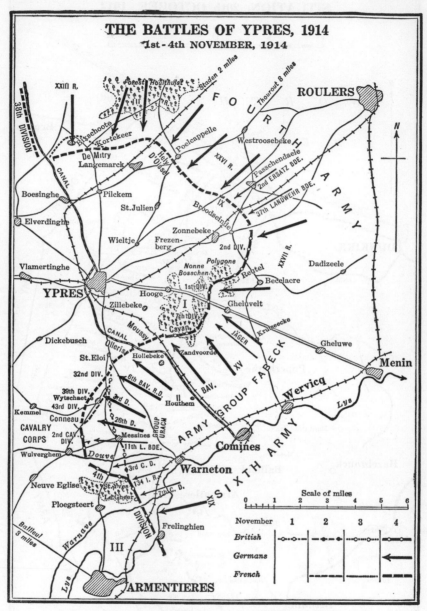

THE BATTLES OF YPRES, 1914
1st - 4th NOVEMBER, 1914

Redrawn from a map in "History of the Great War," published by
The Macmillan Company.

[470]

INDEX

INDEX

INDEX

INDEX

INDEX

INDEX

INDEX

INDEX

INDEX

INDEX

INDEX

INDEX